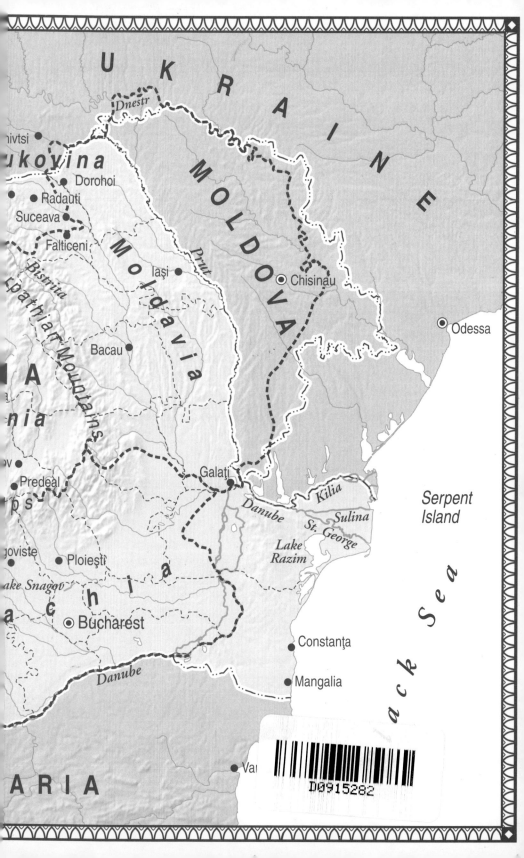

UKRAINE

Dnestr

ukovina

Dorohoi

Radauti

Suceava

Falticeni

Bistrita

Carpathian Mountains

Iași

Prut

MOLDOVA

Chisinau

Odessa

Moldavia

Bacau

IA

nia

v

Predeal

ps

Galați

Kilia

Danube

Sulina

St. George

Serpent
Island

Lake
Razim

goviste

Ploiești

ake Snagov

achia

Bucharest

Constanța

Mangalia

Danube

ack Sea

Var

D0915282

ARIA

BUCHAREST DIARY

Bucharest Diary

*Romania's Journey from
Darkness to Light*

An American Ambassador's Memoir

ALFRED H. MOSES

BROOKINGS INSTITUTION PRESS
Washington, D.C.

Copyright © 2018
THE BROOKINGS INSTITUTION
1775 Massachusetts Avenue, N.W., Washington, D.C. 20036
www.brookings.edu

The Brookings Institution is a private nonprofit organization devoted to research, education, and publication on important issues of domestic and foreign policy. Its principal purpose is to bring the highest quality independent research and analysis to bear on current and emerging policy problems. Interpretations or conclusions in Brookings publications should be understood to be solely those of the authors.

Library of Congress Cataloging-in-Publication data are available.

ISBN 978-0-8157-3272-3 (cloth : alk. paper)
ISBN 978-0-8157-3273-0 (ebook)

9 8 7 6 5 4 3 2 1

Typeset in Adobe Caslon

Composition by Elliott Beard

To the men and women of the United States Foreign Service

Contents

Acknowledgments   *ix*

Foreward   •   U.S. Senator Christopher Van Hollen   *xi*

Preface   *xv*

Part One

MY INTRODUCTION TO ROMANIA

1   Ceauşescu, Romania's Jews, Chief Rabbi Rosen, and Me   3
2   Looking Back to Explain Present-Day Romania   46
3   The Curtain Rises   60
4   Jumping in As Ambassador   75

Part Two

ROMANIA STRUGGLES

5   Building the Case in Washington for the Bilateral Relationship with
Romania and Speaking Truth to Power in Romania   91

6 Former President Bush in Bucharest 117

7 Negotiating Romania's Treaty with Hungary 132

8 Romania's President Comes to the Oval Office 166

Part Three

ROMANIA'S DEMOCRACY IN ACTION

9 A New Year, Step-by-Step 203

10 Washington Pays Attention 219

11 A Visit from Hillary Clinton 232

12 Run-up to the General Election 253

Part Four

CHANGING OF THE GUARD IN ROMANIA

13 New Faces, Old Story Lines 279

14 More Peace and More Business 307

15 A Bountiful Harvest 334

Epilogue
Romanian History in the Making 359

Glossary of People and Places 365

Index 379

Acknowledgments

This book has been in the offing since I returned to Washington in 1997 with vague notions about a future book. In the intervening years many people helped me focus on how I might turn my notes into a book. I benefited enormously from their advice.

Thanks are owed to Nadine Epstein, editor of *Moment* magazine, and my friend and former colleague at Promontory Financial Group, Kinney Zelesne, as well as two other friends and former colleagues at Promontory, Peter Bass and Colleen Brennan, who were by my side from beginning to end.

My friend and the former Romanian ambassador to the United States, Sorin Ducaru, did fact-checking on the Romanian side. My friend Bonnie Boxer served as my Israeli conscience.

My agent, Ron Goldfarb, and his assistant, Gerry Sturman, provided wise advice.

Among those who provided valuable suggestions or read the book in draft, I thank my former colleagues in the American Embassy in Bucharest, Mihai Carp, Susan Jacobs, Richard Rorvig, Sarah Solberg, and Robert Whitehead; my friend and former "Miss Abby," Diane Crowley Hano; Dartmouth College professor Dan Benjamin, who read the text and contributed much; and my synagogue pal, the literary critic and political commentator Leon Wieseltier, who read an early draft and recommended the book to Brookings.

At Brookings I thank the triumvirate who led the charge: William Finan, Janet Walker, and Elliott Beard, later joined by Phil Schwartzberg, cartographer extraordinaire, and my editor, Katherine Scott.

My son-in-law, Mark Mann, a world-renowned photographer, reproduced the photographs in this book.

I also want to thank those who endured the most—my wife, Fern Schad, and my four children and twelve grandchildren.

Thanks also to Senator Christopher Van Hollen, who contributed the foreword and has been my soulmate since he first entered public service three decades ago.

Most important, I thank my friend and assistant for more than fifty years, Paula Brenneman, who transcribed the text from dictation and managed the enterprise.

Foreword

U.S. SENATOR CHRISTOPHER VAN HOLLEN

Alfred Moses arrived in Bucharest to assume his duties as the U.S. ambassador to Romania in December 1994. At that point, five years after the revolutions that swept communism from Eastern Europe, anyone handicapping the prospects of the nations of the region for successful development into democracies with market economies would have placed Romania at or near the bottom of the field. Romania was a land of 40-watt light bulbs, freezing apartment blocks, and desolate, overcrowded orphanages. It was the only country to emerge from the Eastern Bloc through violence: after the briefest of trials, on December 25, 1989, longtime dictator Nicolae Ceauşescu and his wife, Elena, were executed by firing squad.

Ceauşescu had long charted a course of semi-independence from Moscow, and in the last stage of his rule, he was determined to free his country of the demands of Western creditors by reducing the country's debt load. In its turn toward autarky, Romania seemed to be modeling itself more on North Korea than on the states of communist Eastern Europe. The country was an impoverished shambles. With unresolved border issues, restive minorities, sclerotic bureaucracies, and no sustained history of democratic governance—the government had even summoned masses of coal miners from the countryside to put down demonstrations in 1990—a measure of skepticism about the future was appropriate.

Though not a diplomat by profession, Moses came to the job with open eyes. A successful Washington attorney who had served in the Carter White House, he had been visiting Romania for almost twenty years in his capacity as a Jewish community leader. Romania's willingness to stray from Moscow's line beginning in the 1960s had opened up opportunities for engagement for American Jewish organizations eager to support the small Jewish community that had survived the Holocaust. Moses had led negotiations with the regime, pressing successfully for the right of Romanian Jews to emigrate. An observant Jew, he came to his new post with a fondness for the Eastern Europe of his forebears and no illusions about what it would take to move Romania toward a more secure and prosperous future.

Fast-forward to the present: Romania's GDP jumped from $30 billion in 1994 to $188 billion in 2016, almost a sixfold increase in a period when its population fell by almost 20 percent. Life expectancy has increased by five years, to almost seventy-five, not far off Western European levels. Foreign direct investment has grown roughly twelvefold. Poverty remains a problem, but as a member of the European Union, the country is poised for continued long-term growth. In 2004, well before Russia began menacing its neighbors, Romania achieved newfound security as a member of NATO. Compared to some of its neighbors, where nationalism, xenophobia, and anti-Semitism are gaining ground, Romania looks reasonably well rooted in democratic principles and on a positive trajectory.

No one, least of all Al Moses, would claim sole credit for Romania's relative success. Yet he played a critical role in steering the country's leaders and U.S. policy in a constructive direction. As a central participant in the pivotal years of the mid-1990s and as gifted and shrewd observer, he has produced in Bucharest Diary a remarkable account, one that deserves a prominent place among the histories and memoirs recounting U.S. policy of the period.

The book is enlivened by a keen wit and colorful depictions of some of the key American and Romanian figures of the period. Al Moses has a well-earned reputation for blunt, direct speech, and it served him well during his time in Bucharest and as an author. Reflecting, for example, on Romania's second elected head of state, he writes with winning economy, "President Constantinescu, with all his good intentions, was at heart a geology professor, not a businessman." He also has a deep sensitivity for the ravages that the twentieth century brought to the once large and flourishing Jewry of Romania. He seems to have visited every major and minor community in the country.

For historians of the period, *Bucharest Diary* yields trenchant insights into how persistently the United States and its Western European partners pressed for a reformist agenda in the former Eastern bloc. In some countries, such as Poland and the Baltic nations, new leaders came to power who had studied in the West or had drunk deeply of Western free market economics, and who adopted reformist programs rapidly. In more isolated countries such as Romania, foreign envoys worked tirelessly, for example, to press leaders to relinquish control over state-owned companies and seek compromises with neighbors on matters of autonomy for minorities despite the difficult politics of post-communist societies in which the lid had been lifted off long-repressed ethnic tensions. They also worked relentlessly to cut through the red tape so that American investors willing to take a chance in the new democracies could get the opportunity.

For students of American statecraft, *Bucharest Diary* provides a first-class lesson in how a chief of mission pursues his agenda by diligently working all the parties and all sides of an issue. Though he was not a Foreign Service officer, Al Moses's experience as a Washington attorney gave him skills as a counselor to the powerful and negotiator between conflicting parties— within Romania, the region, and, not least, the U.S. bureaucracy—to make a real success of his tenure. When NATO membership looked out of reach, he devised a special partnership between the Alliance and Bucharest to sustain the momentum. He worked deftly across borders and with Washington to resolve the thorny matter of rights for Romania's Hungarian minority. Political appointees to ambassadorships are often criticized as lightweight campaign contributors, and sometimes this is the case. But, as the proud son of a superb Foreign Service officer, I confess that Moses (who was not a Bill Clinton contributor) demonstrates another relevant point—that on occasion, accomplished individuals from law, business, and the academy, can bring skills to the job of ambassador that can match those of the finest career diplomats.

Al Moses left Bucharest in 1997 aboard Air Force One after an extraordinary visit by President Bill Clinton. The Romanian capital was the final stop of Clinton's journey from Madrid, where NATO leaders had agreed to admit Poland, Hungary, and the Czech Republic to NATO. Other stops were in Copenhagen and Poland, and the visit was a kind of consolation prize for Romania and encouragement to continue the hard work of reform so that it might win entry into NATO in the ensuing years. At least half a million exuberant Romanians turned out—other estimates were much higher—to greet the American president, even though their country was not yet being admitted to NATO along with others in the region. The event was a dramatic reaffirmation of Romania's decision to join the West despite all the obstacles.

Therein lies the overriding lesson of Bucharest Diary. At a time when many watch in horror the growth of illiberal democracy in countries like Hungary and Turkey, Moses's account is a powerful reminder of what the U.S. and its partners can do to promote democracy and market reforms when they dedicate themselves to the cause. We risk making a fateful error if we assume that the resurgence of popular nationalism and ethnic chauvinism is foreordained and unstoppable.

America's economic might and the soft power value of its culture and example in world affairs can again play a decisive role in international affairs. Al Moses did a masterful job in Bucharest deploying these tools to achieve the nation's policy goals. Bucharest Diary is a compelling reminder that, several decades later, we can do so again if we choose.

CHRISTOPHER VAN HOLLEN is a U.S. senator from Maryland. He is Co-Chair of the Senate Foreign Service Caucus and a member of the Foreign Operations Subcommittee of the Senate Appropriations Committee.

Preface

A full account of what happened in Eastern Europe after the Berlin Wall fell in 1989 and communism disappeared in that part of the world is yet to be written. I have tried with this book to fill in that part of history for one country, Romania, the second largest in Eastern Europe, where I served as the American ambassador from December 1994 to mid-July 1997.

My association with Romania began in the 1970s, when a chance encounter with young Jews on the streets of Bucharest led to my heading a movement to pressure Romania's communist dictator, Nicolae Ceaușescu, to let Romanian Jews emigrate to Israel. We succeeded. My work getting Jews out ended when Ceaușescu was executed, on Christmas Day, 1989—the only violent ending to communism in Eastern Europe. With the end of communism, Jews and others in Romania were finally free to leave.

On November 9—six weeks before Ceaușescu was executed—joyous young Germans tore down the Berlin Wall while East German soldiers stood by and watched but took no action to stop them. The symbol of the Wall coming down spelled the end of communism in Eastern Europe. One by one, the communist regimes rapidly crumbled—except for the Romanian government. Despite what was happening around him, Ceaușescu clung to power for eight more weeks. He was determined to hold on as long as he could. At the time of his execution, on December 25, Romania was already a shambles.

Its economy had plummeted. It was near or at the bottom of the countries of Europe. The next two years were worse. The economy collapsed even further, before starting a slow recovery in 1992.

Under communist rule the state had owned everything, from small businesses to giant industrial complexes, residential properties, and farmland, plus media, transportation, recreation, and tourism enterprises, and all the rest. Once out from under communism, the popular outcry in Romania was "Privatize!" But how? And who would do it? The government was staffed by leftover bureaucrats weaned on a communist diet of central planning. Romania's pre–World War II entrepreneurs were gone—killed, exiled, or impoverished by a repressive Romanian regime that had been brutal even by communist standards.

Political life was similarly in disarray. Romania's pre-communist political parties were a distant memory. Ceaușescu and his communist predecessors had crushed political dissent. There was no one in Romania like Poland's Lech Wałęsa, the leader of the Solidarity Movement, or Czechoslovakia's human rights activist, Václav Havel, to galvanize and guide political rebirth once the communists were gone. Romania had to start from the bottom to rebuild its economy and political institutions.

When Ceaușescu fled Bucharest by helicopter four days before he was executed, a small self-appointed group of Romanians took control of the country with support from the army. The group, headed by Ion Iliescu, a popular former communist, took the name National Salvation Front (NSF). Five months later elections were held to validate its takeover before political opposition could fully organize. Not unexpectedly, it received an overwhelming endorsement from an electorate still celebrating the end of Ceaușescu and communism. Iliescu was elected president of Romania, and Petre Roman, Iliescu's photogenic hand-picked choice, became prime minister.

Inch by inch, foot by foot, the new government set Romania on the path to recovery. Romania's democratic institutions were rebuilt along Western lines, with generous financial support and technical assistance from the United States, Canada, and the European Union. Western experts by the score came to Romania to train a new cadre of government workers to take over the nuts and bolts of government, help Romania establish an independent judiciary, and reorganize its military along Western lines.

The major funding for Romania's currency stabilization and economic restructuring came from the International Monetary Fund and the World Bank (officially, the International Bank for Reconstruction and Development). The lenders were tough, but rightly so. The Romanian government bristled at calls for economic reform, dragged its feet, one day shouted defiance, the next day cried for mercy, but in the end it had no choice but to comply with the IMF and World Bank mandates.

This book chronicles the long struggle from darkness to light in Romania, the internal conflicts and rivalries among Romania's leaders, the roles played by the Clinton White House, the U.S. State Department, the American military, and other agencies, and the job performed by the U.S. embassy in Bucharest, which was at the epicenter of the U.S. effort to rebuild Romania.

As might be expected in a country that had suffered so much and had so far to travel to recover, there were periodic economic and political crises. But somehow the political center held. Since Ceauşescu fell, Romania has held six national elections (not counting the "quick" election in May 1990), with centrist parties of the left and right winning all of them. Unlike its neighbors Poland, Hungary, and Greece, Romania has not veered to the extreme right or left. It has contributed troops to a half dozen or more United Nations and NATO peacekeeping missions around the world and enjoys the status of "strategic partner" of the United States. It is not a coincidence that Romania today hosts the largely U.S.-staffed North Atlantic Treaty Organization missile shield on the Black Sea. It is a member of both NATO and the European Union.

In the early years after the revolution, economic restructuring and privatization moved much too slowly, especially privatization. When President Bill Clinton visited Bucharest in July 1997, his only public criticism of Romania was its slow pace of privatization. Addressing a cheering crowd of more than 500,000 in Bucharest's University Square, he exhorted Romania to accelerate the pace of reform, telling his listeners that countries "that reform the fastest make the most progress for their people." To its credit, Romania quickened its pace of reform to the point where by 2017 its economy was the fastest growing in Europe. Still more amazing, in 2017 the average per capita income in Bucharest was higher than in Berlin.

Despite its laudable successes, Romania's recovery has been uneven. Its large rural population continues to live at low economic levels not much different from those of previous generations. Also weighing down Romania's economy are the thousand or so remaining large state-owned enterprises (SOEs) and *régies autonomes* (RAs)—semi-autonomous entities, subsidized by the government, adding to the country's budget deficit. These economic dinosaurs are sapping badly needed resources from the economy. Sadly, successive Romanian governments have lacked the political will, and often the resources, to reorganize or shut down these inefficient relics, whose justification is that they provide employment for hundreds of thousands of Romanians—but at a high price.

Romania has many ills. It remains deeply scarred by corruption, a historic problem Romania may never shake. The economy, for all its successes, is still lumpy. The transportation and energy industries need revamping. Intercity travel by road or rail is often difficult. Medical services are inadequate, and underpaid staff depend on "extra payments" from patients to supplement their pitifully low salaries. But on balance, Romania's successes outweigh its failures. Looking at Romania today, one has to marvel at how far the country has come in just three decades—in one generation.

I was present at the beginning of Romania's recovery at a time when the United States was riding the crest of popular acclaim for ridding Eastern Europe of communism. Nowhere was the United States more popular than in Romania, which considered the United States its savior and its protector from a Europe that had not historically been kind to Romania, a non-Slavic country surrounded by Slavic neighbors. Unlike their languages, Romanian has Latin roots.

Romania also has a long history of subservience to surrounding empires— Ottoman, Russian, and Austro-Hungarian—followed by European alliances that cast Romania in the role of junior partner with no control over its destiny. This gave rise to the adage among Romanians that their country has only two friends, Serbia and the Black Sea—and later they added the United States.

In December 1994, when I arrived in Romania as U.S. ambassador, the United States was the shining city on the hill, the country Romanians looked up to and wanted to hold fast to. This gave me the opportunity to help Romania build a free and democratic country closely allied with the United States. At the end of my ambassadorship I initiated a strategic partnership between the United States and Romania that benefits both countries, has endured for twenty years, and continues to grow.

Before I became ambassador, Romania was not on Washington's list of important countries. It was not considered a country whose president should be invited to meet the U.S. president; yet, after I became ambassador that is exactly what happened. In September 1995 Romania's President Ion Iliescu met with President Bill Clinton in the Oval Office. The next year First Lady Hillary Clinton came to Bucharest, followed a year later by President Clinton, who was officially welcomed in Bucharest by Romania's newly elected president, Emil Constantinescu, and by 500,000 cheering Romanians. American secretaries of state and their Romanian counterparts exchanged visits, as did respective heads of intelligence, military commanders, and legislative leaders, including the former senator and Republican Party leader Robert Dole. Former president George H. W. Bush and Barbara Bush, America's business leaders, sports figures, and well-known persons from all walks of life came to Bucharest for various reasons, each requiring the support of the American ambassador and embassy staff. On the lighter side, I gave a pre-wedding party in my residence for Romania's Olympic gymnast Nadia Comaneci and her husband-to-be, the Olympian Bart Conner. Each event contributed its own story to an interesting time to be the American ambassador to Romania.

Like most stories, this one has both heroes and rogues. The U.S. contribution to the rebuilding of Eastern Europe after the fall of communism was simply enormous. From 1989 onward, the United States opened its heart and pocketbook to help the countries of Eastern Europe recover from the dark days of communist economic stagnation and political oppression. Nothing on this scale had been undertaken since the Marshall Plan, forty years earlier, which rebuilt Western Europe after the defeat of Nazi Germany. The U.S. role in post-communist Eastern Europe, however, went far beyond helping Romania and other countries rebuild their devastated economies. After the fall of communism, the United States took the lead, in partnership with the European Union, to help these countries stabilize their currencies, rebuild their finances, carry out labor and fiscal reforms, build independent judiciaries, adopt Western taxation systems, modernize their military, build and protect independent media, train professional cadres in the ways of democracy, upgrade health systems, train local entrepreneurs, and provide financing for small and medium-size businesses. In other words, not just economic support but a comprehensive approach was taken to enable these countries to align with the West and be part of a free and democratic Europe. This was the United States at its best. Nowhere was America's help needed more than in Romania.

On the Romanian side, credit goes to the country's leaders, who never wavered in their commitment to democracy. For twenty-eight years—from President Ion Iliescu in 1990 through Romania's president as of 2018, Klaus Iohannis—Romania has stayed the course, rejecting anti-democratic forces active elsewhere in Eastern Europe. Not to be overlooked are the Romanian people themselves, who suffered so much for so long. Only they can answer the question, "Has it been worth it?," though I think the call is not a close one.

Over the years there were naysayers in the United States as well as in Romania who, had they prevailed, would have taken Romania in a different direction. They are discussed in this book. Some officials in Washington had reservations about the wisdom of helping Romania, a country with a checkered past and an uncertain future. Some questioned the value of foreign assistance in principle. Others distrusted Romania for reasons related to their own identification with other countries in Eastern Europe, primarily Poland and Hungary, which they considered more worthy of U.S. support. There were also a small number of Republican congressmen who wanted the United States to have nothing to do with Romania's President Ion Iliescu, who in their eyes was irredeemably tainted by his communist past. Better to wait, they said, for a government led by Romania's Christian Democrats. In reality, they were saying to the Romanian people, we, not you, should choose your leaders.

After Ceauşescu was overthrown in December 1989, the future political direction of the country was uncertain. Corneliu Vadim Tudor's Romania Mare (Greater Romania) party was most vocal in opposing the country's mainstream political parties. Tudor had been Ceauşescu's court jester and poet. After Ceauşescu fell, Tudor trumpeted a call for the reestablishment of "Greater Romania," a reference to the interwar (1920–39) Romania, when, in addition to its present territory, it included Bessarabia (now Moldova), Northern Bukovina (now part of Ukraine), and the Dobruja (now part of Bulgaria). Greater Romania was twice the size of present-day Romania. Tudor and his party—xenophobic, anti-Semitic, nativists, populists, and jingoists—were a constant thorn in the side of mainstream Romanian politics. Tudor's star rose for a time; he challenged President Iliescu in the runoff for president of Romania in December 2000, only to lose badly, after which his political star faded. He died in 2015.

This book tells the story of Romania under Ceauşescu and my involvement in facilitating the emigration of Romanian Jews to Israel, which was how I became the American ambassador to Romania. I provide a brief overview of Romanian history, to set the scene for the Romania I encountered on arriving in Bucharest as ambassador, followed by a tell-all account of my tenure as ambassador. Recurring themes during my ambassadorship were Romania's start-and-stop economic reform efforts; its strong desire to join Western institutions, principally NATO; the jockeying for power on the Romanian political scene; Romania's relations with its neighbors; my efforts to help Romania conclude basic treaties with two of them, Hungary and Ukraine; the inner workings of the political and bureaucratic scene in Washington that shaped our relationship with Romania; daily life in Romania; and the way the American embassy functioned during my service.

My ambassadorship was unexpected for two reasons. I was neither a Foreign Service officer nor a political contributor to the presidential campaign, the usual paths to an ambassadorial appointment. I was a partner in a major Washington, D.C., law firm that I joined fresh out of law school in 1956 after serving forty months in the U.S. Navy as an intelligence officer. I was also active on behalf of Jewish causes and had served a short stint in the Carter White House, but none of this was a traditional path to an ambassadorship.

My hope is that my Romanian saga will come alive for you, as will the people I write about, what they did and how they did it, the choices they made and why they made them. Is Romania's story unique, or is it part of a larger history of humanity's search for freedom and prosperity? In truth, it is both.

For those readers wishing to read a firsthand account of the fascist years in Romania, I recommend Mihail Sebastian's *Journal 1935–44*, first published in Romanian in 1996 and republished in English by Rowman & Littlefield in 2012. For those interested in a fictional but accurate narrative of Romanian life in communist times, *The Land of Green Plums* (Rowohlt, 1994; Metropolitan Books, 1996), a novel by the Nobel laureate Herta Müller, describes the harsh life for Romanians under an oppressive communist regime.

PART ONE

My Introduction to Romania

Ceaușescu, Romania's Jews, Chief Rabbi Rosen, and Me

MY FIRST YEARS IN ROMANIA, 1976–1989

In early 1976 I received a phone call from New York asking me to lead an American Jewish Committee delegation to Bucharest in late February. I immediately said yes. I was on the AJC's National Board. As far as I knew, none of my ancestors had ever set foot in Romania, yet the country had always fascinated me. I remembered reading about Romania's joining Nazi Germany and Fascist Italy in World War II. In college, I read about the Congress of Berlin, where in 1878 the Great Powers recognized Romania's independence from the Ottoman Empire.

I also read about Romania's role in the slow unraveling of the European order after the Congress of Berlin, its defeat by Germany in the Great War (World War I), and its triumphal return to the war on the Allies' side a few days before the Armistice was signed in Versailles in November 1918. I even had a vague picture in my head of what Bucharest, Romania's capital, looked like. I knew that Romanians called it the Paris of the East, and that in reality it was shabby and decadent compared to the City of Light on the Seine. For whatever reason, shabby, decadent Bucharest appealed to me. Maybe it was the allure of the unknown or a romantic notion of life in a distant spot on the globe about which I knew almost nothing.

Reality hit me when my wife, Carol, and I boarded a Tarom Airlines (the Romanian national airline) flight from Greece to Romania in late February 1976. I was moving into the unknown, and the plane didn't look any too airworthy, but we landed safely in Bucharest. Once inside the terminal, we entered another world. There was an air of harshness mixed with corruption and melancholy so pervasive you could feel it. In the airport, the metal detectors did not work and the baggage conveyor was broken. Our luggage was tossed onto creaky cardboard tables by disgruntled, unshaven airport workers in dirty overalls. Corruption was on open display wherever we looked—jostling by airport attendants, customs officials searching for contraband to seize and probably sell on the black market.

Outside the airport, the sense of desolation grew deeper, with hushed conversations on street corners, bugged hotel rooms, paid informers, and soldiers lolling about smoking cigarettes and asking for "gifts." The streets were dimly lit to save energy in a near-bankrupt country. Room temperatures were bone-chilling.

We stayed at Bucharest's once fabled Athenee Palace Hotel, its pre–World War II grandeur faded almost beyond recognition. When Carol and I exited the elevator the next morning, we saw middle-aged and older women on their hands and knees scrubbing the badly scuffed lobby floors. Carol firmly pronounced, "I am never coming back here." Neither of us could have imagined that eighteen years later I would return to Romania as the U.S. ambassador.

Over the next few days we saw much of Bucharest, but our principal focus was on the city's Jewish community. Before the war it had numbered some 100,000; now that number was down to about 20,000, mostly elderly. Our first stop was at the Jewish Federation's offices adjoining the Choral Synagogue, a short distance from the hotel. The synagogue, built in the late 1800s, was the historic seat of Romania's chief rabbi.

Although it was February, the synagogue, like most buildings in Bucharest, was unheated. Despite its being without heat and badly in need of repair, the building's faded beauty and great dignity were there to see. Looking at the bema with the "eternal light" flickering over the Torah scrolls and the familiar Hebrew inscription above it, I felt at home. There is a sameness to traditional synagogues that is familiar and welcoming to those of us raised in Jewish homes. Memories and feelings travel with us, even when hidden beneath the surface. They are rekindled on occasions like this, visiting a once magnificent synagogue.

The federation offices were in a yellow stucco two-story building across a narrow cobblestone driveway from the synagogue. There we were met by a delegation of community leaders carrying flowers and the traditional Romanian gift of greeting, a large beautiful twisted loaf of bread and salt. The delegation immediately apologized for the absence of Chief Rabbi Moses Rosen, who at that time was out of the country on his annual visit, with his wife, to a kosher hotel in Switzerland. It was clear from words and tone that Rabbi Rosen was the real power in this Jewish community, both venerated and feared. I would meet Rabbi Rosen for the first time a few years later when I returned to Bucharest to take up with Ceauşescu the cause of Romanian Jewry, which by then had become my cause as well. The Jewish community leaders did their best to explain how the highly organized Jewish community functioned under Rabbi Rosen's direction. Much of what we heard was oft-rehearsed, exaggerated rhetoric intended to impress foreign visitors with the vibrancy of the community and the religiosity of its members. We were told there were functioning synagogues throughout Romania, kosher kitchens, Talmud torahs (schools), a Jewish-Yiddish theater, and more.

In truth, the description was more like a Potemkin village than reality. Jewish life was literally dying out. Most Jews were Jewishly illiterate. Older Jews could read and speak Yiddish but not Hebrew. Their recitation of the Jewish prayers was by rote; few of them could actually understand the Hebrew prayers. Younger Jews knew even less. The Jewish community was principally supported by the American Jewish Joint Distribution Committee—the Joint, for short—which each year contributed about $2 million, a major share of the community's total budget, and helped the dwindling Jewish population survive.

The rest of the day was given over to visiting the Jewish Community Center a few blocks from the Choral Synagogue, followed by shorter stops at two other synagogues. One was the Sephardic Synagogue, now largely a museum with pictures of the slaughter of Romanian Jews by the Nazis and Romanian fascists in the early 1940s. The other was the dark, dank "Great Synagogue," no longer used for daily services but housing a small Jewish pre-school. Already feeling gloomy, we moved on to the Jewish community's old-age home, where many Holocaust survivors lived, barely able to talk or get about without help. From what we could tell, the staff was kind and caring, but the facilities were old and woefully inadequate.

When not walking around Bucharest, our mode of transportation was an old bus that coughed and chugged but somehow managed to get us where we were supposed to be eventually. February was not the ideal month to be in Bucharest, particularly, as in our case, after a heavy snowfall. Phalanxes of men and women in office clothes were on the streets shoveling snow. Our Romanian guide explained to us that they were "volunteers" doing their patriotic duty on behalf of the Socialist Republic of Romania. These poor souls, dragooned from their offices, had to shovel snow in the bitter cold.

Bucharest in 1976 was caught in a time warp that began in the nineteenth century and ended in the late 1930s. Horse-drawn carts were commonplace on the cobblestone streets. Other modes of transportation were equally dated—rattling, coughing old trucks, underpowered Romanian-made Dacia automobiles, and an occasional foreign car that looked out of place. Bucharest's once handsome buildings were in disrepair, with peeling paint on the outside and rotting wood protruding through openings. In the streets, no one said hello or acknowledged our presence but instead averted their gaze. Gray skies added to the gloom, as did the ever-present smog from coal-burning furnaces that cast a permanent yellow haze over the city. One could smell the smog as well as see it.

Then something unexpected happened that would forever tie me to Romania. Three young Jewish boys in their teens approached Carol and me on the sidewalk outside our hotel. With downcast eyes, one of them asked me in English if I was American. When I said yes, he asked if I was Jewish. When I again answered yes, he blurted out, "Don't believe what they tell you. The situation here is terrible, especially for Jews. We are blamed for everything that goes wrong. Help us get out. There is no future for Jews in Romania. Everything you hear is a lie, a lie, a lie." From that moment on, I was hooked. Over the next thirteen years I built a cottage industry in the United States with one goal—getting Romania's dwindling Jewish community out of Romania.

It is hard for people in the West, even Jews living today, to understand what it was like to be a Jew in nineteenth- and early twentieth-century Eastern Europe. Jews were a community apart, living together in small Jewish communities, shtetls, and later in largely Jewish cities or parts of cities with their own community leaders and sometimes their own police and tax collectors. Eastern Europe was not a melting pot for Jews. Jews in Romania lived like their fellow Jews in neighboring Ukraine, Galicia (Poland), and Russia. Before World War II, they numbered 800,000, more than 4 percent of the population (less than 2 percent of the U.S. population is Jewish). They were lower-middle-class artisans, metalworkers, tailors, and shopkeepers. After the Congress of Berlin in 1878 and the slow lifting of restrictions on Jews, they entered the liberal professions—law and medicine—primarily in Bucharest and larger Romanian cities. Romania's original Jews came from Poland; later, Jews fleeing the Inquisition in Spain and Portugal came to Romania. There were still Sephardic—Spanish-Portuguese—synagogues in Romania when I arrived in the 1970s that traced their ancestry to Jewish communities on the Iberian Peninsula. Other Jews in Romania may have been descended from the Khazars, a nomadic Turkic people living in what is today Kazakhstan, who converted en masse to Judaism in the ninth or tenth century. The region was overrun by the Mongols in the thirteenth century.

A rich culture surrounded Jewish life in Romania. The Yiddish theater began in Romania, and even in my day a large number of *chazanim*, cantors, in the United States were born in Romania. Maybe the fusion of Roma gypsy music with Jewish liturgical melodies accounted for the profusion of Jewish music in Romania. But unlike their coreligionists elsewhere in Eastern Europe, Romanian Jewry did not produce great scholars, writers, nor even notable Jewish lay leaders. The establishment of famous yeshivas, religious schools, in nineteenth- and twentieth-century Lithuania, Belarus, Poland, and Ukraine did not occur in Romania. This led Jews elsewhere to consider Romanian Jews a Jewishly uneducated, backwater society, left behind by the wave of modernity that swept over Europe.

After World War II, most Romanian Jews emigrated to Israel, in all about 400,000. This began immediately after the war, when Jewish survivors of the Holocaust and fascist Romania left in waves for the soon-to-be Jewish state of Israel, later entering the country under Israel's "right of return," which applied to Jews worldwide. Another large wave of Romanian Jews left for Israel in the early 1960s; after that, a slow trickle followed each year.

Israel was closer and easier to get to than the United States and did not require an immigration visa. Moreover, applying for a U.S. visa was time-consuming, with an uncertain outcome. As a political matter, Romania's communist regime rationalized that Jews emigrating to Israel were "return-ing" to their historic homeland. This was less of a black eye for Romania's communist leaders than Jewish emigration to a Western country, especially the United States. Romanian Jews had been among the early Zionists who emigrated to Palestine more than a hundred years before.

When I visited Romania with two of our daughters in the early 1980s, we saw synagogues in Moldavia (one of Romania's two historic principalities that at one time had a large Jewish population) with primitive hand-painted art depicting biblical scenes in ancient Israel as imagined by the artists. As Rabbi Rosen liked to say, "Our Jews go to Israel, not Philadelphia." It was true then and continues to be true today.

JEWISH EMIGRATION FROM ROMANIA TO ISRAEL: A COMPLEX COLLABORATION

Over time, I became the point person in the United States for Romanian Jewish emigration—not that there was much competition. I eventually built a network among American Jewish organizations, members of Congress, and the executive branch. I spoke not only for myself but also on behalf of the American Jewish Committee and the Conference of Presidents of Major American Jewish Organizations (Conference of Presidents), the umbrella or-ganization that was then comprised of some thirty or so organizations but now has many more.

Other Jewish organizations helped, particularly B'nai B'rith International. We worked together meeting with senators and officials in the White House and the State and Commerce Departments, interceding with the Romanian ambassador in Washington and, on three occasions, directly with Ceaușescu and his ministers. Over those thirteen years, the Carter, Reagan, and Bush ad-ministrations supported our efforts, as did the American embassy in Bucharest.

In the Senate, Senators Adlai Stevenson III (D-Ill.) and John Danforth (R-Mo.) were particularly helpful. The Israeli government also pitched in, but

I had no idea at the time that it was paying Romania a flat fee for each Jew allowed to emigrate to Israel. I did not learn about the Israeli payments until I read Radu Ioanid's book, *The Ransom of the Jews: The Story of the Extraordinary Secret Bargain between Romania and Israel*, published in 2005. (Ioanid is the archival director at the Holocaust Museum in Washington, D.C.) I later learned that the Federal Republic of Germany paid a head tax to Ceaușescu as well to allow German nationals to emigrate from Romania to West Germany.

Ceaușescu allowed people like Rabbi Rosen to travel abroad with the implicit understanding that they would not use their freedom to criticize Romania. By the time I arrived on the scene, Israel's Romanian efforts were coordinated by Nehemiah Levanon, in the prime minister's office. I met with Levanon in my Washington office in 1979 in what turned out to be an unpleasant few hours. Neither then nor later did he or any other Israeli official clue me in on the secret Israeli payments. In effect, Ceaușescu was collecting at both ends for the same thing—cash from Israelis and trade benefits from the United States. I blame the Israelis as much as Ceaușescu, first, for not telling me, and second, for paying a head tax for nothing. Our group in the United States had the muscle to get Jews out, and we did.

Our leverage was most favored nation (MFN) trade status for Romania, which came up each year for renewal in the U.S. Congress. Under the Jackson-Vanik Amendment to the 1974 trade law, which governed U.S. trade relations with communist countries, the president was required to review Romania's MFN status annually. If the administration recommended renewal, it became law unless Congress voted to reject it. In some years the House of Representatives passed legislation rejecting MFN status for Romania, but the Senate did not concur. My and my colleagues' efforts were focused on the Senate.

The Ford administration first recommended MFN status for Romania in 1975, largely in recognition of Romania's acts of independence from the Soviet Union in some aspects of foreign policy. For example, Ceaușescu continued diplomatic relations with Israel during the 1967 Six-Day War when the Soviet Union and the rest of the communist world broke off relations. A year later he denounced the Red Army's crushing of the Prague Spring and kept Romania's military out of the Warsaw Pact High Command.

Ceaușescu also tweaked the nose of Soviet leaders in the Kremlin by periodically visiting China, where he was welcomed with lavish displays of friendship fit for a true world leader, far exceeding Ceaușescu's relative insignificance on the world stage. Ceaușescu was an unintended beneficiary of the Sino-Soviet conflict. The Chinese poured on the flattery as a way of showing that the Soviet Union was not the world's only communist power. In Peking, Ceaușescu met with the Chinese Communist leader, Mao Zedong, and, after he died, with his successor, Deng Xiaoping. He also regularly traveled to Belgrade to meet with Yugoslavia's president, Josip Broz Tito, who had taken Yugoslavia out of the Soviet camp in 1948.

Ceaușescu's "freelancing" got Washington's attention, with White House meetings and official state dinners for him hosted by Presidents Nixon, Ford, and Carter. Presidents Nixon and Ford also visited Romania, where they were greeted by large, enthusiastic crowds. The crowds may not have been entirely spontaneous—the communists knew how to turn out the masses—but the huge numbers of Romanians lining the streets and the enthusiastic popular receptions were impressive. The popular reaction was duly noted in Washington and set off alarm bells in Moscow. As Washington saw it, MFN status was the "reward" for Romania's not hewing to Moscow's line. The annual MFN review by the administration and Congress gave me and the other proponents of Jewish emigration the leverage to prod Romania, a country hungry for hard, freely convertible currency, to let its Jews go.

Ceaușescu knew that Jewish opposition would end MFN for Romania, and without MFN, Romanian goods could not compete in the U.S. market. High U.S. tariffs would have kept Romania's exports out of the country. This was a real threat. Members of Congress on both sides of the aisle had reason to want to block MFN for Romania. For some, it was ethnic politics. Hungarian Americans were vocal in their opposition, which stemmed from historical tensions between ethnic Romanians and ethnic Hungarians in Transylvania, which before 1918 had been part of the Austro-Hungarian Empire.

The majority of people living in Transylvania were ethnic Romanians, but those in power before 1918 were mainly Hungarian. In the peace treaty that followed World War I, Transylvania became part of Romania, but the anger and dismay of ethnic Hungarians, who saw themselves as Transylvania's rightful rulers and cultural elite, remained. Other members of Congress seeking to block MFN for Romania were responding to pressure from American businesses that would be hurt by cheap Romanian imports. For still others, it came down to their rightful distrust and disapproval of Ceaușescu and fear and hatred of communism.

Despite these pressures, Democratic and Republican administrations recommended to Congress that Romania's MFN status be renewed, and Congress went along. In return, Romania committed to Jewish emigration and gave lip service to its commitments under the 1975 Helsinki Accords to respect the human and religious rights of all its citizens. But annual renewal was never a slam dunk, and without Jewish support, the outcome would have been different. To guard against slipups, I and a handful of advocates would meet with key senators each year to urge their support and during the voting would stand off the Senate floor corralling votes.

Meetings with Nicolae Ceaușescu

Until Ceaușescu's overthrow and death at the end of 1989 and Rabbi Rosen's death four years later, the two men had been the key players for me—Ceaușescu because he controlled everything in Romania, and Rabbi Rosen because he was the voice and leader of the Romanian Jewish community. Ceaușescu was the country's coach and quarterback—he called every play and then passed or ran with the ball—so it was not a contest between equals. But what Rabbi Rosen lacked in political power, he made up for in wiliness and connections, particularly in the United States, that impressed the peasant-born Ceaușescu. By supporting MFN, Rabbi Rosen found a way to be valuable to Ceaușescu and in exchange gained modest benefits for Romania's Jews.

Despite Ceaușescu's relative independence from Moscow, or perhaps because of it, Romania was one of the most oppressive countries in the communist bloc. Ceaușescu modeled his rule on the North Korean dictator Kim Il-sung, whom he visited in 1971. The U.S. policy of containment of the Soviet Union by both Democratic and Republican administrations sought engagement with communist dictators such as Ceaușescu who might either challenge Moscow or support the United States at Moscow's expense. Ceaușescu played it both ways, sidling up to the West to curry favor without cutting his ties to his ultimate partner in Moscow. Détente made for strange and sometimes odious bedfellows. The United States and other Western countries showered Ceaușescu with blandishments, even though they had to know that Ceaușescu's trappings of independence were just that. Ceaușescu, the boorish, conniving peasant, with his wife, Elena, at his side, even received an honorary knighthood in 1978 from Queen Elizabeth II at Westminster Abbey.

Elena was even more detested in Romania than her husband. Neither was educated, but she laid claim to being a chemist, and her all-powerful husband appointed her head of the Romanian Academy of Science, a venerable and highly respected Romanian institution. Her appointment was a joke among Romanians and a national embarrassment. To complete the charade, the communist propaganda machine attributed to her numerous inventions that she had never even seen and was probably incapable of understanding. Nevertheless, in Ceaușescu's later years and with his health failing from diabetes, Elena appeared publicly by his side, more and more taking on the trappings of being a co-equal ruler with her husband.

Who was Ceaușescu? Peasant-born, largely uneducated, like Josef Stalin, he worked his way up the Communist Party ladder. He had no obvious intellectual gifts and, unlike Stalin, did not engage in ideological debates. On his route to power he was subservient to his bosses, but once he reached the top, he was brutal to those below him. Ceaușescu valued power for power's sake, not ideology. In his younger years he was known as a brawler, but by the time I met him, he was flabby, with a receding hairline of grayish white hair and a pudgy, colorless face. He was peasant-smart, wily, determined to maintain control of the Communist Party and, through it, Romania. Like Stalin, he forsook religion at an early age. Over time, the Romanian Orthodox Church was subjugated to his will and, along with other institutions, infiltrated by informers. The church in Romania was central to national identity. Like communist leaders elsewhere, Ceaușescu was wary of openly breaking with the church for fear of antagonizing the faithful. In the eyes of Romania's communist leaders, an infiltrated, compromised, and therefore subservient Orthodox church (starting at the top with the patriarch) was better than one that might challenge the government. Ceaușescu undoubtedly looked with concern at what was happening in Poland when Cardinal Karol Józef Wojtyła, later Pope John Paul II, openly challenged communist authority.

My first meeting with Ceaușescu was in April 1978 in New York City's grand Waldorf Astoria Towers. It was arranged by Romania's ambassador,

Nicolae Nicolae, who believed the anti-Semitic canard that Jews were at the epicenter of the business world. He implored me to bring a group of Jewish business leaders to discuss investment opportunities with Ceaușescu. I had been in frequent contact with Ambassador Nicolae on behalf of Romanian Jewry, and he probably assumed (wrongly) that I had great sway within the Jewish community.

Not to disappoint him, I persuaded some dozen prominent Jewish business and financial leaders to meet in New York with Ceaușescu on his way back to Bucharest after official meetings in Washington and a state dinner at the White House. Our group, some of whom had never met each other, huddled in the Waldorf Towers lobby long enough for me to explain our mission and to make sure we stuck to the script—tell Ceaușescu that Jewish investment in Romania depended on his government's allowing Romanian Jews to emigrate. All nodded agreement, whereupon we walked across the lobby to a secure elevator that took us to the heavily guarded forty-seventh floor.

When we entered Ceaușescu's suite, we were greeted by Ambassador Nicolae and Romania's foreign minister, Stefan Andrei (much later sentenced to two years in jail for ordering the army to shoot demonstrators in the uprising that toppled Ceaușescu in 1989). To say that Ceaușescu was unimpressive would be an understatement. What little he said was without emotion or conviction. He conveyed minor annoyance at our constant harping on the right of Jews to leave Romania but otherwise seemed distant and uninterested. After the meeting, Ambassador Nicolae registered disappointment that we had focused on Jewish emigration, not business opportunities in Romania, which was the reason for his arranging the meeting. I suppose that was a victory for our side. The only takeaway from the meeting was Ceaușescu's affirmative grunt when I asked him to acknowledge that Romania's Jews were free to emigrate to Israel.

Ceaușescu may have been grumpy for another reason. Zbigniew Brzezinski, President Jimmy Carter's national security adviser, had called me earlier that morning to tell me that President Carter had raised the issue of Jewish emigration with Ceaușescu in their meeting at the White House. This was in response to my raising the issue with Brzezinski a few days before. Ceaușescu angrily rejected President Carter's intervention, saying that emigration was an internal Romanian matter—in effect, "This is none of your business." President Carter replied unsmilingly, with his well-known icy blue-eyed stare, "I want you to understand, President Ceaușescu, that in the United States, the concern of American Jews for their co-religionists in Romania has a bearing on U.S. government policy toward Romania." It was a not very subtle hint of things to come if Ceaușescu steered Romania off course.

The Israeli Government Gets Involved

After the Ceaușescu meeting, things went well for a while. Then the Israeli government got involved, and it was a whole new ball game. I had not heard before from the Israelis on Romanian Jewry. I had assumed Israel was staying away from the issue largely as a quid pro quo for Romania's helping Israel on other matters. I was wrong. The Israeli government decided to use its muscle in the United States to oppose renewal of MFN for Romania unless it agreed to allow 2,500 Jews to emigrate by the end of 1979. I later learned that this was part of a larger strategy to convince the Soviet Union to take seriously its obligations under the Jackson-Vanik Amendment to the U.S. Trade Act that mandated communist countries to allow free emigration as a condition of receiving MFN status.

While Israel paid Romania to allow Jews to leave, MFN was the only tool available to the Israelis to prod the Soviet Union to allow its Jews to emigrate. And the numbers were huge: An estimated 2 million Jews lived in the Soviet Union, making the Jewish population in Romania seem minuscule by comparison. The Israeli government had decided that the Soviets would view pressure on Romania as a sign that the Soviet Union needed to open its spigot or risk losing MFN. This cockamamie thinking puzzled me. Israel was desperate to speed Jewish emigration from the Soviet Union to Israel. This depended on MFN. No one was foolish enough to think that Israel or its friends would fool around with Jackson-Vanik as it applied to the Soviet Union.

It was a hollow gesture on Israel's part even to suggest this possibility, let alone make it a threat. Soviet diplomats in Washington and their colleagues in Moscow were not spending their time worrying about what was happening in Ceaușescu's Romania, for which they had no love. Moreover, blocking MFN for Romania would have harmed Romanian–United States relations and probably Romanian-Israeli relations. The Jewish community in the United States would have been blamed for pushing a parochial interest, at the price of the larger national interest, and it would have placed the Romanian Jewish community in an impossible position, held hostage by Ceaușescu and likely blamed for Romania's failure to get MFN. Bilateral trade between the United States and Romania at the time was around $1 billion a year, not a huge number, but MFN was important to Romania, a country desperate to get hard currency to pay down its external debt and to improve economic relations with the United States and Western Europe.

I tried to explain this to Nehemiah Levanon, the point man in the Israeli prime minister's office, when he came to my office in Washington in late April to convince me to take a hard line with Romania. Several prominent Jewish organizations, not previously concerned with the plight of Romania's Jews, had been persuaded by Levanon to follow Israel's lead and take an active role opposing MFN for Romania. Levanon spoke with great authority and did not hesitate to mention the names of important Israelis as he made the rounds speaking to Jewish organizations. On matters affecting distressed Jewish communities around the world, American Jews tend to follow Israel's lead on the assumption that Israel knows more about what is happening in those countries than they do. While often true, there are exceptions, and this was one of them. By looking at potentially large Jewish emigration from the Soviet Union, and trying to use Romania's Jews as leverage, Israel was putting much at risk for nothing. In the end, we were able to come up with a decent outcome to avoid what would have been a loss for all concerned.

When word reached Bucharest that renewal of MFN was in serious trouble, the Foreign Affairs Ministry sent to Washington its head of the North American Section, a former Romanian ambassador to the United States, Corneliu Bogdan, a Romanian Jew who had forsaken his Jewish roots. Theodore Mann, the president of the Conference of Presidents, asked me to chair the meeting with Bogdan. There were to be three of us: George Spectre, associate director of B'nai B'rith International, Mark Talisman on behalf of the Federation of Jewish Philanthropists, and me. Spectre, Talisman, and I met fifteen minutes before the scheduled meeting to plan our strategy. Both men turned to me, the Washington lawyer, and expressed the hope that I could think of something before the meeting began. When Bogdan arrived, I put together a three-part proposal that survived the heat of the negotiations and became the cornerstone of the agreement we reached.

Bogdan had served as Romania's ambassador to Washington from 1967 to 1976, longer than any other person. He was well regarded in the United States, where he had reached out to the American public, including the Jewish community. (Bogdan later broke with Ceaușescu and was sacked by the Foreign Ministry. Out of work and money, he turned to the Jewish Federation in Bucharest for help.)

In our meeting, I proposed to Bogdan that Rabbi Rosen (whom I had not yet met) be authorized to announce publicly throughout Romania that any Jew wishing to emigrate would be permitted to do so and that the Romanian government would furnish me with regular reports on the number of applications filed and the dates they were filed. The last part of the proposal called for Jews seeking to emigrate to Israel to register with the Israeli embassy in Bucharest.

Following several days of brinksmanship and an all-day session on July 4 at the Romanian embassy, we had an agreement. Bogdan had resisted at each step of the way, but after checking with Bucharest at the end of the day on July 4, he finally agreed to our proposal while conveying his unhappiness and that of his government.

The agreement was put on paper in an unsigned aide-mémoire. As a private person negotiating with a foreign government, I knew I would need State Department support, so with Bogdan at my side, I presented the agreement to the State Department. The department forwarded it the same day to the U.S. embassy in Bucharest, after which I sent a letter to Congressman Charles Vanik (R-Ohio), chairman of the House Ways and Means Subcommittee on Trade, reporting on the successful negotiations and endorsing the renewal of MFN for Romania. With American Jewish support, a resolution in the House to block MFN was defeated and not even introduced in the Senate.

In October Rabbi Rosen proudly announced to a full synagogue of worshippers in Bucharest on Yom Kippur (Day of Atonement) that any Jew wishing to emigrate to Israel could register with the Romanian Jewish Federation. Within days, more than 600 people registered. Rabbi Rosen thought the initial burst would become a trickle, but by year-end the number reached 1,000. Importantly, after the July agreement there was only one case of an applicant being demoted in her job after applying for a passport—previously a common occurrence. Rabbi Rosen interceded, and the applicant, an English teacher, received her passport and emigrated to Israel.

For the next four or five years things went reasonably well. Each year President Ronald Reagan's administration recommended renewal of MFN for Romania and Congress did not oppose it. Each month I received from Bucharest a list of passport applicants with dates of their applications. I went over the names, checked on the time it took for an applicant to receive a passport, and helped those in need to settle in Israel.

Enter His Eminence, Chief Rabbi Moses Rosen

In December 1979 I learned that Congressman Vanik would be heading a congressional delegation to Eastern Europe in January and that his trip included a two-day stop in Bucharest. Congressman Vanik was a strong supporter of Jewish emigration from communist countries and was rightly proud that his name was attached to the famous Jackson-Vanik Amendment to the Trade Act. I also heard that Congressman Vanik's delegation would meet with Ceaușescu, an opportunity I did not want to miss.

With encouragement from Congressman Vanik's office, the Conference of Presidents asked Jack Spitzer, the president of B'nai B'rith, and me to go to Bucharest. We were to meet with Rabbi Rosen and the Romanian Jewish community and then join the congressional delegation during its two days in country. Before leaving for Romania, I met with Congressman Vanik, State Department counselor Matt Nimetz, and Carl Schmidt, director of the Office of Eastern European Affairs at the State Department, to get an update on happenings in Romania.

For four years I had been promoting the right of Jews to leave Romania, and I felt a personal responsibility to see it through. For Jack Spitzer, Romania was a new experience. But what he lacked in knowledge of Romania and its Jews, he made up for in enthusiasm. Once in Bucharest, our first stop was the Jewish Federation offices adjoining the Choral Synagogue, where I had met the federation's leaders, but not Rabbi Rosen, four years before. This time Rabbi Rosen was the first to greet us, which he did with great warmth.

It was late afternoon on a cold January day. He quickly ushered Jack and me into his office to plan a trip the next day to Predeal in the Carpathian Mountains, where Ceaușescu was vacationing. We knew there could be no meaningful meeting with Ceaușescu concerning Romania's Jews without

Rabbi Rosen's presence and participation. This was the beginning of my close collaboration with him, which continued until his death in March 1994.

Rabbi Rosen's role as chief rabbi of Romania bore little resemblance to that of an American rabbi, even a prominent one. Rosen was Orthodox, but not Hasidic. Yet despite a steady drop in the number of Romanian Jews, to about 20,000 in 1976, Rabbi Rosen maintained the trappings of a traditional Hasidic rebbe, with a royal court of attendants, including a chief of protocol, a government relations specialist (fixer, I suppose), an appointments secretary, a sermon writer, another writer to edit the community's weekly newspaper with articles signed in Rabbi Rosen's name, plus personal attendants, secretaries, and a driver for his black Mercedes.

As the political and religious head of the Jewish community, he automatically had a seat in the Romanian Parliament. (Under the Romanian constitution adopted after the communists came to power in 1947, Jews were one of fourteen recognized "cults" whose leaders were entitled to membership in Parliament.) In short, he thought of himself, and acted, as a notable potentate.

Much about Rabbi Rosen's persona raised questions. His father had been a rabbi in Moldavia, a historical Romanian principality, and Rabbi Rosen claimed to have received rabbinic ordination in Vienna, but the details were sketchy. He survived World War II as a rabbi in Moldavia, where Jews were relatively safe under Ion Antonescu (1882–1946), the authoritarian prime minister and dictator of Romania during World War II who condoned murdering Jews in Bessarabia and Northern Bukovina, both of which had been annexed by the Soviet Union before World War II, but not in the historic Romanian principalities of Wallachia and Moldavia.

Among Rabbi Rosen's detractors was Alexandru Şafran, Rosen's predecessor and later the chief rabbi of Geneva, Switzerland. He had been deposed as Romania's chief rabbi by the communists in 1948 in favor of the more communist-compatible Rabbi Rosen. Rabbi Şafran later wrote a tell-all book about his life in Bucharest and his role as Romania's chief rabbi during World War II, sharply criticizing Rabbi Rosen's "takeover" as chief rabbi.

Rabbi Rosen clearly thought of himself as not just part of the Jewish community but as its undisputed—and unquestioned—leader whose directions others should follow even if he did not always follow them himself. To illustrate the point, he frequently talked about the obligation of childless Romanian Jews to bequeath their property to the Jewish Federation, but this apparently did not apply to him. When he died in 1994, his sole beneficiary was his wife's nephew.

Imperfections aside, Rabbi Rosen was an engaging, energetic operator who kept alive and sustained the Jewish community in Romania. What he did was not always pretty or strictly kosher, but he was courageous and shrewd. He made a Faustian bargain with the communists that they would not interfere in the affairs of the Jewish community, and in return he would see to it that the Jewish community did not cause trouble for the government.

Under this unwritten pact, Romanian Jews lived as traditional Jews, practicing their religion, but were expected to stay out of politics. They were also under constant surveillance. One of my favorite photographs, taken in the Choral Synagogue in the late 1980s, shows me in the front row during the annual memorial service for Jews murdered by Romania's Iron Guard in 1940. On one side is Roger Kirk, the American ambassador. Seated next to us is the ambassador from Poland and to his left the Canadian ambassador. On my right is a Securitate agent sent to observe and record everything we said and did.

As far as I know, Rabbi Rosen never spoke truth to power in Romania, but given his role and responsibilities, this was understandable. The penalty for dissent in Romania was severe, with little to be gained. One either went along with Ceauşescu through silent acquiescence or ended up in prison under a penal system that was at best harsh and often brutal. At the same time, when outside Romania, Rabbi Rosen was not an apologist for Ceauşescu and did not sugarcoat the bad things that happened in Romania. I suppose he could get away with this because Ceauşescu saw the value of having someone speaking freely abroad who was not a Ceauşescu puppet, but Rabbi Rosen knew his limits.

No Jewish community in postwar Eastern Europe had an easy time, but Romania posed particular challenges. Romania's communist leaders, first Gheorghe Gheorghiu-Dej, then Ceauşescu, came to power at the point of Soviet bayonets. Lacking a homegrown base, communism in Romania progressively turned inward, as its leaders sought to stoke feelings among its indigenous nationalities of pride in the country's traditions and culture. This put Jews, as an ethnic and religious minority, under suspicion of being less than "purely Romanian." In the eyes of non-Jewish Romanians, Jewish traditions and culture were different. They were linked to a separate Jewish existence in a Jewish world that did not include Romania.

In the same vein, from time to time Ceauşescu would allow, and perhaps encourage, virulent anti-Semitic articles in the tightly controlled Romanian press. These were written by his non-Jewish court poet-jester, Corneliu Vadim Tudor, who after Ceauşescu's death continued his anti-Semitic diatribes as the founder and leader of the crypto-fascist political party Romania Mare (Greater Romania). This went on for fifteen or so years after Ceauşescu's death, until he did a complete turnabout, becoming philo-Semitic—perhaps influenced by an Israeli campaign strategist he had hired who had previously advised prominent Israeli politicians. Truly, there is nothing new under the sun.

The meeting in Predeal was scheduled for 9 a.m. This meant a 6 a.m. departure from Bucharest for the three-hour drive to Predeal, high in the Carpathian Mountains. It was January and still pitch dark when we left Bucharest. Once in Predeal, the sun's welcome rays provided the first warmth of the day. We were high in the Carpathians with several feet of newly fallen snow— before us, young people walked to the lifts carrying their skis on their shoulders, and children whizzed down the snow-covered slopes on old-fashioned sleds. The few cars on the roads maneuvered to avoid pedestrians. Once inside Ceauşescu's compound, we were greeted by Romania's minister of cults, the word "religion" being taboo. He explained that there were fourteen cults in Romania. Two such groups, the Old Believers and the Evangelical Church of the Augsburg Confession, were unknown to me.

Minutes later we were ushered into Ceauşescu's villa, whereupon Rabbi Rosen whispered to me, "It is unbelievable for me, a Romanian Jew, to be received by Romania's president with a government minister waiting in the snow to greet me, a room set aside for me to recite the morning prayers" (which by tradition cannot be said before sunrise). He then excused himself, went into an adjoining room, and said the morning prayers.

After prayers, we were ushered into Ceauşescu's living room to meet the president. Ceauşescu was wearing a baggy turtleneck sweater and a pair of ill-fitting pants held up by elastic. The room was filled with baskets of withered flowers extending as far as the eye could see. We were told they were gifts from Romania's "grateful" workers to his wife, Elena, in honor of her birthday two days before.

The meeting lasted more than two hours, common in Romania where brevity is not considered a virtue, but it was not uplifting. The absence of a common language and the delayed translation tended to produce stilted, largely hollow statements by Ceaușescu. He sought to persuade us that Israel needed to be more forthcoming in solving the Palestinian issue, a theme I was to hear at home and abroad for the next forty years. He also spoke boastfully about the importance of his role in facilitating Egyptian President Anwar Sadat's historic trip to Jerusalem in November 1977. Before the trip, Sadat had asked Ceaușescu whether Israel's prime minister, Menachem Begin, was a strong leader and trustworthy. Ceaușescu answered yes to both questions. (In my meeting with President Sadat five months later at his home in Mit Abu al-Kawm, Egypt, he told me that Ceaușescu had indeed given him the assurances he was seeking, but that he had decided before his meeting with Ceaușescu to go to Jerusalem.)

As for Jewish emigration, Ceaușescu repeated more clearly the assurance he had given me in New York that any Jew wanting to emigrate to Israel would be allowed to go "in accordance with Romanian law." But here was the rub: Under Romanian law a Jew seeking permission to emigrate first had to go to the local police station to request an application for a passport. The application form was only given after a local committee tried to persuade the applicant not to apply. This had the intended chilling effect, particularly for Jews intimidated by a local committee of non-Jews in a country with a long history of virulent anti-Semitism. I had not been aware of this when I met with Bogdan in Washington the previous July.

Now was the time to fix this last part of the emigration problem. I asked Ceaușescu to change the procedure so that any Jew who wanted to emigrate would receive an application directly from the Interior Ministry. He agreed. The change was made and the number of emigrants went up. Again, it was hard to equate this Ceaușescu with the one who was the absolute ruler of an authoritarian communist country. When speaking, he did not exude the strength or the drama of Anwar Sadat, or the passion and steely determination of Menachem Begin.

It became clear from my meeting with Ceauşescu in Predeal that the agreement we had made the previous July in Washington reinforced for Romania the reality that on matters affecting Jewish communities abroad, American Jews had a legitimate and important say in U.S. government decision-making. Nothing short of this could account for the leader of a communist country spending more than two hours with two private American citizens discussing his country's emigration policies, for the courtesies shown to Rabbi Rosen, Jack Spitzer, and me.

Once the meeting was over, Rabbi Rosen took charge. Back in Bucharest after a three-hour drive, we went directly to the Jewish community's dining hall where more than 1,000 meals were served daily, mostly to persons who paid little or nothing. By the time we arrived, it was already past 2 p.m. The kitchen was closed, but a few elderly Jews remained to sit in the heated room and enjoy one another's company. We had now been awake since 5 a.m. and were getting wobbly.

Taking no notice of our fatigue, Rabbi Rosen proudly marched us through the kitchen and storage facilities and then up a long flight of stairs to a meeting hall complete with a stage where I would later see performances by the community's amateur actors. Next the indefatigable rabbi insisted we visit the Moses and Amalia Rosen Jewish Old Age Home—a replacement for the dilapidated Jewish Home for the Aged I had visited in 1976—which was a thirty-minute drive from the dining hall. We were due back at the Choral Synagogue at 5 p.m. for Friday night services.

Despite the rush, I was struck by the Old World manners surrounding us. The Romanians addressed Rabbi Rosen as "Your Eminence," an honorific seldom bestowed on Jewish clerics. Peasants doffed their caps. In the synagogue, children rose unprompted in complete silence when Rabbi Rosen entered. Distinguished people from the world of music and government kissed Amalia Rosen's hand, a chivalrous gesture from another era. It seemed stiff and formal to me, but I said to myself, "Hey, this is the world of my ancestors."

As the sun set, Rabbi Rosen ushered us into Bucharest's faded synagogue. Leading the Friday night service was the cantor, a distinguished older gentleman with the familiar, non-Romanian name, Willie, who, despite his age, had a magnificent, resonant voice. None of the well-known modern Israeli melodies had crept into the service. When I closed my eyes and listened to the cantor and choir, I was magically transported to the synagogue I had attended as a boy in Baltimore. Seated on the bema, I was also conscious that I was wearing new yellow boots my daughters had given me before I left for Romania. Sartorial splendor was not a Romanian distinction, but even in Romania, yellow boots stood out as less than decorous. My only consolation was the realization that I had not asked to sit on the bema; I was there because Rabbi Rosen put me there.

Following the service, we waited in the federation's offices next to the synagogue for the arrival of the U.S. congressional delegation. Again, I wondered how the Romanian government felt when such an important delegation decided that the first person it would see in Romania was Rabbi Rosen. Congressman Vanik had insisted on this. The seven-member delegation included my congressman, Joseph Fisher (D-Va.), and two congressmen friends from my Dartmouth days. Rabbi Rosen gave a virtuoso performance, summarizing the situation in Romania, focusing on the Jewish community.

The only negative voice came from Congressman Richard Schulze (R-Pa.), who led the opposition in the House to the renewal of MFN for Romania. He took out of his pocket several Israeli newspaper articles critical of Romania and Rabbi Rosen and, after standing up to add emphasis, sharply questioned the rabbi about the stories. Rabbi Rosen replied, in typical Talmudic fashion, with questions of his own. "Why ask me about stories in the Israeli press? Why not ask the persons who wrote them? I am only a rabbi, not a storyteller." Schulze quickly realized he was in a fight he was not going to win and sat down. The meeting ended with all seven U.S. congressmen, assorted congressional staff, U.S. Ambassador Reuben Aggrey, members of the American embassy staff, and others raising champagne glasses and toasting Rabbi Rosen with "L'chaim!"—To life!

The last stop was the Intercontinental Hotel, less than a mile from the synagogue. Because it was now the Sabbath, Rabbi Rosen had to walk on a bitter cold night through the snow-covered streets of Bucharest. I accompanied him out of respect and admiration. Once inside the hotel, we joined the congressional delegation being feted by the Romanian National Orchestra in the ballroom. It was totally incongruous, a luxurious floor-lit room with glass walls and chandeliers and a small all-male orchestra decked out in white ties and tails to honor the chief rabbi of Romania, in a historically anti-Semitic country run by communist toughies.

Dinner did not end until well after midnight. Congressman Vanik announced that the delegation would leave at 8 a.m. the next morning for a meeting with the minister of trade. In the morning, a bleary-eyed congressional delegation stumbled through a meeting intended to discuss trade between our two countries, but which quickly became a speechathon that filled the allotted time with meaningless oratory. From the Ministry of Trade we proceeded en masse to two of Bucharest's architectural relics a few miles away, the parliament building, home to the Grand National Assembly, and, next to it, the Patriarchal Cathedral.

The parliament building was historic but not functional. The straight-back wooden chairs were unusable. The socialist realism art interspersed with portraits of long-deceased parliamentarians, with unlifelike faces and stiff poses, was out of place. A garish National Socialist Republic shield in the entrance hall added a further discordant note, reminding us that the doctrine of separation of powers did not exist in communist Romania. Ceaușescu's wishes became law in form and in fact. A visit to the cathedral next door did not dispel my gloom. A peasant woman in a black dress and shawl was squatting on the floor while a similarly dressed woman hovered over the communion offerings.

The congressional delegation quickly moved on, to meet with Ceaușescu. By prearrangement, Jack and I headed to the Foreign Ministry to meet with Corneliu Bogdan, still head of the North American Section, and his deputy from his Washington days, Mircea Raceanu. There we were joined by the deputy director of the Office for Passports in the Interior Ministry. (Raceanu was later convicted of treason and sentenced to death for giving classified documents to the CIA. He was pardoned in 2002.)

The next morning we were whisked from our hotel in downtown Bucharest to Otopeni Airport (now renamed Henri Coandă International Airport), where we were escorted to the Tarom plane to New York. As we boarded the plane, the flight attendant handed me Romanian newspapers with front-page pictures of Jack and me meeting with Ceaușescu. When I arrived home, I proudly showed the pictures to one of my daughters, who remarked dismissively, "It's easy to be famous abroad," to which I wearily nodded assent.

Rabbi Rosen Comes to Washington

After arranging our January 1980 meeting with Ceauşescu in Romania, Rabbi Rosen came to Washington each year, and the two of us met with senators and administration officials to bolster MFN. Rosen, in his rabbinic garb, would shuffle from office to office explaining, with impressive theatrics, that despite communist oppression and the despotism of Ceauşescu's totalitarian government, Romanian Jews were free to emigrate to Israel. Congress was not Rabbi Rosen's only stop. We regularly met with State Department officials, including the deputy secretary of state, John Whitehead.

Secretary Whitehead never seemed to tire of Rabbi Rosen's stories, and the meetings would often run into overtime, driving his staffers to distraction. Not the least disturbed, Rabbi Rosen would keep on talking about the perils of Jewish life in communist Romania. Secretary Whitehead knew a great deal about Eastern Europe from his frequent visits to the region and was an innovative thinker and doer in U.S. efforts to wean the satellite countries of Eastern Europe away from the Soviet Union.

In meetings with Americans, neither Rabbi Rosen nor I defended Ceauşescu or his government. In fact, in my only congressional testimony on MFN, I described the situation in Romania as "horrible." This obviously did not endear me to the Romanian government, but it needed American Jewish support for MFN as much as we needed leverage to persuade Romania to allow its Jews to emigrate to Israel. It was a workable but never comfortable arrangement—diplomacy is rarely about negotiating with friends.

In recognition of Rabbi Rosen's activism, in 1982 the Romanian embassy hosted a lunch in his honor. Rabbi Arthur Schneier and I were invited to attend. Schneier, born in Austria, was a close friend of Rabbi Rosen. In addition to being the senior rabbi at one of New York's large Orthodox synagogues, he was chairman of the Appeal of Conscience Foundation, an interdenominational group of clerics and business leaders operating worldwide. The conversation at lunch was the usual exchange of pleasantries, but then, as we were about to get up from the table, Rabbi Rosen remained seated, took from his pocket a prayer book, and proceeded to chant in Hebrew the entire Birkat Hamazon, the blessings after a meal. As in Predeal, our communist Romanian hosts waited for the rabbi to finish his prayers.

I matched Rabbi Rosen's trips to Washington with trips of my own to Bucharest to check on emigration and remind the Romanians the deal was a two-way street. American Jewish support for MFN required Romania to allow its Jews to emigrate.

Hanukkah in Romania

One of the benefits for me of my involvement in helping Romania's Jews emigrate to freedom was to receive an invitation to visit small Jewish communities throughout Romania as part of Rabbi Rosen's annual Hanukkah tour.

In 1983 and 1984, two of my daughters and I joined Rabbi Rosen for his annual Hanukkah tours of Jewish communities. During the eight days of Hanukkah we traveled from sunup to late at night, crisscrossing Romania by bus, visiting four or five synagogues each day. Our little caravan with a police escort was led by Rabbi and Mrs. Rosen, who were seated in the back seat of his Mercedes. Amalia Rosen, an attorney by profession, preferred to speak French. The rabbi was at home in six languages: Romanian, German, French, Hebrew, Yiddish, and English.

Among our dozen or so travel companions were a CIA official attached to the American embassy and Avram Burg, later speaker of the Israeli Knesset and, still later, head of the Jewish Agency worldwide. The sixty-person Romanian Jewish choir, traveling on a separate bus, would sing at each stop. Then someone in our delegation would speak, followed by the rabbi. The drama was repeated at every stop. Elderly Jews waited in cold, half-empty synagogues, sometimes for hours, for the triumphal entrance of the chief rabbi in his full rabbinic regalia, a purple robe, gold chain around his neck, holding a large Star of David, and wearing a miter hat fit for a bishop or someone of high ecclesiastical rank—quite fitting for someone addressed as "Your Eminence." Combining an inspirational retelling of Hanukkah, the story of the Maccabees as brave defenders of Jewish traditions against the intrusion of Greek culture, with exhortations as to how Romania's Jews must now preserve and protect their Jewish way of life by emulating the Maccabees, his talks were masterful, reaching a high point in fifteen minutes or so.

This was followed by the lighting of the Hanukkah candles, Rabbi Rosen's dramatic exodus from the synagogue, the choir singing, and the congregants looking with tear-filled faces as their spiritual leader walked slowly, ever so slowly, out of the synagogue. For me, it was both an emotional drain and an endurance contest. Emotional because seeing mostly elderly Jews listening to a Romanian rabbi in unheated synagogues in a far-away country called up in my imagination pictures of centuries of Jewish life in Eastern Europe. And an endurance contest because to stay awake for an hour or longer listening to speeches in Romanian was an ordeal in itself, particularly after only a few hours' sleep the night before.

The rabbi invariably called on me to speak after introducing me in flowery style as a world Jewish leader and adviser to U.S. presidents. I would then speak for five or ten minutes about Jewish history and the unity of the Jewish people. The mere fact that I was from the United States and had traveled behind the Iron Curtain to Romania for Hanukkah was all the congregants needed to hear in order to welcome me, but Rabbi Rosen was not to be dissuaded from extolling my virtues, many of which were unknown to me.

One such evening stands forever engraved in my memory. It was in Iasi, a historic city in eastern Romania, where the congregation had been waiting for three hours for the appearance of His Eminence. We were very late and did not arrive until after 9 p.m.; the rabbi was exhausted. He was counting on me to speak first so he could rest, but fate was not kind to him. I, too, was exhausted, so instead of giving my usual speech, I quoted the Jewish saying "From Moses to Moses there was no one like Moses." The reference was to "Moshe Rabenu," the Moses of the Bible, and the "Rambam," Moses Maimonides, a famous twelfth-century Jewish philosopher. I continued, "Whereas the Jewish people had to wait three thousand years from Moshe Rabenu to the Rambam, tonight you will only have to wait thirty seconds from this Moses to Chief Rabbi Moses Rosen." An unhappy Rabbi Rosen rose slowly to his feet.

Rabbi Rosen never ceased to amaze me. On the first night of Hanukkah in 1983, we traveled by train from Bucharest to Falticeni, deep in Moldavia, where Rosen had served as a young rabbi in the 1930s. When we exited the train at 5 a.m. and entered the small wooden Falticeni train station, only a few Romanians were there, all huddled around a wood stove to protect them from the winter cold. Rabbi Rosen suddenly stopped, turned around to our little group trailing behind, raised his cane, and announced in a loud voice,

"Morning prayers will begin at seven in Falticeni's synagogue," but then he added, "For those of you who prefer to say prayers in your rooms, breakfast will be served at eight thirty." To no one's surprise, the rabbi and I were the only ones who made it to synagogue.

Most of the synagogues in small villages we visited had been recently refurbished. The newly polished floors glistened. They had not been trod upon for one reason: There were no Jews left. They had gone to Israel. Despite the absence of Jews, Rabbi Rosen saw it his duty to preserve the artifacts of Jewish life in a Romania that had once existed. It was different in Iasi, Cluj, Timişoara, Targu Mureş, Bacau, Braşov, and other larger communities where Jewish life continued, but, with a few exceptions, the small shtetls had disappeared.

The two exceptions I saw were in Dorohoi and Piatra Neamt. I visited both as part of the rabbi's Hanukkah tour. Dorohoi, a small village nestled close to the Ukraine border, still housed a small functioning wooden synagogue. The Jewish community was led by Reb Wasserman (in the Orthodox tradition, the honorific "Reb" is bestowed on a learned person who is not a rabbi). Reb Wasserman was like a character out of a Sholem Aleichem play, with his gray beard, dark, penetrating eyes, and ill-fitting gabardines. He seemed ageless. On this particular morning, he led the service, which was attended by the few Jews still around plus our caravan of seventy or so. When we filed out of the small synagogue, curious villagers were peering over wooden fences gazing at these Jews who had come to Dorohoi in December to celebrate "their Christmas."

Piatra Neamt in Moldavia was less isolated and far bigger, but the synagogue was even older. Built centuries before of rough-hewn unfinished logs on the outside, the small synagogue was warm and welcoming inside. It dated from the time of the Baal Shem Tov, the founder of the Hasidic movement in the early eighteenth century, who is thought to have visited Moldavia on one of his historic missions to the Jews. According to legend, the Baal Shem Tov prayed in this synagogue later in the eighteenth century. After evening services in what the local Jewish community called "Baal Shem Tov's shul," we were invited to a private home next door for dinner. As I was walking over, Amalia Rosen whispered to me, "The knaidels"—potato dumplings—"are 'the best in the world.' They go down like ice cubes."

This was repeated at dinner, and sure enough, the knaidels went down as smoothly as ice cubes.

Last Meeting with Ceaușescu, February 1986

By 1986 the winds of change were already blowing across the communist world. The previous year, Mikhail Gorbachev had taken over leadership of the Soviet Union after two infirm, aging leaders in the Brezhnev mold died in rapid order. With Gorbachev came *glasnost*, openness, and *perestroika*, restructuring; the reins of communist control began to loosen across the region. The more communism buckled elsewhere, the more Ceaușescu tightened his control in Romania, leading to new economic lows and political oppression. Those of us in the United States who tried to help Romania's Jews were worried. After consulting with others, Jack Spitzer and I decided to return to Bucharest for another visit with Ceaușescu. It was to be my third and last meeting with Romania's dictator.

Ceaușescu received us in his office at Communist Party headquarters in Bucharest, the same building from which he would flee by helicopter three years later. In addition to Rabbi Rosen, we were accompanied by the American ambassador to Romania, Roger Kirk, a great supporter and warm friend. He and his wife, Betty, insisted I stay with them in Bucharest. In our meeting, Ceaușescu agreed to allow the Baptist Bible to be printed in Romania, to free two imprisoned Christian clergymen, and to allow the Romanian Jewish choir to travel to Washington a few months later to sing in the rotunda of the Capitol at the annual congressional Holocaust memorial ceremony. When I raised the issue of the choir's travel, Ceaușescu first responded that it was up to Tarom to decide whether or not to fly the choir to the United States. This was patently false. Ceaușescu controlled Tarom and everything else in Romania. When I mentioned that a favorable word from him could be helpful with Tarom, he grumpily acknowledged that might be so—and on this occasion, it was.

The Romanian Jewish Choir Visits Washington

On a bright sunny morning in May 1986, seventy young Romanian Jews walked down the ramp of a Tarom Boeing 707 at New York's Kennedy Airport, along with Rabbi Rosen and his wife, Amalia, the choir director, Izu Gott, and three Romanian Jewish community leaders with fancy titles I had come to know from my many trips to Bucharest. A man named Zilberstein was the only one who spoke English and was fittingly given the title of chief of protocol.

I had raised the money for the choir's visit from prominent Jewish donors, including Edgar Bronfman, president of the World Jewish Congress and CEO of the Seagram Company Ltd.; we "shook hands" on it over the phone. A few weeks later when I called back to get the money, my call was transferred to Israel Singer, the secretary general of the World Jewish Congress. Singer had a reputation of trying to walk back, if not reverse, Bronfman's commitments, and this was no exception. He told me that Bronfman had decided to cut his commitment in half. Knowing Singer's ways, I had expected as much and was prepared: I told him that if Bronfman did not pay the full amount, the Romanian choir would picket outside New York City's Seagram Building on Park Avenue holding placards reading, "Edgar Bronfman won't give us the money to fly home." Singer mumbled that I would receive the money—and I did.

Once the choir landed in New York, representatives of the American Jewish Committee shepherded the young singers around the city with stops at the usual tourist attractions—the Statue of Liberty, the Empire State Building, and the United Nations. The next day the choir sang in Philadelphia's Independence Hall before traveling to Washington for an evening's performance at the Israeli embassy. This, too, had its difficult moments. The Israeli ambassador, Meir Rosenne, born in Romania, had concerns about Rabbi Rosen's having cozied up to Romania's communists.

Now in Washington, the Romanian choir, with Rabbi Rosen in the lead, headed down the steps of the tour bus and into the Israeli embassy. The atmosphere was frosty. But all changed when the choir, young Jews who had never set foot outside Romania, began to sing their program of Yiddish, Romanian, and Hebrew songs. I looked over to see Ambassador Rosenne and his wife, their eyes filled with tears. A few moments later, the choir director, Izu Gott, raised his accordion and began playing the hora. There was Meir in the middle of the circle dancing with Rabbi Rosen. After that, Rosenne and Rabbi Rosen became friends. Rosenne wisely understood that regardless of any putative taint in Rabbi Rosen's political past, he was the person keeping Jewish life and culture alive in Romania.

The choir's performance of the same program the next day in the rotunda of the Capitol was equally moving, ending this time with an English rendition of "Oh, Susannah!" This was the first time a choir from behind the Iron Curtain had appeared publicly in Washington, and it was widely reported in the press and on television. I was interviewed on ABC's *Nightline* about the visit. The next morning the choir performed for Vice President George H. W. Bush at the White House before leaving by bus for a cookout at our home in McLean, Virginia. When the hamburgers were on the grill, our daughter Amalie put out a tray of bananas. Within seconds, all eighty bananas were gone, snatched by the eager hands of those with painful memories of empty stomachs. It was a telling indicator of the sad conditions in Romania.

The Waning of Ceaușescu's Reign and Saving the Great Synagogue

Romania's Jews shared their countrymen's fate as victims of Ceaușescu's ever-increasing megalomania. One of his grand schemes in the 1980s was to eliminate Romania's foreign debt to show foreign lenders he did not need them. This was after they refused to expand Romania's credit lines. Over the next decade, Romania repaid its entire foreign debt, but the Romanian people paid the price, not Ceaușescu. Imports were slashed, and whatever in Romania could be sold was sold. Harsh austerity drastically reduced Romania's already low standard of living. Imported goods disappeared from store shelves. Long lines formed outside food stores whenever there was a rumor that meat or some other scarce commodity might become available. Streetlights everywhere in Romania were permanently dimmed.

The prevailing economic gloom, combined with Ceaușescu's delusional self-promotion as the "Genius of the Carpathians," led him to embark in the 1980s on an insane project to construct a massive Romanesque government center in downtown Bucharest dedicated to the glory of socialism. The outrageous $2 billion price tag was staggering for a country whose citizens were without food, housing, and heat. But the Genius of the Carpathians could not be denied.

One of the historic buildings slated for the wrecking ball to make way for Ceaușescu's building program was the Great Synagogue, built in 1845. On a July morning in 1986, I received a frantic telephone call from Rabbi Rosen telling me that he had just come from a meeting with the Israeli ambassador, who had met that same morning with the mayor of Bucharest. The ambassador had sought the mayor's assurance that the Great Synagogue and the historic Sephardic Synagogue, built by descendants of Jews who had left Spain after the Inquisition, would be spared demolition. The mayor told the ambassador not to worry; both synagogues would be preserved. Thinking all was well, the ambassador planned to walk by the Sephardic Synagogue on his way back to his embassy. Rounding the corner, he was shocked. The Sephardic Synagogue was gone; it had been demolished the night before. When Rabbi Rosen heard the news, he rightly feared that the Great Synagogue would be the next to go. He immediately called me, asking for help.

After I hung up, I called the State Department. Within an hour I was seated in the office of Thomas W. Simons Jr., regional director for Eastern European affairs (later the American ambassador to Poland), along with his deputy, Mark Palmer (later our ambassador to Hungary), and the Eastern European area director, Martin Wenick. All agreed that if the Great Synagogue were destroyed, it would irreparably damage our relations with Romania. The situation was serious enough for us to get on the calendar that day with Rozanne Ridgway, assistant secretary of state for European and Canadian affairs. On this occasion, as on others, Roz was fully on board. She took the matter to the top, briefing Secretary Shultz, also a stalwart on human and religious rights. He pressed the matter a few weeks later at a meeting with Romania's foreign minister, Ioan Totu, on the margins of the annual UN General Assembly session in New York. Roz reported that Secretary Shultz told his Romanian counterpart that if the Great Synagogue were destroyed, the U.S. government would reexamine its relations with Romania. That did it. The Great Synagogue was spared and is still in use today. Completely renovated, it is an architectural and historic gem fully functioning as a synagogue.

Later the same year, the saga of the Great Synagogue produced another unexpected call, this time from my friend Elyakim Rubinstein, at the Israeli embassy. Ely, a highly respected retired justice and former deputy president of the Israeli Supreme Court, was then the Israeli chargé in the absence of Ambassador Meir Rosenne. An Orthodox Jew and great storyteller, Ely was all business that day as he read to me what he called "an official statement from my government." The statement was along the lines of "Mr. Moses, we know you are very active in efforts to save the Great Synagogue in Bucharest. Please be advised that the Government of Israel has a special relationship with the Government of Romania and that this special relationship is in danger of being compromised because of your activities on behalf of the Great Synagogue. Please bear this in mind in your future dealings."

Apparently, the Jewish state of Israel was fearful of offending Romania if I spoke up in defense of the historic synagogue. It was pressuring me to back off. At first I was speechless. Then I asked Ely if there was anything more he wanted to say. When he said no, barely containing my anger I said that I appreciated his government's words, but that I intended to do all I could to save the Great Synagogue. Not to be outdone, Ely replied, "I have read you my government's message. Now I will add my personal words; I agree with you," and hung up.

The years 1987 to 1989 were even darker for Romania. Fewer and fewer Westerners visited Romania, a country that seemed to be withdrawing within itself. Rather than expose his country to withering criticism in the U.S. Congress, Ceauşescu renounced MFN, thereby virtually closing the door to Romanian exports to the United States. Street riots and demonstrations followed. The end was near. The only thing not known was how soon and by whom Ceauşescu would be overthrown.

POST-CEAUŞESCU ROMANIA AND MEETING NEW PRESIDENT ION ILIESCU

On Christmas Day, 1989, Carol and I were in the Bahamas with our four children and first grandchild, belatedly celebrating my sixtieth birthday, when we saw the trial and execution of Elena and Nicolae Ceauşescu on television.

I assumed that the end of the Ceauşescu regime and the fall of communism signaled the end to my efforts on behalf of Romania's Jews, who would now be free to emigrate. But I soon found that my ties to the Jewish community and particularly to Rabbi Rosen were enduring. He continued to ask for my help in caring for the dwindling Jewish community and ensuring his own safety and well-being.

Three months after the revolution, I was back in Romania. Soldiers were on the streets; order had broken down; the economy barely functioned. Inflation was rampant. Rabbi Rosen was full of stories about the personal dangers he faced during the revolution when hundreds of people were killed. His concern—not unfounded, considering the history of anti-Semitism in his part of the world—was that the chaotic conditions would result in violence against Romania's Jews, and that his dealings with Ceauşescu would lead to his denunciation by Ceauşescu's successors. Fortunately for him, the new Iliescu-led government did not hunt down former Ceauşescu go-betweens. Moreover, Rabbi Rosen was nimble enough to join the anti-Ceauşescu crusade, publicly condemning Ceauşescu immediately after his downfall.

I had never heard of Ion Iliescu before seeing him interviewed on television as the newly chosen head of the National Salvation Front and then of the Provisional Government of Romania. However, when I went to Romania a second time after the revolution, Rabbi Rosen arranged for me to meet newly elected President Iliescu and other government officials, including the new minister of religion. For close to an hour President Iliescu and I chatted amiably in a large formal room in Cotroceni, the newly refurbished presidential palace, a beautiful transformed monastery set in a botanical garden.

My first impression of President Iliescu proved a lasting one. He was down-to-earth, open, and plain-speaking and had none of the airs of a self-important head of state. He thought of himself as a man of the people. The only other person present in our meeting was the president's adviser, Ion Mircea Pascu, who laughed loudly at my weak attempts at humor. (In 2001 Pascu became Iliescu's defense minister; he is now vice president of the European Parliament.)

At the end of the meeting, President Iliescu suggested that I meet with Prime Minister Theodor Stolojan, who had been Ceauşescu's head of central planning. Stolojan had succeeded Prime Minister Petre Roman after a second coal miners' raid on Bucharest resulted in a split between Iliescu and Roman. Five years later those raids contributed to Iliescu's losing his bid for reelection. It was a cold, rainy day and already dark when I was driven through the unlit streets of Bucharest to the prime minister's office. Stolojan was sitting at his desk, which was lit by a single bulb. His skin was ashen, his gray hair was thinning, and he had a weary look on his face. He was struggling with a railway workers' strike and a huge budget deficit with no prospect of increasing government revenues. It was quickly apparent that neither of us knew why President Iliescu had sent me to him. We chatted aimlessly for a few minutes, then I left.

I later heard that the railway workers' strike was settled, but I never learned what the strikers received in return for going back to work. Prime Minister Stolojan's real accomplishment came a few months later when he steered through Romania's Parliament a new constitution modeled on the constitution of France's Fifth Republic. Prime Minister Stolojan resigned after the 1992 Romanian elections and joined the staff of the World Bank in Washington as a senior adviser, where I saw him from time to time. We remain friends.

I met with President Iliescu again when he came to Washington in May 1993 for the dedication of the Holocaust Museum. I hosted a lunch for him with U.S. government officials and others at my law offices on Pennsylvania Avenue. The same year, I met with Romanian Foreign Minister Adrian Nastase. I gave a lunch for him, and he in return gave a dinner for me in Bucharest when I visited in October 1993. After serving as prime minister ten years later, Nastase lost his bid for president in 2004 and subsequently went to prison, convicted of corruption while in office.

It was now late 1993, and again I thought my mission to Romania was over. Rabbi Rosen was safe, and the Jewish community in Romania was no longer in danger of anti-Semitic outbursts. Moreover, it was now up to Romania to decide its future. I turned my attention to my law practice. Two years before, I had been elected national president of the American Jewish Committee, a demanding job in itself. And by then Carol and I had six grandchildren! But life for me took a different turn, and Romania called me back.

ON THE AMBASSADOR TRACK

Little in Washington happens by chance. It all depends on timing and the people in a position to make things happen. Sometimes it is an influential member of Congress, other times a major business leader with close ties to the top rungs of government, but it can also be someone in government who, because of his or her position or relationships within government, can make things happen. This was borne out by my becoming the American ambassador to Romania.

On a gray, rainy day in November 1993 I had lunch with my friend Marc Grossman at Kinkead's, a well-known restaurant in downtown Washington. Marc and I had worked together in the Carter White House.

When I arrived at the White House in 1980, I did not know President Jimmy Carter, but the administration was in trouble as a result of an ill-considered vote in the UN Security Council strongly deploring Israel's settlement policy in the "occupied Arab territories including Jerusalem." The resolution as it applied to Jerusalem was contrary to assurances President Carter had given to Prime Minister Menachem Begin the previous year that the status of Jerusalem would not change without Israel's concurrence. Without giving the matter much thought, President Carter had approved Secretary of State Cyrus Vance's recommendation that the United States vote in favor of the resolution. The UN vote took place on Saturday, March 1, 1980. On the following Monday morning the Jewish community and its supporters in Washington were up in arms. President Carter issued a mea culpa that made him look either incompetent or uncaring. He was neither, but the president had badly botched this one, and his relationship with a constituency that was important to his reelection hopes was under strain.

With the administration in full retreat, three White House wise men, Lloyd Cutler, the president's counsel, Sol Linowitz, a close confidant of the president, and Stuart Eizenstat, the president's domestic affairs adviser, put their heads together. I was told that Sol suggested that someone like Al Moses join the White House staff as special adviser to the president for Jewish affairs—the post was suddenly vacant as the result of a medical emergency—whereupon Stu piped up and said, "That's a good idea. Let's get Al." And so it was.

The job was two-hatted: advising the president on matters affecting Jews and reaching out to the Jewish community in an effort to calm the waters on behalf of the administration. To keep abreast of critical Middle East issues affecting Israel, so important to the Jewish community, I needed the State Department's help. The White House asked Hal Saunders, the assistant secretary of state for Near East affairs, to dispatch someone to the White House to advise me. The short straw fell to Marc Grossman, a highly regarded junior Foreign Service officer who had recently served in Pakistan and was now Assistant Secretary Saunders's hand-picked assistant. For the next ten months, until the end of the Carter administration, Marc did his best to keep me informed and out of trouble in a three-way tug-of-war among the White House, the State Department, and the Jewish community. Those White House years cemented our friendship, which continues to this day. Marc had a spectacular State Department career culminating in his appointment as under secretary of state for political affairs, the third-ranking position in the department and the highest that career officials (as opposed to political appointees) can attain. Later he served under President Barack Obama as special envoy for Afghanistan and Pakistan. He also knew Eastern Europe and Romania from his frequent trips to the region and knew of my activities in Romania. When we met for lunch in November 1993, Marc was the executive secretary of the State Department.

At lunch our conversation started with the usual convivial niceties about family and career. Suddenly Marc looked at me, his eyes half closed, a faint smile on his face, and said, "Al, are you still interested in Romania?" I said yes, thinking it was a harmless statement leading nowhere. I was wrong. Marc continued: "Our present ambassador to Romania, John Davis, has been in Washington for a year undergoing medical treatment and will not be returning to Bucharest. Do you have an interest in being ambassador?"

I blurted out, "Marc, that's a great idea, but I don't know anyone in the White House. I did not contribute to President Clinton's campaign, and anyway, I am not a Foreign Service officer, so the State Department will not support me." Marc in his usual calming voice said, "Well, Al, think it over. You know a lot about Romania. Why don't you speak to people who can help," meaning, I thought, people I knew from my Carter days, members of Congress and others in and out of government who might be helpful. There was no suggestion or indication that the State Department would support me or any real likelihood that the White House would either. Nevertheless, I was intrigued and decided to give it a try.

The position and function of executive secretary to the State Department are little known outside Washington cognoscenti. The executive secretary is at the center of the written communications hub at the department. Fortunately for me, no one was more adept at moving pieces on the State Department chess board than Marc, who, despite his quiet, unassuming manner, had extraordinary bureaucratic skills and deftness. Marc's encouragement was enough to get me thinking about being ambassador to Romania. Rabbi Rosen was still chief rabbi, and I knew Romania's president, Ion Iliescu, and a few others at the top in Romania.

I was then a senior partner in the Washington, D.C., law firm of Covington & Burling, one of whose distinguished partners had been the former secretary of state, Dean G. Acheson. When I was a young lawyer, I revered him as the architect of post–World War II U.S. foreign policy. My most memorable recollection of Mr. Acheson was a chance encounter with him in January 1961 when I entered the downtown building where the firm had its offices early the Monday morning following John F. Kennedy's inauguration the previous Friday. A foot of snow had fallen the night before the inauguration, and it remained bitterly cold three days later.

Just as I entered the building, the six-foot-two, mustachioed former secretary of state strode into the lobby wearing a pearl gray fedora and a full-length black overcoat while vigorously clapping his gloved hands. As we rode up together in the elevator, he was in obvious high spirits, talking about the dinner he had attended on Saturday at the White House. He said, "It was a wonderful evening; the president was there." This struck me as odd: Of course President Kennedy was there; where else would he be? Only later did I realize that "the president" meant Harry Truman, whom Acheson had served for four years as secretary of state. To Acheson, "the president" would always be President Truman.

Acheson's words resounded in me. I thought about the excitement of public life and the opportunity to shape history that comes with it. As a young man, I aspired to be a part of that legacy, although I could scarcely fathom its actual contours then.

After my lunch with Marc, I planned first to speak with Carol, who had been in Romania with me seventeen years before and had vowed never to return.

As it turned out, our oldest daughter, Barbara, a lawyer in New York, was home for the Thanksgiving holiday, so I decided to try out the idea on her. She liked it. With this encouragement, I screwed up the courage to ask Carol, who surprisingly did not say no; she only said, "You're crazy. You have no chance of being appointed." Then, with her usual high spirits, she added, "If you want to try, it is fine with me."

Looking for Support

My first call was to President Carter at the Carter Center in Atlanta. In addition to my White House hat advising him on Jewish affairs, I had been lead counsel to the president in the "Billygate" affair in which the president's brother, Billy Carter, had caused a huge political problem for the president that gripped the nation for a few months. As lead counsel I was immersed in it from the beginning: spending a weekend with President Carter at Camp David working on his speech to the nation, reporting to Congress as special counsel to the president, representing witnesses at congressional hearings, dealing with a Justice Department investigation and press briefings in the White House. Eventually Billygate was buried and forgotten—just another one of our nation's "much ado about nothings."

From this crucible a strong personal bond developed between President Carter and me. I liked him and he clearly trusted me. When I called in late 1993 to ask for his support of my bid to be appointed ambassador to Romania, he immediately offered to write to President Clinton on my behalf.

I next reached out to my old friend Lane Kirkland, head of the AFL-CIO, whom I knew socially in Washington and with whom I had traveled in Israel. It is difficult to explain today the power and weight that the leader of the nation's largest labor union had in official Washington then, particularly with a Democratic administration in the White House. Kirkland's dedication on Jewish issues came from the heart as well as the head. Lane's wife, Irena, and her identical twin sister had been born in Czechoslovakia and had survived Auschwitz. Kirkland had been in the Merchant Marine in World War II and still talked like an old salt. When I called explaining that I wanted to talk to him about being ambassador to Romania, he replied with his usual bonhomie, "Al, come on over." As soon as I entered his cavernous offices on Sixteenth Street, a block from the White House, he exclaimed, "Al, you will be a great ambassador to Romania. It is the best thing those bastards in the White House ever did." Kirkland was still upset with the Clinton administration for its championing the North American Free Trade Agreement, NAFTA, among the United States, Canada, and Mexico, which the AFL-CIO vigorously opposed. Lane mentioned the names of union leaders in Romania and promised to get behind my nomination. He, too, sent a message to the White House, which was eager to mend its fences with the AFL-CIO.

Support came from others in government, such as Connecticut's senior senator, Joseph I. Lieberman. We first met when he arrived in Washington as a junior senator in 1988. Our common domain was the Jewish world and our regular attendance at a small Orthodox Jewish synagogue in downtown Washington where we schmoozed after (and sometimes during) services. Unexpected support also came from Senator Paul Simon of Illinois. I did not know the senator personally, but his chief of staff had worked with me on Romanian matters when he was at the State Department. On his own initiative, he drafted a letter for Senator Simon to send to President Clinton. It was a classic, saying, in effect: "I have been to Bucharest, and if Al Moses wants to go there as ambassador, send him."

I have often thought that the most consequential endorsement may have been one that came from an unlikely source, a former law client, Louis Ramsey, the chairman of Simmons National Bank in Pine Bluff, Arkansas. Simmons's bank had gotten caught up in the early 1980s in a savings and loan scandal, and I was lead counsel to the bank in the follow-on investigation. Ramsey had been chair of the board of trustees of the University of Arkansas when Bill Clinton graduated from Yale Law School and returned to Arkansas to launch his political career. Clinton had been hired to teach law at the university. Now, Ramsey wrote directly to Clinton, which at least helped with his Arkansan inner circle and possibly with the president himself. In time, others at the White House such as the president's adviser, Rahm Emanuel (now mayor of Chicago), and my longtime friend Richard Schifter, then serving as a senior official on the National Security Council staff, gave me a big boost. By January 1994, I was sufficiently confident that I would become ambassador that when Rabbi Rosen visited Washington late that month, I told him, in confidence, that I expected to be nominated. He was thrilled to hear the news. Sadly, he died two months later, before I took up my posting.

As it turned out, there was a last-minute hiccup. Tony Lake and Sandy Berger, the president's national security adviser and deputy national security adviser, had proposed one of their senior staff as our ambassador to Romania. Again, Richard Schifter came to my rescue, persuading Sandy that I was a better fit for Romania based on my experience there and my prominence in the Jewish community.

The president signed off on my nomination in August, and my name went to the Senate a few days later. After a routine hearing before the Europe Subcommittee of the Senate Foreign Affairs Committee, presided over by Senator Joseph R. Biden (D-Del.), my name, along with those of four other proposed ambassadors, went to the Senate. In late September our nominations were unanimously confirmed.

Much later I learned that I was not just the White House's but also the State Department's choice for ambassador. Since I was not a Foreign Service officer, this was unusual and was due entirely to Marc Grossman's support. It was not the last time Marc would work his magic on my behalf. Five years later I became President Clinton's presidential special envoy for the Cyprus conflict. At the time Marc was the assistant secretary of state for European affairs and suggested my appointment to Secretary of State Madeleine Albright, whom I also knew from our days together in the Carter White House.

Back to School—Ambassador School

After our confirmation by the Senate, the next step was "ambassador school." Five of us attended—Marc Grossman, ambassador to Turkey; Charles E. Redman, Germany; Johnnie Carson, Zimbabwe; and Jerome Gary Cooper, Jamaica—and our wives. We represented the "new look" at the State Department. Marc and I were Jewish; Johnnie and Gary were African American; only Charles Redman was cut from the traditional Foreign Service cloth.

Ambassador school was run by two veteran Foreign Service officers. Langhorne A. Motley had been U.S. ambassador to Brazil, and Sheldon J. Krys had been our ambassador to Trinidad. They were highly entertaining and gave sound advice based on their personal experiences. Lacking prior State Department service, I was the one who had the most to learn about the bureaucracy and what was expected of an ambassador. I received lots of practical advice, such as when to cable to Washington and when not, how to mark my cables so they were not read by everyone in the State Department and outside, how to lead and inspire embassy staff, and how to deal with foreign press and political leaders in my soon-to-be host country.

We spent the last day of the two-week course at Fort Bragg, North Carolina, where we were indoctrinated into the mission of the U.S. Special Forces, who would come to our rescue if we were seized by terrorists. Wives did not participate in this part of the training, which included use of live ammunition and demonstrations of hostage taking and rescue operations.

I remember thinking that terrorists might be a problem for Johnnie in Zimbabwe or Marc in Turkey, but not for me in Romania. A terrorist attack was not high on my list of concerns in 1994. The greater danger, I thought, would be serving as the first Jewish American ambassador to a country with a long history of anti-Semitism, marked by the death of 400,000 Romanian Jews during World War II, one-half of them killed by Romanians in concentration camps in Transnistria (now technically the Pridnestrovian Moldavian Republic), the other half killed by Germans at Auschwitz. My friend, the late Nobel laureate Elie Wiesel, was one of a small number of Romanian Jews to survive Auschwitz. He had been deported from his home in Sighet, in northern Transylvania (then briefly part of Hungary), to Auschwitz at age fifteen, along with the rest of his family. Only he and two older sisters survived. Against this backdrop, it was both supremely ironic and quintessentially American that it was my Jewish activism that had led to my being chosen as ambassador in the first place.

The second part of my indoctrination was a breakfast meeting with the legendary Richard A. Holbrooke, then assistant secretary for European and Canadian affairs. Once I became ambassador, Dick was not officially my boss—technically the president is an ambassador's boss—but Dick was the person to whom I reported. The day after I was confirmed by the Senate, Dick called. We had met in Germany when he was ambassador a few years before, and prior to that in the White House, when Carter was president. He was charming, telling me how pleased he was that I was going to Romania and how important Romania was for our country, neither of which was entirely true.

As we talked further, it became clear that Dick knew little about Romania, but he was a remarkably quick study and with broad brushstrokes painted a picture of what our country hoped to achieve in Central and Eastern Europe. Dick set great store by personal relationships and expected American ambassadors in Europe to look primarily to him as assistant secretary. In "Washington-speak," Dick was an empire builder. He possessed an enormously forceful personality, prided himself on the scope of his Rolodex, and made no secret of his own unquenchable ambition to become secretary of state, but he died in 2015 without achieving his ambition. Right or wrong on a given issue, Dick was exciting, action-oriented, and interesting.

A few days after I was confirmed, Senator Jesse Helms (R-N.C.), the ranking Republican member of the Senate Foreign Relations Committee, received a letter signed by six Romanian senators, five of whom were members of a right-wing xenophobic, anti-Semitic Transylvania-based political party, the Romanian National Unity Party, asking him to vote against my confirmation. They claimed I had been too close to Nicolae and Elena Ceaușescu and added a not-too-subtle reference to my being Jewish. The American and Israeli press termed the letter anti-Semitic, as indeed it was.

The fact that I had never laid eyes on Elena Ceaușescu and that my only dealings with Nicolae Ceaușescu were anything but cordial was beside the point. As far as I know, Senator Helms never replied to the letter, probably because by the time he received it, I had already been confirmed. The day I arrived in Romania as ambassador in December 1994, I was asked at an impromptu press conference about my reaction to the letter. As it happened, I was attending an interdenominational service in a Roman Catholic Church and was able to reply, truthfully, "I never discuss politics in church."

My Trip to Saudi Arabia, October 1994

Before setting the date for my swearing in and subsequent departure to Bucharest, I took time out for a seven-day trip to Saudi Arabia and Israel. I was invited to visit the Kingdom of Saudi Arabia as a guest of King Fahd, in my capacity as president of the American Jewish Committee. The Oslo Accords between Israel and the Palestinians, signed the previous year on the White House lawn, ushered in a diplomatic thaw by the Saudis, who were taking their first tentative steps toward building a wider peace in the Middle East.

Four days in Riyadh were an eye-opener for me. Unlike the Arab leaders

I had met in Egypt, Jordan, Iraq, and, of course, Israel, the Saudis seemed to have no problem with the existence of Israel as a Jewish state, provided the conflict with the Palestinians could be resolved. We delivered the Saudi message to Prime Minister Rabin and Foreign Minister Peres a few days later in Jerusalem.

Two Steps Forward, One Step Back

On my return from my seven-day trip to Saudi Arabia and Israel, I was greeted with a devastating shock: Carol was at home in bed with severe abdominal pains. We had spoken by phone every day I was away. She never mentioned illness, but as soon as I saw her, I knew something was wrong and insisted we immediately go to the hospital. After a battery of tests, the doctors reported that Carol had a growth in her abdomen that would require surgery both to remove it and to ascertain whether the growth was malignant.

Washington is big on celebrations, and friends of newly appointed ambassadors customarily give lunches or dinners for them. Carol's doctors urged her to continue her normal life pending the operation, scheduled for early November, so we accepted four or five invitations. The first was for dinner at the residence of our friends the German ambassador, Immo Stabreit, and his wife, Barbara. At the Stabreits', Carol and I were surrounded by old friends and government officials we knew and liked.

The next day, ten of my Dartmouth classmates gave a lunch for me at the Cosmos Club, a private club in Washington that prides itself on having distinguished literary members, among others. As we sat together in a private dining room drinking and retelling undergraduate escapades of long ago (some of them no doubt imagined), the intervening four decades melted away in a spirit of camaraderie and an alcoholic haze.

A few days later, Carol endured a two-and-a-half-hour operation at Georgetown University Hospital. She was diagnosed with stage 4 ovarian cancer. The surgeon said that treatment would entail six months of intensive chemotherapy.

I was stunned. The sonogram Carol and I saw at the doctor's office a week before the operation showed the growth, but the doctor downplayed its seriousness as probably nonmalignant. Carol knew better. While still in the recovery room she whispered to me, "It's bad, isn't it?" I stayed at the hospital the next three nights, sleeping on a chair in her room. Her recovery from the surgery was difficult and she was not strong enough to undergo chemotherapy for another three weeks.

After Carol's operation and diagnosis, I decided to forgo Romania and stay home with her. When I called Deputy Secretary of State Strobe Talbott to tell him my decision, he asked me to meet him the next day at the State Department. When I arrived, Holbrooke was there. He had gotten word from Strobe of Carol's illness and knew I had decided not to go to Romania. Dick would not hear of it. He insisted I go, saying that we had not had an ambassador in Bucharest for over a year, and that we needed an ambassador there now even if I could only stay a month or two. He went further, saying that I should consider the Bureau of European Affairs at State (known as EUR) my administrative "home" and return to Washington whenever Carol needed me. Strobe nodded in agreement. This meant that EUR would cover the special costs incurred by the medical situation.

After I told Carol what Dick had said, we decided that I would remain in Washington for her first chemotherapy treatment two weeks later, then go to Romania, and after that return for her five scheduled follow-on chemotherapy sessions. As it turned out, she had a hard time with chemotherapy and stopped earlier than planned. She continued on a nonchemotherapy regime as an outpatient at the National Institutes of Health, living a fairly normal life for almost nine years. She was able to join me in Bucharest only three times for short stays, otherwise staying close to the NIH's essential medical services. For the next three years, I returned home every month for ten days or so.

At first, EUR paid for my travel, as Dick had proposed, but early on I decided that I should pay, not the State Department. Several years after I returned to Washington for good, there was an investigation prompted by a complaint about my frequent trips home. There was also a rule that all chiefs of mission must request permission to leave their posts. The complainants did not know that I paid for the travel myself and that each time, before leaving Bucharest, I received permission from the State Department. When investigators asked Dick about this, he confirmed that he had authorized the travel. Dick was at that time the American ambassador to the UN and had a lot of clout. I never heard anything more about my travel.

 **2**

Looking Back to Explain Present-Day Romania

Romania's history explains why Romanians view the world as they do and the impact that this worldview has had on Romania's foreign and domestic policies.

There is probably no country in Europe with a sadder history than Romania. Romanians have long memories and speak passionately about the ills that befell their country at the hands of others. Victimhood is central to Romania's self-identity.

THE DESTINY OF AN ETHNIC CROSSROADS

Even Poland, divided three times in modern history, has a proud past. Romanians, by contrast, throughout history have been looked down on by the rest of Europe. Generally speaking, the prestige slope in Europe runs west to east. Germany's nineteenth-century chancellor, Otto von Bismarck, summed up Europe's feelings in his often quoted remark, "The Balkans aren't worth the bones of a single Pomeranian grenadier."

Romania's eastern border is the Black Sea. It shares to the west a border with Hungary and Serbia, and to the south a border with Bulgaria, across the Danube River. Romania also shares borders with Moldova (a region earlier known as Bessarabia) and Ukraine, both parts of the former Soviet Union.

Unlike most of the Balkans, Romania is neither Slav nor Magyar (Hungarian). If you ask Romanians to tell you their origins, they are likely to say that their national story began in the second century with the Roman emperor Trajan and his legions. Actually, Persian soldiers preceded Trajan and his legions in Romania, but legends are not to be denied. The Romans heavily colonized ancient Dacia, much of the eastern region of present-day Romania, and exploited its rich gold and silver deposits. They left behind a language with Latin roots, mixed in with some Slavic and other non-Romance-language words. Nevertheless, the language is a sufficiently close relative of French for France to claim Romania as a Francophone country and, when it suits its purposes, as a Francophile country politically. Before World War II, educated Romanians spoke French. After the war, when Romania became part of the Eastern bloc, instruction in Russian was mandatory for high school students, but was little used. Romanians have traditionally disdained everything Russian, referring to Russians as "the guests who come for dinner and never leave."

In its principal religious profile, Romania aligns with Serbia, Russia, Bulgaria, and Greece, having its own Romanian Orthodox Church, which follows the Eastern rite. This differentiates it from Poland, western Ukraine, Hungary, Slovakia, and Croatia, where Catholicism predominates, and Muslim Bosnia and Turkey. Thus, Romania has something of a hybrid culture.

After the Roman legions left, Dacia was invaded by Goths, followed by a succession of nomadic tribes who lived alongside and intermarried with the local population. In the Middle Ages, the people now known as Romanians lived in Wallachia, Moldavia, and a third principality, Transylvania, to the west. The three principalities became the heart of what is now Romania. Two other peoples lived in Transylvania, the Saxons, a Germanic people, and the Székelys, a subgroup of the Hungarian population, in parts of Transylvania. After the Magyars conquered Hungary, Transylvania became part of the Kingdom of Hungary, but a majority of the population remained ethnically Romanian. To this day, the memory of ethnic conflict in Transylvania between Romanians and Hungarians (Székelys) plays a role in the political life of Romania.

Next came the Turks. After the Ottoman Turks conquered Constantino-
ple in 1453, Wallachia came under Ottoman suzerainty, as did Moldavia and,
a short time later, Transylvania, but all three preserved considerable internal
autonomy. At the end of the sixteenth century, Mihai Viteazul—Michael the
Brave—united Wallachia, Moldavia, and Transylvania in a ceremony at Alba
Iulia, in Transylvania, to form the newly named Kingdom of Romania. Thus
King Michael was Romania's founding father. After the Turks were defeated
at the gates of Vienna in 1683, Transylvania became part of the Hapsburgs'
Austrian empire, where it remained until the end of World War I, when it was
reintegrated into an independent Romania.

Before the reunification of Romania following World War I, Braşov,
Sibiu, Sighişoara, and other Saxon cities ringing the Carpathian Mountains
did not allow Romanians to spend the night in their cities, partly out of fear
that a Romanian majority would replace the Saxons and partly out of prejudice against ethnic Romanians. In 2014 a descendant of these Saxons, Klaus
Iohannis, mayor of Sibiu, became president of Romania.

ROMANIA ENTERS THE MODERN AGE

Modern Romania's origins go back to 1859, when the mercantile leaders
of Wallachia and Moldavia elected Alexandru Ion Cuza to be their ruling
prince. Seven years later Cuza was exiled and replaced by a member of the
royal German family (Hohenzollerns), who became Prince Carol of Romania and later King Carol I, ruling Romania with his German wife, Queen
Elizabeth. Following Russia's defeat of Turkey in 1878, Romania declared
independence and was officially recognized as an independent state by the
Great Powers of Europe at the Congress of Berlin. In return, Romania agreed
to cede Bessarabia, present-day Moldova, to Russia. Transylvania remained
part of the Austro-Hungarian Empire and thus, with its majority ethnic Romanian population, bordered the newly independent Romania to the east.

After King Carol I died, in 1914, his nephew Ferdinand became king. His
wife, Queen Marie, was a star in the West. A granddaughter of England's
Queen Victoria, she was regal and beautiful—but she was not Romanian by
birth or culture. Nevertheless, most Romanians adored her.

Romania's role in World War I was complicated. Romania first declared neutrality. Two years later, being assured by France that if Romania joined the Triple Entente, the alliance of Great Britain, France, and Russia, it would get back Transylvania from a defeated Austria-Hungary, Romania declared war on Austria-Hungary. Dreams of victory were short-lived. Two-thirds of Romania, including Bucharest, was occupied by the Central Powers. As a consequence, in December 1917 Romania signed an armistice and withdrew from the war. But a year later, when both the Austro-Hungarian and Russian Empires were disintegrating, Romania rejoined the Triple Entente. Romania had its eye on regaining Bessarabia, which it had lost to Russia in 1878, and Transylvania and Northern Bukovina, which had been incorporated into the Austro-Hungarian Empire.

THE INTERWAR PERIOD: GREATER ROMANIA REDUX, 1918-39

In the peace that followed the Great War, Romania regained all three territories, thereby creating Romania Mare, Greater Romania. Without waiting for formal peace talks, the union of Transylvania with the Kingdom of Romania was proclaimed on December 1, 1918, in Alba Iulia—the same city where, 350 years before, King Michael the Brave had welded Wallachia, Moldavia, and Transylvania together in a union that lasted a little more than a year. Nevertheless, King Michael was viewed as Romania's equivalent of George Washington, Alba Iulia as Romania's historic capital, and December 1 as its July Fourth.

Between the two world wars, Romania enjoyed relative prosperity, owing principally to petroleum exports. Amoco and Shell Oil had major Romanian oil and gas concessions. With oil money flowing into the country, large government buildings and private mansions were built, lending support to Bucharest's claim to be the "Paris of the East." A faux arc de triomphe, made of wood and smaller than the original but still impressive, was constructed in central Bucharest. It was later redone in stone. For more than a decade, Romania enjoyed political stability. Power resided in the monarchy. King Ferdinand I was followed by his son, Carol II, who appointed the prime minister, whose designation was regularly confirmed in national elections. The prime minister's role was filled successively by the Bratianu family's Liberal Party and by Iuliu Maniu's National Peasant Party. It was Romania's Golden Age, but it was short-lived.

King Ferdinand died in 1927 and was succeeded by his son, Carol II, who had a messy personal life. His first marriage, to a commoner, the daughter of a Romanian general, was annulled. He then married Princess Helen of Greece, who gave birth to a son, the future King Michael I (Mihai). Michael I returned from exile to live in Romania and died in December 2017 at the age of ninety-six. Carol II's second marriage was not a happy one, and he spent the rest of his life in a relationship with Elena Lupescu, a divorced Roman Catholic whose parents were Jewish. Elena, whose Romanian name was Magda and whom King Carol eventually married while in exile, had a much-talked-about past, giving rise to the limerick

> *Have you heard about Magda Lupescu*
> *Who came to Romania's rescue?*
> *It's a wonderful thing to be under a king.*
> *Is democracy better, I ask you?*

Politically, all went well for a time. But a decade later, Romania experienced a rise of fascist anti-Semitic parties, the largest and most dangerous of them being the Iron Guard, also known as the Legion of the Archangel Michael, or Legionnaires. Carol tried to co-opt them. When he failed, he turned against the Iron Guard and ordered the execution of their leader, Corneliu Codreanu. Codreanu's followers blamed this on Romania's Jews, pointing to—you guessed it—Madame Lupescu as the prime villain.

Meanwhile, events elsewhere in Europe were closing in on Romania. In August 1939, as part of the infamous 1939 Molotov-Ribbentrop Pact that divvied up Poland between Germany and the Soviet Union, Romania was forced to cede Northern Bukovina and Bessarabia to the Soviet Union. A year later, Hitler, fresh from defeating France, compelled Romania to return a large part of Transylvania to Hungary, thus ending the short duration of Greater Romania. In 1940, under extreme pressure from pro-fascist elements, Carol II abdicated in favor of his nineteen-year-old son, Michael. But the real power resided in Romania's Marshal Ion Antonescu, who ruled Romania initially with the Iron Guard, and then in 1940 turned on the Iron Guard, after which he ruled alone.

Antonescu remains a hugely controversial figure. To some he was a Romanian patriot and military leader. To most he was an anti-Semite and fascist. All agree he was authoritarian and strong-willed.

WORLD WAR II: FASCISM RISING AT HOME AND ABROAD

In January 1941 the Iron Guard stormed through Bucharest's Jewish quarter, killing and beating up whomever they encountered, looting and burning shops and homes. Jewish worshippers were dragged from the Choral Synagogue and taken to a slaughterhouse, where they were brutally murdered, their corpses hung on meat hooks with signs reading "Kosher." Six months later, on the eve of the German invasion of the Soviet Union, Romanians rounded up 12,000 Jews in Iasi, on the border with the Soviet Union, and stuffed them into sealed railroad cars pulled by locomotives until the "passengers" were dead. The massacre may have been instigated by German SS troops, but the perpetrators were Romanian.

On June 22, 1941, Germany invaded the Soviet Union. More than 3 million German soldiers, supported by the bulk of the Romanian army, took part in the largest military operation in World War II. With Soviet military forces in full retreat, the Romanian army quickly recovered Northern Bukovina and Bessarabia and advanced with German troops, occupying Odessa, where they slaughtered the city's Jews, before the Red Army stopped them, and the German invaders, at Stalingrad in the winter of 1942–43.

This was the turning point in the war. After that, Soviet troops moved steadily west and by August 1944 were massed on the Romanian border. Romania sued for peace. Antonescu was overthrown, and on August 23, 1944, Romania joined the Allies. As a consequence, Romania regained Transylvania from Hungary, but Northern Bukovina and Bessarabia remained part of the Soviet Union. So too Dobruja, a small area on the Black Sea that Romania had been forced to cede to Bulgaria at the outset of World War II, remained part of Bulgaria. After World War II, there was no "Romania Mare." After Soviet troops occupied Romania, Antonescu was tried and executed.

ROMANIA IN THE SOVIET BLOC, BUT
FOLLOWING A DIFFERENT DRUMMER

Once Soviet troops occupied Romania, it was only a matter of time before the communists took over the country. In 1947 King Michael involuntarily abdicated and fled by rail to Switzerland. The head of the Communist Party, Gheorghe Gheorghiu-Dej, ruled the country until he died of cancer in 1965. By the time he died, Romania had already departed from Soviet economic policy and inaugurated a period of relative economic openness. In response, the United States and other Western countries invested in Romania. Gheorghiu-Dej also persuaded the Soviet Union to withdraw its troops from Romania, which allowed him and his successor, Nicolae Ceauşescu, the leeway to act independently of the Soviet Union when it suited their purposes. Internally, Gheorghiu-Dej and Ceauşescu brutally suppressed internal dissent, Ceauşescu most intensely after his trip to North Korea in 1971, following which he adopted a new role model—Kim Il-sung.

After Mikhail Gorbachev came to power in the Soviet Union in 1985 and declared his policies of *glasnost* (openness) and *perestroika* (restructuring), Ceauşescu still continued to trumpet his own hard-line communist policies. This led in 1987 to massive protests by Romanian workers in Braşov, a center of heavy industry in Transylvania. The protest was quelled by the militia and Ceauşescu's Securitate, but the handwriting was on the wall. Yet even after the Berlin Wall came down on November 9, 1989, Ceauşescu, blinded perhaps by self-regard, tried to cling to power.

A few weeks later, while Ceauşescu was out of the country visiting Iran, a demonstration in Timişoara in western Romania got out of hand, swelling to more than 50,000 demonstrators shouting "Down with Ceauşescu!" The next morning the city looked like a war zone. Still in Iran, Ceauşescu ordered the military and Securitate to open fire on demonstrators. Thousands of demonstrators were killed or wounded. The "Timişoara massacre" became a headline around the world; the media likened it to the Tiananmen Square massacre six months earlier in Beijing.

On December 20, 1989, the demonstration leaders called a general strike in Timişoara. This time the military refused to intervene, and the next day the army withdrew. With the authorities in Bucharest powerless to put down the Timișoara uprising, communist Romania was unraveling. Ceaușescu flew back from Iran to take personal control. The next day, December 21, he spoke from the balcony of Communist Party headquarters facing a large open square in the center of Bucharest.

In the past such public speeches had worked. The communist way of demonstrating popular support for the party's leader was for Ceaușescu to stand on the balcony at Communist Party headquarters, wave to the crowd below, and deliver a long speech haranguing the faithful workers, who, having been bused into Bucharest for the speech, would cheer and applaud on cue. Not this time! Ceaușescu was greeted by loud protests and random shooting. At first he paused, seemingly unable to comprehend what was happening. When he tried to resume speaking, he was interrupted by a loud uproar and more shooting. He was completely flummoxed. This had never happened before. His bodyguards formed a protective ring around him and led him inside party headquarters.

A short time later, he and Elena Ceaușescu fled Bucharest by helicopter. Four days later, on Christmas Day, the Ceaușescus, who had been apprehended by the Romanian army, were summarily tried and executed at an army base in Targoviște, about sixty miles north of Bucharest, on orders from the National Salvation Front, the ad hoc group that had taken charge of the country when the Ceaușescus fled. It was the only violent removal of a communist leader in Eastern Europe.

AFTER CEAUȘESCU: FILLING THE VOID

With the hated Ceaușescus gone, Romania was left in disarray. Unlike in other former Soviet satellites, there was no democratic or dissident government-in-waiting ready to take over. Crudely speaking, Ceaușescu had bought off the United States and much of the West with his policy of independence from the Soviet Union, leaving him with a free hand to eliminate all organized internal opposition or dissent. Ceaușescu's flight from Bucharest left a political vacuum in Romania, but it was soon filled by Ion Iliescu and others. The exact details of the political developments after December 21 are murky, and the full facts may never be known. The account that follows is based on what

President Iliescu and other eyewitnesses to the events told me. Some of them later split with Iliescu and joined the political opposition.

Upon hearing that Ceauşescu had fled the city, Iliescu walked a few blocks from his office in Bucharest to the government television station, where a large anti-Ceauşescu protest was taking place. When he arrived, the demonstrators recognized him and told him about a meeting then in progress of self-appointed leaders at Communist Party headquarters. When he arrived at the meeting, those assembled quickly deferred to him. This is not surprising: Iliescu possessed qualities of leadership combined with a twinkle in his eye, a ready smile, and a self-assurance that bespeaks confidence. He was elected head of the Provincial Council of the National Salvation Front (NSF), the name chosen by the assembled group that had assumed control of the country.

After he was chosen to head the NSF, Iliescu wanted someone with a fresh face, not tainted by a communist past, to lead the government as prime minister. A large student demonstration in University Square, three blocks from Communist Party headquarters, was shown on national television. In the middle of the crowd, standing on the pedestal of a monument, could be seen Petre Roman, a professor of engineering at Bucharest Polytechnic Institute. Roman had been walking home when he saw the student demonstrators and joined them, waving a Romanian flag with the hammer and sickle cut out. The flag became the symbol of the revolution. Seeing the student demonstrators on television, Iliescu recognized Roman as the son of Valter Roman, a Jew who had been born Ernst Neulander and who had fought with the Republican Army in 1938 in the Spanish Civil War. President Iliescu later told me that he said to himself, "This is my future prime minister. He was not tainted by Ceauşescu and has the looks and pedigree to become prime minister." And so he did.

The hated Ceauşescus were gone, but the new caretaker government faced huge problems. When I visited Bucharest in March 1990, a few months after the revolution, the army was still patrolling the streets in armored personnel carriers, and demonstrators in University Square were holding up antigovernment signs demanding free and open elections and the banning of former communists from government—a demand that could not be met without eliminating a large swath of the Romanian bureaucracy.

Elections were held in May 1990. Iliescu's NSF, now the National Salvation Party, won with around 85 percent of the vote, but the results were widely contested, with charges of voter fraud and other irregularities.

However courageous President Iliescu might have been in defying Ceaușescu, he was not accepted by the surviving leaders of Romania's pre-communist-era National Peasants Party. Regardless of his personal merits and the fact that he was only fifteen years old when the communists took control of Romania, in their eyes he was guilty of being a loyal communist under a leadership that had sentenced them to seventeen years of harsh imprisonment. Some of their colleagues died in jail; others were broken in health or spirit. Those who survived and eventually were released from prison such as Corneliu Coposu and Ion Diaconescu were silenced by an oppressive communist regime.

Once Ceaușescu fell, the leading surviving pre-communist-era political figure was Corneliu Coposu, the then ailing seventy-five-year-old leader of the party that had been formed from a merger of the National Peasants Party and the Christian Democratic Party: the PNT-CD. After the revolution he refused to strike a political bargain with Iliescu and led his followers into the streets, where they sounded a constant drumbeat denouncing Iliescu and his government as communists. The hurried elections in May 1990, which Iliescu and his National Salvation Party won handily, did not ease the tension. No one in Romania's new government, including President Iliescu and Prime Minister Roman and other ministers, had held high office under Ceaușescu, but most of them had some connection to Romania's communist past.

The Western press, suspicious of the genuineness of the revolution, bought into the story. But had it not been for two coal miner raids on Bucharest engineered by President Iliescu, the first in June 1990, the second in September 1991, he might in time have been accepted by the West as a reformed former communist on the model of Hungary's post-revolution Prime Minister Gyula Horn or Poland's President Aleksander Kwaśniewski. But this was not to be. TV images of soot-covered miners from Romania's Jiu Valley brought to Bucharest by the government, savagely beating and on occasion killing students and other antigovernment demonstrators, left the impression that little had changed in Romania.

After the second coal miners raid, in September 1991, a badly shaken Petre Roman resigned as prime minister, split from President Iliescu, left the

Romanian Social Democratic Party (PDSR), and started his own Democratic Party (PD). Bringing in the coal miners permanently tarnished President Iliescu's image, but it jump-started the political career of Emil Constantinescu, who defeated President Iliescu in the 1996 presidential election. In 1991, when students were being beaten by the miners, Constantinescu, then Bucharest University's rector, ordered that the university's doors be opened to allow injured students to escape. For this he was lionized by the PNT-CD leader, Corneliu Coposu, who chose him to run as the PNT-CD candidate for president in 1992 and again in 1996. He lost badly to President Iliescu in 1992 but triumphed four years later, when Petre Roman swung his PD party behind Constantinescu and the PNT-CD to form a coalition government that was characterized in the West as center-right.

ROMANIAN HISTORY UP CLOSE AND PERSONAL

As ambassador I often witnessed firsthand how Romanians revisit their history every day, nursing old grudges and burnishing their brief moments of glory.

Following a speech I gave at Black Sea University a short time after I became ambassador, a professor and former Romanian ambassador to the United States asked me whether Americans were aware that "we Romanians are descended from Emperor Trajan and his Roman legions," to which I replied, "Most Americans do not know who Trajan was." But, eager to understand the country and its past, I later traveled the length of the Danube River Delta, the path crossed by nomadic tribes, and walked over Roman ruins dating back to the time of Trajan.

Americans have heard about the legend of Dracula, a creation of Western literature, but most know little about the historical basis of the legend. The legend of Dracula owes its origins to the forty-seven-year reign of Vlad III, the Prince of Wallachia but better known to history as Vlad the Impaler, in the fifteenth century. In 1996 I raised the legend of Dracula with Mugur Isarescu, the governor of the National Bank of Romania, while on a visit to a church dating back to the Middle Ages on an island in Lake Snagov, outside Bucharest. Pointing to a crypt in the church floor, Governor Isarescu said, "Here lies Dracula." He explained that Vlad the Impaler, notorious for impaling his victims, was less than five feet tall, and was beheaded—thus spared the fate of his victims. The bones inside the crypt were those of a short man without a head, thereby giving birth to the supposition that these remains were those of Vlad the Impaler.

When I visited the historic home of the Bratianu family (now a museum honoring the Bratianus' memory), situated outside Pitești, an industrial city an hour's drive west of Bucharest, it made me think again about the Paris Peace Conference and the return of Transylvania, Northern Bukovina, and Bessarabia to Romania in 1920. Ionel Bratianu, a Romanian statesman, was prime minister and the principal Romanian negotiator in the talks that led to the restoration of Transylvania, Northern Bukovina, and Bessarabia to Romania after World War I.

When in Sighet, I visited the Nobel laureate Elie Wiesel's birthplace and spoke in the Sighet jail, where Iuliu Maniu of the National Peasants Party and Gheorghe Bratianu of the Liberal Party died in 1953 under unclear circumstances.

I heard stories from Romanian families living on the border between Romania and Ukraine about family members who crossed the Tisza River to visit neighbors the morning the Soviet Union closed the river border in May 1944. They never returned.

When I was in Bucharest in 1980 to meet with Ceaușescu, I attended the memorial service at the Choral Synagogue for the Jewish victims of the January 1941 pogrom. As ambassador, I returned to the Choral Synagogue each year to speak at the annual memorial service.

I heard accounts from eyewitnesses to Romania's horrific twentieth-century tragedies and moments of national joy.

I listened to accounts of the anti-Ceaușescu labor protests in Brașov, the demonstrations in Timișoara, and the riot that erupted when Ceaușescu spoke in Bucharest on December 21, 1989. I sat in the room at the former Communist Party headquarters (later the Romanian Senate) where Iliescu and others gathered after Ceaușescu fled. Eyewitnesses at the headquarters that day told me what happened, minute by minute. The most detailed account was that of Silviu Brucan, born Saul Bruckner, a prominent communist ideologue and onetime ambassador to the United States, who had been placed under house arrest for a time by Ceaușescu but later had been allowed to travel abroad.

Princess Margareta, King Michael's daughter, visited me in the American embassy, at my invitation, which led to my incurring the displeasure of President Iliescu and his government. This was at a time when the political opposition was calling for the restoration of the monarchy. In fact, the restoration of the monarchy became one of the planks in Emil Constantinescu's 1996 "Contract with Romania."

I interceded with President Iliescu to stop former Iron Guard Legionnaires and their followers from building monuments in memory of Marshal Ion Antonescu, who had made the fateful decision to join Nazi Germany in the invasion of the Soviet Union in 1941 and who gave the orders that led to the killing of 200,000 Romanian Jews deported to Transnistria.

President Iliescu and others told me about their pre-revolution efforts to overthrow Ceaușescu. Iliescu consorted with a high-ranking army general and Virgil Magureanu, the post-Ceaușescu head of the SRI (Romania's internal security service), who resigned in 2007 amid allegations of wrongdoing. They were secretly planning to overthrow Ceaușescu, but they gave up when they failed to muster the support of the military and security services.

I heard separate eyewitness accounts of the two coal-miner raids from President Iliescu, Petre Roman, and President Constantinescu, journalists, Ion Ratiu (the opposition leader whose home was ransacked), and others.

The Christian Democratic leader Corneliu Coposu and Bishop Tokes of Hungary (whose removal by Romania's communist government led to the December 1989 demonstrations in Timișoara and Ceaușescu's loss of power) contacted me seeking my support in their political battles. I sympathized with them—recognizing their personal suffering and their service to democracy— but in my view, both went too far in trying to enlist me, the American ambassador, in their political battles. Bishop Tokes wanted me to agree that the treatment of Hungarians by Romanians was a second Holocaust. I refused for the simple reason that it was not true, and for the less simple reason that equating all tragedies to the Holocaust distorts history and cheapens the memory of those lost to genocide. Romanians did not send Hungarians to gas chambers, systemically kill Hungarians, or murder them as the Nazis did Jews. Coposu wanted the American government to condemn President Iliescu as an illegitimate usurper of power intent on restoring communism. This, too, was untrue. In 1992 President Iliescu was reelected in free and fair elections. He knew that communism was finished and that Romania needed to join the West.

I experienced constant reminders of the prominent role of the Jewish community in pre–World War II Romanian life. I attended Jewish religious services, occasionally convening them myself, in small, deserted synagogues throughout Romania that formerly served thriving Jewish communities.

President Iliescu never tired of telling me, or anyone else who would listen, about the discrimination against and, sometimes, persecution of Romanians at the hands of Hungarians in Transylvania. Knowing Iliescu's propensity to lapse into his set anti-Hungarian speech, I implored his diplomatic adviser to persuade him in advance of his meeting with First Lady Hillary Clinton in July 1996 not to repeat his Hungarian speech, but to no avail! Halfway through the meeting, out came the Hungarian speech. To her great credit, Hillary sat there impassively and, to my amazement, later told me she found Iliescu's account interesting.

In the run-up to the 1996 elections, former prime minister Theodor Stolojan returned to Romania from Washington, reportedly to support President Iliescu's reelection bid. He initially supported Iliescu, but then did a turnabout and supported the opposition. Such political flip-flops are not uncommon in Romania, as a quick perusal of the long list of Romanian political parties and their leaders shows.

President Constantinescu explained to me two days after he took the oath of office why it was important for him as president of Romania to be in Alba Iulia on December 1, a historic location and a historic date.

When I ended my tour as ambassador, Iliescu, no longer president but still a Romanian patriot, gave me a hand-carved two-foot-high figurine of Michael the Brave astride his horse.

 3

The Curtain Rises

When I took up my ambassadorial duties, I was only vaguely aware of official happenings on the ground in Romania or what our government expected me to accomplish. Except for my one breakfast meeting with Dick Holbrooke, which was chiefly a hello and a pat on the back—Dick had never been to Romania—no one briefed me on goings-on in Romania or discussed our policy and goals. Career U.S. Foreign Service officers have a big advantage in that they know the ropes and are plugged into the State Department system. My two-week course at "ambassador school" focused on procedure, not substance. There was nary a word about Romania. John Davis, my predecessor as ambassador, had been back in the United States for a year and, although extremely friendly and supportive, was by nature laconic and did not tell me what was happening in Romania or what he thought our policy should be.

THE PLAYERS

From day one, I was largely on my own trying to formulate a coherent and consistent policy with clear objectives consonant with U.S. interests. Once on the job, I benefited greatly from the support of our embassy staff and from official Washington, including the White House, the State Department, the Department of Defense, the Commerce Department, and the CIA— in short, of all relevant departments of the executive branch of government. The same was true of the international financial institutions, principally the World Bank and International Monetary Fund, with which I worked closely in Bucharest and Washington on economic matters.

The only negative vibes came from some members of Congress on the political right who were hostile to President Ion Iliescu, a former communist, and disapproved of my working with him, even if it enabled us to strengthen Romania's democratic institutions, promote economic reform, and build a relationship of cooperation and trust between our two countries. This was a recurring problem. Three Republican members of the House—David Funderburk (R-N.C.), Frank Wolf (R-Va.), and Chris Smith (R-N.J.)—had close ties to the Christian Democratic (CD) Party in Romania (later allied with the National Peasants Party to become the PNT-CD), led by the ailing Corneliu Coposu, who had survived seventeen years in prison under the communists. He died in the fall of 1995 after a long illness and is still looked upon today by many Romanians as a national hero. Coposu was uncompromising in his denunciation of President Iliescu and his government, refusing to form a national coalition or otherwise bend in his opposition. For him it was keeping faith with his dead mentor, Iuliu Maniu, the historic leader of Romania's National Peasants Party (PNT), who died in a communist prison in 1953.

Congressman Funderburk, a protégé of Senator Jesse Helms (R-N.C.) and a one-term congressman, had served four controversial years as the American ambassador to Romania under President Ronald Reagan. He bitterly denounced all efforts by our government to work with Romania's new government. He enlisted to his cause the International Republican Institute (IRI), a congressionally funded NGO that was active in Romania and other countries in Eastern Europe. Individually and collectively they had no impact on our policy, but they were a constant irritant and, at times, troublemakers.

THEIR PARTIES

When I arrived as ambassador in December 1994, Romania was still haunted by the Ceauşescu days and the messy succession that followed the dictator's execution. Iliescu had been reelected president for a four-year term in 1992. His opponent, Emil Constantinescu, the rector of Bucharest University with no previous political experience, had been handpicked by Coposu to run against him. Constantinescu lost with 38.73 percent of the votes against Iliescu's 61.27 percent. In the parliamentary elections, Iliescu's Social Democratic Party of Romania (PDSR) won a plurality of the seats, but not a majority. After the elections Iliescu proposed to the PNT-CD that it join PDSR in a national unity government, but Coposu refused, hoping that the government would flounder and be replaced by a PNT-CD government. He was right, but he had to wait another four years.

Rejected by the center-right parties, Iliescu's PDSR entered into a voting arrangement in Parliament with extremist parties on the left and right, one of which, the Romanian National Unity Party (PUNR), a Transylvania nationalist party, was also a member of the government. By the spring of 1994, PNT-CD was ahead of PDSR in nationwide polls and had a strong following in Bucharest and other major cities, but President Iliescu held the reins of power and remained popular in rural areas and with industrial workers. (The scene has not changed dramatically since then. As of 2017 the center-left Social Democratic Party still depended on rural areas and workers for support; the center-right opposition drew support from Bucharest and other urban areas.)

In December 1994 the political temperature was at a low boil. Romanian society was simply broken. After two generations of communism, a middle class no longer existed. In its place, workers, peasants, former nomenklatura, and hangers-on clamored for attention as they sought to influence policy. The political opposition called for President Iliescu's impeachment, terming him and his political allies "crypto-communists," a charge echoed by many in the Romanian émigré community in the United States, particularly those who had left Romania after the communists seized control. Not to be outdone, the Romanian government referred to the opposition in Romania as "crypto-fascists." Both terms resonated in Romania, a country that had lived through the horrors of both fascism and communism.

For two years my principal dealings on economic matters were with Finance Minister Florin Georgescu, Economic Reform Minister Mircea Cosea, Secretary General of the Government Viorel Hrebenciuc, and Governor of the National Bank of Romania Mugur Isarescu. They did not speak with one voice, as will be seen throughout this book.

Finance Minister Georgescu, a former Romanian footballer (soccer), worked for a time at the U.S Federal Reserve. He had a forceful personality and definite views tinged with a socialist caste. He was a member of PDSR, Iliescu's party. The political implications of economic decisions were never far from his mind. The same was true of Secretary General Hrebenciuc, but he did not think of himself as an economist. He was "Mr. Fix-It." He knew the ins and outs of Romanian politics, was always available for a meeting, and usually gave straight answers. Economic Reform Minister Cosea, an economics professor, was a member of PUNR, so he was not in the PDSR political circle. Well-intentioned, he was bypassed by others in government and in the end accomplished little. After the 1996 elections, Georgescu, Cosea, and Hrebenciuc were replaced by a less colorful set of ministers. But as of the writing of this book, National Bank Governor Isarescu was still head of the National Bank of Romania and was the world's longest-serving national bank governor.

On matters pertaining to foreign policy, defense, and security, the lineup had more players but was blander. President Iliescu sat at the top of decision-making in all three areas. The foreign minister, Teodor Meleşcanu, was an urbane, friendly, pro-American career diplomat. Our relations were excellent from day one. He was a favorite of Secretary of State Warren Christopher. As of 2017, twenty-one years after he left the Foreign Ministry in December 1996, he was back as foreign minister at age seventy-six. The defense minister was Gheorghe Tinca, a Foreign Ministry career diplomat whom President Iliescu chose to be his defense minister for reasons that were not readily apparent other than the fact that he spoke English and was acceptable to the West.

Responsibility for security was divided between the Internal Security Service (SRI) and the External Security Service (SIE). The director of the SRI was Virgil Magureanu, an inscrutable man viewed by many in the West as a sinister figure. His only bias that I was aware of was a deep fear of Russia.

He was always on the lookout for KGB operatives. I worked with him on highly sensitive matters but was never sure whose side he was on. The SIE was directed by Ioan Talpes, a close ally of President Iliescu and avowed pro-American. He was a friend and confidant of Romania's ambassador to the United States, Mihai Botez, who was also pro-American but, tragically, died in the summer of 1995.

This was the foreign policy, defense, and security team: Foreign Minister Meleșcanu and SIE Director Talpes were on our side, along with a more guarded Defense Minister Gheorghe Tinca. SRI Director Magureanu was harder to read. He never put all his cards on the table. President Iliescu and I developed a strong bond that has continued, but Iliescu was and is his own man, answering to his deeply held belief in an egalitarian society and distrustful of the wealthy.

There was one other player, Adrian Nastase, chairman of PDSR and president of the Chamber of Deputies. I met Adrian in Washington when he was foreign minister, preceding Meleșcanu in that role. In his new position as president of the Chamber of Deputies he assumed great self-importance. He was later prime minister. He was generally progressive and helpful on much-needed reform legislation.

Here is the lineup of major players from 1994 to 1996:

> Ion Iliescu, president of Romania
> Teodor Meleșcanu, foreign minister
> Gheorghe Tinca, minister of defense
> Florin Georgescu, minister of finance
> Adrían Nastase, president of the Chamber of Deputies
> Mircea Cosea, minister of economic reform
> Viorel Hrebenciuc, secretary general of the government
> Mugur Isarescu, governor of the National Bank of Romania
> Virgil Magureanu, director of SRI
> Ioan Talpes, director of SIE

Lesser lights were Prime Minister Nicolae Vacaroiu and Oliviu Gherman, president of the Romanian Senate.

NEW DEMOCRACY, NEW ECONOMY

Despite the rawness of its politics, by December 1994 Romania was a functioning democracy. Its new constitution, adopted in 1992, provided for a popularly elected president as head of state, a bicameral parliament consisting of co-equal Senate and Chamber of Deputies, a government headed by a prime minister, and a government of ministers. All ministers were appointed by the president and confirmed by the Parliament. People could say what they wanted to whomever they wanted. There were more than 100 newspapers reporting the news, or their versions of the news, most of them anti-government, and freedom of religion was respected.

Romania's main problem was not its democracy but its economy. Throughout my ambassadorship, economic reform was the most difficult problem facing the country. Under Ceauşescu, the economy was one of the most highly controlled and centralized in Eastern Europe—a Stalinist model that had previously been abandoned by other countries in the region. Its state-owned sector was dominated by heavy industry operating under rigid quantity targets. Employment was redundant and inefficient. Steel and aluminum mills, truck manufacturing, heavy machinery manufacturing, cement plants and the like dominated the economy and sucked up its resources long after many other communist countries in the region had introduced a limited market economy.

Once Ceauşescu was gone, the government looked for ways to transfer the tightly controlled, heavily industrial economy to a market-based system. The strategy adopted was a gradual approach in the hope of avoiding the pain of rapid change and downsizing. Gross domestic product contracted in the years from 1990 to 1992 and only started to recover in 1993. The recovery was largely a result of "spontaneous" development by privately owned small and medium-sized businesses. Larger state-owned enterprises (SOEs) and *régies autonomes* (RAs)—primarily utilities and quasi-governmental entities engaged in essential industrywide production—remained in government hands and were inefficient and unprofitable. Romania's GDP is shown in IMF figures:

Year	Real GDP
1990	(5.6)
1991	(12.9)
1992	(8.8)
1993	1.5
1994	3.9
1995	7.1
1996	3.9

Source: International Monetary Fund, "Staff Country Report No. 98/123," p. 3. Parentheses indicate a decrease from the previous year.

Shortly after the 1989 revolution, most housing and retail businesses were privatized, including 80 percent of agricultural land, but seed, fertilizer, equipment, supply, storage, marketing, and financing remained under government control. By the end of 1995, privately owned businesses were numerically the majority of businesses in Romania, but most were small, and the SOEs and RAs continued to account for the dominant share of employment and practically the country's entire industrial production. Badly needed adjustment was resisted, and these enterprises continued to drag down the economy.

Direct foreign investment in Romania in 1994 was only a few hundred million dollars, well below Romania's target of $1.5 billion. Its hard currency reserves were close to zero. As a result, Romania was forced to look to the IMF and the World Bank for loans and grants. Romania survived as a ward of the West.

During my three years in Bucharest, I witnessed and participated in numerous efforts by Romanian governments to reform the economy: first, the PDSR and its center-left coalition under Iliescu; followed in December 1996 by the PNT-CD and its center-right coalition headed by Emil Constantinescu and his prime minister, Victor Ciorbea. There were encouraging starts and abrupt stops, disruptions and detours, disappointments and frustrations. The international financial institutions, the United States, and other Western countries always said to the Romanians, "Do more. Go faster." But enormous obstacles—political, societal, historical, and cultural—stood in the way, making reform difficult to enact, and even more difficult to implement.

There were lots of reasons why economic reform did not move faster in Romania. For one thing, the SOEs and RAs were creatures of the communist regime that President Iliescu and other former socialists were reluctant to disavow entirely, believing that big businesses should be owned by "the people," not by a new entrepreneurial class headed by "rich people." There was also the fear that profitable government-owned enterprises would be gobbled up by foreign investors at bargain prices. Call it national pride, native populism, or whatever, it recurs throughout history and crosses borders, including our own.

Also standing in the way of reform was a lack of know-how. Romania did not have the in-country expertise to carry out wholesale privatization and was forced to look abroad for guidance, primarily to the World Bank. This set off a bureaucratic war, with competing international and Romanian "experts" vying for the last word.

Another issue was the fear among Romanian politicians that rapid privatization would lead to wholesale job losses, an economic turndown, and resultant losses at the polls for incumbent officeholders. The PDSR tried to grease the skids leading up to the 1996 national elections by employing various economic schemes to boost the economy, but they all failed.

In the process, economic reform was held hostage to a losing cause. Even with needed legislation, the amended Mass Privatization Program, in place in late 1995, the political determination to implement privatization and other reforms was lacking. Starting in 1997, with a new government in place, better things were expected. Sadly, this did not happen fast enough. Two years after the new government came to power, the pace of privatization was slightly lower than it had been the year before the change in government. Again, timidity, lack of know-how, and political maneuvering left things little improved from PDSR days. National Bank Governor Mugur Isarescu, an economist, not a politician, became prime minister in 1999 and imposed draconian economic measures to squeeze inflation out of the economy (as Federal Reserve chair Paul Volcker did in the United States in the early days of the Reagan administration). He also accelerated the pace of privatization. After that, Romania's economy started to grow on a sustainable basis. From 1999 to 2004 there was an impressive increase in GDP moving from $36 billion in 1999 to $76 billion in 2004, thereafter peaking at more than $208 billion in 2008.

FOREIGN POLICY CONSIDERATIONS

Romania's foreign policy largely boiled down to one word or, rather, acronym, NATO. Thinking in the West on how and when to enlarge NATO began in late 1994, with the United States and Germany the main drivers. The United States hoped that enlargement would forge a "peaceful and undivided Europe," President Clinton's words in a speech he gave earlier in the year. Germany looked to NATO enlargement, focusing on Poland, to fill the security vacuum between Russia and Germany and to reposition Germany at the center of an enlarged NATO rather than remaining exposed on its eastern flank.

From the moment NATO enlargement became a possibility, Romania made a beeline dash to NATO's door, and made early entry a national passion. Romanians saw NATO membership as the answer to centuries of victimization at the hands of more powerful neighbors that had held the whip hand: first the Ottoman Empire, followed by Russia and Austria-Hungary. Being part of a united Europe in NATO, a military alliance that included the United States and Canada, was highly appealing to a country with a long history of foreign invasions and domination.

It was no surprise that Romania's initial position on NATO expansion was maximalist: all the former satellite countries should be admitted simultaneously. This was not magnanimity on Romania's part but practicality, stemming from Romania's realization that if NATO were to pick and choose among former Soviet satellites, Romania would not be at the top of the list. When it became clear that NATO would expand in stages, Romania's foreign policy had only one objective: early admission to NATO. It shaped everything Romania did in its external relations and military planning.

DECEMBER 1994: ENTER, STAGE WEST

On December 9, I said a tearful good-bye to Carol and flew from Dulles Airport to Vienna, where I met up with our oldest daughter, Barbara. She would accompany me to Bucharest, staying until I returned home at the end of the month. The next day, a cold, snowy morning, Barbara and I took off through heavy clouds for Bucharest. As we crossed the snow-covered Carpathian Mountains, the weather cleared. Below was a broad flat plain with Bucharest to the north and the storied Danube River to the south, meandering to the Black Sea.

When we arrived, waiting for us at the bottom of the airplane steps was the American embassy "country team," composed of senior embassy officers. Instinctively, I took the arm of the smiling consul general, Nancy Pelletreau, a thirty-year Foreign Service veteran whose friendly face radiated warmth. Together we strode arm in arm into the airport lounge. It was Sunday, and the airport was deserted. Parked on the side of the runways were old Russian planes no longer airworthy, now relics. The airport, Romania's finest, had the appearance of a junkyard for airplanes.

I do not know what the country team thought of its new ambassador, and I had almost no idea what was in store for me, but I was confident and enthusiastic and the senior embassy staff were warm and welcoming. Several of them had come to see me in Washington and apparently brought positive words back to Bucharest. Jonathan Rickert, the chargé d'affaires at the embassy for over a year in the absence of Ambassador John Davis, had also gotten in touch with me and we exchanged notes. He knew of my prior involvement in Romania and spread the word that the new ambassador knew the country. This, too, was helpful.

The embassy had performed superbly in the absence of an ambassador, its staff taking on tasks that would have normally fallen to the ambassador. This was particularly true of Jonathan, a highly competent Foreign Service officer on his second tour of duty in Romania. He graciously relinquished the leadership role to me on my arrival.

After brief hellos and handshakes in an ornate, paneled room at the airport, built by Ceaușescu to impress foreign dignitaries, reality struck when we proceeded into Bucharest. On the fifteen-mile ride from the airport to my official residence, the ambassador's car, a 1987 Cadillac, stalled at every traffic light, finally stopping with a *chug-chug* a block from the ambassador's residence. Barbara, a successful New York lawyer, and I carried our suitcases to the residence, which both of us thought was just fine. It was also a fitting beginning to service in a country struggling to catch up.

Our ride into Bucharest was eventful for another reason. The road from the airport to Bucharest was more a death trap than a highway. Cars crossed the road without warning, traffic slowed for horse-drawn carts carrying hay and people, the street lighting was poor to nonexistent.

The ambassador's residence was a handsome house constructed in the early 1900s that had formerly been the home of Ana Pauker, Romania's first communist foreign minister, serving from 1947 to 1952. She lost her job, as did other Jewish communists, in 1951, when Jews were expelled from the top ranks of the party on Stalin's orders. Inside the residence, the embassy team introduced Barbara and me to the house staff, and the members of the embassy team described their duties and the problems they faced. After this, I drove an embassy car—not expected of new ambassadors—to a nearby Catholic church, where, unrelated to my arrival, the embassy was hosting a Christmas concert with lots of holiday songs, and a few Hanukkah melodies added to round out the program in the spirit of American ecumenicalism. At the end of the service there was an impromptu press conference, which gave me an opportunity to make the comment about "never discussing politics in church."

After the concert Barbara and I went for a walk in downtown Bucharest. Our first stop was Revolution Square, where Ceaușescu had made the speech that sparked the revolution in December 1989. We stared at the damaged buildings with bullet holes everywhere and exteriors pockmarked by shells. From Revolution Square we proceeded down to that part of Bucharest destroyed by Ceaușescu as part of his Victory of Socialism madness, now rebuilt with immense neoclassical buildings. The empty buildings looked grotesque and out of place. Our last stop was the Choral Synagogue, where I had spent long hours with Rabbi Rosen attending services, speaking to the congregation, and planning ways to help Romanian Jews emigrate to Israel.

Several years earlier, after one of Rabbi Rosen's annual Hanukkah tours, our daughter Amalie had lived in an apartment adjoining the synagogue. This time the synagogue gates were locked. The guard muttered in Romanian something about our being out of luck. We stood around for a few minutes wondering what to do next, when a man emerged from the synagogue, said something to the guard, and in we went. Barbara handed the guard a $20 bill, probably a week's pay.

As in the past, visiting the synagogue had an emotional effect on me as my mind traveled back over the centuries thinking of Jewish life in Romania, faded now by time, yet kept alive by the miracle of Jewish survival.

The next day I met one-on-one with the entire embassy staff, beginning with the consular section, a hardworking and often overlooked part of the embassy. Five mornings a week, Romanians lined up around the block seeking U.S. immigration or visitor visas. Each applicant was interviewed by one of eight U.S. consular officers, who then, on the basis of the papers filed and a brief interview, told the applicant yes or no. The process for a visitor took barely fifteen minutes but much longer for immigrant visas; in both cases, however, it was hugely consequential for the applicant, who was approved or denied largely on the basis of the consular officer's judgment as to whether the applicant would overstay the six-month limit for a tourist visa or, once in the United States, would try to remain permanently. For immigrant visas the issues were financial sustainability and character. The consular office is often the first foreign post for a new Foreign Service officer. It was instructive and perhaps sobering for young diplomats to see, early in their careers, how desperate people were to emigrate to our country.

The next stop was the U.S. Information Agency (USIA), which had an extensive and effective Romanian program of public diplomacy. It brought the American message of democracy and freedom in the form of lectures, films, and an impressive and heavily used library. The USIA's familiar theme was "Romania turns its eyes to the United States to help transform the country from communism to democracy."

It was a short walk from the handsome USIA cultural center to the General Service Office, housed in what was once the Yugoslavia embassy but now looked more like a warehouse than an embassy. This was where carpentry and automobile repair work was done plus all the other things that went into maintaining the U.S. government's complex of about a dozen buildings in downtown Bucharest.

After that came the CIA station. Before leaving Washington I had been told at the State Department to expect CIA officers to bridle at any suggestion that the ambassador had authority over them. This was not the case for me in Romania. To a person, the CIA operatives were totally open to my initiatives and supportive.

It was now evening and I was off to a reception given in an ornate hall by the Romanian-American Chamber of Commerce. I was introduced to a group of about 100 members and then went around the room introducing myself and hearing stories about what it was like to do business in Romania.

There were lots of complaints, most involving red tape, indecision, multiple decision-makers, and corruption. On the last point, the complaint was not corruption per se. Surprisingly, these American businessmen did not care about Romania's endemic corruption. Their complaint was that corruption made it hard for them to compete for business. In other words, they felt hampered in their ability to conduct business in Romania and not make expected payments to Romanian sticky fingers because of the restrictions placed on them by the U.S. Foreign Corrupt Practices Act. At that point I pulled myself up to my full height and in a starchy voice announced that if the embassy got wind of violations of the FCPA, we were required by law to report them to the Department of Justice. This was not what the chamber's members wanted to hear, but it is what the law required, so I said it.

With per capita annual income in Romania hovering around $1,300 and the Romanian government hard pressed to stay afloat economically, there were not many opportunities for Americans to start legitimate businesses in Romania. Total American investment in Romania was around $100 million, with Coca-Cola and Amoco accounting for about half this amount. Those who did start businesses needed to take a long-term view.

On successive days I was introduced to the joys of the U.S. foreign aid bureaucracy. The U.S. Agency for International Development (USAID) had a large office on Magheru Boulevard, one of Bucharest's main thoroughfares, two blocks from the embassy. The building had been damaged in the 1986 earthquake and was abandoned a year or two later. USAID dispensed over $30 million annually in Romania, supporting more than thirty projects, including health care, democracy building, economic planning, fiscal reform, legal and judicial reform, infrastructure aid, transportation, and many more. The problem was that in tackling so much, USAID ended up accomplishing little—too much of the money went for administration.

Over the next three years I tried to persuade USAID in Washington and Bucharest to focus on four or five key projects with genuine accountability that would give us the opportunity to leverage our funds. For example, I suggested, "Let's train the trainers," meaning let's double leverage by spending U.S. dollars to train Romanian professionals to train others, not continue cookie-cutter programs designed in Washington on the theory that one size fits all. When Central and Eastern Europe opened up after the fall of communism, USAID was anxious to start immediately with its assistance programs and employed contractors on a regional basis, many of whom were former USAID staffers who took the opportunity to move to the private sector with higher pay. The USAID team in Bucharest, and presumably in other countries, was not really managing the programs. They were directed from Washington on a regional basis. In time my message got through, and USAID focused on fewer projects with more leverage.

I also visited our IMET (International Military Education and Training) mission, which was working to downsize the Romanian military by retiring about half of its bloated officer corps and upgrading its fighting strength by increasing the number and quality of noncommissioned officers. The program aimed, three years down the road, to achieve a slimmed-down military with improved interoperability and communications, reduced from 150,000 to 75,000 uniformed military personnel, which eliminated conscripts and relied upon longer-serving volunteers (comparable to the U.S. volunteer military). Without slimming down and modernizing its army, Romania was ill prepared to join NATO. Three years later Romania's army had climbed to the top among NATO aspirants. This was just one of the many ways that the United States helped Romania move from the back of the line to the front.

The Peace Corps had more than seventy volunteers in Romania. Many of the volunteers were middle-aged or older, people who as students had been inspired by the vision of John F. Kennedy when he created the Peace Corps. They shared a common enthusiasm and eagerness for everything from teaching schoolchildren and adults to working on farms to cleaning polluted rivers and building homes. This was truly inspiring. These Americans, most of whom were highly accomplished professionals, had left their homes in the United States, and often their families, to help people in a far-away country. They did not come for money or glory but to help people in need.

Each branch of the U.S. military—the army, the navy, and the air force— had a senior attaché in Bucharest under the command of U.S. Army Colonel Frank Boyd Jr., whom I first met when he visited my home in McLean, Virginia, a few weeks before I left for Romania. He called in advance for directions. We then met unexpectedly on the road. I was jogging and he, in civilian clothes, stopped his car to ask directions. We were both surprised—he because he did not expect to see an ambassador jogging and I because I was not expecting an African American army colonel. Frank and his wife, Alberta ("Bert"), became close friends and valued colleagues, greatly admired by the embassy staff and by Frank's counterparts in the Romanian military. An additional American military presence in Bucharest was a security detachment of eight U.S. Marines assigned to the embassy to protect U.S. government property. I frequently went to Marine House to work out in its gym and afterward to join the Marines for dinner.

The main embassy building, the chancery, was the locus of the mission's core diplomatic functions, including political, economic, and administrative sections, each headed by a senior Foreign Service officer plus Deputy Chief of Mission Jonathan Rickert (after August 1996, Michael Einik). Jonathan steered me through my early days in Bucharest and was a model Foreign Service officer, highly knowledgeable, possessing sound judgment and eminent fairness. Mike was equally gifted and became a close friend.

Alfred Moses shaking hands with President Jimmy Carter, May 1980, one of many Oval Office meetings.

From left to right, Defense Minister Victor Babiuc, Foreign Minister Adrian Severin, Prime Minister Victor Ciorbea, President Clinton, the author, and U.S. National Security Advisor Sandy Berger near the stairs of *Air Force One*, July 11, 1997.

From left to right, the author, B'nai B'rith president Jack Spitzer, and Nicolae Ceausescu, Communist Party Headquarters, Bucharest, the author's last meeting with Ceausescu, February 1986.

Chanukah celebration in the Falticeni synagogue, Romania, 1984. In the front row are Rabbi Moses Rosen; the author; Scott Edelman, U.S. Embassy official; and Rabbi Menachem Hachon from Israel.

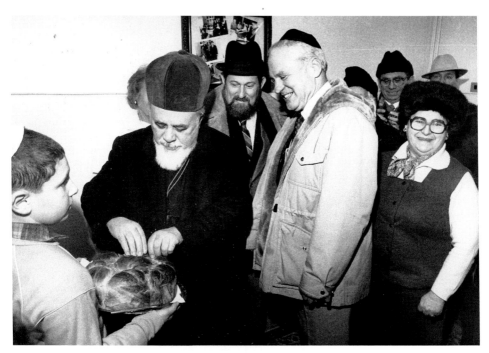

In 1984, Chief Rabbi Rosen breaking challah after the synagogue service. Looking on are Rabbi Menachem Halchon and the author.

Members of the Romanian Jewish Federation Choir
singing in the Rotunda of the U.S. Capitol on Yom
Shoah, Holocaust Remembrance Day, May 1986,
in front of the statue of Abraham Lincoln.

Chief Rabbi Moses Rosen discussing an issue with the author, 1986.

Romanian President Ion Iliescu and Alfred Moses pose for a photo after the author presented his credentials as ambassador, December 1994.

Meeting in the Oval office during President Ion Iliescu's visit to Washington. September 26, 1995. On President Clinton's left are Vice President Albert Gore, the author, and Deputy Secretary of State Strobe Talbott. On the president's right are Iliescu, followed by Foreign Minister Melescanu, Diplomatic Adviser Traian Chebeleu, and Romania's ambassador to the United Nations, Ion Gorita.

Chairman of the U.S. Joint Chiefs of Staff General John Shalikashvili,
the author, and Romanian Chief of Staff General Dumitru Cioflina
posing outside the Defense Ministry in Bucharest, February 1996.

First Lady Hillary Clinton and the author in
Revolution Square, Bucharest, July 1, 1996, during
the First Lady's two-day visit to Romania.

The author with embassy officials Susan Jacobs and Mihai
Carp at Romania-Ukraine border, February 1997.

Merry Cemetery in Sapanta, Romania, February 1997.

The author greets World Bank president James Wolfensohn in
front of the Choral Synagogue in Bucharest, May 1997.

The author with Romanian President
Emil Constantinescu, May 1997.

Romanian Patriarch Teoctist with the author at
the American Embassy, July 4, 1997.

During his visit to Romania on July 11, 1997, President
Clinton greets former Romanian President Ion Iliescu.
Romanian President Emil Constantinescu looks on.

President Clinton and the author addressing the
American Embassy staff, July 11, 1997.

During a visit to Romania in 2005, former president Clinton
poses with his daughter, Chelsea Clinton, the author,
and Romanian president Traian Basescu at Cotroceni.

After tennis: Foreign Minister Teodor Melescanu, Romanian security official, former president George Bush, former Romanian Davis Cup player Sever Muresan, and the author, Bucharest, 1995.

President Clinton and the author with the U.S. Marine Detachment,
American Ambassador's residence, Bucharest, July 11, 1997.

President Iliescu (and clockwise around the circle), the author,
former American ambassador to Hungary Mark Palmer,
PRO-TV Director Adrian Sarbu, Diplomatic Adviser Traian
Chebeleu, former Romanian Davis Cup captain Ian Tiriac, and
cosmetics heir Ronald Lauder, Bucharest, February 1995.

From left to right, Romanian Securitate agent, Israeli ambassador Yosef Govrin,
U.S. ambassador Roger Kirk, the author, Canadian ambassador Saul Grey, Polish
ambassador, and Avrum Burg (head of the Jewish Agency in Israel), Hanukkah 1985.

Standing next to *Air Force One* are, from left to right: Prime Minister
Victor Ciorbea, U.S. Embassy personnel Peter Lapera, Paul Womer,
Mihai Carp, Abigail Womer, the author, Susan Jacobs, President Clinton,
Michael Einik, Sarah Einik, Robert Whitehead, and Charles Kinn.

President Clinton greeting Priscila Nzunga (whose father was an
American Embassy employee), and the author, July 11, 1997.

Painted Church, Suceava County, Northern Moldavia.

Jumping in As Ambassador

With Christmas fast approaching, I had a lot of ground to cover before Romanians started celebrating and I needed to return to Washington for Carol's next round of chemotherapy. Romania's number one problem was its economy. On the must-do list were meetings with the IMF and the World Bank, Romania's financial lifelines. The IMF provided currency stabilization loans to Romania to prevent a run on the Romanian leu, and in 1991 the World Bank made a $400 million structural adjustment loan (SAL) to enable Romania to begin privatizing its heavy industry.

Sadly, three years after the SAL funds were disbursed, there was little to show for it. The heavy industrial dinosaurs were still state-owned. The IMF had imposed tight monetary restraints on Romania, which brought inflation down from over 300 percent in 1993 to less than 70 percent the following year, but Romania's finances were still shaky. The leu was not freely convertible. If it had been, there would have been a run on the leu and its value would have plummeted.

To the government's credit, when President Iliescu first assumed power, it immediately proclaimed the restoration of democracy, personal freedom, the revocation of Ceauşescu's hated ban on abortions and contraception (a crude

attempt to increase Romania's birth rate), and the dismantling of the Securitate. Soon after, most residential properties, including apartment buildings,
were privatized. A year later the government adopted a land reform program
that by 1991 had returned more than 80 percent of agricultural land to 5.5
million owners. However, large farms and poultry and meat producers plus
the means of production, storage, marketing and, most critical, financing remained under the control of the government of Romania.

The first privatization law was enacted in 1991 creating the State Ownership Fund (SOF) to hold 70 percent of the shares of to-be-privatized
companies and five private ownership funds (POFs) that were allocated the
remaining 30 percent. Certificates, and later vouchers, were issued free to
more than 15 million adult Romanians, representing ownership interests in
the POFs. But the process was complicated, the progress slow.

After four years, fewer than 25 percent of commercial companies had
been privatized, employing about 600,000 workers out of total employment of
more than 4 million. Most privatized companies were small, employing fewer
than 500 workers. It was thought that the shares held by POFs transferred to
the public would be tradable on a to-be-created U.S.-sponsored RASDAQ
(Romanian Association of Securities Dealers Automated Quotations), modeled after the U.S. NASDAQ (National Association of Securities Dealers
Automated Quotations), but this was not operational until 1996.

The SOF's ownership interests were to be sold for cash initially by means
of management-employee buyouts intended to speed up privatization of
small enterprises, those with fewer than 500 employees. MEBOs proved
popular and were later extended to larger enterprises, but the government
priced the shares of the large commercial companies out of the market, and
privatization ground to a halt. Legislation to create the accelerated Mass
Privatization Program (MPP) was passed in June 1995, but progress was still
slow. The World Bank tried to help by setting privatization milestones as a
condition for disbursals under a $280 million Financial Enterprise Struc-
tural Adjustment Loan, but it was not signed until December 1995 and soon
encountered its own set of obstacles when the Romanian side failed to live
up to its promises.

The IMF and World Bank representatives I met with during my first week
in Bucharest could not have been more different in appearance and tempera-

ment, but both were talented and dedicated. The IMF's Josh Green hailed from Philadelphia and was open and friendly. Arna Hartmann, the World Bank representative, from Germany, was earnest and reserved, but deeply committed to helping Romania.

In early 1995 the Romanian Senate passed the MPP legislation, but the bill remained stalled in the Chamber of Deputies. As ambassador I spent a lot of time urging Adrian Nastase, president of the Chamber of Deputies, to pass the law. Once the bill passed in June 1995, the real work would begin.

It took a long time for Romania to privatize or shut down its large SOEs and RAs, which were hemorrhaging money. It was apparent to me when I first became ambassador, and was reinforced later, that the country would have been better off taking drastic action early and enduring the short-term political pain from layoffs and production losses as the price to be paid for creating long-term economic growth. Economists understand this, but there is a reason economists do not run for office: it is not a popular message. Romania's politicians dragged out reform, thereby lengthening the period of pain. As a result, even after the government slowed down economic reform and increased spending in the hope of winning the election, the public threw out President Iliescu and his party in 1996. The new center-right government of Emil Constantinescu and his prime minister, Victor Ciorbea, did not do enough fast enough, and in December 2000 Iliescu was back in power.

FIRST OFFICIAL MEETINGS—SANS CREDENTIALS

My first official meeting was with Foreign Minister Meleşcanu—a breach of protocol, as I had not yet presented my credentials to President Iliescu. According to international diplomatic protocol, one is not an ambassador until his or her official designation is presented to the host country's head of state and officially accepted. In my case, this was a letter on White House stationery signed by President William J. Clinton, addressed to Romania's President Ion Iliescu. The meeting with Meleşcanu was his idea. I knew him from the year before, when he had represented Romania at the UN General Assembly in New York and I, as president of the American Jewish Committee, met him on the fringe of the annual General Assembly session. Meleşcanu spoke excellent English and was one of Romania's most capable ministers.

His message was simple: "NATO, NATO, NATO," meaning Romania wanted to be in the first wave of new members. He went on to explain that, as Romania saw it, the United States was key to Romania's NATO membership. If it were left to the United Kingdom, France, or other NATO countries, Romania would not be admitted—although perhaps he adjusted his message for ambassadors from other NATO member nations. This was my introduction to the "NATO chant," which I would hear from the beginning of my days in Bucharest to the end.

The following morning was given over to the formal ceremony in the presidential palace, Cotroceni, in which I presented my credentials to President Iliescu. The immediate schedule was a far cry from the practice in the United States, where foreign ambassadors often wait for months to present their credentials in a brief ceremony in the Oval Office. In Romania the timing was different, undoubtedly owing to the relative importance of the American chief of mission in Bucharest compared to that of my Romanian counterpart in Washington.

The day before the ceremony, Romania's chief of protocol came to my residence to prepare for the big event. The two of us reviewed a diagram he had prepared showing where President Iliescu and I would each stand and the choreography that was to follow. I was instructed to hold President Clinton's letter designating me as the American ambassador to Romania in one hand, walk across the room to where President Iliescu would be standing, present the letter to him with my left hand, and then shake hands using my right hand, at which point the cameras would flash and the deed would be done. As is typical in Romania, the next morning there was a new diagram and a new choreography.

Before we left for the ceremony, I had in mind a picture of the American ambassador to the Court of St. James riding through the streets of London, wearing a top hat and formal attire, sitting on the back seat of a magnificent black coach with gold embossing, the carriage drawn by eight prancing white horses, on his way to present his credentials to Her Majesty the Queen. This mental picture was more than a little askew. The carriage that took us to the ceremony was a small antiquated Dacia, modeled on a vintage French Renault, made in Romania. The chief of protocol and I sat on the Dacia's broken backseat, and off we went. Our little convoy was led by a Romanian police car, also a Dacia, its siren blaring, then our Dacia, followed by two embassy cars carrying Barbara and five senior embassy officials.

Pedestrians did not spare us a glance as we drove down Bucharest's main boulevard, Calea Victoriei. We proceeded through the gates of Cotroceni, up a long circular driveway into the courtyard of the palace, where I was saluted by the president's "praetorian guard," as I called them, all of whom were over six feet tall and wore eighteenth-century Prussian helmets and uniforms more suitable for stage than guard duty. We proceeded into the waiting room, and then, at the designated moment, into the ceremonial hall. It seemed like something out of a Victor Herbert light opera. The sweaty-palmed protocol officer was tense. I forgot my opening line, "Good morning, Mr. President," and Iliescu forgot his. Finally, I came through with the magic words "Mr. President, I have the honor and privilege to present to you my credentials signed by President William Jefferson Clinton designating me to be the United States ambassador to Romania and the letter of recall of my predecessor, Ambassador John Davis." Not a hard script to follow. With flashbulbs popping and television cameras rolling, I walked the eight paces and handed the letters to President Iliescu. The revised protocol demanded that this be done in a two-handed performance. So I shoved the letters toward President Iliescu, both hands extended, and he accepted them with two hands. It was done!

After the ceremony, President Iliescu, Foreign Minister Meleşcanu, U.S. Deputy Chief of Mission Jonathan Rickert, and I went into an adjoining room for a more intimate conversation that lasted over an hour. To the Romanian press waiting outside, the importance of the meeting was measured by its length. The time exceeded the substance. The discussion was friendly but did not cover new ground. I brought up the negative effect in the United States of Romania's efforts to rehabilitate its former dictator, Ion Antonescu. I also referred to the issue of Romania's Hungarian minority, a problem that loomed large in the United States.

President Iliescu, for his part, went over old ground. It was a two-part history lesson. The first part was a retelling of the ills suffered by ethnic Romanians in Transylvania under the Hungarians with their capital in Budapest, who for 300 years held the reins of power. The second part was about Romanian triumphs, not victimhood, starting with Romania's founder, Michael the Brave, followed by the story of Romania's discovery of oil long before it was found in Titusville, Pennsylvania, in 1859. The latter caused much Romanian head scratching as they tried to locate Pennsylvania on a map. Then fast-forward to World War I, when a Romanian inventor synchronized the firing of a machine gun mounted on the fuselage of an airplane with rotating propeller blades, a claim that sounded more like an article of faith than a marvel of science.

Like Foreign Minister Meleşcanu the day before, President Iliescu gave the NATO chant and Romania's need for foreign investment. Meleşcanu weighed in from time to time, mostly with humor. The Romania side had no doubt rehearsed their lines. We had not. It was their show, not ours, and yet nothing we heard was unexpected or unwelcome. We wanted Romania to become part of NATO as much as the Romanians did. The question was whether Romania could make the grade. We were there to help, but it was up to Romania to step up to the plate.

A near diplomatic faux pas followed. I found myself finishing lunch at the residence a little after 1:30 p.m. without realizing that my next appointment with Defense Minister Georghe Tinca was at 2 p.m. When I finally got word, there was less than twenty minutes to go. Fortunately, my driver put on a virtuoso performance, heroically driving on the wrong side of the street, weaving through and around traffic and depositing me at the steps of the Defense Ministry building with two minutes to spare. A nervous, sweating (in winter, no less) Colonel Frank Boyd was waiting for me at the bottom of the steps. Together we dashed up the two flights and entered Defense Minister Tinca's office just as the clock struck two.

Defense Minister Tinca, Romania's first civilian defense minister, had pursued a prior career in the Foreign Ministry. Romania had been required to make the switch to a civilian defense minister when it joined the U.S.-initiated NATO-preparatory Partnership for Peace the previous January. Tinca described our bilateral military relationship as "quite good." Romania was anxious to acquire American military equipment, in Tinca's words, "not to fight anyone but rather to build a deterrent force," the words every defense minister uses.

Romania's immediate procurement need was for four excess U.S. C-130 cargo planes, made available by the United States at a total cost of $12 million. Hungary had turned down a similar offer, but Romania was going ahead, hoping the cost could be spread over three to four years, in which case Romania would buy the four planes (it did). Romania was also negotiating with Lockheed-Martin to buy radar equipment for air defense and hoped to co-produce the U.S. Cobra helicopter in Romania under an agreement with Bell Helicopter. The Cobra was no longer a state-of-the-art aircraft, but export sales still required U.S. government approval. Romania wanted to buy ninety-six helicopters for its own use. The alternative for Romania was co-production of a French-built helicopter, which would mean loss of business for the United States and loss of American control over helicopter exports from Romania. The Cobra deal, after a promising start, had a long and disappointing journey. The deal cratered when the IMF raised objections and my successor as ambassador turned negative on the deal, not realizing its strategic and morale value for Romania. A state-of-the-art modern helicopter assembly plant in Romania would have transformed the country's manufacturing capabilities and would have set a standard of excellence badly needed in post-Ceauşescu Romania. A Romanian military with ninety-six Cobras would have been the leading military force in Eastern Europe, one closely allied with the United States. The helicopters would have given Romania a military capability it lacked because of the numerical limitation on tanks in its military under the Conventional Armed Forces in Europe Treaty signed in 1990 by twenty-two countries, including Romania, which governed the number and composition of forces in Central and Eastern Europe.

The following day I was back on schedule with Foreign Minister Meleşcanu. Six of us from the American embassy plus Barbara attended a two-and-a-half-hour lunch—a Romanian ritual—at the Diplomatic Club, not far from my residence. The table was too wide for serious conversation, but at the end of lunch Foreign Minister Meleşcanu handed me a document that diplomats call a "non-paper": an official document, usually drafted on plain paper without letterhead so its provenance supposedly cannot be traced, and not requiring an official response. This non-paper outlined Romania's position on democracy building, the economy, security, and, most important, NATO expansion. Strangely, the main message on NATO expansion came from the Foreign Ministry, not the defense minister, with whom I had met the previous day.

The non-paper made clear that Romania's principal concern was that NATO would close its door with Romania remaining on the outside, the paper's point being this would hurt the government politically, making it vulnerable to criticism from the political right in Romania by blaming the political left government. It would also give the ethnic Hungarians in Transylvania reason to complain that if Transylvania were still part of Hungary, it would be in NATO—sort of like saying if the elephant were a giraffe, it would not be an elephant. The paper further argued that if NATO's boundaries stopped short of Romania, it would subject Romania to increased pressure from Russia. This was a real fear for Romania with its deep anti-Russian feeling; Foreign Minister Meleşcanu also knew that the Russian argument would resonate well with opinion makers in the United States such as former national security adviser Zbigniew Brzezinski, Professor Frank Gaffney of the University of Maryland, and others who feared Russian efforts to reassert Russia's Warsaw Pact–era influence in Eastern Europe.

In truth, NATO was an effective tool for us to use to persuade Romania to do the things it should do anyway. Whether Romania qualified for NATO membership or not, the decision in Washington on enlargement would be driven by domestic political considerations. This was true in other NATO capitals as well. The step-by-step planning process at State and within the American defense establishment was necessary for its own sake but was secondary to political considerations.

Two years later the decision made by the White House was that only three countries, Poland, the Czech Republic, and Hungary, would be admitted in the first wave of NATO enlargement. As the White House saw it, more than three might tip the scales against NATO treaty approval by the Senate, concerned as it was with the cost of NATO enlargement and the extension of security guarantees that the United States would need to make to new members under the NATO Treaty.

Next on my agenda was the political opposition leader and future president of Romania, Emil Constantinescu. We met in an ornate room at Bucharest University in which pictures of Romania's King Ferdinand hung on the wall. Constantinescu was courtly but clung to positions that seemed badly out of date, such as restoration of the monarchy. He denied that the PNT-CD leader, Coposu, had held out for unrealistic demands as the cost of joining a coalition government following the 1992 elections. Constantinescu claimed that he himself had recently offered to form a coalition government with Iliescu, but no one had taken him up on his offer. It was truly an empty gesture made on television long after the elections. Constantinescu told me that he expected to be the opposition presidential candidate again in 1996; to my mind, if the present government continued to muddle along, Romanians might vote for political change.

My next meeting was with Adrian Nastase, president of the Chamber of Deputies and the titular head of the Social Democratic Party of Romania, PDSR, the successor to Iliescu's National Salvation Front. As president of Romania, Iliescu could not be a member of a political party, but there was no doubt that he was the real boss of the PDSR. I knew Chamber of Deputies President Nastase from his time as foreign minister. Not known for his modesty, he started out telling me that recent opinion polls showed him to be the most popular politician in Romania (a month later he had dropped down in the polls). Then in his mid-forties, he spoke with great earnestness and gravity but was thought to be opportunistic, even corrupt. (Fifteen years later he was in jail.) Our conversation covered all the issues, but no new ground.

Later that day I met with Oliviu Gherman, the president of the Senate. Under Romania's constitution, Gherman, not Nastase, was first in line to succeed President Iliescu. Unlike Chamber of Deputies President Nastase, Senate President Gherman was modest, apolitical—more of an éminence grise than a politician, which fitted his background as a professor of physics at Babeș-Bolyai University in Cluj.

Senate President Gherman was of German descent, and this may have been a factor in President Iliescu's choosing him as his successor under Romania's constitution, to distinguish Romania's present leadership from Ceaușescu's ethnic Romanian apparatchiks. Gherman told me how much he missed his students and looked forward to the day when he could return to the university. In the meantime, he would soldier on, proud of the Senate's recent approval of the MPP, which was unfortunately being held up in the Chamber of Deputies.

The next morning began with a meeting with Economic Reform Minister Mircea Coșea, a member of the Romanian National Unity Party (PUNR), who was responsible for guiding the restructuring of the Romanian economy. He was courteous but indecisive and in the end accomplished little in the way of economic reform. This may have been attributable to his being a member of PUNR, a coalition partner, not PDSR, Iliescu's party, which controlled the government. Coşea was not an accepted insider in a country where personal relations and trust were needed to get things done.

Coşea acknowledged that Romania's economic problems were enormous, stating that "less than 5 percent of Romanian industry could compete with Western Europe." The solution, as he saw it, was direct foreign investment led by the United States and by the enactment by the Chamber of Deputies of the MPP, even though it would cover only 3,900 SOEs, leaving much of Romania's industrial capacity in government hands, including 44 large RAs and many smaller RAs of less significance.

Coşea was well aware of the opposition to downsizing, let alone closing, uneconomic state-owned businesses. He cited a recent government effort to close two antiquated steel plants that led to a general strike and a no-confidence motion in Parliament. He volunteered that the enormous payroll increases agreed to by Prime Minister Nicolae Vacaroiu a day or two before on behalf of the government to settle the strike made it difficult to privatize similar money-losing transportation and energy companies that had bloated payrolls. On the energy front, he was counting on a new nuclear power plant, furnished with American-made reactors, scheduled to come online the following year in Cernavoda in southeastern Romania, to make Romania a net exporter of energy. He was also looking to privatize Tarom, as well as the country's banking system. He was candid, adding that it was easier to modernize by buying computers and new office equipment than to change the mentality of Romania's business leaders. All of this was bold talk, music to my ears, but did not portend badly needed action.

The last meeting of the day was with Prime Minister Vacaroiu, who had just returned from settling the steel workers strike that Coşea had referred to earlier. The press reported that Vacaroiu had caved in to the workers' demands and agreed that the government would invest $47 million to modernize the two antiquated plants. This was money the government did not have. Vacaroiu was an economist in the Central Planning division under Ceauşescu and had been President Iliescu's third or fourth choice for the prime minister job. The others, who had turned him down, spoke English and had commendable achievements to their credit. Not so Vacaroiu, who struck me as the old-line communist bureaucrat he was. My impression might have been colored by the fact that he did not speak English. As a result, our conversation was stilted. He seemed to be delivering a set speech similar to those I had heard from Romanian bureaucrats in Ceauşescu's days.

The day ended with a press conference at the American Cultural Center. Present were journalists from Romanian State Television, Bucharest's three independent television stations, most of Romania's national radio stations, all the major dailies, and resident correspondents from five international news services, including Reuters and AP. The new American ambassador meeting the press was as close to star billing as there was in Romania. The next day the leading Bucharest independent paper, *Adevarul*, ran a headline quoting my reference to Romania as a "stable country in an unstable region." Even the leading opposition paper, *Romania Libera*, ran a headline quoting me saying, "Romania is an important country from a strategic point of view." More important, a *Romania Libera* editorial captured the theme of my remarks in an editorial titled "Romanian-American Relations: Everything Depends on Us." The editorial stated, "What is most important is that his statements at the press conference made it clear that the new ambassador is not only an exceptional diplomat . . . but a strong believer that Romania should go toward democracy, the rule of law, and a market economy. . . . We can be confident and even optimistic about the future of Romanian-American relations in the following four years, as long as Ambassador Moses is in Bucharest. The general impression at the end of this first press conference was that in case anything goes wrong between Bucharest and Washington this will not be his fault in any case." This would be my message for the next three years, but I was still in the honeymoon phase.

My last night in Bucharest before heading home to be with Carol, I hosted the ambassador's annual Christmas party at the residence. There was a huge turnout, no doubt attributable to Foreign Service nationals (Romanians) working at the American embassy and others on the embassy staff wanting to see the new ambassador.

In less than a week I had met for over an hour with President Iliescu, three times with Foreign Minister Meleşcanu, and had had separate meetings with the prime minister, defense minister, economic reform minister, the World

Bank and IMF representatives, the press, and the embassy staff. To the extent personal relations make a difference in diplomacy, I was off to a good start, but it was still early days. Moreover, I was keenly aware that access was not the same thing as influence. As the American ambassador, I had virtually unlimited access to the president, prime minister, and everyone else in the Romanian government and to Romanian society at large. If access was total, my influence was decidedly less, even though Romania was looking to the United States as its lifeline to the West and to the fulfillment of its NATO dreams.

Romanians across the political spectrum were sincere in reaching out to the United States, but only up to a point. Despite the bestowal of florid kisses on both cheeks and loving words, like all other foreign ambassadors I would always be an outsider dealing with a tangle of relationships, many barely discernible to outsiders, and with personal and political interests that were difficult for an outsider to understand. This reality was made clear to me time and again over the next three years. The dilemma was not unique to Romania. The only difference was that in Romania the national culture was beguiling in its warm welcome and expressions of sincerity, mystifying in its opacity, and frustrating in its unwillingness to match words with deeds.

There is another national characteristic that had a bearing on my Romanian experience. Romania is seductive. It draws you into its chamber, like the sirens beckoning Ulysses, with plaintive pleas and an apparent openness combined with expressions of sadness that appeal to the heart in ways that need to be experienced to be understood. The melancholy feeling it evokes is different from anything I experienced elsewhere in Eastern and Central Europe. Romania's calls for help tugged at your heartstrings, causing even diplomats at times to lose objectivity.

Until I became ambassador, I associated this phenomenon with Rabbi Rosen, who was exciting, highly animated, and personally compelling in ways that no other Jewish figure I knew could match. His personality and role as the leader of a Jewish community that retained its historic Jewish identity drew me in, even if it existed largely on the surface. For me, what I saw in Rabbi Rosen and the Jewish community was the real thing: *Yiddishkeit*— Eastern European Jewish culture that most of us had read about but not seen. Now it was there in front of my eyes to see and touch. In time I came to learn that the appeal was quintessentially Romanian.

BACK TO WASHINGTON: FINE-TUNING THE NATO CHANT

My first return to Washington set the pattern for the remainder of my ambassadorship. The routine consisted of about twenty days in Romania followed by a shorter stay in Washington to be with Carol and to attend meetings at State, the White House, the Pentagon, the CIA, and other government agencies.

Once back in Washington I realized that Romania's "NATO chant" was a hook we could use to spur positive change in Romania. The Romanian government understandably focused on Article 5 of the North Atlantic Treaty, which provided that an armed attack on one of the member countries would be considered an armed attack on all members. In short, this meant spreading the United States' nuclear umbrella over Romania, but not without a price. The preamble to the treaty reaffirmed the parties' adherence to the principles of "democracy, individual liberty and the rule of law," later enshrined in the Perry Principles, named for U.S. Secretary of Defense William J. Perry, for aspiring members to be eligible for NATO enlargement. These principles included civilian control of the military, no existing border or other disputes with neighboring countries, possession of a military force able to contribute to the joint defense, respect for human rights, a functioning democracy, and adherence to a free market economy. For me, these general principles as they applied specifically to Romania implied the following conditions:

1. Rejection of political extremism. No harking back to Romania's communist or fascist past or toleration of the notion of Greater Romania or building statues in memory of Romania's fascist leader, Marshal Antonescu.

2. Respect for the political rights of the opposition. The dismissal of local officials from opposition parties had to stop.

3. Respect for the rights of Hungarians, Roma, Jews, and other minorities.

4. Reform of Romania's military with an emphasis on interoperability and an upgrade in communications.

5. Building from the bottom up Romania's private economy while at the same time privatizing state-owned enterprises and ending subsidies for government-owned economic dinosaurs. A rising economy would promote political stability and a national feeling of "can do," important for a country's self-image and magnanimity.

6. Ending political interference in the judicial system and building a competent, independent judiciary.

7. Privatizing national television and making it available without government restriction to viewers throughout the country.

8. Ending border and other disputes with Romania's neighbors and entering into basic treaties with Hungary and Ukraine.

9. Enhancing and protecting the democratic rights of Romanian citizens by ensuring free and fair elections.

10. Returning to rightful owners community and personal property taken by the communists.

11. Raising standards of health care, education, and public transportation.

12. Strengthening democratic institutions across the board.

The United States would do its part with technical, financial, and political assistance and support, but it was up to Romania to seize the opportunity to change the course of its history, not stay mired in the past. I was convinced that Romania's sense of victimhood would leave it behind its neighbors. It was time for change. This became my mantra for the next three years.

NATO was there, but Romania needed to step up to the plate. I said this repeatedly in meetings with President Iliescu, President Constantinescu, and other Romanian government officials, in press conferences, speeches to university audiences, and at diplomatic functions, as well as in articles and op-ed pieces that appeared in the Romanian and Western press. In time others took up the mantra and repeated what I said—editorial writers, commentators, political pundits, and high-ranking U.S. government officials, including President Clinton and Vice President Gore. However, in December 1994, I was standing alone, still at the starting line.

PART TWO

Romania Struggles

1995

 **5**

Building the Case in Washington for the Bilateral Relationship with Romania and Speaking Truth to Power in Romania

WINTER 1995

Still in Washington in early January, I first met with Thomas A. Dine, deputy USAID administrator for Eastern and Central Europe, and then with Assistant Secretary of State Richard Holbrooke. I knew Tom from his days as the executive director of the American Israel Public Affairs Committee. Tom was supportive on all counts, including a commitment to provide USAID funding to build what became the RASDAQ (Romanian Association of Securities Dealers Automated Quotations), an essential piece of the Romanian government's economic reform plan that called for privatizing 3,900 government-owned businesses. This required a stock exchange to allow investors to buy and sell shares in the to-be-privatized companies. Expertise in building the RASDAQ would come from market experts at the U.S. Securities and Exchange Commission, with USAID picking up the tab. Tom also agreed to fund U.S. experts in banking and insurance. Since Romania's communist vintage National Health Plan had cut the market out from under would-be private health insurers, employer-provided life and disability insurance was unknown in Romania. This would now change.

Private banking was also behind Western standards. There were a few start-up banks, Banca Tiriac and Banca Dacia Felix being the largest, but neither was able to compete with Romania's large state-owned banks. Ion Tiriac, a Romanian former Davis Cup star who controlled Banca Tiriac, had reportedly attracted German money for his start-up. He lived in Germany, where he owned Mercedes Benz dealerships. Dacia Felix was a different story. It started with "hot" money from former Securitate operators. The front man, Sever Mureşan, a well-known Romanian Davis Cup tennis player, was thought to be a figurehead only. Two years later Mureşan was gone and Banca Dacia Felix closed. Big banks in Romania were still government owned, including the Postal Bank, the Development Bank, the Commercial Bank, Banca Agricola, and Bancorex. Banca Agricola and the Commercial Bank were used by the government to subsidize agriculture and the money-losing large state-owned enterprises (SOEs) by extending to them government-funded credit. Sooner rather than later, the logjam had to be broken and a privately owned, modern banking system created in its place. This meant shutting down or privatizing the money-losing state-owned banks—an enormously difficult task.

HOLBROOKE AND NATO

Assistant Secretary of State Holbrooke, a rapid speaker and thinker, liked to bark out orders with machine-gun rapidity. He chaired the U.S. European Security Interagency Working Group, a fancy title for a group tasked with taking the first step in formulating our NATO expansion strategy. In November 1994 President Clinton had publicly stated that the issue was not whether NATO would expand, but when and how. This produced a race by the twelve countries in Eastern Europe, the exact number depending on the results of the final breakup of Yugoslavia, to see who would be the first to join. Romania wanted to make sure it was not left out. It was the first country to join the Partnership for Peace, designed by the U.S. Department of Defense to serve as the stepping-stone to NATO for former Soviet bloc countries.

Holbrooke was the point man at State on NATO expansion, a designation that did not happen by accident. Dick was a power-seeking bureaucrat and an experienced Washington hand. The working group, composed of high-level officials from the Department of Defense, the CIA, the U.S. Information Agency, and the State Department, met at State in early January with Dick as chair and me as his invited guest. It soon became clear that there was no agreed-on direction for implementing President Clinton's decision. Two weeks before, President Boris Yeltsin had blasted the proposal to expand NATO, calling it "directed against Russia," a charge that was not unfounded. It had fallen to Vice President Albert Gore, an advocate of NATO expansion, to try to persuade his Russian counterpart, Prime Minister Viktor Chernomyrdin, that NATO expansion was not a threat to Russia's security and that promoting stability in Eastern Europe would actually aid Russia's security. This would be a hard sell.

In January 1995, two months after Clinton's speech, the United States was coming to grips with the difficult task of formulating a policy for NATO expansion. The impetus for NATO expansion was initially centered on Poland, not on the Balkans or the former Yugoslavia. Germany was becoming increasingly uncomfortable being on NATO's eastern border, while Poland feared, from its tragic history, that it might not survive long between Germany and Russia. Sooner rather than later it would have to choose one side or the other as its ally, and, with the possible exception of Romania, there was probably no former Warsaw Pact country more enthusiastic about joining the United States and the West than Poland. This was reinforced by Poland's many friends in Washington, including outspoken supporters such as Jimmy Carter's national security adviser, Zbigniew Brzezinski. There was little doubt that Poland would be the first country admitted to NATO, with or without others following.

Assistant Secretary Holbrooke's working group was the start of a long and difficult undertaking with pressures both pro and con at home and abroad. It was highly doubtful that NATO would expand in the first wave beyond Poland, the Czech Republic, and Hungary, unless Russia again became a real threat to the stability and security of Europe. Then the rush would be on to push ahead rapidly to reassure the former Soviet satellite countries that the West's commitment to their security was solid, thereby preventing a repetition of the instability that existed in Eastern Europe between the two world wars. The irony, of course, was that a rush to expand NATO could trigger a resurgent Russia, escalating the problem into a crisis, and thus become the curse the former satellite countries feared. The thought in Washington was: better do it now, while Russia was weak, not wait until Russia recovered.

Ultimately, the decision on NATO expansion was made at the White House by Deputy National Security Adviser Sandy Berger, not at State. Sandy decided that the first wave of enlargement should include only Poland, Czechoslovakia, and Hungary. This decision was based on his reading of sentiment in the Senate, which would need to approve an amendment to the NATO Treaty, and his conclusion that the Senate would not go along with more than three countries in the first wave for reasons of money and the extended commitment by the U.S. military.

THE ECONOMIC FRONT

While in Washington in January 1995, I also spent time at the World Bank. The bank had played the key role in restructuring the Romanian economy, first with the Structural Adjustment Loan (SAL) in 1991 and later with the negotiation of the follow-on Financial Enterprise Structural Adjustment Loan, which was signed in January 1996. The World Bank was critical of the deal Prime Minister Nicolae Vacaroiu had made with the workers in the two steel plants in December and was pressing the Romanian government to restructure and privatize its money-losing state-owned enterprises and *régies autonomes* (RAs). Even with the active support of the United States, it would be a long, tough struggle to get the Romanian government to agree to the World Bank's restructuring plan with its steep short-term political cost.

In the second week of January I flew to Cleveland to attend the White House Conference on Trade and Investment in Central and Eastern Europe sponsored by the U.S. Commerce Department as part of our effort to nudge Romania to speed up economic reform. Economic Reform Minister Mircea Coşea headed the Romanian delegation, which also included Finance Minister Florin Georgescu and National Bank Governor Mugur Isarescu, but not Viorel Hrebenciuc, the secretary general of the Romanian government.

There were genuine expressions of interest on the part of American businesses in Romania's to-be-privatized companies as well as in greenfield (start-up) opportunities, but much needed to happen in Romania before dollars would flow.

U.S. Secretary of Commerce Ronald H. Brown, an old friend from his early days in Washington with the Urban League, gave the principal address. Ron was masterful both onstage and off. Later in the day he chaired a bilateral meeting with the Romanians in which he told them what they needed to do to attract American investment, emphasizing economic reform, streamlining the investment process, eliminating the bureaucratic maze, and clamping down on corruption. He was direct and forceful, speaking with charm, even when his words made the Romanians wince. (Brown was killed a year later in a plane crash during a trade mission in Croatia.) Ron's theme was not new or different from what the World Bank and I had said in Bucharest the month before, but for the Romanian ministers to hear it again from the American secretary of commerce added weight.

RETURN TO BUCHAREST

Gray skies greeted me on my arrival back in Bucharest from Washington on January 16. Romania was beginning to take some tiny steps to help itself. U.S. Army officers were now teaching at the Romanian Military Academy. In one class were three women, two of them journalists, and a Hungarian officer, all new faces. Political opposition leaders were also enrolled at the academy, a further sign that political life in Romania was evolving in ways that had been forbidden under the communists.

COUNTRY TEAM MEETING

The standard U.S. embassy practice worldwide was to start the week with a "country team meeting" in which the embassy's section heads met with the ambassador to review events of the past week and looked ahead to the coming week. For security reasons, the weekly team meetings were held in a "bubble" with a sound machine muffling voices so that the staff's words could not be heard by Romanian intelligence devices—even though most matters discussed at the meetings were either already known to the Romanian government or were not particularly sensitive. Despite my aversion to big "huddles," I found the country team meetings valuable in building teamwork and closer coordination among embassy staff. This routine would be repeated every week I was in Bucharest.

THE PRESIDENT'S ANNUAL DIPLOMATIC RECEPTION

Later in January, President Iliescu hosted Romania's presidential New Year's reception for the diplomatic corps. This was an elaborate affair in Cotroceni, the presidential palace, with more than sixty foreign ambassadors attending plus another twenty or so chargés d'affaires, together with a gaggle of high-ranking Romanian officials. The reception was in the same room where I had presented my credentials the previous month, a large chamber with fifteen-foot ceilings, marble floors, and alabaster fluted columns. As often happens in Romania, the evening had its light side. It is customary in the diplomatic world for the most senior ambassador in residence, the "doyen," to respond to the host president's speech by extending greetings on behalf of the foreign diplomats. In Bucharest the Zaire ambassador was the doyen, but he had not been paid for months, maybe years, was destitute, and did not own a suit. So the lot fell to the ambassador from Lebanon, the next in line. President Iliescu spoke in Romanian, after which the Lebanese ambassador responded in French.

When he concluded his remarks, President Iliescu came over to me to inquire about Carol and to discuss the White House conference in Cleveland. He asked if Secretary Brown would be willing to visit Romania. I tried to explain that a visit by Ron on his own would not accomplish much. What was needed was for American businesses to come to Romania to invest, for contracts to be signed with dollar amounts attached, and then for Secretary Brown to announce results. This would get headlines not only in Romania but also in the United States and would encourage visits by other U.S. businessmen. This was hard for President Iliescu to understand; he attached great importance to personal appearances by major public figures, particularly Americans, quite apart from a larger strategy.

As I went down the receiving line, Ioan Talpes, head of Romania's External Security Service, pulled me aside to tell me he wanted to reassure me that the SIE had closed its intelligence operations in the United States; the contrary thought never occurred to me. Talpes told me the present Romanian ambassador to the United States, Mihai Botez, had made shutting down SIE's operations in the United States a condition to his agreeing to become ambassador. I later arranged for Talpes to visit CIA headquarters in Washington. The CIA was convinced that he was reliable and that we should cooperate with the SIE in areas where it could be helpful, focusing on targets in Iran and Iraq.

Next in line was Adrian Nastase, the president of the Chamber of Deputies, who wanted to comment on my statement in a Voice of America broadcast a day or two before to the effect that the American government would prefer a strong centrist governing coalition in Romania rather than the present grouping in which the center-left PDSR relied on three extremist parties. Nastase blamed the PNT-CD and its leader, Corneliu Coposu, for declining Iliescu's 1992 offer to form a national unity government, which had left the PDSR with no alternative but to work with the two right-wing national parties, the Romanian National Unity Party (PUNR) and Romania Mare (PRM), and the Socialist Party of Romania (PSM). PRM and PUNR attacked me with similar anti-Semitic tropes. PRM's leader, Corneliu Vadim Tudor, was particularly vitriolic. In a signed editorial in PRM's newspaper, *Romania Mare*, he referred to me as a Zionist, a code word for Jewish, as though it were a slur and not a point of pride, which it is for me. In the next sentence he called Romania's center-left Democratic Party (PD) a Zionist party. The supposed reason was more ironic than factual. The head of PD was Petre Roman. His father, Valter Roman, was Jewish by birth. He married a Catholic from Spain whom he met during the Spanish Civil War in the late 1930s. Their son, Petre, prominently wore a large crucifix. But in Tudor's eyes, he was still Jewish.

The evening was not without a discordant note. The Belgian ambassador, Ignace van Steenbergen, brought up the letter from the six Romanian senators to Senator Helms urging him to oppose my nomination as ambassador. Steenbergen told me in a low voice that he had spoken with one of the signers of the letter, who revealed to him that I had helped Jews but did not help others. Even worse, he said I had been involved in paying Ceaușescu to get Jews out. Neither was true. I helped Jews and non-Jews get out of Romania and was never involved in, or even knew of, any payments. Our conversation went downhill from there. "Tell me, Ignace," I said, "if I saved Belgian Jews from the Nazis during World War II, would I be blamed for not saving others?" No reply. Thus emboldened, I added, "Ignace, what did you do during World War II to save Belgium's Jews?" Again, no response. Steenbergen, who revealed himself to be a right-wing anti-Semite, was later recalled by his government for incompetence.

TIME TO DO BUSINESS

The following morning I met with Commerce Minister Christian Ionescu. There was a lot of verbal sparring, but no punches landed. Romania wanted to increase its trade with the United States from $450 million this year to $800 million next year. This was certainly possible. U.S. textile imports from Romania alone would increase the following year by $80 million to $100 million as a result of an increase in the U.S. textile quota for Romania. A lot of the discussion that followed was centered on my complaint about Romania's imposition of minimum resale prices on poultry imports from the United States. This hurt U.S. exporters such as Tyson Foods and Perdue Farms. The Romanians claimed that minimum prices were needed to protect Romania's nascent poultry industry, even though minimum prices were no longer permitted under the recent Uruguay Round of the World Trade Organization signed by Romania. In its place, Romania would probably impose higher tariffs, which are permitted; the effect would be the same, keeping U.S. poultry exports out of Romania and prices artificially high. While it was hard to attack the Romanian position, since we impose duties on Romanian textile imports, Romania would be the loser on both counts. The U.S. textile quotas were directed against cheap Asian imports, not textile imports from Central Europe, but other countries in Central and Eastern Europe had higher U.S. textile quotas than Romania. Romanians would end up selling fewer shirts in the United States and paying more for their chicken dinners at home.

ROMANIA'S INTERNAL POLICE SERVICE

On January 18 I had a long meeting with Romania's interior minister, Doru Taracila. Included in his ministry's responsibilities was oversight of Romania's national police force, a service widely thought by our government to be corrupt. Taracila was a Romanian insider. He was active in the revolution and was present at the military trial of the Ceauşescus and, later that day, when they were shot. Now Taracila insisted that he had cleaned up the force. Gone, he claimed, were Ceauşescu-era strong-arm thugs, replaced by a professional force of over 1,000 new officers, of whom at least 7 percent were ethnic Hungarians. When I asked about Roma officers, he said, "We have one high-ranking officer who is Roma." (Sound familiar?) In general, despite occasional complaints by human rights groups, our embassy believed that the gross abuses of the past were gone. The ministry cooperated with the FBI in Washington, and the following month several Romanian police officers were slated to go to Budapest for training at an FBI-friendly academy in dealing with counterfeiting and drug smuggling. We had major concerns in both areas and needed Romania's cooperation.

Taracila had seldom met a foreign ambassador and seemed flattered that I called on him. This gave me the opening to mention the lingering negative image of the Romanian police in the United States, making the work of his ministry of continuing interest to our embassy. I suggested ways to reduce street crime and get rid of the professional beggars who camped out near Romania's better hotels, in railway stations, and in principal shopping areas, where they jostled and harassed passersby. Taracila followed through. A few days later the sidewalks of Bucharest were clear of the annoyances that had plagued foreigners and discouraged tourism. The former street scenes had hurt Romania's reputation in the West almost as much as Ceauşescu's goons. This was a small part of the whole in furthering Romania's move toward the West and eventual NATO membership, but each step helped.

GOVERNMENT OFFICES IN ROMANIA

U.S. government offices in Washington vary in style and degree of splendor, but compared to those in Romania, they were opulent. With the exception of Cotroceni, government offices in Romania were uniformly decrepit or worse. To illustrate, on my visits I would routinely be ushered into a minister's anteroom for a ceremonial coffee or juice while seated on a dirty or tattered couch pocked often with holes, its sad condition a dim reminder of its elegance sixty or seventy years before. All ministerial offices were furnished with the same vintage pieces in the same state of disrepair. Telephones on ministers' dark wooden desks looked like props from a silent movie. The receiver sat on a cradle four or five inches above the base containing an old-fashioned rotary dial with only numbers. While Ceaușescu spent billions of dollars building his monstrous Palace of the People, Romania's public buildings had been crumbling for decades. Now the cupboard was bare.

THE HUNGARIAN MINORITY: AN EVER-PRESENT TENSION

As long as Romania is Romania, it will have a Hungarian issue. The ethnic Hungarian minority represents 6 to 7 percent of the population, heavily concentrated in Transylvania, with its own political organization, the Democratic Union of Hungarians in Romania (UDMR). Ethnic political leaders often took extreme positions to maintain their hold on voters, harping on incidents that might otherwise have passed as inconsequential. Shortly after my arrival in Romania, there was a public call by Bela Marko, the chairman of the UDMR, for territorial autonomy in the parts of Transylvania with large Hungarian populations. This produced a demand by the equally strident Transylvania-based PUNR to outlaw UDMR. The matter escalated when PUNR tried to enlist the PDSR, the coalition leader, in the demand. PDSR wisely refused to be drawn into the fray. Its decision did not endanger its coalition with PUNR. The three PUNR ministers in the government were not leading the anti-Hungarian charge. They left this to Gheorghe Funar, chairman of PUNR and mayor of Cluj, the largest city in Transylvania. Later, in June, I met Mayor Funar in his office in Cluj before I delivered a speech at Babeş-Bolyai University in Cluj. To my surprise, the mayor made me an honorary citizen of Cluj, complete with a plaque and certificate.

In January 1995 the Hungarian problem was back on the front burner. In response to Bela Marko's territorial autonomy demand, Romania's justice minister, Iosif Chiuzbaian, a member of PUNR, called for a ban on UDMR as punishment for having called for Hungarian territorial autonomy. I met with him to defuse the issue. He denied the newspaper reports of his wanting to outlaw UDMR, blaming them on inaccurate coverage of his remarks in the press, but this was unlikely. He proceeded to criticize Bela Marko while at the same time boasting of his personal friendship with Hungarians. Justice Minister Chiuzbaian talked a lot and listened little. Luckily, our conversation turned to the need for an independent judiciary, improving Romania's prison system, the current political scene in Romania, and his decision to join the PUNR after he became justice minister. His explanation was straightforward: he owed his appointment to PUNR and felt an obligation to join the party.

To balance the scales, I next met with Marko, who was more sophisticated and less outspoken than Chiuzbaian. He, too, had moved away from his previous statement about territorial autonomy, claiming that he had only called for regional autonomy. When I asked him what this meant he hesitated, then replied: more education in the Hungarian language, returning Babeş-Bolyai University in Cluj to its former Hungarian status, deleting the law requiring public meetings to be conducted in Romanian, and printing more street signs in Hungarian. None of this was new. Romania's King Michael named the university Babeş-Bolyai in honor of two Romanian Hungarian scholars in 1947 (it is cosmmon for universities in Central Europe to be named after a person instead of a place). Marko stated plaintively that he would be satisfied if, in any future Hungarian-Romanian Basic Treaty, regional autonomy was referred to as something to be achieved in the future. Regional autonomy could only come about, I thought, if Romania decentralized its administration to give more authority to counties, mayors, and other locally elected officials. As things stood, most regional and even local governmental matters were handled out of Bucharest.

MY JEWISH SOUL

Wearing both my American and Jewish hats, on January 27 I attended a five-hour ceremony at the Polish embassy commemorating the fiftieth anniversary of the liberation of Auschwitz by the Red Army in January 1945 (ironically, the Russian ambassador was not in attendance). Seated next to me was the Israeli ambassador, Avshalom Megiddon, a quiet diplomat with whom I would often meet. A day later there was a memorial service at the Choral Synagogue. This time I sat between the Israeli and Polish ambassadors and listened to the same Jewish choir I had heard eight years before singing in the Rotunda of the U.S. Capitol. At the Polish embassy and the next day at the Choral Synagogue there were speeches by Auschwitz survivors, many from Transylvania. In my travels I met frequently with Auschwitz survivors. Each occasion brought tears to my eyes as they recounted the horrors they had endured. Tragically, some were too broken in mind and spirit to do more than shake my hand and thank me for helping them.

Friday night is the beginning of the Jewish Sabbath, called Shabbat. In Virginia I traditionally stayed home on Friday nights, and I continued this practice in Romania, inviting guests to join me for dinner. This particular night, January 27, my guests were Izu Gott, the director of the Romanian Jewish Choir, and his wife; Emily Hachomi, the deputy chief of mission in the Israeli embassy and her husband, Itzak; and Josh Green, of the IMF, and his wife, Dora. Josh played the piano and Gott accompanied him on the accordion. Everyone sang, which was uplifting, but the most moving moment came when Itzak recounted his experiences as a boy of eight trekking the 2,300 miles from Samarkand, in Central Asia, to Jerusalem with his twelve-year-old brother. It took them two and a half years. Twenty-three years later his mother was finally allowed to leave the Soviet Union. When her plane landed at Ben Gurion Airport, Itzak bounded up the stairs to meet her. Most of the passengers had deplaned. Seated in the rear of the plane were two old Russian women. As he approached, one of them turned to the other and said, "See that man? He is my son." She had not seen him for twenty-three years. She had sent him and his brother to Jerusalem, telling them they would sit under fruit trees and figs would fall on their heads. She believed that Israel was the land of milk and honey, Jerusalem the Holy City, and that "no one would disturb you" in the land G-d gave to the Jewish people.

CULTURAL OFFERINGS IN BUCHAREST

One of the advantages of serving in a European capital was the rich selection of cultural events. During my tour I attended theatrical productions of Gershwin's *Porgy and Bess*, several operas, and the Yiddish theater and listened to rhapsodies composed by George Enescu, Romania's most famous composer. These performances were held either in Romania's ornate Opera House, near the Dambovita River in the center of Bucharest, or at the Athenaeum, a restored classical hall resembling a Greek basilica next to the Athenee Palace Hotel and across from Romania's National Art Museum. I was also treated to a concert at the American Cultural Center featuring American show tunes. Joshua Green with the IMF was the pianist and a superb baritone from the Romanian Opera Company sang. It seemed incongruous for me to sit in Bucharest and listen to American show tunes, but American music reminded me how much our culture is, perhaps, our most cherished and valuable export.

MY FIRST MEETING WITH MR. FIX-IT

High on my list of people to meet was Viorel Hrebenciuc, the secretary general of the government who had been President Iliescu's campaign manager in 1992. Hrebenciuc was known throughout Romania as Mr. Fix-It. He had a mixed reputation in Romania. Some called him corrupt, venal, and unconscionable—"the fountain of corruption"—but he was also engaging, a source of useful information, and a real doer. For every problem Hrebenciuc had a solution. I was hopeful that as the chair of the Romanian Minority Rights Council, which dealt with Hungarian and other minority issues, he would live up to his Mr. Fix-It nickname. When I met with him on January 21, he confirmed my impression that the Hungarian-Romanian conflict was more a calling card of PUNR and UDMR party leaders than an everyday problem for Romanians. Hrebenciuc wanted to solve the Hungarian call for Babeş-Bolyai University to return to its 1947–59 status as a Hungarian institution by reserving some 300 seats for Hungarian students. He was confident the places would not be filled, but reserving places would ease the tension. But this never happened.

Hrebenciuc had just returned from Israel, where he discussed with the

Romanian exile community in Israel the restitution of Jewish community property in Romania. He was prepared to deal with this issue as well as claims for the restitution of private Jewish property, but only together with the claims of other minorities who had lost their property to the communists. The restitution of Jewish personal and communal property turned out to be a long-term affair, still not fully resolved twenty years later, but it, too, was an issue Romania needed to acknowledge and deal with. President Clinton raised the issue in his historic speech to the Romanian people in July 1997. Secretary General Hrebenciuc was concerned that if Jews were singled out for favorable treatment, it would produce a huge outcry in Romania. Maybe so.

THE ROMANIAN OPPOSITION LEADER, CORNELIU COPOSU

In his capacity as the leader of PNT-CD, Corneliu Coposu was the de facto head of the Romanian opposition. He came to my residence on January 24 carrying a large sheath of documents. Then age eighty, bent over and in obvious ill health, he had been jailed for seventeen years, from 1947 to 1964, by the communists in the same prison as Gheorghe Bratianu and Iuliu Maniu. Coposu, a purist, remained a prisoner of the past long after his release from jail. He was a fervent monarchist and advocated bringing King Michael back to the throne. He refused to have anything to do with President Iliescu or the political parties cooperating with PDSR, calling them all Marxist-Leninist. When I asked about his party's political platform, he answered that PNT-CD's platform had to remain a secret "so that Iliescu does not steal it."

Coposu died in November 1995. After his death he was recast as a patron saint who had suffered imprisonment under the communists for his democratic beliefs. The suffering part was true, but the Coposu I knew was wedded to the ideology of his mentor, the former Peasant Party leader, Iuliu Maniu, who had been dead for more than forty years, and did not speak to the needs of post-Ceaușescu Romania. Maniu was a true hero, opposing first the fascist Iron Guard and Ion Antonescu and later the communist boss, Gheorghe Gheorghiu-Dej. Companions from Coposu's early days claimed he had been Maniu's bodyguard, not a person of stature. This may have been unfair and reflected personal rivalries. Whatever Coposu's relationship to Maniu was, by the time I knew him, he was the moral and political leader of what was left of Romania's democratic past.

CINDERELLA STORY

I had been on the job only two months when I realized I needed to get word to the West of Romania's reform efforts. I wrote an op-ed, "Romania, a Cinderella Story?," got the State Department's approval to publish it, and sent it to the *International Herald Tribune*. Appearing on March 17, 1995, it had the intended effect both in Romania and elsewhere. The article was part of my three-year push to move Romania ahead and ally it firmly with the West. It closed with the following paragraph: "Romania is now at a critical point in its negotiations with the IMF and the World Bank. The outcome of these negotiations will determine whether Romania, like Cinderella, gets a chance to dance with Prince Charming or goes back to living with the mice in the kitchen."

It was not ordinary fare for an American ambassador to go public, telling a foreign country—and the president of that country—what it should do, but this was the role I played for the next three years. Diplomatic? No, but I thought it was essential, and the Romanian public and our administration in Washington allowed me to do it.

HELPING PREPARE ROMANIA TO JOIN THE WEST

Following the January White House conference in Cleveland, I had expected the economic reform minister, Coşea, to give me a laundry list of things he wanted from the United States. Instead, at our meeting on January 30, he asked me what Romania should do. Improvising as I went along, I suggested that the government appoint an economic czar to cut through Romania's impenetrable red tape, start planning now for the privatization of 3,900 businesses, and set up duty-free industrial zones for foreign investors. Coşea saw himself as this future economic czar . He inquired about direct U.S. government aid. In response, I suggested he think about requesting technical assistance for economic restructuring, educating Romanians on the modalities of privatization, and encouraging them to move ahead with aggressive programs to spur the growth of new small and medium-sized businesses.

In the course of our discussion, it became clear that the Romanian side was short on ideas, perhaps as a result of forty-plus years of communism, which had sidelined two generations of would-be entrepreneurs. After the fall of communism the country depended on the World Bank, the IMF, the EU, and the United States to finance restructuring and implement economic reform. At the same time, ideas not homegrown were deemed "foreign," with a decidedly pejorative connotation that engendered resistance, reflecting a mixture of national pride, resentment at being lectured to by rich countries, and wariness that foreign investors would swoop in as they had in the 1920s and 1930s and grab up the country's wealth. As non-Romanians, we were never able to penetrate the Romanian subculture that was self-protective, clannish, and suspicious. Trust among Romanians was not in long supply, either.

Later in the day Romania's ambassador to the United States, Mihai Botez, stopped to see me on his way to meet with President Iliescu. It was a dry run for my planned meeting with President Iliescu in February, at which I intended to set forth the things Romania needed to do to be accepted in the West. I gave Botez a copy of a letter I had written to Secretary General Viorel Hrebenciuc in which I raised the issue of the planned monument to Marshal Antonescu, which I had first mentioned in my meeting with President Iliescu and Foreign Minister Meleşcanu after I presented my credentials back in December. I also took advantage of the occasion to raise four or five other issues concerning Romanian domestic issues, the most important being the government's flirting with the PRM (anti-Semitic) and the PSM (former communist), and its uneasy marriage with PUNR (anti-Hungarian). I stated that President Iliescu could not have it both ways—be seen in the West as the leader of a liberal democracy and at the same time depend on extremist parties to maintain his voting majority in Parliament.

I also raised concerns regarding the government's dismissal of scores of mayors across the country on what seemed to be trumped-up charges of financial irregularity. Almost all the mayors were members of the political opposition, and the general assumption was that the dismissals were politically motivated (which later was proudly admitted to me by a PDSR minister). I also touched on the desirability of licensing a national television channel that would not be government owned and decentralizing the national government to improve efficiency and to help with the Hungarian issue. Botez agreed on all points. (I would revisit these issues, adding a few more, when I returned to Washington to meet with Dick Holbrooke and others at the State Department and later in my gloves-off meeting with President Iliescu.)

This was a list of the high-priority steps that Romania needed to take. Other important steps that Romania need to take, such as undertaking economic reform, modernizing the Romanian military, solidifying Romania's democratic gains, and signing basic treaties with Hungary and Ukraine, would take more time. I put all these points in a detailed "non-paper" that I crafted to show to President Iliescu after I ran it by the State Department. If I were to be more than a figurehead ambassador making the usual rounds, I wanted to use the enormous influence and prestige of the United States to help Romania chart a path to democratic institution building and economic reform as the preconditions to its joining NATO and the EU.

However, when I showed the non-paper to Holbrooke in Washington in February, he wisely suggested that I deliver the message orally in person. I was quickly persuaded that Holbrooke was right. I was too new on the job to be laying down a non-paper. Instead, I would see President Iliescu and deliver the message. So the non-paper became a non-non-paper.

MEETING ROMANIAN ROYALTY

Royalty came to the American Embassy on February 1 in the person of Princess Margareta, the oldest child of King Michael I. She was the head of the Princess Margareta of Romania Foundation, which helped with the enormous problem of Romania's 100,000 or so abandoned children left behind from the Ceaușescu days as a result of Ceaușescu's population policy: he believed that increasing the population was key to strengthening the economy and country, so he banned contraception and abortion and taxed the childless. The result was the abandonment of thousands of children by impoverished families. The high number of abandoned or orphaned children was often cited with dismay by visiting Americans.

But the foundation was only one area of Margareta's interest—her principal goal was to restore the monarchy. King Michael I returned to Romania twice after the revolution. The first time he drew enthusiastic crowds in downtown Bucharest. The second time he only got as far as the airport. The government refused to let him enter the country. Margareta, an attractive, friendly person in her mid-forties, was still recovering from a hip operation and walked with a cane. She planned to return to Romania in a month or two, at which time I told her I would join her at the foundation's orphanage in Bucharest for picture taking; the foundation could use the photos to raise funds. I was supportive of the foundation, but the notion of restoring the monarchy was close to madness—one thing Romania did not need was a king. In my view, the government had been hard-headed in its dealings with King Michael I. But he nevertheless remained a symbol of national legitimacy and was an anti-communist icon. Two years later Princess Margareta kindly invited me to her wedding.

WASHINGTON, FEBRUARY 3–19: STREAMLINING ASSISTANCE

On February 2 I flew from Bucharest to D.C. While there, in an effort to break through the stalemate in Bucharest on economic reform, I cooked up the idea of convening a meeting in Romania that we would host with Romania's economic ministers, the IMF, the World Bank, the European Bank for Reconstruction and Development, and the EU. The purpose of the meeting would be to review the privatization program, which had stalled in Parliament, and to decide on first steps Romania should take once the law was enacted.

I coordinated this with Ralph Johnson, USAID's coordinator for Eastern European assistance. He was enthusiastic and committed to support the effort with USAID money and experts. Ralph and I also agreed to reduce the number of USAID contractors in Romania to less than a dozen and to concentrate on programs that would have a maximum multiplier effect. Banking was surely one of them. Also, we needed to fund programs that would train management and provide seed capital for small and medium-sized businesses, and encourage the Romanian government to implement the privatization program once it was passed.

Following our meeting in Washington, Ralph sent a USAID team to Bucharest to take a look at Romania's privatization program. The team returned to Washington with a comprehensive proposal covering implementation of the Mass Privatization Program reform of capital markets and restructuring of industry. The full program would cost $42 million the first year, of which the U.S. portion would be approximately $30 million. The rest was to come from the EU's PHARE (Poland and Hungary: Assistance for Restructuring their Economies) assistance program, created in 1989.

This was an ambitious undertaking, but if it worked it would be a game changer. In the end, the EU said no, unwilling to be second chair to USAID. The Romanians also declined, not wanting USAID or any other third party looking in Romania's closet at its deal-making and raw politics. The Romanians preferred to keep control of the method and pace of privatization and not answer to others who would not have to pay the political price the Romanians would pay if the economy tanked.

Bank privatization was a tricky business. Romania's state-owned banks carried sizable non-performing loans made to large industrial state-owned enterprises and to the agricultural sector at the behest of the Romanian government. Before any of Romania's five large state-owned banks could be privatized they had to be "cleansed" of these loans, which would be written off or placed in another state-owned bank. Until this was done, Romania's banking sector would not be able to provide the credits needed to support a growing economy.

While in D.C. I also stopped at the Pentagon to meet with Joseph S. Nye Jr., assistant secretary of defense for international security affairs, and Joseph J. Kruzel, deputy assistant secretary of defense for Europe and NATO policy. Nye had been in Romania a few days before, but I had already left for Washington. He told me he came away from Bucharest with positive feelings about Romania, and that it would receive a $10 million U.S. grant under the Pentagon's "Warsaw Initiative," designed to help the nations of Central and Eastern Europe participate in the Partnership for Peace program. The same amount would go to the Czech Republic and Hungary. Only Poland was slated to receive more, $25 million.

Once the money was received, Romania would use it to maintain the four Lockheed C-130 Hercules transport aircraft that the United States planned to transfer to Romania. Even more important than the much-needed grant was the symbolism of Romania grouped together with Poland, the Czech Republic, and Hungary, the leading candidates for NATO accession. Assistant Secretary Nye touched on two other issues. First, Romania needed to move ahead with a site survey that was required for the country to be eligible to receive classified information, a must for NATO membership. (It was completed the following year.) Second, Nye told me that he was hoping that Romania's admission into the Australia Group (to assist in fulfilling country obligations under the Chemical Weapons Convention) could be favorably resolved in the next few months. It took a year and a strong push from me and other proponents of building a stronger U.S.-Romanian bilateral relationship to get the job done. This was all part of the larger plan to bolster the American-Romanian relationship and help Romania get across the NATO finish line. (Joseph Kruzel was tragically killed, along with two other U.S. diplomats, in an accident involving his armored convoy in Bosnia in August 1995.)

TACKING UPWIND

Senator Jesse Helms (R-N.C.), chairman of the Senate Foreign Relations Committee, continued to have an interest in Romania, which was spurred by his North Carolina protégé, Congressman David Funderburk. One of Helms's staffers, Ann Smith, who covered European affairs for Senator Helms, called the State Department in early February to complain about the Romanian government's dismissal of mayors and other local officials. At State's request, I reviewed with her the Romanian political scene, pointing out that Romania was mostly shades of gray, not black and white.

She acknowledged that the Hungarian lobby in the United States, which regularly complained to Helms about Romania, was highly emotional and far from objective. Senator Helms wanted to know who his ideological allies in Romania, the Christian Democrats, were. I gave her a rundown of the opposition parties, but her focus was on PNT-CD, which most closely mirrored Senator Helms's views. I told her that I thought PNT-CD might win the elections in 1996 and form the next government. This brought a smile to her face.

She also mentioned the letter to Senator Helms about me from seven Romanian senators, which had arrived after I was confirmed as ambassador: Father Gheorghe Calciu-Dumitreasa, who had been imprisoned by the communists for twenty-one years for criticizing Ceauşescu, was either the author of the letter or its instigator. By this time he was the clergyman in a Romanian émigré church in Northern Virginia. I had mentioned Calciu-Dumitreasa's imprisonment as an example of human rights violations by Ceauşescu when I testified before Congress in 1986 and had asked Ceauşescu to release him the last time I met with the dictator. Calciu-Dumitreasa was subsequently released and allowed to emigrate to the United States. His role in spearheading the letter to Senator Helms to sink my appointment is a good example of the axiom that no good deed goes unpunished. I was later told by a prominent Romanian high church official that Calciu-Dumitreasa, like his patriarch, Teoctist, had become a communist informer, and that this greatly troubled his conscience, which might explain his erratic behavior.

MY LONG MEETING WITH PRESIDENT ILIESCU

On February 20, the day after my return to Bucharest, I met with President Iliescu at Cotroceni to communicate to him the substance of my non-paper. Jonathan Rickert, our deputy chief of mission, accompanied me. President Iliescu graciously departed from the customary formality and met with us, along with his diplomatic adviser, Traian Chebeleu, in a small sitting area outside his private office. I began by talking about the improvement in our countries' bilateral relationship and expressed the hope that further improvement would lead to permanent MFN (most favored nation) status for Romania, expanded U.S. technical support for privatization, and more high-level visits.

After the good news came the tough message: The U.S. government was concerned about the extremist parties' role in the government following the signing of the 1992 political protocol that laid the foundation for a voting coalition in Parliament among the PDSR, the PUNR, the PRM, and the

PSM. The United States strongly supported a basic treaty between Romania and Hungary in order to advance the integration of both countries into Western military and political structures—namely, NATO and the EU. We were concerned about the resuscitation of the reputation of the pro-Nazi dictator Marshal Antonescu and the arbitrary dismissal of opposition mayors. I addition, we encouraged Romania to facilitate the establishment of a privately owned national television channel and to move ahead with privatization.

President Iliescu listened patiently, but then went into high gear. His face turned florid, and his words poured out. He was no longer in total control. I looked over at Jonathan, who was sitting on the edge of his chair biting his lower lip, a worried expression on his face. Finally, President Iliescu said, "Mr. Ambassador, not even Brezhnev talked to us this way." I replied, "Mr. President, I hope I am a better friend of Romania than Brezhnev." He acknowledged that was true, and the meeting proceeded in a more friendly way. Iliescu stated that he had been very frank because he considered me a friend, to which I nodded affirmatively.

On the specific issues, he responded, "We will find a way to solve these problems." And for the most part, he did. As we were leaving, he commented, half smiling, on the double standard that the United States imposed by treating Romania differently from other Central European countries. I silently agreed, but this was the reality, and both countries needed to do the things required to change the way Romania was viewed in the United States. Romania needed to start with the things I had just mentioned, and the United States in return needed to support Romania's reform efforts and larger legitimate aspirations. I was pressing the limits of protocol for an ambassador, but I had concluded that losing Romania to extremism was not an option for the United States.

A few weeks later the astute German ambassador, Anton Rossbach, commented that Chancellor Helmut Kohl of Germany had never met Iliescu and did not intend to meet him for reasons that Rossbach found illogical and unfair. Kohl did not accept President Iliescu's legitimacy, but, as Rossbach pointed out, different criteria were being applied to Romania than to Hungary. Kohl still considered Romania a communist country, but if that was so, then Rossbach thought Kohl should apply the same standard to Hungary's Prime Minister Gyula Horn, a former communist whom Kohl accepted. But

Kohl continued to ignore President Iliescu. It was hard to escape the conclusion that a cloud hung over Romania.

Later, President Iliescu also let me know that he was disappointed in not having been officially invited to meet with President Clinton in the White House. He explained that the opposition press in Romania made much of this, overlooking the fact that he had met with President Clinton in the White House in 1993 in connection with the opening of the Holocaust Museum and again in New York the year before. I was surprised that President Iliescu was concerned about views in the opposition press. I thought he would care less about what the opposition thought than where he stood with the public at large. Romanians paid scant attention to political attacks in the press by one party or another, seeing them as a source of amusement, not news.

Despite these rough edges, President Iliescu and I continued our close collaboration. He delivered, and so did I. The following year Congress approved permanent MFN status for Romania. Gone were the annual reviews that Romania considered demeaning. Six months after my meeting with President Iliescu at Cotroceni, he was invited to Washington to meet with President Clinton in the Oval Office. Former president George H. W. Bush and his wife came to Bucharest for a highly celebrated visit, and First Lady Hillary Clinton arrived the following year, as did other important Americans, most particularly members of the American military. The U.S. government also flooded Romania with technical experts to help with privatization and with building democratic institutions. In time, all the issues I raised with Iliescu were solved, with the single exception of economic reform, which continued to lag.

Not all my efforts to bring headliners to Romania were successful. After my meeting with President Iliescu, I cabled Washington, urging Vice President Albert Gore to visit Romania for a day on his way to or from a scheduled trip to Moscow in June. I realized that this was a long shot but worth the effort. There had been presidential and vice presidential visits to most major capitals in Central and Eastern Europe, including Riga, Latvia, and even Sofia, Bulgaria, a country a third the size of Romania. The absence of a stopover to Romania from a high-level U.S. visitor when the country was unabashedly pro-American gave rise to daily comments in the Romanian press asking why the United States treated Romania differently. A visit by Vice

President Gore would have done much to dispel Romanian feelings of unrequited love. Vice President Gore's staff seriously considered the visit, but the trip was axed for security reasons after the Secret Service recommended that the vice president fly directly from Moscow to Washington with no stopovers.

A year later I suggested to former president Jimmy Carter that he open a Habitat for Humanity project in Romania. After leaving the White House in 1981, Carter gave a big push to Habitat for Humanity, helping to build low-income housing in the United States. The idea caught on, and Habitat for Humanity projects sprang up around the country and then overseas. When the former president was scheduled to open a Habitat for Humanity project in Hungary in February 1995, I suggested that he combine his Hungarian visit with a stop in Romania. He promised to consider the suggestion, but in the end he did not come.

SEEKING "HIGH-LEVEL" MEETINGS

On February 22 Adrian Nastase, the president of the Chamber of Deputies, asked to see me. He wanted my help in arranging high-level meetings for him on a visit he planned to make to Washington in early March. His objective was to create favorable publicity at home. A few days later, I met with Bob Understein, the American businessman in Bucharest who, I found out, was paying for Nastase's trip to Washington. Understein saw himself as the go-between for Marriott Hotels and Nastase. There were then a half dozen or so such "shadow" American businessmen in Romania, some of questionable character, hoping to find deals. There was a certain naiveté among Romanian government officials. They were used to relying on private "fixers," not understanding that official visits by foreign government officials worked best using government channels.

Marriott was looking to purchase the Intercontinental Hotel, the only large modern hotel in Bucharest. It was slated to be sold to a strategic foreign investor as part of Romania's privatization, but Romanian hands got in the way, and it ended up going to a Romanian insider, George Paunescu, Ceaușescu's former Securitate operator in Italy. Understein saw Chamber of Deputies President Nastase as his wedge to get into the deal and arranged, through a Republican lobbyist, for Nastase to meet Republican congressmen on Capitol Hill, even though they were not of Nastase's political persuasion. This was not a good way for the president of the Romanian Chamber of Deputies to meet people in Washington.

Despite his protestations that he would not come to the United States without high-level meetings—with Vice President Gore, Secretary of State Christopher, and House Majority Leader Newt Gingrich—Nastase showed up in Washington on schedule. He met some people on the Hill and in the administration but not the big names he wanted. I attended his meeting with Deputy National Security Adviser Sandy Berger at the White House. Sandy asked the right questions, about the basic treaty with Hungary, the Partnership for Peace, and privatization. Chamber of Deputies president Nastase was there for show, a photo op, not substance, and had little to say. At the end of the meeting he complained about the level of his meetings in Washington this time, compared with a previous visit in 1990, when he had met with Secretary of State James A. Baker III. Explanation: then he was Romania's foreign minister; now he was not.

HOLBROOKE PLUS ONE

On the afternoon of February 22, Assistant Secretary Holbrooke and his fiancée, Kati Marton, arrived in Bucharest from Ankara. I was on hand to meet them at the airport, together with senior members of the embassy staff and the Romanian Protocol Office. A police escort accompanied Dick and Kati to my residence, where they stayed. A quick drink, a swim for Kati, then off to a downtown restaurant. This was my first go at a post-revolution restaurant. It was quite good. We wisely ordered Romanian dishes, including *mamaliga* (a cornmeal-based Romanian porridge), another first for me. At Holbrooke's urging, Kati told me about her life growing up in Hungary; her fleeing the country after the aborted 1956 revolution; her later discovery that her grandparents on both sides were Jewish; and the death of one set of grandparents at Auschwitz. After dinner, we took a windshield tour of Bucharest and looked at Ceauşescu's monstrosities. Kati astutely commented that Ceauşescu must have intended the massive buildings to dwarf human beings. Kati was in the process of getting a divorce from Peter Jennings, of ABC News. She and Dick were married the following November in a ceremony in the American embassy in Budapest.

Holbrooke was masterful at meetings the next morning with President Iliescu, Foreign Minister Meleşcanu, and Nastase, sailing through without recourse to briefing papers. Afterward I hosted a lunch in Dick's honor at my residence, attended by most of official Romania, including Meleşcanu, Nastase, Defense Minister Tinca, Secretary General Hrebenciuc, and the opposition presidential candidates Emil Constantinescu and Petre Roman. In my introduction I mentioned that during Dick's seven months as assistant secretary of state for European and Canadian affairs, there had been no "noticeable deterioration" in our relations with Canada. Dick managed a pained smile, but Kati obligingly laughed. Following lunch, Holbrooke delivered a superb lecture at the Euro-Atlantic Council attended by the press and forty prominent Romanians.

Two days later, on February 24, I flew to Budapest for the Conference of Central European and American Ambassadors, chaired by Holbrooke. There was time before the conference for me to meet with the Hungarian foreign minister, László Kovács, to discuss the Hungarian-Romanian Basic Treaty and to hear the Hungarian side. For the Hungarians, the sticking point was Council of Europe Recommendation 1201 of the European Convention on Human Rights, as an added protocol to the Strasbourg Convention which referred to autonomy, a term that was anathema to the Romanians. Fortunately, the language in Recommendation 1201 was sufficiently ambiguous to allow each side to claim victory when the treaty was finally signed a year and a half later. In the text of the treaty the contracting parties agreed that Recommendation 1201 did not require territorial autonomy or refer to group rights.

6

Former President Bush in Bucharest

SPRING 1995

HELPING WITH NASTASE'S TWO PROBLEMS

Adrian Nastase, the president of the Chamber of Deputies, was my guest for lunch in March. Although I had known him since he first visited the United States in 1991, and he was usually on the attack, this time he was playing goalie. Legislation was pending in the Romanian Parliament to outlaw flying foreign flags and singing foreign national anthems in Romania. He had been rightly warned that this would be seen abroad as retrogressive nationalism and implored me to come up with alternative language that would allow the supernationalists in Parliament to save face without putting punitive legislation on the books that would be sharply criticized in the West.

The stratagem we agreed to was an official letter from me to him as president of the Chamber of Deputies, intended to cool the ardor of Romania's supernationalists and lead to acceptable language. The letter read as follows:

Dear Mr. President:

Permit me to share with you our serious concern about the amendments to the criminal law, passed recently in the Senate and pending before the Chamber of Deputies, that are intended to enforce respect for state symbols and to limit the display of foreign flags and the playing of foreign national anthems. There can be no legitimate disagreement that national and cultural symbols should be treated with respect. Indeed, in recent years questions over flag-burning have prompted much debate in our country.

Nevertheless, the amendments proposed by the Senate would infringe on an individual's constitutionally guaranteed freedom of expression by providing criminal sanctions, which can be deemed as being disproportionately severe in cases concerning the display of foreign flags and the playing of foreign anthems (especially article Nos. 7 and 14). The amendments proposed to the criminal law have the potential for official abuse.

If the provisions of the criminal law are enacted in their present form, it would be justifiably seen as contravening the democratic safeguards and respect for the free expression of views that Romania has strived to establish since the revolution.

Experience shows that legislation of this sort not only fails to inhibit the objectionable conduct but often becomes a means whereby protestors draw attention to their cause. By staging incidents designed to evoke a governmental reaction that produces the desired publicity for their cause, protestors may succeed in casting the government in the role of a repressor. In short, such legislation is more harmful than helpful to the objective sought by its proponents.

I do not presume to suggest to the Romanian parliament how legislation in this delicate area should be framed. However, I trust that you and your colleagues will consider carefully whether new legislation should be enacted at all in light of the effect that such legislation will have on Romania's image abroad and at home at a time when Romania is seeking to strengthen its democratic institutions and to integrate its human rights policy with Western practices and norms.

With deep respect.

We also discussed the problems that had arisen with the absence of an effective Romanian copyright law. American films were shown on Romanian television without payment of copyright fees. The U.S. Motion Picture Association in Washington, headed by my longtime friend Jack Valenti, succeeded in getting Romania added to the U.S. watch list of countries violating copyright law. Jack sent me a handwritten note asking me to intervene. Otherwise, if Romania remained on the list the following year, the U.S. trade representative would be compelled by law to seek punitive damages. In the end I was able to come to the rescue by persuading the Romanian Parliament to adopt the copyright protection law that answered the needs of an important segment of American business—book publishers, the motion picture industry, television producers, and the creative arts generally; it was another step on Romania's road to NATO membership.

The rest of the lunch was given over to Nastase's complaints about "unfair" criticism of him in the Romanian press. He told me that the press had reported that he owned four apartments, whereas in fact he owned only two. He blamed the misinformation on Romanian Internal Service Director Virgil Magureanu—more of Romania's endless political infighting.

PUSHING ECONOMIC REFORM

I met regularly with Arna Hartmann at the World Bank Bucharest offices, joined by other World Bank representatives such as Michael Wiehens, the head of the World Bank's Central European office. Wiehens was pessimistic about reaching agreement on the FESAL (Final Enterprise Structural Adjustment Loan). As he saw it, with Romania refusing to meet essential conditions for successful privatization, many months of arduous negotiation lay ahead.

As a follow-up, I invited World Bank, IMF, and EU representatives to a meeting to discuss whether the Romanian government had the will to accelerate privatization and sign the FESAL. It was clear the Romanian agency in charge of privatization, the State Ownership Fund (SOF), did not have the manpower to administer such a large privatization program. The SOF was headed by Emil Dima, appointed by the Romanian Parliament, not the Romanian government. The U.S. accounting firm Coopers & Lybrand had mistakenly come up with the idea of parliamentary selection, intending it to insulate the SOF from politics. In practice, it had the opposite effect. Dima was principally interested in protecting Romania's redundant workers from losing their jobs as a result of downsizing and did everything he could to thwart privatization. The upshot of our meeting was that we would draft a joint démarche to President Iliescu, but a day or two later, Karen Fogg, the EU representative, demurred, insisting that she had to check with the French ambassador. France at the time held the EU presidency. As expected, the answer was no.

In the end, after my efforts at a multilateral approach failed, I met alone with President Iliescu's economic adviser, Misu Negritoiu, an economist and reformer. He agreed that now that the EU had dropped out, World Bank and IMF representatives along with me should meet with President Iliescu to urge prompt enactment of the Mass Privatization Program amendment, and agree on procedures for its implementation following passage.

Still pushing economic reform, on February 27 I had met Mr. Fix-It, Viorel Hrebenciuc, the secretary general of the government, at my residence for dinner. He was still the favorite to implement the MPP once it passed. "No" was not a word in his vocabulary. This time was no exception, but even Mr. Fix-It proved powerless to implement economic reform. Too many private interests stood in the way. Moreover, I doubted that the mechanism for implementation had been thought through by Hrebenciuc or anyone else.

TERROR THREATS

In March the FBI thought it had identified an Arab terrorist living in Romania who was involved in the 1985 TWA Airline hijacking. While en route from Athens to Rome, the plane was forced to land in Beirut by Shiite Hezbollah terrorists. On March 14 I accompanied the FBI to a meeting with Virgil Magureanu, the head of the Romanian Internal Security Service, the SRI, who agreed to cooperate in confirming the suspect's identity. If the suspect checked out, we would fly him directly to the United States on a CIA plane. It would be a major story, but the CIA station chief and I doubted that the suspect would turn out to be the culprit. Most likely we were being set up by an informer for payment with no delivery. This turned out to be the case. Unfortunately, it was not the first time the FBI paid an informer for a scam.

The informer was known by the SRI to be a fraud and it told the FBI this, compounding the bureau's embarrassment, in my view.

Later that month, we had another counterterrorist operation, this time involving the Japanese Revolutionary Army. This one was real, but our response was complicated by the need to cooperate with the Japanese, who were even more bureaucratically muscle-bound than we were.

On a bright, cold early Sunday morning in March, I was called to the embassy to respond to an urgent cable about an antiterrorist operation in Bucharest. After a brief huddle with our regional security officer and the CIA station chief, we drove the ten miles to SRI headquarters outside Bucharest to meet with Magureanu. At my urging, he gave orders to the SRI to pick up the suspect in her Bucharest apartment. To cover my tracks, I immediately briefed Romanian State Secretary Marcel Dinu at the Foreign Ministry without giving him the details. I wanted to avoid a diplomatic flap over why the American ambassador was involved in the arrest of a Japanese terrorist in Romania. He had only one question: Did it involve the Kurds? When I said no, he did not ask anything further. I sent a reporting cable to the State Department and the trap was set for the suspect. Two days later she was arrested by the SRI and detained, awaiting necessary papers for deportation to Japan. The Japanese were quite inept in this instance; but for my intervention with Magureanu, the suspect might have slipped out of the country.

A few months later two Secret Service agents and a CIA operative briefed me on their efforts to nab a Palestinian in Romania who was peddling the counterfeit $100 U.S. bills that were called supernotes. They thought he could lead them to the source of the notes, a printing press in Lebanon's Beqaa Valley, which was protected by Syria. The suspect, if caught, might not talk—he had been in an Israeli prison for years without talking. We tried to enlist the help of Ioan Talpes, the head of the SIE, and other Romanian sources, but never found the printing press. The United States undertook the rare step of altering the design of the $100 bill to make counterfeiting more difficult.

HIS HONOR THE MAYOR

Big-city mayors are a special breed: consummate politicians and adept power jugglers who adhere to U.S. House Speaker Tip O'Neill's adage that "all politics is local." Mayor Crin Halaicu of Bucharest was no different. Sitting in his faded late nineteenth-century office in downtown Bucharest in March 1995, "Hizzoner" could easily have been mistaken for the mayor of New York or Chicago. He was big and direct, and kept telling me that he liked to solve problems. Taking him at his word, I mentioned two to him. The first involved street crime. I thought to myself that this was a problem the mayor could easily handle, but alas, the buck did not stop at the mayor's desk. He told me that this was the responsibility of the Ministry of the Interior. In other words, the national police.

Another problem struck even closer to our embassy. We needed a permit to build a passageway between the embassy and the U.S. consulate. Mayor Halaicu told me he could handle this one and he did, but it took another six months to get the permit for the embassy to break through the wall adjoining the consulate building. We finally took a sledgehammer to the wall in December 1995.

A NIGHT TO REMEMBER

President Iliescu rarely hosted or even attended private dinners, but the night of March 20 was different from other nights. The occasion was a visit to Romania by Ronald Lauder, the son of Estée Lauder, the founder of the cosmetics firm bearing her name. The other guests were Mark Palmer, my State Department friend and the former American ambassador to Hungary, now Lauder's business partner; Ion Tiriac, the former Romanian Davis Cup tennis star living in Germany but with extensive business interests across Europe; and Adrian Sarbu, a Romanian businessman tapped by the businessmen Lauder, Palmer, and Tiriac to apply for a national television station license and head up the new station.

The dinner was held in an official government villa near Herăstrău Park on the north side of Bucharest. Despite the ample size of the room, the powerful men barely squeezed in. Tiriac boasted of his friendship with former

U.S. Senate majority leader George Mitchell and other major figures. Not to be outdone, Lauder talked about his friendship with Senator Robert Dole and the upcoming presidential election in which Dole would be the Republican presidential nominee. Lauder told President Iliescu that he strongly supported General Colin Powell as Dole's running mate. In his enthusiasm, Lauder overlooked the fact that General Powell had not yet declared whether he was a Democrat or a Republican, or whether he had any interest in being vice president.

In an effort to catch up, Palmer stated that he ranked ninth in a recent Hungarian poll of the ten most popular people. With a straight face, he said how amazing this was, since he was neither Hungarian nor had spent time in Hungary since he resigned as its American ambassador in 1990. President Iliescu simply listened politely.

The next day I hosted a lunch at my residence for the four stars of the previous evening. With no Romanian officials present, we talked about tactics to use in seeking the television license. Lauder's was the only American-backed group applying, so I was able to pledge Ron my strong support. In the end, his group won the license and the station, PRO-TV, became the number one privately owned TV channel in Romania. This gave Romania a privately owned national television station for viewers throughout the country, which was a positive step in Romania's westward advance.

APRIL: GEORGE H. W. AND BARBARA BUSH'S VISIT

The embassy closed for Easter, and when it reopened, our focus was on the upcoming visit of former president George Bush and Mrs. Bush, a private trip sponsored by a Romanian businessman, Sever Mureşan, now a banker and the largest stockholder in Banca Dacia Felix in Cluj. Dacia Felix got off to a splashy start, but its star soon fell. Mureşan and his fellow bankers hoped to boost their status in Romania by showcasing the U.S. ex-president and his wife. Despite his claimed wealth, Mureşan dressed like a typical Romanian, wearing a shiny, ill-fitting, unpressed suit and cheap, light brown shoes that clashed with his dark suit. Rotund, with thinning dark hair and a round face, he looked more like an American ex–football lineman than a tennis star, let alone a banker.

I met with President Bush's advance team. Unfortunately, it was the little things that caused trouble, such as who would ride in the U.S. embassy Cadillac with President and Mrs. Bush from the airport to the parliament building, where President Bush was scheduled to deliver his speech. The car belonged to the embassy and was for the exclusive use of the ambassador. It was armored and had bulletproof windows. By law I needed to be in the vehicle whenever it carried passengers, but, as I saw it, my first responsibility was to protect President Bush. So I made a presidential decision. The Bushes would ride in the Cadillac with Mureşan, who insisted that he be seen next to them. Under the circumstances, the only alternative would have been for the Bushes to ride with Mureşan in an unprotected car. If anything had happened to the Bushes, I would have held myself responsible. In return, Mureşan agreed to absent himself the next night when President Bush had a private meeting with President Iliescu, Foreign Minister Meleşcanu, and me.

When the Bushes' private plane, paid for by Mureşan, arrived, there was a ceremonial welcome at the airport, after which the motorcade proceeded to the parliament building for President Bush's speech to an audience of 400 assembled by Mureşan. The motorcade itself was over the top, featuring outriding cars with hooded security guards armed with Uzis, which stuck out the windows. President Bush was not a strong speaker, but the audience reacted positively to the person who was president of the United States when communism fell and Ceauşescu was overthrown. He then took questions and did a television interview, following which we proceeded to the residence for an hour of "quiet time." The staff at the residence had managed to find a picture of President Bush when he was president, which they prominently displayed in the entranceway. He asked me, "Where did you find that relic?" Julius, the ever-courteous Kenyan butler, kissed Mrs. Bush's hand. I showed the Bushes to their bedroom, modest by presidential standards, but Mrs. Bush shrugged it off, saying, "You should see where George took me when we were first married." With that comment, the two males headed for the sauna, where we exchanged the usual ribald stories. He told me a funny story about a mutual friend who, after passing out at a dinner in Palm Beach, was revived by his second wife. President Bush knew I had worked for President Carter and said he admired Carter's dedication and his good deeds but was skeptical about his "Lone Ranger" missions to Haiti, North Korea, and most recently Bosnia.

The problem with Carter, Bush said, was that he did not follow instructions. He believed he was more effective operating on his own, taking measure of the person he was dealing with and then trying to personalize the relationship. This is what he did successfully with Sadat and Begin in negotiating the Egyptian-Israeli Peace Treaty, but that was when he was president. It was harder to carry this out now that he was no longer president.

We left the residence a short time later for a dinner hosted by President Iliescu. The first hour was given over to conversation between the two presidents, Foreign Minister Meleşcanu, and me. President Iliescu retold the story of the revolution and Romania's post-revolution saga. It was a bit revisionist, but not bad. Toward the end, President Iliescu complained about Romania's treatment in Washington. It was no different when George Bush was president, a fact somehow lost on President Iliescu. The Romanians needed to stop complaining. The more they talked about being treated as a second-class nation, the more likely it would continue.

Of greater interest was President Bush's flat denial of widely circulated press reports that he and the Soviet Union's Mikhail Gorbachev had plotted in Malta in 1989 to overthrow Ceauşescu. By contrast, Bush was defensive about his decision not to intervene in the Serbian uprising in Bosnia in 1992. He claimed that Secretary of Defense Dick Cheney and Chairman of the Joint Chiefs Colin Powell had told him at the time that a minimum of 250,000 American troops would be needed in Bosnia to end the fighting without an exit strategy for U.S. forces and with no assurance that the number was adequate. President Iliescu, like most Romanians, was pro-Serbian and distrustful of the Muslim population in Bosnia. He listened politely but did not comment.

The conversation at dinner was the usual pleasant banter. The original seating chart put together by Mureşan's people had him sitting next to Bush. The Romanians rightly took charge of their dinner, and Mureşan ended up halfway down the table. One of Emil Constantinescu's first acts after being elected president in December 1996 was to order Mureşan's arrest on corruption charges.

The next day the American embassy staff together with spouses and children, some 200 strong, greeted the Bushes at the residence at 8:30 a.m. Bush was great, signing autographs and having his picture taken with each family.

He liked embassy people, and it showed. Both Bushes spoke to an apprecia-
tive audience, commending them for their public service and reminding them
that the Bushes had served in Beijing from 1974 to 1976, when George Bush
was our unofficial ambassador to China (formal diplomatic relations were established in 1979). Next stop: center court at the Romanian tennis stadium. I
played in one set, but even with Mureşan as my partner, we lost to Bush and
Meleşcanu. Mureşan later told me, "It is hard to be a great tennis player and
a great host at the same time."

It was a good visit for the Bushes, and for Romania. The Bushes had a
splendid time. Bush liked President Iliescu and invited him to visit him in
Houston. When I later took President Bush aside to ask him if he was serious,
he said yes. And he was.

TENNIS DIPLOMACY

On a balmy evening in early May, Chamber of Deputies President Nastase
and Foreign Minister Meleşcanu joined Jonathan Rickert, our deputy chief
of mission, and me for tennis, followed by dinner with their wives. The tennis
ended up a diplomatic 6–6 tie. Nastase arrived late, so we were unable to
finish the set before the wives arrived for dinner. I have often been told that
behavior on the tennis court is indicative of character. If so, both Meleşcanu
and Nastase came off well. Meleşcanu was gracious and quick with humorous
remarks, often self-deprecating. Nastase was earnest and characteristically
humorless, but he made the right line calls, the true test of character.

The banter carried over from the tennis court to drinks and then dinner.
The mood was helped by Meleşcanu's having forgotten his shoes. It is not
often that a foreign minister attends a diplomatic function wearing rubber
crepe sandals without socks. Nastase was tieless, also uncharacteristic for
Romanians.

Without Carol with me to arrange things properly, I depended on the
residence staff to handle place cards at meals. That night there was a slipup.
Meleşcanu was seated opposite me and Nastase was at the end of the table.
As president of the Chamber of Deputies, Nastase was the third in diplomatic
rank behind President Iliescu and Senate President Oliviu Gherman, a fact

he generously shared with others. As foreign minister, Meleşcanu was some-where down the official pecking order. As we walked into the dining room, I recognized the faux pas and announced I did not know where people were to be seated—it was such a small group that people should sit wherever they wanted. Nastase was polite, but I knew he was miffed.

The dinner began with Dana, Nastase's wife, announcing that it was her fortieth birthday and asking everyone to wish her happy birthday. From the expression on her face, it was obvious that her husband had forgotten her birthday and she wanted to make a point of it. To smooth things over, I of-fered a toast and everyone sang happy birthday, somewhat leadenly. At the end of dinner Nastase tried to recoup his losses by proposing a toast to his wife with words about how honored the two of them were to be celebrating her birthday with such good friends. It seemed to prove the adage that if you are in a hole, the first rule is to stop digging!

The dinner conversation touched on the Romanian-Hungarian Treaty and led to a modestly positive outcome. Slovakia had previously agreed in its draft treaty with Hungary to specific references to Council of Europe Rec-ommendation 1201. I remarked that now it might be hard to persuade Hun-gary to agree to something less with Romania. The way ahead was to go back to Foreign Minister Meleşcanu's earlier suggestion that the parties agree that these provisions did not call for recognition of group rights or territorial au-tonomy based on ethnicity. Meleşcanu agreed, but said that much depended on the Romanian Parliament. I then turned to Nastase with a questioning look. When he voiced his support for the concept, Meleşcanu beamed. When I met later with Meleşcanu, he told me that with Nastase's support he could persuade Hungary to agree on the formula we discussed at dinner. As it turned out, this was the deal that was struck in September 1996.

Nastase then launched into his "unrequited love" spiel: Romania had reached out to the United States and done its part without reciprocity from America. When I tried to explain that Romania and the United States were not equal world powers, Nastase shot back that Romania could be our best friend and then asked rhetorically, "What has the United States ever done for Romania?" Exasperated, I blurted out, "It sent me as ambassador." Others laughed, but Nastase looked defeated.

THE RESTITUTION OF JEWISH PROPERTY

I met with Secretary General Hrebenciuc at his office in late May in his capacity as the government minister for minority rights, one of his many titles. He was in shirtsleeves and, as usual, puffing on a cigarette. Being six inches taller than he, I put my arms on his shoulders and persuaded him not to put on his jacket, and I immediately took off mine. He began by telling me how much he had enjoyed the dinner at my residence a few nights before with Prime Minister Vacaroiu and Finance Minister Georgescu, particularly Vacaroiu's positive reaction to my importunings on economic reform. In return, I commended him for his stellar performance as tennis referee and assured him that he had the job as long as I remained ambassador. (Vacaroiu and Georgescu were avid tennis players. Hrebenciuc did not play, so I put him in the referee's chair.)

I was there to discuss the restitution of Jewish community property, an increasingly high-profile issue. Israel Singer of the World Jewish Congress (WJC) and Neftali Lavie of the Jewish Agency in Israel were pushing the issue throughout Central and Eastern Europe. Stu Eizenstat, the U.S. ambassador to the European Union, had been in Hungary and Poland the week before, having been appointed by Dick Holbrooke roving U.S. ambassador for the restitution of Jewish property in Europe. The situation was complicated on both sides of the table. The WJC and the Jewish Agency wanted to establish the principle that Jewish community property should be returned or compensation paid. The Jewish Agency wanted the money go to Israel; the WJC was looking for confrontation to produce headlines. The third party, the Jewish community in Romania, wanted compensation but was fearful of an anti-Semitic backlash if it was seen to be receiving "special treatment."

For Hrebenciuc, Mr. Fix-It, there was (almost) no problem he could not fix. He had determined that synagogues were functionally different from churches and therefore synagogues could be dealt with differently from Uniate churches, which the communists had turned over to the Romanian Orthodox Church (Uniate churches followed the Eastern rite but acknowledged the pope as their supreme pontiff). The distinction in Hrebenciuc's mind was that synagogues had a communal, cultural function that went beyond strict religious observance. The distinction escaped me, but I did not argue the point.

In the interest of finding a solution, I was willing to accede to Hrebenciuc's status as a leading authority on religious practices in Romania, even though he had probably never stepped foot inside a synagogue or a Uniate church.

On the basis of his synagogue/church distinction, Hrebenciuc was prepared to start returning Jewish community buildings without waiting for an act of Parliament. I looked to Stu to keep Jewish organizations abroad from creating a mess with the Romanian Jewish community becoming the loser. The WJC's secretary general, Israel Singer, was traveling around the Balkans displaying a letter drafted by him but ostensibly from congressional leaders to Secretary of State Christopher calling for the restitution of Jewish communal and private property in Central and Eastern Europe, with the veiled threat of holding up U.S. assistance for countries that did not comply. As expected, the reaction in Eastern Europe was uniformly negative, and in a poor country like Romania, nothing was likely to happen quickly. As I left, Hrebenciuc smiled, looked me in the eye, and said to tell the CIA he was "not Ukrainian." Where this came from I never knew, but it may have had something to do with his being born in Suceava County, on the Ukrainian border, which had a significant Ukrainian population. I never thought of him as anything other than Romanian, but now that he called my attention to it, his last name was Ukrainian. When I asked him who suggested he was Ukrainian, he said "Fine." There was nobody with that name in the embassy so he must have been referring to Zvi Feine of the Joint (American Jewish Joint Distribution Committee), an American-born Israeli now living in Tel Aviv. Still smiling, he told me he was not Ukrainian, nor was his father or grandfather.

ROMANIA'S ÉMINENCE GRISE

Sylviu Brucan, an old-line communist who had been held under house arrest in the last years of the Ceaușescu regime, had been ambassador to Washington in the early 1960s under Gheorghiu-Dej, largely because he was an urbane communist who could speak English. Even when he later became persona non grata under Ceaușescu, he was permitted to travel to Moscow and Western countries. When we met in Bucharest in May 1995, he was close to eighty and no longer wielded power or influence, but his name commanded respect as well as occasional criticism for his "cozy" connection to communist Romania. He was an intellectual and an idealist, and had been referred to pejoratively in communist times as "cosmopolitan."

On a balmy spring day, Silviu Brucan stopped by the embassy to chat. In Ceauşescu's day, his link to the American embassy had given him security. He now wanted to preserve this connection for prestige, contacts, and relationships.

His old Romanian Communist Party member card dated back to the 1930s, but by 1988 he had determined that communism had failed politically and economically. In his words, technology had reduced the role of the worker to the point where workers no longer counted for much. The Romanian Communist Party could not reform from within as Gorbachev and others had believed and therefore deserved to fail.

Brucan took credit for the appointment of Petre Roman as prime minister. According to Brucan, President Iliescu's first choice had been Ilie Verdets, a prime minister under Ceauşescu. Brucan said he had strongly opposed Verdets and supported Roman after he appeared on television standing with students in University Square proclaiming the revolution. Roman was young and attractive, and was the right symbol for the time. Brucan said Roman later became arrogant and acted unwisely: "Now he has no chance to be prime minister, but perhaps he can be a future foreign minister in a coalition government." This turned out to be true.

The only person Brucan had good words for was former prime minister Theodor Stolojan, then in Washington with the World Bank. Brucan predicted that President Iliescu would easily be reelected in November 1996 "because there will be no serious opposition." He thought that several businessmen such as Dan Voiculescu might run in order to use the platform for their own aggrandizement but that no credible political leader would run. Brucan was critical of the present government: Prime Minister Vacaroiu was not a politician and could only discuss economics; Foreign Minister Meleşcanu was able but had dropped the ball at the Council of Europe, in Strasbourg, when he was stationed there in Ceauşescu's last days, implying, I suppose, that Meleşcanu should have denounced Ceauşescu. A wholly absurd idea. Meleşcanu had at the time been serving in Ceauşescu's government and had even less independence than Brucan, who in private life was nevertheless circumspect in what he said about Ceaușescu. Brucan predicted that after the elections, Chamber of Deputies President Nastase would not emerge as prime minister (the position he wanted, having earlier turned it down in favor of someone with more experience in economic matters, Romania's number one priority), even if PDSR received a plurality of the votes. The next government, he said, was likely to be a coalition with PNT-CD. Brucan lamented the absence of young political leaders but saw a new cadre emerging in ten to fifteen years and cited as possibilities three or four of his present students at Bucharest University, where he said he taught, but he did not elaborate further. Brucan enjoyed the role of public critic. With vast experience and a record of personal integrity and of being right more often than wrong, he was looking for respect and was desperate to find people who would listen to him and praise his "wisdom."

Negotiating Romania's Treaty with Hungary

SUMMER 1995

TRANSYLVANIAN INTERLUDE

Like most capital cities, Bucharest offers an imperfect lens on the rest of the country. One must leave the capital occasionally to understand what is happening elsewhere in the country. In this spirit, the U.S. Information Agency (USIA) arranged for me to spend a June day in Cluj-Napoca, Cluj for short, the capital of and largest city in Transylvania. Debra Towry from the consular section and I left Bucharest on a vintage Tarom turboprop that held about fifty passengers. Every seat was taken. Judging from their attaché cases, most of our flight companions were businessmen looking like early morning weekday travelers in our country.

Cluj is a university city that dates back to Roman times and was probably named by them; it is thought that "Cluj" derives from the Latin word for "ravine." The city retains its medieval walls, and its central square has a traditional Central European look, similar to those of cities in Slovakia and Hungary.

My first meeting was with Prefect Grigore Zanc (PDSR); Mayor Georghe Funar, the chairman of the Romanian National Unity Party (PUNR);

132

and County Council President Romulus Constantinescu (PUNR)—three very different people. Zanc, a scholar, detested Funar and regularly put him down, invalidating his outlandish anti-Hungarian decrees. As prefect, Zanc had jurisdiction over the mayors in his *judet* (county). Constantinescu, a professor who studied for a time in the United States, was now an elder statesman. Funar was a firebrand. He struck me as unsure of himself, not serious. Exploiting Romanian-Hungarian tensions for his own political gain, he did his utmost to keep anti-Hungarian hatred alive among his ethnic Romanian constituents. Each of the three began by reading a prepared statement, first Zanc in Romanian, then Funar in English, telling me at the end that he was not an extremist. In reply I said it was not for me to call anyone in Romania extremist. That was for Romanians to decide, but his statements were extreme, producing interethnic tension much as Bishop László Tökés's statements had on the Hungarian side. His rhetoric, I told him, was harming Romania at a time when Romania was seeking closer ties with the West. Funar took all this in silence and, surprisingly, did not attack me in the press.

From the prefect's office we walked the half mile or so to the USIA office, passing centuries-old neoclassical buildings and the famous statue of King Mathias, the focal point of Romanian-Hungarian tensions in Cluj. Each side claimed it owned the statue of Mathias, who was half Romanian and half Hungarian. Now he was principally a symbol for Hungarians protesting Funar's threats to remove the statue and to erect statues of pureblood Romanians in its place.

A roundtable discussion with local political leaders had been arranged in the USIA office. I immediately suggested to them that they work together to lessen Hungarian-Romanian tension, which would enable them to capture votes from the ultranationalist PUNR in the upcoming parliamentary elections in November 1996. When I asked the local political leaders who would run for mayor against Funar, they replied that they would run a single candidate so as not to split the vote. When I asked who this would be, they replied it was a secret. I thought it was a little late for secrets, the same thing I told the PNT-CD leader Corneliu Coposu when he had informed me a short time before that his party's platform for the parliamentary elections was still a secret. Romania was not the United States, but it is hard to win elections anywhere with a secret candidate or a secret platform.

Next was a press conference at the university. Some non-journalists showed up. The questioners focused on Hungarian-Romanian issues, the basic treaty between the two countries, and minority rights. Romanian journalists were not adept at asking questions, nor did they follow up their questions as their American counterparts did, making it much easier for the speaker. However, there was an occasional diversion: midway through, one man, not a journalist, stood up and made a plea for the restoration of the monarchy. Another non-journalist asked for American funding for his favorite charity.

PASSAGE OF THE MASS PRIVATIZATION PROGRAM LEGISLATIONS AND THE IMMEDIATE AFTERMATH

In mid-1995 Parliament passed the Mass Privatization Program (MPP) legislation (Law 55/1995), marking the beginning of the phase of the larger privatization plan. It was to be implemented in three ways:

1. Sale of shares through direct negotiation

2. Management/employee buy-outs (MEBOs), initially the government's preferred method, giving preference to management and employees

3. Public offering of shares at a fixed price

The modalities of economic reform were primarily a World Bank creation. The FESAL would provide funding in tranches, but the Romanians needed to agree to the World Bank's conditions for signing. This eventually occurred, but it took years to implement. Privatizing state-owned enterprises (SOEs) and *régies autonomes* (RAs) proved difficult. (As of the time of writing of this book, SOEs and RAs still accounted for 9 percent of Romania's GDP and employed 10 percent of its workforce.)

As soon as the MPP was signed, Richard Rorvig, the U.S. economic counselor, and I met with Emil Dima, the head of the SOF. Before the MPP passed the Parliament, the SOF announced it would privatize 1,500 companies by the end of the year. In the first six months of the year, only seven companies were privatized, so it was clear that the SOF's announced goal would not be met. By year-end 1995, 648 companies had been privatized. The same was true for privatizations the following year. Fewer companies were privatized than the government announced at the beginning of the year, and those privatized tended to be smaller companies structured as MEBOs paid in installments over three to five years..

Foreign companies were invited to make cash tenders for companies to be privatized, but that did not happen for two reasons. First, the SOF owned only 70 percent of the shares in the companies to be privatized. The remaining 30 percent were held by the five private ownership funds (POFs), whose shares were represented by certificates, later vouchers, that had been distributed free to adult Romanians. This greatly added to the complexity and slowed the pace of privatization.

In addition, Finance Minister Georgescu kept insisting that the SOF not sell its ownership interest in large companies at prices determined by the market but only at a minimum price determined by the government, thereby effectively pricing shares out of the market. This was a populist measure that blocked the inflow of the foreign investment capital Romania needed to re-structure its money-losing SOEs and RAs and reduce its current account deficit, which had imploded due to increased imports in the period leading up to national elections in November 1996.

INCREASED AMERICAN INTEREST IN ROMANIAN INVESTMENT, BUT ONLY A FEW DEALS CLOSE

When I first arrived as ambassador in December 1994, most American busi-nessmen in Bucharest were middlemen trying to connect Romanian busi-nesses with American investors. With nothing to offer themselves, they were trolling for fish with unbaited hooks. After the initial wave of privatizations, real businessmen started to show up. In March 1995 a high-level team from Crane Corporation, a large American industrial products company, came looking to expand its existing relationship with a Romanian valve manufac-turer. The team was led by Crane's chief financial officer, a sign that Crane was serious. But no deal was made, for the reasons previously discussed.

A short time later, Peter Ehrenwald, director of Boeing Aircraft's commercial aircraft group, sought the embassy's support for the sale of Boeing civilian aircraft to Tarom. Unfortunately, Tarom was broke. A sale would require financing from the U.S. Export Import Bank, which in turn required a Romanian government sovereign guarantee, which I explained to Ehrenwald was unlikely. Tarom had a large operating deficit. It needed to become profitable before a government guarantee would be available.

U.S. government policy was to encourage direct American investment abroad. When in Washington, I routinely reached out to U.S. companies to inform them of investment opportunities in Romania. My calls were answered at the top—the presidents of Bear Stearns, GE Capital, Lockheed Martin, Colt's Manufacturing, and many others. Some CEOs indicated interest (no one said no), and a few sent people to Romania to look at prospects. Although one or two deals came close, none was made in the first half of 1995. The answer was always the same: there were better opportunities elsewhere—less risk, greater legal certainty, and a friendlier business climate. A breakthrough came later in the year, when Procter & Gamble bought a detergent plant in Timişoara, following which Reynolds Tobacco built a manufacturing plant outside Bucharest and McDonald's opened for business in downtown Bucharest.

THE CONTINUING STRUGGLE TO PRIVATIZE THE ECONOMY

A short time after the MPP passed, in late June Finance Minister Georgescu showed me a draft letter he was proposing to send to the World Bank. It made clear that the Romanian government was not willing to downsize state-owned money losers as long as they were government owned. The letter hedged on the question of privatization but rejected the World Bank's call for automaticity in implementing the MPP. The letter also proposed to reduce from 400 to 100 the number of companies to be sold to strategic investors, meaning primarily to foreign companies in similar or related businesses.

The World Bank negotiations were the traditional tug-of-war between two strong-willed parties—Romania and the World Bank—but there was also a heightened sense of national pride on the Romanian side and a distrust of those it could not control, namely, the World Bank. In the end, Romania would be the loser, but it was hard to get this message across.

Privatization was the most critical part of the economic puzzle, but not the only one. Romania was far behind the West in management skills, technology, modern equipment, and virtually every other aspect of economic life. In the ensuing two years, the United States did much to help bring high-level financial, management, and technology experts to Romania to advise the government and train new management and professionals.

THE DIPLOMATIC SCENE IN BUCHAREST

The United States, together with the large European countries, dominated the diplomatic scene in Romania, but not to the total exclusion of others, mainly Russia, China, Japan, and South Korea.

The Russian ambassador's residence was across a tree-lined boulevard from mine. Russia's ambassador, Yevgeny Ostrovenko, had most recently been ambassador to Afghanistan. After the Soviet army left Afghanistan in 1989, Soviet diplomats were next to leave, but Ostrovenko's plane sat for hours on the runway at Kabul, the passengers not knowing their fate. The plane in front of them was blown up by the mujahideen. Hours later Ostrovenko's plane took off and landed safely in Moscow.

Before serving in Kabul, Ostrovenko had been stationed in Iran, then in Ghana, where he picked up his English. He was avuncular and friendly but hard-line, especially on NATO expansion, claiming that it would harm President Boris Yeltsin and the reformers in Moscow. He stated: "An expanded NATO would draw a line across Europe for the second time in the last fifty years with unforeseeable consequences. Russia and the United States are partners today (even if not allies); why change this?" He did not accept that it was in Russia's interest to bring stability to Central Europe, and that incorporating Romania and others in the region in a democratic security framework would benefit Russia.

I asked Ostrovenko about Prime Minister Chernomyrdin's cancellation of his scheduled visit to Sofia, Bulgaria, in March. His answer was that Yeltsin had scheduled a meeting in Moscow at the same time and that Chernomyrdin was needed at the meeting. The Bulgarians saw it differently: the Russians were balking at paying $100 million owed to Bulgaria and were upset by the recent trip to Washington of Bulgarian President Zhelyu Zhelev and the trip to Bulgaria by U.S. General George Joulwan, commander in chief, U.S. European Command and Supreme Allied Commander. When Ostrovenko saw that his explanation was not working, he came up with a second one: "Yeltsin was leaving the country and Chernomyrdin needed to remain."

When Ostrovenko and I met for a second time, in June, the conversation began where it had left off three months earlier, with Ostrovenko weighing in against NATO expansion. He offered the same arguments: it would divide Europe anew, strengthen Yeltsin's opponents on the right, and be seen in Russia as a hostile act. He rejected the argument I had offered before, that NATO expansion would promote stability in Central Europe. The tone was friendly but the meeting was not productive. Earlier, in Moscow, Russian officials had spoken about "conditions" for NATO expansion that would make it acceptable to Russia. Now it was a flat no, owing more to the upcoming presidential elections in Russia in 1996 than to anything else.

China had a large embassy compound on the northern edge of Bucharest that was built in Ceauşescu's time, when China and Romania were close allies. Romania sided with China in the Sino-Soviet border conflict that persisted from 1969 to 1991, and in turn Ceauşescu sought China's support to protect him from Moscow. With Ceauşescu gone, Romania no longer needed China's support against Russia. As a result, the staff in the Chinese embassy was down from over 100 to 30, including technicians, all living within the embassy compound.

China's ambassador, Li Fenglin, had visited the United States as part of a foreign exchange program in the mid-1980s. He told me he had spent all his time in Kansas City and knew little about the rest of the country. In response to my question about internal conditions in China, he gave the party line, citing the need to preserve discipline; otherwise, China would face chaos. He maintained that the Chinese economy was now largely privately owned, with "peasants," comprising 85 percent of the population, prosperous and content.

Japan's ambassador, Yoshiki Sugiura, a career diplomat, whispered to me "in confidence" that he had been waiting three years without success for

Japanese businessmen to come to Romania. The Japanese invested elsewhere, such as Hungary, the Czech Republic, and Poland, but not in Romania. In these three countries, they encountered tough German competition. He commented wistfully, "Luckily for us, the Germans are not in Romania." But neither were the Japanese. He added, "Who knows? If one large Japanese company comes, maybe others will follow." None came.

Unlike the Japanese, South Koreans proved to be risk takers. South Korea's ambassador, Paik Nak-whan, joyously confided to me that Daewoo Motors, a South Koran automobile manufacturer, had committed to invest $500 million in an automobile plant in Romania. If this panned out, Daewoo would be the largest foreign investor in Romania. The plant was built, but closed within a decade when sales failed to meet projections.

THE HUNGARIAN-ROMANIAN BASIC TREATY AND THE BEGINNING OF TALKS WITH UKRAINE

To comply with the Perry Principles for NATO enlargement, both Romania and Hungary knew they had to sign a basic treaty ending their historical dispute. This was difficult, politically and culturally, for both countries. President Iliescu never stopped talking about the injustices that ethnic Romanians suffered in Transylvania at the hands of ethnic Hungarians. Later, when NATO membership became a real possibility, he shifted gears and became a proponent of the treaty. Hungarian nationalists, for their part, clung to the memory of a Greater Hungary that included Transylvania and parts of Slovakia and Yugoslavia.

In March 1995 Hungary's state secretary came to Bucharest to begin discussions on a basic treaty, but the two sides could not agree on autonomy for ethnic Hungarians in Transylvania. Romania proposed language that called for decentralization and autonomy for individuals at the local level. Hungary did not buy into this. In return, on March 16, Romanian Foreign Minister Teodor Meleşcanu traveled to Hungary to meet with his Hungarian counterpart, László Kovács, but the two again failed to reach agreement. In Budapest, the Liberal Party, part of Prime Minister Gyula Horn's Socialist Party coalition, opposed the treaty, as did the Democratic Union of Hungarians in Romania (UDMR). The best Romania could salvage from Meleşcanu's trip was agreement that neither side would blame the other for the failure and that the two sides would continue to talk.

To complicate matters, Slovakia caved in during its negotiations with Hungary and was ready to sign a basic treaty with Hungary that included a reference to the Council of Europe Recommendation 1201, which provided local autonomy for ethnic minorities. The Slovaks were covering up their capitulation by relying on side language about group rights not being recognized. But this gave the Hungarians a victory that put Romania in a difficult position, trying to hold to their stance that the clarifying language about group rights and territorial autonomy should be in the treaty itself.

A few days later, on April 6, I delivered an "oral note"—actually, I had drafted it—from Secretary of State Warren Christopher to Foreign Minister Meleşcanu urging Romania to move ahead with the basic treaty with Hungary (an oral note is written down to ensure clarity and precision but is delivered orally). Meleşcanu hoped to break the impasse on autonomy by taking some, but not all, of the language from Recommendation 1201 or, alternatively, accepting the language of Recommendation 1201 but with an agreed interpretation appended that would exclude territorial autonomy and group rights. In other words, rights would apply to an individual but not to a group.

Then Romanian-Hungarian negotiations hit another hurdle, fueled by ethnic politics on both sides of the border. This time, UDMR, controlling about 7 percent of the national vote, threatened to make extremist statements that would provoke a similar response from Romanian nationalists, principally Cluj's Mayor Gheorghe Funar and his allies in PUNR. That would have poisoned the atmosphere and made it difficult politically for the Romanian government to move ahead with the treaty. It would take time for the two sides to wear themselves out. The Hungarians needed to recognize that the treaty would not recognize group rights or territorial autonomy based on ethnicity. For the Romanians, the big gulp would be their recognizing the individual rights of ethnic Hungarians to preserve their cultural heritage.

The Romanian government was also in active negotiations with Russia and Ukraine on basic treaties to resolve post–World War II disputes and to disavow the Molotov-Ribbentrop Pact between the Soviet Union and Nazi Germany, which had forced Romania to cede Northern Bukovina and Bessarabia to the Soviet Union in the period leading up to the German invasion of the Soviet

Union. Foreign Minister Meleşcanu told me that Romania realized it could not regain the territories lost to the Soviet Union, and that politically neither Russia nor Ukraine would accept a formal nullification of the Molotov-Ribbentrop Pact, which would leave them open to future territorial claims by Romania. Later, a formula was found to repudiate the moral justification for the Soviet Union's land grab, but that did not change the facts on the ground.

Negotiations on a Romania-Ukraine friendship treaty took numerous turns before an agreement was reached in June 1997. President Iliescu did not oppose the treaty when he was president, nor was he a strong advocate for it. Negotiations were proceeding in two channels: one between the Ukrainian foreign minister, Hennadiy Udovenko, and the Romanian foreign minister, Teodor Meleşcanu; the other through the two countries' intelligence services—SIE Director Talpes and Ukraine's national adviser for security, Volodymyr Horbulin. Talpes's understanding was that Romania would give up its territorial claims to Northern Bukovina, now part of Ukraine but formerly part of Romania, in return for Ukraine's condemning the Molotov-Ribbentrop Pact. There was also a dispute over ownership of Serpent Island, in the Black Sea near the Danube Delta—sometimes described as a pile of rocks. Romania would agree that it belonged to Ukraine, but the two countries would have equal exploration rights in the Black Sea, which was the real game. Director Talpes told me that there were two factions in Ukraine, one headed by President Leonid Kuchma that favored National Security Director Talpes's proposal, and the other (not identified) that was opposed. Early in 1996, Romania's Prime Minister Vacaroiu met with Ukraine's Prime Minister Marchuk in Kiev, hoping for a breakthrough, but nothing came of it.

Foreign Minister Meleşcanu later showed me maps that largely focused on ownership of Serpent Island and the effect ownership of the island would have on oil exploration rights in the Black Sea. The issue was not the island per se, but the mineral rights in the Black Sea that under international law derived from ownership of the island. Later, in Washington, I reviewed maps of the Black Sea with maritime counsel in the Office of the Legal Adviser at the State Department, looking for a solution, which we later came up with, thanks to Ukraine's ambassador in Bucharest, Oleksandr Chaly.

In the spring of 1996, the treaty with Ukraine was still stuck on the issue of the condemnation of the Molotov-Ribbentrop Pact. Russia, Ukraine, and Moldova formed a united front objecting to any reference to the pact in the treaties. The Ukrainians wanted to protect Northern Bukovina and the Moldovans wanted to hold on to Bessarabia. For Russia it was a question of national pride. At one point, the Romanians thought that the treaty with Ukraine could be initialed but not signed in the run-up to the Romanian elections in late 1996. If only initialed, the treaty would not need to be submitted to Parliament or made public.

The Ukrainian ambassador to Romania, Oleksandr Chaly, was my eyes and ears on the other side. He saw the treaty with Romania as necessary for Ukraine's own NATO ambitions. It may seem far-fetched today to think of Ukraine as a member of NATO, but in the early 1990s, with a weak Russia and a Western-leaning Ukraine, it was thought possible. Ukraine was willing to give in on some key issues, including a reference to the Molotov-Ribbentrop Pact; this was even without an explicit renunciation by Romania of its claims to Northern Bukovina. Left unresolved was the question of Serpent Island. Even on this, Chaly indicated that Ukraine would give in, submitting the issue to the International Court of Justice at The Hague or, perhaps, agreeing to joint Ukraine-Romania exploration and production rights in the oil and gas fields under the Black Sea.

The problem, as Chaly saw it, was the lack of political will on the Romanian side to conclude the treaty. He was right. Corneliu Coposu of the PNT-CD, among others, condemned any compromise by Romania on Black Sea issues.

After Coposu's death, Romania's position remained at first unchanged. Ironically, it was a protégé of Coposu, Emil Constantinescu, who, once he became Iliescu's successor as president in December 1996, was a strong advocate for a Romania-Ukraine friendship treaty. This did not happen by accident. A week after he was inaugurated, Constantinescu met in Lisbon with U.S. Vice President Gore, who made the Romania-Ukraine treaty the number one priority on his list of things Romania needed to do. President Constantinescu took this to heart, not knowing that I had written the vice president's talking points. The Romania-Ukraine treaty was signed the following June after a strong push from President Constantinescu. The treaty provided that if the parties failed to reach agreement on the demarcation line for oil and gas exploration in the Black Sea, either side could submit the issue to the International Court of Justice. This happened, and in 2009 the court awarded nearly 80 percent of the disputed territory in the Black Sea to Romania.

VISITS BY HIGH-RANKING U.S. MILITARY

In the course of my service in Bucharest, American military chiefs routinely visited. The first, on March 20, 1995, was four-star General Ronald R. Fogleman, Air Force chief of staff, and his wife, "Miss Jane," together with the Air Force's number two, Lieutenant General Richard E. Hawley, and his wife. This was an official visit at the invitation of the Romanian Defense Ministry and the Romanian army's chief of staff, General Dumitru Cioflina.

After a welcoming lunch at the residence, I accompanied the two U.S. generals at meetings with General Cioflina and Defense Minister Tinca. In General Fogleman's telling, the Romanian military came off well, primarily in the categories of sincerity, commitment, and a strong desire to modernize and adopt American military doctrines. The problem for Romania was money, not willingness.

Later in the afternoon, General Fogleman and I marched shoulder to shoulder in a foot of snow to lay a wreath at the Monument to the Heroes of the Air, not far from my residence. General Fogleman and his wife were from a small town in Pennsylvania's anthracite coal district. They were typical Americans—straightforward, earnest, professional, and dedicated. To my mind, the character of our military had much in common with the character of the American Foreign Service: the motto was service.

Before leaving, General Fogleman asked me what he could do to thank me for my hospitality. My answer was "Send the U.S. Air Force Band to play at the embassy's upcoming Fourth of July party." He said he would, and he did, but not without first maneuvering around Air Force Secretary Sheila E. Widnall. She had issued an order prohibiting U.S. Air Force bands from playing at Fourth of July celebrations abroad, but General Fogleman had given me his word and this officer was also a gentleman. The Air Force Band arrived on schedule and was a big hit.

NATO COUNTRY AMBASSADORS' LUNCHES

From time to time each of the thirteen NATO country ambassadors in Bucharest hosted a lunch at which a high-ranking Romanian official was invited to speak. The first ambassadors' lunch I attended had been on April 4. Foreign Minister Meleşcanu was the invited speaker. He was eloquent but had a hard time persuading the NATO country ambassadors that Romania should be in the first wave of countries to join NATO. Germany's ambassador to Romania, Anton Rossbach, was the most direct, telling Meleşcanu that in his view Romania was in the queue behind the Vişegrad Four (Poland, the Czech Republic, Hungary, and Slovakia), and it was unrealistic for Romania to expect to be in the first wave.

This was hard for Foreign Minister Meleşcanu to swallow. A skilled diplomat playing the only card he had, Meleşcanu fell back on Romania's fear that, if left behind, it would be swallowed up by the "Russian bear." Official Washington had not begun to think about what it needed to do to support countries that were not admitted in the first round. It was important that countries left out not give up hope or, in U.K. Prime Minister Margaret Thatcher's words on another occasion, go "wobbly." Two years later when NATO admitted Poland, the Czech Republic, and Hungary in the first wave, we had an answer, at least for Romania: the United States–Romania Strategic Partnership.

The NATO ambassadors convened again informally two days later, on April 6, at the French embassy. This time the focus was on the Hungarian-Romanian Basic Treaty and, as at the last meeting, on Romania's efforts to be included in the first wave of countries admitted to NATO. My position carried the day. If, as expected, Romania was not in the first wave, we needed to encourage Romania to move toward the West and reward it with tangible benefits. Some ambassadors wanted to defer the issue of reaching out to Romania until after the meeting of the North Atlantic Assembly in Bucharest in the fall. One or two went so far as to criticize the decision already made to hold the next North Atlantic Assembly in Bucharest. This would have been self-defeating. If we told the Romanians they were not fit to sit at the same table with the West, the outcome was assured: political forces in Romania opposed to the West, primarily Romania Mare and the Socialist Party of Romania, would prevail, and Romania would conclude that despite its best efforts to become part of the West, it would not be accepted. We needed to use carrots, not just sticks.

Opinions on Romania in other countries varied. Germany was the least friendly. This changed after Emil Constantinescu became president in December 1996. Constantinescu, a Christian Democrat, had strong ties to Germany's Christian Democratic Party, headed by the German chancellor, Helmut Kohl, as had Constantinescu's mentor, Corneliu Coposu. The Norwegians, Dutch, Belgians, and Danes were generally unfriendly, a holdover from Ceaușescu's day reflecting also an anti-communist stigma that carried over to President Iliescu. The British were "British": proper but not forward-leaning. The French were paternalistic and patronizing toward Romania without offering real support. Italy, Greece, Spain, Portugal, and Turkey were opportunistic, looking for economic opportunities in Romania, but not otherwise engaged. The United States, Canada, the British ambassador, Andrew Bache, and the German ambassador, Anton Rossbach, saw Romania as too big and, potentially, too important to give up on.

My third lunch with NATO ambassadors was on a hot, sunny day in June; it took place outdoors in the garden at the German embassy. Fortunately, we were in the shade overlooking an extensive rose garden and a gracefully shaped decorative pool, in which Germany's iconoclastic ambassador, Anton Rossbach, plunged for a swim each morning, weather permitting. Our guest was Ion Ratiu, a leader of the Peasant Party who during communist rule lived in London, traveling widely in the West and reputedly making a lot of money. Now, at age seventy-eight, he was back in Romania. In his outlook, manner, and appearance he was more Western than Romanian, silver-haired and urbane. He was critical of most things in Romania including President Iliescu, the PD leader, Petre Roman, and his own PNT-CD, starting with its leader, Coposu. Ratiu saw himself as the rightful heir to the former National Peasants Party of Iuliu Maniu, but by fleeing to London during the communist period, he had forfeited his chance to succeed Maniu and ended up publishing an expatriate newspaper, *Cotidianul*, printed on presses paid for by USAID. Pro-West, he was an articulate spokesman for Romania in the North Atlantic Assembly, one of the few Romanians who could hold his own in Western-style debate. Ratiu, a warm colleague, was a frequent guest at my residence.

ARRANGING ILIESCU'S INVITATION TO THE OVAL OFFICE

In late April, when I returned to Washington, I had immediately gone to see Deputy National Security Adviser Sandy Berger at the White House. He was a strategic thinker, able to put policy pieces together to create a workable design that was imaginative and practical. Sandy, President Clinton's principal gatekeeper, agreed to a fall meeting for President Iliescu with President Clinton in the Oval Office. Once the invitation was set, I called Iliescu in Bucharest to give him the good news he had been requesting for months. In a matter-of-fact voice, he responded, "When the invitation arrives in writing, I shall be pleased to accept." Iliescu had suddenly become "Mr. Cool."

Taking advantage of the Oval Office invitation to President Iliescu, I met with him immediately upon my return to Bucharest. Bounding into the room in Cotroceni, dispensing with protocol, he immediately asked about the White House meeting, now planned for September. He was also encouraged by the outcome of his recent meeting with Max Watson, deputy director of the IMF: Iliescu's take-away from the meeting was that Romania would soon sign the standby loan with the IMF, which would provide Romania with the liquidity it needed to buy foreign currency. But then he quickly added that reaching agreement with the World Bank on the FESAL remained doubtful. Returning to the subject of presidential meetings, I conveyed to him former president Bush's invitation for him to meet with an energy group in Houston. Again there was a big smile and a loud yes. He planned to be in New York for the UN General Assembly the last week in October but preferred to fly to Houston after the White House meeting ("sooner rather than later" were his words).

Iliescu's high spirits did not last through my recital of things he might do in advance of his upcoming White House meeting. I started off with the restitution law for private dwellings. Apartment units had been privatized immediately after the revolution, but the privatization had been widely criticized in the West for limiting restitution to persons living in Romania. He spoke with great emotion about not wanting to benefit former owners, some of whom owned multiple dwellings and were now living abroad. He mentioned, among others, Ion Ratiu, who, he claimed, owned thirty-seven buildings in Bucharest before the war and during Ceaușescu's reign had lived in

London making money. Ratiu's home in Bucharest had been attacked during the miners' strike in 1991. In President Iliescu's words, "Romanian emigrés should come back to Romania if they want compensation. Otherwise, too bad; they did not suffer like the rest of us." As he often did on such occasions, he exclaimed that he did not want to be dictated to by "Brezhnev and the Germans" and, without saying it, by me. My answer was the obvious one: "I am not dictating nor am I in a position to dictate. You and your government have to decide what is best for Romania. But, as you have repeatedly told me, Romania's future lies with the West; there are certain norms Romania needs to live up to if it is going to be part of the West. Respect for private property is one of them." President Iliescu quieted down and nodded approval of some of my other suggestions, such as getting on with the Hungarian-Romanian Basic Treaty, the IMF and World Bank agreements, and business privatization. The long saga continued.

A few days later, on June 16, President Iliescu asked me to return to Cotroceni to discuss his upcoming trip. Should he go only to Washington, or to three or four other cities to meet with Romanian-American business groups and local politicians? Should his trip to Washington be official only, or should he try to promote trade and investment? Should he bring private businessmen or only government officials? He also wanted to visit Los Angeles, where his "adopted" son, Mihai Sion, the Romanian consul, lived with his movie-star wife. (Sion had been orphaned at an early age and Ion Iliescu and his wife, Nina, who were childless and close neighbors, helped raise Mihai.) Sion wanted to schedule high-level West Coast meetings for Iliescu. I suggested Washington, followed by Los Angeles, leaving the rest of his U.S. itinerary for his return in October, when he would be attending the UN General Assembly in New York. I tried to balance Ambassador Mihai Botez's desire that President Iliescu visit only Washington with the strong pull of Los Angeles. Iliescu agreed with this plan. The remainder of the meeting was taken up with more substantive issues. Number one was signing the Hungarian-Romanian Basic Treaty. I explained to him that this would help Romania's NATO quest and also relieve some of the anti-Romanian pressure coming from the Hungarian lobby in the United States. Next we discussed agreement with the World Bank on the FESAL. Other hardy perennials included privatization under the MPP and the benefits that would flow from it. The long meeting went well, with President Iliescu taking notes and only occasionally digressing with "history lessons"—usually berating Hungarians.

EXXON SAYS NO TO ROMANIA

When I was in Washington later in the summer to conclude the details for President Iliescu's White House visit, I spoke with Norman Schuld, Exxon's head of international economics and planning, the upshot of which was that Exxon was not likely to pursue investment in Romania. In 1994 Exxon had set up a "new business development group" to look at potential investments in seventeen countries. Romania was not on the list. Like other American petroleum companies, Exxon was waiting for Romania to decide how and when it was going to privatize its extensive upstream and downstream petroleum industry, whether it was going to establish an integrated oil company, and, if it did, whether it would allow a free market to operate side by side with the integrated company. Until these matters were sorted out, large multinational oil companies were not coming to Romania. Exxon promised to incorporate these views in a white paper I could deliver in Bucharest to let the Romanian government know what it needed to do to attract strategic investors. Other countries such as Malaysia were stepping up their support of foreign investment, leaving Romania further and further behind.

MY COLLISION WITH WASHINGTON POWER POLITICS

The array of government and quasi-government agencies charged with spending U.S. taxpayers' dollars dispensing foreign aid has few rivals for bureaucratic complexity and red tape. At the time, the principal U.S. aid agency, USAID, was housed in the same building as the State Department. Although each guarded its prerogatives, they closely coordinated their operations. After the fall of communism, USAID inaugurated cookie-cutter-like programs throughout former communist Europe but wisely added technical assistance to advise Romania and other recovering economies on everything from capital markets to bank privatization and more. It also administered enterprise funds established by Congress for each of the former communist countries of Eastern Europe. The Romanian American Enterprise Fund was set up in 1995 with $61 million in seed capital. Larger funds were established in Poland ($255 million), the Czech Republic ($65 million), and Hungary ($73 million). Added to the foreign aid mix was the U.S. Trade and Development Agency, the Overseas Private Investment Corporation, plus the old standby, the Peace Corps (providing assistance but not financial aid).

Not to be left out of the aid business were our two national political parties, which persuaded Congress to establish and fund the National Democratic Institute (NDI) and the International Republican Institute (IRI) to promote economic and political reform in Central and Eastern Europe. As far as I knew, the NDI played by the rules that prohibited it from engaging in partisanship politics. Not so the IRI. In the run-up to Romanian elections in the fall of 1996, the IRI funneled funds and advice to the political opposition, principally the Christian Democratic Party (PNT-CD) favored by Senator Jesse Helms (R-N.C.) and his protégé in the House, Congressman Funderburk (R-N.C.). PNT-CD was heavily funded by the Christian Democratic Union in Germany. When I raised objections to the IRI's funding PNT-CD, all hell broke loose. The IRI stopped its other programs in Romania, all perfectly legal, and, like an ill-tempered child, picked up its marbles and went home. This led to an exchange of letters between IRI's president, Lorne Craner, and me. The administration backed me, but Craner's tirades led to angry calls to the White House from Congressman Robert Livingston (R-La.)—he later resigned after confessing to adultery—and in 1997 from the redoubtable John McCain (R-Ariz.), with whom I met at the request of National Security Adviser Berger to explain to him why I had done what I did. Nothing came of it, but I learned a lesson: in Washington being right is not enough.

THE HUNGARIAN-ROMANIAN BASIC TREATY: THE VIEW FROM WASHINGTON

As expected, in June President Clinton raised the issue of the Hungarian-Romanian Basic Treaty in his White House meeting with the Hungarian prime minister, Gyula Horn, and Secretary of State Christopher followed up the next day, telling Horn that Romania would agree to a specific reference to Council of Europe Recommendation 1201 in the basic treaty providing there was interpretive language excluding application of group rights or territorial autonomy based on ethnicity. (I had cabled this language to the State Department after the dinner with Chamber of Deputies President Nastase and follow-up with Foreign Minister Meleşcanu.) Horn bobbed and weaved, saying he could accept the proposed language only if the interpretive part was in a separate document signed by the two foreign ministers. This was a potential stumbling block. If the Romanian side dug in and insisted that the interpretive language be in the basic treaty itself, I argued we should weigh in on the Romanian side. After all, the Romanians were making the major concession. State agreed. A year later in July 1996, Hungary agreed. The delay was due mainly to the concurrent negotiations between Hungary and Slovakia in which Slovakia agreed to the formula proposed by Hungary's Prime Minister Horn in his June meeting with Secretary Christopher.

CHALLENGES TO PRIVATIZING ROMANIA'S ECONOMY

Petty jealousy, intramural competition, and jockeying for power on the Romanian side continued to complicate efforts to accelerate economic reform. Finance Minister Georgescu had the same aversion as President Iliescu to downsizing SOEs and privatizing them by sales to strategic investors. SOF president Dima was not helpful. This left it up to Economic Reform Minister Mircea Coşea and Secretary General Hrebenciuc, one with an official title, minister for economic reform, and the other with political power but with a nebulous title, secretary general, that suggested everything and nothing. I met with the two in their offices on July 8. This time Secretary General Hrebenciuc was wearing blue jeans and boots, a real Romanian cowboy. Coşea was wearing a tie and jacket, no cowboy he. (Later, when I mentioned Hrebenciuc's outfit to Coşea, he said disdainfully that Hrebenciuc had only come to the office to meet me, whereas he, Coşea, had a full day's work ahead. One-upmanship was an intramural sport in Romania.)

Hrebenciuc had been steering a deal through the Romanian government, put together by George Paunescu, to buy the Intercontinental Hotel from the

SOF. He tried to persuade me that Marriott Corporation had made a mistake in looking to Chamber of Deputies President Nastase for help. The subtext here was that, unlike Hrebenciuc, Nastase was not part of the old boy network of former communists and Securitate. At the same meeting, I went over the proposed USAID program for privatization, market reform, and capital markets, a package worth $42 million. I told Hrebenciuc I was prepared to push it, provided the Romanian government signed on and understood that if performance goals were not met, the money would stop. Hrebenciuc said yes, but then he always said yes. In the end, nothing came of it. Both the Romanian side and the EU nixed it.

Marriott Corporation lost the Intercontinental Hotel deal but was later chosen, at our urging, to manage a new Grand Hotel next to the Defense Ministry in Bucharest, a 500-room hotel and office building. The financial partner was an Austrian group that brought Romanian "insiders" into the deal. We still needed to overcome Defense Minister Tinca's objections that the proximity of the hotel to the Defense Ministry would allow "spies" to electronically eavesdrop or use high-powered telescopes to read confidential documents. I persuaded him that this was unlikely. But then, one never knows in Romania whether such concerns are genuine or a ruse. Our diplomats in Paris have long voiced unease at the proximity of the Hotel Crillon across the narrow street from our embassy.

The atmospherics were very different in the case of McDonald's. When McDonald's' Golden Arches first opened in Moscow on January 30, 1990, it made the front page of the *New York Times*, complete with a picture. McDonald's' opening in Bucharest in June 1995 did not make it into the *New York Times*, but for Romanians it was a big story. One headline read: "Finally the Americans have come to Bucharest; we have been waiting 50 years for you"—a reference to the 1945 Yalta agreement. McDonald's' Golden Arches were a welcoming sight in drab, still communist-looking Bucharest. McDonald's planned to open 100 eateries in Romania by the end of the decade. It was one response to the unrequited love expressed by Chamber of Deputies President Nastase and other Romanians when they asked, "Where are the Americans?"

DEFENSE MINISTER GHEORGHE TINCA
GOES TO WASHINGTON

The meeting in Washington between the civilian defense minister, Georghe Tinca, and his Washington counterpart, Defense Secretary William Perry, on June 22 was a historic occasion. Perry was impressed with Tinca, and the two of them, with their civilian and military aides, had a productive meeting. The principal focus was on bilateral military cooperation, and here the groundwork was laid for the "strategic partnership" that emerged two years later and its subsequent implementation, leading to the deployment in 2016 of U.S. forces in the Black Sea and the advanced positioning of U.S. military equipment in Romania.

Tinca focused on nineteen interoperability plans, which he hoped would lead to further science and technology cooperation with the U.S. government, with emphasis on research and development to support reform of the Romanian army. This would also help the Romanian defense industry to restructure, increase employment, and upgrade technology across the board. Tinca was fashioning specific proposals from the Perry Principles that fit U.S. military doctrine. He also talked about a role for Romania in enabling a small U.S. naval presence in the Black Sea. In this regard, he offered the Mangalia Shipyard, on an inlet of the Black Sea, for use by the U.S. Navy as well as a modern military hospital near the Black Sea. Added to this was his offer of two firing ranges on the Black Sea shore, equipped for use by missiles with electronic measuring monitors. The NATO chant came up in the form of Tinca's proudly stating that the Romanian Parliament had unanimously approved a government decision to "integrate" with NATO (which was half the battle) and commended Perry's repeated assurances that there was "no short or long list" for membership. He concluded by saying that Romania would endeavor to meet the criteria for admission—whereby he overlooked Romania's foot-dragging on economic reform.

The only sour note was Tinca's weak reply to Perry's question about two U.S. official reports, one on Romanian arms sales to Iran, Iraq, and other pariah countries, and the second on Romanian missile stockpiling. Tinca said merely that his investigation was continuing but that Romania's arms exports were small in today's numbers. The issue was credibility, not numbers. Tinca admitted that Romania had missiles with a range under 300 kilometers. He then added that Romania had no chemical or bacterial weapons or materials. The questions relating to Romania's dealings with Iran and Iraq had been prompted by me. Perry had not been previously briefed on what Romania had been doing, nor did he know that Tinca himself was involved in the negotiations with Iran.

A few weeks later we received information that Romania was selling steel bars to Iraq, in violation of the UN embargo. At my urging a demarche was delivered to the government of Romania demanding that it stop the shipment. The government declined, insisting that the destination was Jordan, not Iraq. This may have been technically correct, but the Jordanian company was fronting for Iraq.

THE FOURTH OF JULY

American Independence Day is celebrated in American embassies around the world, affording a unique opportunity to throw a party and combine it with diplomacy. In Bucharest the Fourth of July party was a major event. In the lead-up to the 1995 celebration, we decided to drop the usual formal diplomatic fare in favor of a down-home American party with hot dogs, hamburgers, ice cream, and the rest. When the day arrived, if I had closed my eyes, it would have felt like Iowa. More than 3,000 guests attended, including the president of Romania, most members of the government, Romanian military leaders and clergy, notable Romanians and assorted American ex-pats. American businesses generously pledged cash to help defray the cost of the party or supplied food and drinks. For example, the Mars candy company sent a thousand Mars Bars, McDonald's furnished 1,500 Big Macs, Coke and Pepsi delivered drinks, and Miller furnished 300 liters of beer. Kosher hot dogs came from Dobbs in Chicago, freight free courtesy of Romania's Tarom Airlines.

The number of guests was the largest ever; there were balloons, crepe paper, a twenty-two-piece band, pizza, hot dogs, hamburgers, and beer. It was a marked change from the formal diplomatic receptions of the past, and a welcome one. The official hours were from 6 to 8 p.m., but at 8 p.m. most guests were still milling about, including President Iliescu, who in addition to being warm and friendly spoke good English (unlike Prime Minister Nicolae Voiculescu or Iliescu's successor, Emil Constantinescu). To his credit, after he became president, Iliescu taught himself English. It always puzzled me that President Constantinescu, who had earned a doctorate in geology from Duke University, was only comfortable speaking Romanian and French, not English.

It was also the tradition that a week after the July Fourth party, all Romanian Americans and Foreign Service nationals who worked at the embassy came to the residence for a second party, this time a picnic supper. I was there all three years. It was a wonderful scene, with children of all ages running about, parents and grandparents spread out over the two-acre garden adjoining the residence, playing games, drinking beer, eating, singing, and dancing.

DEATH OF ROMANIAN AMBASSADOR BOTEZ

On July 11 I received a late-night call from the Romanian Foreign Ministry that Mihai Botez, the Romanian ambassador to the United States, had died in a Bucharest hospital. When he had entered the hospital a few days before, his condition was not deemed serious. He was fifty-four years old.

The next day, Mihai's widow, Magda, came to see me at the residence. She was composed but obviously under enormous strain. She asked two things: that I remain ambassador, this being Mihai's wish, and that I try to persuade Dr. Nicolae Cajal, president of the Romanian Jewish Federation, to be the new Romanian ambassador to Washington. It was unlikely that I could fulfill her second wish: Cajal, then seventy-five, was committed to remaining in Romania as head of the Jewish community.

Over the next few months I conferred regularly with President Iliescu and Foreign Minister Meleşcanu on a suitable candidate to be the next Romanian ambassador to the United States. Various names were floated, but for one reason or another—Securitate background, President Iliescu's reluctance to part with key staff, or personal considerations—no suitable candidate surfaced. Three months later I suggested Mircea Geoana, the press spokesman at the Foreign Ministry, be appointed ambassador, but this is a later story.

HIS BEATITUDE THE ORTHODOX PATRIARCH TEOCTIST

More than 90 percent of Romanians are nominally members of the Romanian Orthodox Church. This makes church and nation one in spirit and identity and confirms the importance in Romania of the church's patriarch. Teoctist was elected patriarch by the Romanian Holy Synod in 1986.

When I called on Teoctist on July 10, I was immediately struck by his remarkable physical resemblance to the late Rabbi Rosen: he had the same high cheekbones and round face. Both had Moldavian roots; perhaps in the distant past they even had a common ancestor. Patriarch Teoctist showed me around his residence, beautiful, yet also depressing—heavily laden with Eastern Church iconographic art, which, like minor keys in music, I found soulful but not uplifting. Patriarch Teoctist said I was the first American ambassador to call on him in his ten years in office. He knew I was Jewish. This, plus my being an American, skewed his comments toward the words he thought I wanted to hear—about liberty, justice, tolerance, and so forth.

Teoctist, eighty years old in 1995, had been badly compromised by Ceauşescu's Securitate. After the 1989 revolution, he offered to resign as patriarch, fearing his ties to Ceauşescu would lead to his being denounced, but when conditions improved and the government did not interfere in church affairs, he remained in the post. In our conversation, he made much of his friendship with Rabbi Rosen, whom he considered a fellow "believer." When I told him that two of the seven Romanian senators who signed the letter to Senator Helms asking him to vote against my confirmation were orthodox priests, he expressed surprise and stated that the implied anti-Semitism was contrary to church doctrine and that the clergy had been ordered to abstain from political activity. As far as I know, no one in the church had been disciplined for political activity, including the two priests who signed the letter.

Before I left, Patriarch Teoctist and I toasted each other with cognac, which, he solemnly explained, was strictly medicinal, reminding me of a similar toast with a Romanian Catholic cardinal in Hungary ten years before. Patriarch Teoctist remained a friend and even came to one of our July Fourth receptions, a first for the patriarch of the Romanian church. For an ambassador in Romania, having the national church on your side was a definite plus.

VANDALISM IN BUCHAREST'S JEWISH CEMETERY

During the night of July 12, the Jewish cemetery in Bucharest was vandalized. More than 100 tombstones were overturned. On hearing this, I immediately went to take a look. The cemetery was enormous and offered its own silent and sad story of Jewish life in Romania. In one section were the graves of the 106 Jews massacred by the Iron Guard in January 1941, many of whom had been young, in their late teens and early twenties. As far as I could tell from the tombstones, they were all men, including Romanian Jewish World War I veterans, a distinction that did not save them from the Iron Guard. Tombstones had photographs of the deceased, a common practice in Eastern Europe and Russia. Some other tombstones depicted the craft or profession of the deceased, a cement piano for a pianist, a lathe for a craftsman, and so on. The vandalized section was badly overgrown; the remaining Jewish community was simply too few in number to maintain the vast space. The police arrested a group of youngsters, all under age thirteen, who as minors could not be tried under Romanian law. If these youngsters were the actual vandals, they would have needed tools to cut the heavy metal chain fence and the muscle to overturn heavy tombstones. Incidents like this are hard to unravel. On the one hand, there is a temptation to make more out of them than called for, given the history of anti-Semitism in Romania and elsewhere in the region. On the other hand, to ignore such incidents is to invite repetition. I later held a well-attended press conference to call attention to the vandalism, which was front-page news in Romania; I called on the government to take action to prevent future incidents.

FROM THEOLOGY TO INTRIGUE

The director of Romanian Internal Security, Virgil Magureanu, came to see me on July 11. A starker contrast could not be imagined than that between him and Patriarch Teoctist. Magureanu was anything but soulful. He was sphinxlike, his true personality obscured by an impenetrable veil. He told me the Russian intelligence service was seeking the SRI's cooperation in combatting the Russian mafia in Romania while at the same time using the same mafia to further Russia's political purposes. According to Magureanu, the Russian mafia was smuggling arms through Romania to the Middle East with the cooperation of the Bulgarians. This was probably true. Magureanu, in his own way, generally leveled with me. He wanted our help in combatting smuggling and terrorism. He seemed delighted by my invitation for him to visit FBI and CIA headquarters in Washington in the fall, to build the bilateral relationship. I did not know where Magureanu stood in the internal Romanian hierarchy, but I knew that he had both friends and enemies. Meanwhile, he told me he was writing a "white paper" on the operations of the Securitate from the late 1950s to the late 1970s, including the career of Ion Pocepa, a three-star general and head of the Securitate, Ceaușescu's Romanian Foreign Intelligence Service, who defected to the United States in 1978. According to Magureanu, Pocepa and his fellow "spooks" were engaged in widespread criminal activity, including inveigling dissidents abroad to return to Romania, where they could be eliminated by Ceaușescu's goons. He saw the Russians as being up to their old imperialist game, but owing to their limited power, restricting their efforts to persuading Romania not to move closer to the West. Magureanu claimed that the Russians were using Mayor Funar of Cluj for this purpose. I very much doubted it.

FINAL PLANNING FOR PRESIDENT ILIESCU'S WASHINGTON VISIT

By August, plans for President Iliescu's trip to Washington in September were nearly in place. The White House's NSC staff had put together an interagency team to map out his schedule. Then an article appeared in the *Washington Post* reporting the sale of the Intercontinental Hotel in Bucharest to Romanian "insiders"—the Paunescus—not to Marriott. This did not help the atmosphere for the visit. The article suggested that the Romanian government intended to sell its "gems" to domestic insiders; foreign investors need not apply. This was not far from the truth and reflected the negative thinking of President Iliescu and Finance Minister Georgescu. On the merits, Marriott's offer was better than the Paunescus', but the latter had the inside track. They knew it and so did Secretary General Hrebenciuc, who had told me as much a couple months earlier, saying that the Intercontinental would be sold to the Paunescus. The Romanian government had hired an American public relations firm, APCO, to improve its image in the United States. The sale of the Intercontinental to Marriott would have helped Romania's image a lot more. Now it was APCO to the rescue.

There were numerous follow-up meetings with President Iliescu at Cotroceni to work on his Washington trip. Iliescu was usually outgoing and friendly, crediting me with obtaining the Oval Office meeting and now helping him plan his week in Washington. I suggested he speak at the National Press Club and address the Center for Strategic and International Studies. He readily agreed. This would be in addition to official meetings with Vice President Gore, National Security Adviser Tony Lake, and the secretaries of state, defense, treasury, and commerce. Before going further, I asked him what he wanted to accomplish in Washington. This drew a long pause, followed by words about American investment. In response, I suggested he host a lunch in Washington for CEOs of major American corporations that might be interested in doing business in Romania, such as Procter & Gamble, Amoco, Marriott, PCA, Boeing, Lockheed Martin, and other potentially interested companies. I agreed to ask Commerce Secretary Ronald Brown to speak at the lunch.

The American ambassador is expected to return to Washington when the head of state of the country to which he is posted pays an official visit. The head of state also is supported in most ways by his own country's ambassador in Washington. After the death of Mihai Botez, Romania did not have an ambassador in Washington. The lack of staff and experience on the Romanian side and the importance of President Iliescu's trip led me to take an unusually prominent role in organizing and preparing the visit. President Iliescu's visit would be the first official visit by a Romanian head of state since Ceaușescu's visit almost twenty years before. The Oval Office meeting was set for Tuesday, September 26; President Iliescu was to arrive the night before and stay through Saturday.

Both countries had a stake in the success of the visit, but I also saw President Iliescu's visit as an opportunity to impress upon him and his government the need to move ahead with economic reform and strengthen Romania's democratic institutions. We were counting on President Iliescu to keep Romania on track to join the West. Accordingly, I encouraged Iliescu to focus on present and future plans for his country and to leave Romania's grievances at home. I began drafting language for him to use in speaking at the National Press Club and the Center for Strategic and International Studies, plus talking points for Oval Office and cabinet-level meetings and for his to-be-scheduled breakfast with Vice President Gore. It may seem strange that I was, to some degree, on both sides shaping talking points for both leaders to use, but this passed for normal in the heady days of post–Cold War Europe. President Iliescu was also meeting with the editorial board of the *Washington Post* and with the IMF general director, Michel Camdessus, and James Wolfensohn, president of the World Bank. These were all top-line meetings, and a first for a Romanian president. A lot rode on the outcome: they offered Romania a chance to catch up to its westernizing neighbors.

The preparation routine became familiar: President Iliescu and I would sit together with shirtsleeves rolled up, going over the schedule. I would give him drafts of speeches and talking points for him to revise and approve. At one meeting President Iliescu, to my surprise, did not want to talk about the trip at all, but about a speech he was giving the next day, August 30, on the fifty-fifth anniversary of the Vienna Diktat of 1940, when Hitler forced Romania to cede the Banat in western Romania and much of Transylvania to Hungary. President Iliescu's prepared speech called for Hungarian-Romanian reconciliation. This was a major breakthrough, with President Iliescu publicly acknowledging that there were legitimate interests on both sides. No doubt Romania's NATO aspirations were the reason for Iliescu's change of heart. Our strategy of encouraging reconciliation was paying off.

MAKING THE ROUNDS IN BUCHAREST

August was also a time for catch-up meetings with Ministers Meleşcanu, Georgescu, Coşea, and Diplomatic Adviser Chebeleu. Foreign Minister Meleşcanu gave a tour de force. He had just returned from Belgrade, where he was told that the Serbian government was willing to end the conflict in Bosnia on the basis of a U.S. initiative designed and led by National Security Adviser Tony Lake that summer. This was the first inkling of the beginning of a process that led to the Dayton Accords, which ended the horrific war in Bosnia. Meleşcanu reported that the Serbs were fearful that the recent Croatian military success in Krajina would cause Bosnian Serbs to pressure Serbia to send its army into Bosnia. This would be a major military escalation, likely leading to war between Serbia and Croatia. Serbia knew that Russia—historically Serbia's patron—would not provide it diplomatic cover or support it militarily. In fact, Serbia was convinced that Russia was playing its own game. Meleşcanu's comments were surprisingly accurate and confirmed that the decision by Lake to "unleash" the Croatians had a moderating impact on Serbia, which up to that point had the field largely to itself. Knowledgeable foreign policy experts in the United States later credited Lake, not Holbrooke, with the authorship of the strategy that led to the Dayton Accords and ended the war in Bosnia.

Meleşcanu was also a realist. He knew that Romania would not become a member of the EU anytime soon, nor would it be admitted to NATO in the first round. To stay in the race, he wanted Romania to establish a free trade association with other countries in Central Europe as a stepping-stone to EU membership. Absent NATO's protective umbrella, Meleşcanu saw forging a special relationship with the United States as the logical intermediate step. He touted non-Slavic Romania as a bulwark against Slavic hegemony in Eastern Europe. Meleşcanu rightly claimed that, militarily, Poland and Romania were ahead of the others. Once they became part of NATO, the rest of Central Europe would fall into line, creating a "cordon sanitaire" against Russia extending from the Baltics to the Black Sea. Meleşcanu made the most of his brief but had few cards to play. I explained that his pitch would be a difficult sell in the United States as long as Romania played it both ways: flirting with China, maintaining its previous contacts with the pariah states Iran and Iraq, while posturing as a bastion of democracy in Central Europe. This was not something Meleşcanu wanted to hear, but the message got through.

When I met with Economic Reform Minister Mircea Coşea on August 24, he was his usual plaintive self. He wanted help with bank privatization. Then, after some delay, when he finally met with Jed Smith, our expert from the Treasury Department, the meeting was not a success. Coşea brought in Hildegard Puwak, the ministry's state secretary, number two in the ministry, and a reputed expert on bank privatization. The Romanian and U.S. experts butted heads. The reason: the Romanian government was fearful that large-scale bank privatization would lead to social unrest and political defeat at the polls. There was an added problem with bank privatization. The Romanian government had been using Romania's large state-owned banks to subsidize its agricultural, petroleum, steel, and other industrial sectors. Once the banks were privatized, the loans would move onto the government's books, increasing the budget deficit and endangering Romania's negotiations with the IMF on extension of the standby loan.

THE PRESS AND ME

On August 25, after the meeting with Coşea, I held one of my many press conferences, followed by a separate meeting with Peter Bales, the Reuters bureau chief in Romania. Reuters put out a daily news summary that was widely picked up by the local press. I found Bales to be a straight shooter, which suited me fine.

A short time later, I was interviewed on the government-owned Channel One, which had the largest audience in Romania. I was asked whether I agreed that Romania protected its Jews in that part of Transylvania ceded to Hungary in 1940 under the Vienna Diktat. My answer: "Surely some Romanians helped Jews during World War II, but Romanians were heavily involved in the killing of Jews in Transnistria and elsewhere during the war." This was not what the interviewer wanted to hear. Romanians like to think of themselves as victims, never perpetrators.

RESTITUTION OF JEWISH PROPERTY

On August 27, the U.S. ambassador to the European Union, Stuart Eizenstat, arrived from Brussels to begin negotiations with the Romanian government on the restitution of Jewish communal and personal property. I first took him on a windshield tour of Bucharest, stopping at the Choral Synagogue, which I knew would be of great interest to him. Inside were a group of touring Israelis, who were astonished to meet two American ambassadors, both

Jewish. To compound their amazement, I spoke to them in Hebrew. During the course of the day, Stu— President Carter's former domestic policy adviser and an astute policy guru—became convinced that the Jewish community in Romania should be front and center in the negotiations on restitution. The Romanian government was more likely to agree to give communal properties back to the Jewish community in Romania than to an outside group such as the World Jewish Restitution Organization (WJRO), headquartered in Jerusalem.

As it happened, I urged the Romanians to return some communal properties in advance of President Iliescu's visit to Washington the following month. If they did, Romania would be ahead of Hungary, where the process had been agreed to but nothing had happened. Israel did not care about the Jewish community in Romania. For Israel, it was embarrassing that Jews still lived in Romania, not Israel; if restitution created a backlash in Romania that hurt the Jewish community, so be it, ran the Israeli thinking. Romania's Jews would leave for Israel. This is where Israel thought they should be anyway.

I invited Dr. Nicolae Cajal, the president of the Romanian Jewish Federation, to join Stu and me for breakfast at my residence on August 28. As in the past, Dr. Cajal wanted to avoid a confrontation with the WJRO but at the same time insisted that the Romanian Jewish community be the principal negotiator. He was right. Without consulting the local Jewish community, the WJRO had given Hrebenciuc, in his capacity as secretary general of the government, a four-page statement lifted from a document it used in Hungary. This was a twofold blunder. The document itself was replete with factual errors—Hrebenciuc referred to it in an aside to me as "blah blah blah"—and the WJRO, operating independently from the Romanian Jewish community, was no match for the government of Romania.

Dr. Cajal commanded great respect in Romania for his many contributions to medical science. He was a lovely gentleman and, like many Romanian Jews, was deeply affected by the tragedies that had befallen the Jewish community in Romania throughout history. His watchword was "Avoid confrontation lest it lead to unwanted attention directed against the Jewish community." In the end, Dr. Cajal proved correct. The Romanian Jewish Federation was the beneficiary of restitution payments that enabled it to renovate its synagogues and other communal buildings.

ARRIVAL OF CONGRESSIONAL DELEGATION

Congressional delegations, "CODELs" for short, are regular fare for an American ambassador. The one that arrived in Romania in late August was led by Floyd Spence (R-S.C.), chair of the House Committee on National Security, and two committee members, Solomon Ortiz (D-Tex.) and Steve Buyer (R-Ind.), together with their spouses. Congressman Spence was accompanied by a Navy doctor, a pulmonary specialist who had looked after him for nearly a decade. The group arrived in a U.S. government jet. As was typical for such visits, the CODEL came to my residence for lunch and a briefing before going off to meet Foreign Minister Meleşcanu, Defense Minister Tinca, and Chamber of Deputies President Nastase. After the briefing, which was quite detailed, I expected the CODEL to be loaded for bear. But it was largely hello and good-bye—meaning that either the CODEL had failed to absorb the briefing or the members were uninterested. As an aside, Congressman Spence told me that he had visited 110 countries during his 24 years in Congress. He had forgotten the names of most of them and those he remembered had left little impression. Nastase, being the proud Romanian he was, invited the CODEL to tour the new Hall of the People, the future house of the Romanian Parliament. It was reputed to be the second largest administrative building in the world, an architectural monstrosity resembling a misshapen wedding cake. Under construction for five years under Ceauşescu's direction at a frightful budget-busting cost, it was still incomplete when I arrived. Nevertheless, the CODEL was impressed.

The following night a dinner was arranged for the CODEL by its Romanian hosts. Because it was Friday, the start of the Jewish Sabbath, I was unable to join them. The next morning I walked to the hotel where the CODEL was staying to say good-bye. Everyone was in fine fettle, set for a day visiting the painted churches and monasteries in Bukovina accompanied by Defense Minister Tinca and his wife. Before Congressman Spence left, the press crowded around him asking for a statement. Not entirely sure where he was, he wisely talked about how impressed he was with developments "in your country."

A DAY AT THE BLACK SEA

On August 30 my host in Constanta, Romania's large port on the Black Sea, was Vice Admiral Gheorghe Anghelescu, chief of staff of the Romanian navy. He had invited me on an inspection tour of the Romanian navy at its base at Constanta. Roughly my age, he was due for retirement but was still energetic. The trip from the airport to the Black Sea was memorable as our police escort, driving seventy to eighty miles an hour with horns blaring, scattered cars before us moving in both directions. Admiral Anghelescu patted my knee and whispered, "Welcome to Constanta."

The Romanian navy possessed no capital ships, only one destroyer, commissioned in 1986, a nine-year-old former Russian submarine, and a dozen or so smaller vessels. Shades of *H.M.S. Pinafore*! I was piped aboard the frigate *Mărăşeşti* for a tour of the pride of the Romanian navy. The ship was built in the shipyard at Mangalia to a Romanian design complete with a tiled bathroom that included a gigantic bathtub for Ceauşescu. Lying at anchor most of the time, the only threat the *Mărăşeşti* posed was to the Romanian budget. Like the military everywhere, the Romanian navy had its privileges. Lunch was served at the Romanian Military Hotel. There were the customary toasts, first with Tuical, a distilled Romanian spirit made from plums, followed by wine and champagne. I took a sip each time, but Anghelescu was less temperate, belting them down, becoming more voluble with each glass.

The most interesting part of the journey was a tour of the Constanta Naval Shipyard, which employed roughly 4,000 workers and could simultaneously build two ocean-going ships and repair a third. It was a huge facility. It was still state-owned, needing a government subsidy to survive. The shipyard also needed upgrades and fresh thinking. In communist days, when it had a huge government subsidy, it had built and repaired tankers. Without a subsidy, it was no longer a viable concern.

Later I delivered a speech at Black Sea University in Mangalia, about thirty miles south of Constanta, on U.S. policy in Central Europe, NATO expansion, the EU, relations between NATO and Russia, and what I saw as Romania's role in the new Europe. It was a long speech, but I felt that the message was important. It set forth the criteria for Romania and other aspirants to NATO membership: democracy; no foreign entanglements; civilian control of the military; market economies; free and independent media. A sixth consideration was military preparedness. Here I assigned Romania high marks for its participation in the Partnership for Peace and cited, as major pluses, Romania's recently proposed nineteen interoperability plans. I grouped Romania along with Poland in the first tier for military preparedness and talked optimistically about NATO-Russian cooperation and the viability of an independent, democratic Ukraine. My message was not a personal one but set forth official U.S. policy. Questions followed, then the press had its shot. There was extensive media coverage, headlines, and front-page pictures the next day.

 **8**

Romania's President Comes to the Oval Office

FALL 1995

THE IMF AND THE STANDBY LOAN NEGOTIATIONS

In the summer, the standby loan negotiations with the IMF had started to become unglued. When the IMF team arrived in Bucharest in the fall, it was handed a new set of GDP figures that showed a larger budget deficit than had been agreed. To complicate matters further, according to the IMF team, Finance Minister Georgescu had engaged in one of his soccer-honed negotiating explosions accusing the IMF of playing politics, siding with the PD leader, Petre Roman, and the political opposition. The IMF team left in disgust, recommending against extending the standby loan, meaning that a new agreement would have to be negotiated and submitted to the Romanian Parliament. In other words, a disaster.

I immediately met with Mugur Isarescu, the governor of the National Bank of Romania, who confirmed the accuracy of the IMF's report on the negotiations. There were three issues: the GDP deflator (inflation barometer), the exchange rate for the leu, and huge arrears in the accounts of some of the RAs, principally the electric utility RENEL. Isarescu lamented that Finance Minister Georgescu had fouled up the negotiations. I pointed out that the

IMF board of directors meeting would begin shortly in Washington, and this might be Romania's last chance to get the negotiations back on track. One possibility would be for Finance Minister Georgescu and Governor Isarescu to call the IMF in Washington to try to save the situation. Isarescu agreed, but asked me to get Georgescu's say-so.

I was in Georgescu's office a few minutes later. He was talking on the phone with the prime minister. Georgescu ran a one-man operation. He was the sole decision-maker in the Finance Ministry, and all major economic issues ended up on his desk. When the two of us were alone, I listened patiently to Georgescu's toned-down version of his blow-up with the IMF the day before. In the end, Georgescu agreed to act immediately. Half an hour later he called to tell me that National Bank Governor Isarescu would immediately call the IMF with a revised proposal, agreeing to reduce the 1996 deficit and to accelerate depreciation of the leu (a partial victory). It worked. The IMF agreed to keep talking.

SEPTEMBER 25–29: PRESIDENT ILIESCU'S TRIP TO WASHINGTON

President Iliescu arrived in Washington on September 25, but because it was the first day of Rosh Hashanah, the Jewish New Year, I could not meet him at the airport. Substantive meetings started the next day. I had had a major hand in persuading the White House to invite President Iliescu, and I certainly went all out to support his visit. If Romania was not going to be in the first wave of new NATO members, the Oval Office visit was to reassure Romania that it would not be permanently excluded from NATO and to encourage it to do the things needed to stay on track. I arranged most of Iliescu's meetings in Washington and was at his side throughout his five days in D.C. President Iliescu never forgot what side of the diplomatic table I was on, but I think he saw me as a friend of the new Romania he was trying to build.

President Iliescu's trip to Washington was a success. The meeting in the Oval Office was the high point for him. If a picture is worth a thousand words, that was certainly true for President Iliescu, seen in a photo sitting next to President Clinton in the Oval Office. On the American side, in addition to

President Clinton, those present were Vice President Al Gore, Deputy Secretary of State Strobe Talbott, National Security Adviser Tony Lake, Deputy
National Security Adviser Sandy Berger, Deputy Assistant Secretary of State
Marshall Adair, Dan Fried of the National Security Council, Leon Fuerth,
foreign policy adviser to Vice President Gore, and me. President Iliescu spoke
for about fifteen minutes, touching on NATO, the Romanian-American relationship, the war in Bosnia, MFN, Romania's support for the Partnership
for Peace, and Romania's five-year journey from the death of Ceaușescu to
the present. Unlike Hungary and Poland, he explained, Romania had no external debt in 1989 and in the aftermath of the revolution did not have access
to external capital markets. Its current external debt was just a little over
$4 billion, owed mostly to the IMF and the World Bank. President Iliescu
presented detailed comparisons of Romania's debt to the much larger external debts of other former Soviet bloc countries. This was a theme President
Iliescu would return to many times during his visit.

   President Clinton, in a low-key, friendly voice, said positive things about
Romania's post-revolution progress, its ties to the United States, and the importance of its concluding agreements with its neighbors and assured President Iliescu that the NATO process would be open and that no country or
countries had been selected for early admission. He urged progress on property restitution, citing specifically Jewish property. As for MFN, the president was positive, stating that the administration supported permanent MFN
status for Romania, but that this would require congressional action and that
the administration and Congress did not always see eye to eye. Vice President
Gore said a few words about the environment, President Iliescu having told
him that his book on the environment had been translated into Romanian.
Iliescu had made a point of arranging for the translation in advance of the
visit, commenting that he had read it on his flight to Washington.

   From the Oval Office the two presidents walked together to the front
entrance of the West Wing, where President Clinton introduced President
Iliescu to the press. President Iliescu then stood outside under an umbrella
in a downpour to answer questions, following which the Romanian side plus
Dan Fried and I went to National Security Adviser Lake's office for a follow-
up meeting. The discussion covered no new ground but continued the positive
tone set in the Oval Office.

President Iliescu stayed at the Willard Hotel, two blocks from the White House. After each meeting I returned with him to the hotel.

The next meeting, with U.S. Defense Secretary William Perry at the Pentagon, was the most substantive. Secretary Perry met President Iliescu on the steps of the Pentagon and the two of them entered the building through an honor guard. Secretary Perry was extremely gracious, greeting President Iliescu as a friend and Romania as a valued participant in the Partnership for Peace. The meeting was in the large room adjoining Secretary Perry's smaller private office. Invited to speak first, President Iliescu expressed his condolences on the deaths of Dr. Joseph Kruzel and Colonel Nelson Drew, who along with Robert Frasure, a career Foreign Service officer, had died on August 19 in an armored convoy accident while approaching Sarajevo. He mentioned Romania's interest in procuring U.S. military equipment, emphasizing Romania's role in ensuring stability in Central Europe, along the north–south axis of Poland, Romania, and Turkey.

Perry mentioned his close relationship with Defense Minister Georghe Tinca and congratulated Romania on civilian control of its military. He then turned to the specific issue of the C-130s, with deliveries to start in December 1996 (the United States would work to minimize the cost to the Romanian government). General Dumitru Popa delivered Romania's letter of acceptance of the C-130s. The $10 million grant to Romania under the Warsaw Initiative could not be used for the C-130s and would be better used, Perry said, to improve NATO-mandated interoperability by buying small unit radios, improving language procedures, standardizing ammunition, and rationalizing supplies such as MREs (meals ready to eat). Perry voiced support for Romania's procurement of long-range radar for dual military-civilian use. If asked, the Department of Defense would gladly assist Romania in destroying its Soviet scud missiles, still in Romania (nice way of saying, "Get rid of them"), and expected to provide support for the Cobra project when talks began with Bell on weaponry, engines, and avionics. The United States would also support thirty Romanian students under next year's International Military Education and Training program, a significant increase.

Perry reiterated his unequivocal support for Romania's entrance into NATO but didn't mention a date, noting that no priority was being given to the Vişegrad Four (the Czech Republic, Hungary, Poland, and Slovakia).

NATO would look at each country separately and evaluate it on the basis of the five Perry Principles: democracy, market economy, civilian control of the military, no external conflicts, and interoperability. This did not mean F-15s and F-16s but the ability to operate on the ground stressing communications and the rationalization of supplies and ammunition.

The remainder of President Iliescu's trip was equally productive, starting with a meeting at Treasury with Secretary Robert Rubin. At the State Department, Acting Secretary Talbott greeted President Iliescu at the building's entrance, escorted him to a formal conference room on the prestigious seventh floor, and with great skill established rapport with President Iliescu, recalling his visits to Romania in the early 1970s when he was a *Time* magazine correspondent in Belgrade. An immediate invitation to revisit was extended by President Iliescu and repeated at the end of the meeting. No new issues were raised, but Strobe referred specifically to the pending amendments to the penal code and the U.S. government's position that they were inadvisable. (Strobe knew about President Iliescu's previous assurances to me on the issue that they would "find a way to solve it.")

Encounters on the Hill included an unfriendly session with Congressman David Funderburk in which he accused Romania of a series of actions harmful to U.S. interest. They were not true, and President Iliescu skillfully rebutted them. There was also a meeting with Senators Tom Daschle (D-S.D.), Claiborne Pell (D-R.I.), Hank Brown (D-Ohio), and Chuck Grassley (R-Iowa), the latter being primarily interested in trade issues.

President Iliescu next addressed an audience of 150 at the Center for Strategic and International Studies, a prestigious Washington think tank, and delivered a major address at the National Press Club that was carried nationwide on C-Span.

On the Jewish front, President Iliescu met for a joint breakfast with representatives of the American Jewish Committee and B'nai B'rith and a day or two later visited the Holocaust Museum, where he was greeted with hugs by its chairman, Miles Lerman, a Polish Holocaust survivor. The principal issue of substance at the Holocaust Museum was archival access in Romania that the Holocaust Museum had long sought to fonts (finding aides) covering pertinent Jewish-related documents in the State Archives of Romania (renamed the National Archives of Romania in 1996). President Iliescu's sister-in-law worked in the State Archives, and he defended nonproduction of the fonts, saying that Ceauşescu had destroyed the State Archives building and dispersed its contents. Now that the issue was fonts only, consisting of an estimated 250 pages, the problem could be solved. However, the Romanians continued to stall, citing one excuse after another for reasons that can only be explained as national pride or plain bumbling.

President Iliescu's next three meetings were at the World Bank, the IMF, and the U.S. Export-Import Bank.

Jim Wolfensohn, the president of the World Bank, was charming and supportive. IMF Managing Director Michel Camdessus was less so, where-upon a member of the Romanian delegation turned to me and said, "We prefer the Americans; they are direct and honest."

In Iliescu's meeting at EXIM Bank with its president, Kenneth Brody, the two presidents signed a cooperative financing agreement between the U.S. EXIM Bank and Romania's Exim Bank, another checkmark on the bilateral relations checklist.

Toward the end of Iliescu's week in Washington, Vice President Gore hosted a breakfast for President Iliescu and others in the vice president's mag-nificent official office on the second floor of the east wing of the Old Execu-tive Office Building, built in Second Empire style between 1871 and 1878. Located next to the White House, the OEOB in pre-Pentagon days had been the State, War, and Navy Building. In 1999 it was formally renamed the Eisenhower Executive Office Building. It remains an architectural gem and a tangible reminder of America's emergence as a great power at the turn of the last century. At breakfast, Iliescu gave the vice president a copy of the Romanian edition of his book on the environment. Gore recalled an earlier conversation with Iliescu in which Iliescu had pointed out the similarities between the delta of the Danube and deltas of other great rivers, such as the Nile and the Mississippi, a view Gore shared. The vice president raised the key bilateral issues, pointing out the need for congressional support for MFN without being overly concerned about such bogus issues as seed corn (a reference to Congressman Funderburk's earlier demarche). The real issues, he said, were Romania's relations with Hungary and Ukraine, the situation facing ethnic Hungarians in Romania, NATO enlargement, and restitution of Jewish communal property. In other words, a complete checklist of things

Romania needed to do. President Iliescu got the message and on returning to Romania set about trying to do the things Vice President Gore had told him were needed.

At the *Washington Post*, Iliescu met with the all-star cast consisting of Managing Editor Bob Kaiser, Deputy Editorial Page Editor Stephen Rosenfeld, the columnist Jim Hoagland, and the reporters Jackson Diehl, Tom Lippman, Bob McCartney, and Michael Dobbs. Iliescu made a good impression, explaining why it was necessary to include "extremists" in the government and in the working coalition in Parliament. As on other occasions, Iliescu sought to distinguish between extremists such as Georghe Funar and Vadim Tudor ("not normal people") and those in the Romanian National Unity Party and Romania Mare, who were "normal people." As expected, freedom of the press came up, and here Iliescu, with support from Foreign Minister Meleşcanu, disowned the government of Romania's responsibility for a pending criminal action against two reporters from the Romanian newspaper *Ziua*; in fact, the action was brought by the state prosecutor. Foreign Minister Teodor Meleşcanu later admitted the mistake to me. Iliescu's other media appearances were on CNN's *Worldwide News* and an early morning interview on the Fox Television Network that were not notable.

Later that same day President Iliescu hosted a lunch at the Romanian ambassador's residence for eighteen CEOs from Procter & Gamble, Amoco, Tenneco, Marriott, General Electric, Motorola, General Motors, and others. President Iliescu spoke briefly and appropriately, as did U.S. Commerce Secretary Ron Brown, who was there from beginning to end. Ron also expressed privately to President Iliescu his unequivocal support for graduating Romania to permanent MFN status. It was a first-rate affair. The only regret was that the Romanian side did not take the opportunity to ask each guest to say a few words about his or her company's interest in Romania and put together a suitable press release; tallying the total commitments would have been impressive even if little actually came of them.

A close second to President Iliescu's Oval Office meeting came at the end of his visit: a flight by helicopter from Washington to Norfolk, the headquarters of the Supreme Allied Command Atlantic, where he was greeted by a four-star general, Jim Shannon. He took the salute from a Navy band and saw the raising of the American and Romanian flags with those of NATO members. The sight of the Romanian flag flying alongside those of the NATO members was worth a lot. The highlight was a helicopter landing on the nuclear carrier USS *Enterprise*. It was an impressive show by any standard, but for Romanians whose navy had no capital ships, it was an amazing spectacle. President Iliescu was thrilled to be aboard the *Enterprise*. The helicopters departed for Washington from the flight deck of the carrier, not an everyday occurrence for a Romanian president or for an American ambassador.

President Iliescu was immensely pleased with his Washington visit. Other than when giving formal speeches, he spoke without notes, displaying a good grasp of history, current events, and, on occasion, humor, his favorite line being to encourage "joint ventures," then adding "joint adventures." He combined presidential stature with a politician's love for the crowd. He greeted people and shook hands in American style. He was skillful in difficult or potentially difficult moments such as his meetings on the Hill with Congressman Funderburk and the other members of Congress, and his meeting with the IMF's Camdessus.

Other than television appearances on CNN, C-SPAN, and Fox News, and an article or two in the *Washington Times*, the visit was not covered by the press, something a better-connected embassy could have fixed. The only weak point was the Hill. The Republican leadership—Senators Bob Dole and Jesse Helms and Congressman Newt Gingrich—declined to meet with Iliescu, and those Republicans who did were either hostile (Congressmen Gilman, Smith, and Funderburk) or indifferent. The Democrat senators Daschle and Pell were friendly but largely uninterested.

Important openings were made with the business community, which strengthened Iliescu's position for his upcoming appearance at the energy conference in Houston on October 26. For Romania to take advantage of the opportunity in Houston and beyond, it needed to improve decision-making, reduce corruption, and strengthen the legal framework for investment. It would also need to avoid unforced errors: improvident measures such as the pending amendments to the penal code and the legal proceedings against the two *Ziua* reporters. Looking back, the visit was more impression than substance, but that is typical for visits by heads of state. Americans saw an Iliescu who did not have horns, was open and friendly, and was a huge fan of the United States. President Iliescu saw Americans as favorably disposed to Romania and willing to hear more.

After the president's Washington visit, the major issues confronting Romania were the IMF standby loan extension and the future of the parliamentary coalition that included the PRM and its demagogic leader, Corneliu Vadim Tudor. The Romanian press picked up a *Washington Times* article quoting President Iliescu as likening Vadim Tudor and the PUNR chairman, Georghe Funar, to the Russian ultranational rabble-rouser Vladimir Zhirinovsky. Funar ignored the comparison, but not Vadim. His newspaper, *Romania Mare*, accused Iliescu of selling Romania out to "the Jews and Western interests." President Iliescu reacted angrily, giving his party the green light to break the coalition with PRM. (One down, two to go: PUNR and PSM.)

OCTOBER: THE PRESS, PLOIEŞTI, PETROLEUM, AND PRIVATIZATION

H. L. Mencken famously quipped that the job of journalists is to comfort the afflicted and afflict the comfortable. If so, afflicted Romania was the exception. It received unremittingly harsh coverage. Other than in the *Financial Times*, whose reporter Virginia Marsh took a balanced approach, international press coverage of Romania was uniformly negative. For example, the editorial board of the *Wall Street Journal*'s European edition took a jaundiced view of Romania, skeptical of its progress and suggesting that it had not fully shaken its communist past. The *Economist* regularly bashed Romania, influenced by the Peasant Party's Ion Ratiu, who, despite his advanced age and lack of a political following in Romania, had spent thirty years in London burnishing his image as a major opposition figure.

When Ernest Beck, the *Wall Street Journal*'s reporter covering Romania, tried to convince me that the news side operated independently of the paper's conservative editorial page, I wanted to give him a chance to prove it. Beck looked and acted like a foreign correspondent with his wire-framed glasses, colorful suspenders, and an engaging personality, laced with cynicism (picture Humphrey Bogart in the press room). He wanted to meet President Iliescu, but the president was due to leave in a few days for New York for the UN's fiftieth-anniversary ceremony and then travel to Houston for the energy conference in late October. The only chance for Beck to meet him would be if he got his editors to commit to run a story on Romania in the U.S. edition the week President Iliescu was in New York. Then I would have something to sell to Iliescu and perhaps could begin to turn the tide of negative coverage. I saw Beck later in the week; he was still hoping to see President Iliescu, but with no assurance about a U.S. article, Iliescu's answer would be no.

Ploiești, the oil capital of Eastern Europe, was an hour's drive east of Bucharest, but it was a thousand miles behind the times. It featured prominently in World War II news coverage as American B-25 bombers made regular daytime raids over the oil fields, the principal source of petroleum for Hitler's Wehrmacht. Flying low to see their targets, many of the planes were shot down and American servicemen interned in Romania. By the time I arrived forty years later, Ploiești was still the oil capital of Eastern Europe, but the oil fields themselves were played out. Secondary and tertiary recovery was largely unknown in Romania, and Ploiești's extraction and refining facilities were a generation or further behind the West.

In late October, while President Iliescu was getting ready to visit Houston, I visited Petrobrazi, the largest refinery in Ploiești, built in the 1960s and now operating at less than 50 percent of capacity. Sixty percent of its 7,500 employees were engaged in "maintenance." The plant manager admitted he needed only 3,000 workers; the rest were paid by government subsidies. Petrobrazi was one of five state-owned giant refineries kept afloat by the government. Its catalytic cracker was American brand, Universal Oil Products, vintage 1960. Today, one man with computerized controls could operate the entire system, replacing rooms full of dials, gauges, charts . . . and people.

At another nearby plant I saw the world's largest mobile drilling rig, slated for export to Russia. It was simply enormous. The rig itself was of Romanian design, but the motors were manufactured by Caterpillar USA. The plant where the rig was assembled did not measure up to American standards and survived mainly through sales to a domestic captive market at low prices made possible by a fully depreciated plant and subsistence wages.

Economic backwardness, huge numbers of redundant workers, and government subsidies to support antiquated, uneconomic behemoths held Romania back and prevented it from raising the standard of living of its people and competing in world markets. What I saw in Ploieşti was sadly repeated throughout Romania: steel mills using 1960s Soviet casting furnaces, automobile plants stamping out 1950 models of Dacias with automobile bodies designed in France five decades before, shipyards on the Black Sea that riveted ship hulls using methods out of date in World War II. Privatization was the only answer, even if it meant selling businesses to non-Romanian strategic investors. My take on the sad state of Romanian industrial production weighed on me when, a short time later, I was asked to advise Romanian decision-makers on a new law to facilitate privatization of Romania's petroleum industry.

Privatization of Romania's petroleum industry required a new law that welcomed foreign investment. The task of drafting the new legislation fell to a bipartisan Economic Commission of the Romanian Senate whose members in October sought my advice, no doubt influenced by their realizing that most of the needed capital would come from the United States. I knew something about the issues, having seen Petrobrazi and other outdated Romanian petroleum plants and having been briefed in advance by American petroleum company representatives in Bucharest. I used the opportunity to suggest a provision for international arbitration of disputes, non-revocation of drilling rights except in the case of material contractual default, equal access to the Romanian pipeline, and limitations on the right of the government of Romania to buy oil and gas at other than market prices.

The Romanian senators I met with indicated that the draft law would be amended to incorporate these suggestions, but, as with legislative bodies the world over, anything could happen once the bill reached the Senate floor for a vote. The Romanian Parliament had not adopted procedures such as those in our House of Representatives, where most bills go to the floor under a "closed rule" that limits debate and amendments. To make matters worse, there was little if any party discipline, so each member of the Senate was a voice unto himself or herself. Even so, a few weeks later, in November, the petroleum bill passed without change from our suggested amendments, a major achievement!

ILIESCU'S UN AND HOUSTON TRIP

On October 21, I was in the VIP lounge at Bucharest's Otopeni Airport to accompany President Iliescu to New York when Secretary General Hrebenciuc approached requesting help with the IMF and MFN. As he put it, "It is up to you and Dr. Zinger"—presumably he meant Israel Singer, director of the World Jewish Congress—"to use your influence with Fisher and with the Congress. Dr. Zinger told me he would help when we met in Brussels, and the three of you (including Fisher) have great influence." (Dr. Stanley Fisher was the deputy director of the IMF, and later governor of the Bank of Israel and still later vice chairman of the U.S. Federal Reserve.) What Hrebenciuc was really saying was that we three Jews must know each other because all Jews know each other. The three of us could deliver both the IMF and Congress. Dr. Fischer, a former MIT economics professor and world-renowned economist, had probably never heard of Israel Singer, and if he had, it would have made no difference. Romania's "Mr. Fix-It" was obviously of the view that anyone Jewish had a lifelong bond with the other 12 million Jews around the world and that, collectively, we could fix Romania's financial problems. When I suggested this would not work, he was crestfallen. "How could this be after we went to the trouble to go to Brussels to meet with Zinger and Edgar Bronfman?" Bronfman was president of the World Jewish Congress. The episode highlighted the absurdities that pop up from time to time in the supposedly sophisticated world of diplomacy.

The flight to New York was on an old Boeing 707 that Tarom had sold to a private Romanian airplane leasing company with the right to lease it back for presidential trips. I was seated in the front of the plane across the aisle from President Iliescu. Behind us was a small cabin with a couch on one side and what I assumed were bunk beds for the president and crew. The rear cabin carried the press, a security detail, and the rest of the president's party. In all, there were about eighty on board.

From time to time, two or three "friends of the president" emerged to chat with him. He was in high spirits, talking with journalists and reading an assortment of Romanian newspapers and briefing papers. After lunch, Iliescu, Foreign Minister Meleșcanu, Diplomatic Adviser Chebeleu, and I held a "strategy session" (Meleșcanu's term) on the upcoming trip. I went over the meetings I had arranged and gave President Iliescu an idea what to expect from the editorial boards of the *New York Times* and the *Wall Street Journal* with whom he would be meeting. My advice was to "keep your answers short and forget the history lessons!" It was a tough assignment, but he ended up doing better than he had done the previous month in Washington.

As we approached Kennedy Airport, a cold front moved through, producing strong wind and heavy rain. The plane bounced up and down in the thick cloud cover. Meleşcanu, Chebeleu, and I tightly grabbed our seats, our eyes half closed, but not President Iliescu. He continued reading and talking, seemingly unaware of what was happening.

After we landed I caught up with Iliescu and his official party at the offices of the *Wall Street Journal* for a meeting with the newspaper's editorial staff, followed by an elegant dinner at the Sky Club on the fifty-seventh floor of the old Pan Am Building with a magnificent view of New York City. President Iliescu did well with the *WSJ* editorial board. Peter Kahn, the publisher, attended and seemed to like Iliescu, as did the other *WSJ* editors. Iliescu was at his best. Later, at dinner, he received a "prestigious" award from some supposedly "important" organization. My strong suspicion was that the affair was rigged by APCO, Romania's Washington public relations firm. The attendees were either APCO staff or American businessmen looking for investment opportunities in Romania. If the "sponsoring organization" existed, it was not confirmed. There was mention of similar awards given to Presidents Reagan and Bush, most likely by mail.

Breakfast the next morning was at the Harvard Club in Manhattan, where Iliescu spoke to a group of capital venture firms invited by the Romanian American Enterprise Fund, whose chairman, Bob Wald, a Washington attorney, wanted to find a suitable event to link the fund to Iliescu's two visits to the United States. This was it. Bob, a talented lawyer, did not last long as chairman of the fund. I never figured out whether it was his failing or palace intrigue by the fund's trustees—probably a little of both. When Bob was removed, I had to find a replacement and, luckily, found Harry Barnes, a retired American career ambassador then serving as a consultant at the Carter Center. After a good deal of persuasion on my part, Harry agreed to take the position. Under his direction and the investment know-how of the fund's president, John Klipper, the fund prospered, returning its seed capital to the

U.S. Treasury, with $100 million left over to create a charitable foundation that as of 2017 was still operating in Romania.

From the Harvard Club, on West Forty-Fourth Street, the motorcade moved at glacial speed across Manhattan to the Anti-Defamation League's (ADL) building on the East Side. The ADL's executive director, Abraham Foxman, and its past president, Mel Steinberg, were waiting at curbside to escort us to the top floor of the building, which had a magnificent view of the East River. Abe was a good drill sergeant. He had his people lined up to ask questions touching on issues affecting the Romanian Jewish community. The ADL was more friendly than its usual challenging posture would have intimated. I had prepared a briefing paper for Abe that may have helped a bit.

That afternoon, as soon as we boarded the plane to Houston, Meleşcanu, who was seated next to me, asked who I thought should be the next Romanian ambassador in Washington. Looking up, I saw Mircea Geoana walking down the aisle. From what I had seen of him as the Foreign Ministry spokesperson, I was impressed. His English was perfect. He had done postgraduate work at a French university, and was youthful in both actual age and appearance. In sum, he personified the "new Romania." I looked up, pointed at Geoana, and said to Meleşcanu, "That guy should be your next ambassador." Startled, Meleşcanu turned and said, "Why Mircea Geoana?" My answer was, "Who else do you have?" To which Meleşcanu responded, "Nobody." That was it. Meleşcanu proceeded to the front of the plane with me trailing behind, sat down next to President Iliescu, and said, "Ambassador Moses thinks Mircea Geoana should be our ambassador to the United States." Without looking up, Iliescu said, "Whoever Ambassador Moses wants is fine with me. He is our ambassador in Washington"—an egregious misstatement! Mircea went on to serve five years in Washington, with great success.

President Iliescu's staff insisted that I ride with him from the airport southeast of Houston to his hotel. The ride gave me a chance to gauge his reaction as a first-time visitor to Houston and its oil-created wealth. He was amazed at the sprawling modern city with office buildings reaching to the sky and a feeling of opulence that Romanians could only dream about.

The evening in Houston, hosted by former president Bush, started with cocktails at his home and then dinner at the nearby Bayou Club. President Bush was in good spirits, extremely gracious, first at his home and then at dinner at his private club. Bush's home, an attractive townhouse, was well appointed with antique furniture and the famous needlepoint rug handcrafted by Mrs. Bush, the centerpiece in the living room.

Bush had invited a dozen or so American businesspeople to join us, plus his Bucharest trip sponsor, Sever Mureşan, who somehow got his name on the invitation list. There was a dark cloud hanging over Mureşan in Romania. He had failed to meet his funding obligations to Dacia Felix, and the bank faced serious liquidity problems. Governor Isarescu of the National Bank of Romania had told me that Banca Dacia Felix was in trouble, which had been rumored for some time. As we were flying to Houston, Meleşcanu told me that Mureşan had asked to be named Romania's honorary consul in Dijon, France, where he lived, but that the French government turned him down, raising a question in Meleşcanu's mind as to what the French knew that he did not. The business "mafia" in Bucharest was wary of Mureşan and had not brought him into its deals. Even New York's Mark Meyer, the effervescent chairman of the Romanian-American Chamber of Commerce, had run into problems with Mureşan. Mark was trying to put together a housing deal in Romania involving land that Mureşan had under option but lost when he defaulted on an installment payment. Mark entered into an agreement with Mureşan to purchase his option. Mureşan promised to pay to reinstate his option, but Mark was still waiting for him to keep his word. Secretary General Hrebenciuc later told me Mureşan owed $280 million to Dacia Felix. This was the same figure that Diplomatic Adviser Traian Chebeleu had mentioned to me a couple of days before, but the sum was so enormous I thought he must have been substituting leu for dollars.

A major scandal was in the offing. Everyone would be blamed, from Ion Iliescu to George Bush. Mureşan had bought his way into so many things that no one in Romania would believe that higher-ups were not involved. In former president Bush's case, he was attracted by the opportunity to pick up a check for a speech. Mureşan got what he was looking for: the impression that he had the inside track with important people. After he pushed his way into the dinner that President Bush gave for President Iliescu in Houston, I called President Bush to give him a "beware" signal in dealing with Mureşan.

The energy conference the next day was standing room only. A lot of interest in investing was evident, but in the months that followed nothing came of it, in part because the initial enthusiasm wore off and in part because there were more attractive opportunities to invest in the energy sector elsewhere, such as in Brazil, Russia, Nigeria, and Venezuela.

MEETING THE PRESS

An ambassador's job can involve as much public diplomacy as private. As important as it was to meet with President Iliescu and other senior leaders in the Romanian government and members of Parliament to persuade them to do the things Romania needed to move ahead, this alone would not have made things happen without public support in Romania. I needed to get the word out to the Romanian public and enlist its help. For an ambassador, this was more than unorthodox and audacious; it was outrageous. Still, I considered the risk worth taking, and, luckily, my superiors in Washington did not stop me.

Looking back, I think there was a combination of factors at work. The State Department and the White House seemed content to leave Romania to me as long as the policies I pursued were consistent with our interests and the Romanian government did not complain. Here I had the advantage of a friendly President Iliescu; whatever our disagreements, he recognized that I wanted to help Romania, and that my take on Romania would become American policy. I also had good friends like Foreign Minister Meleșcanu and his press person, Sorin Ducaru (later Romania's ambassador to the United States, and still later an assistant general secretary of NATO), who supported me when needed.

Shortly after President Iliescu returned from Washington, I held a press conference for Romania's print media and its three principal television stations. The conference was widely reported in Romania. Typical of the coverage was an article by Reuters' Romanian correspondent, who after the ouster of PRM from the parliamentary coalition, wrote on October 22:

> Romania's ruling party has cut adrift an extreme nationalist ally which shored up its coalition government but had become an embarrassment abroad and a liability ahead of elections next year.
>
> President Ion Iliescu's Party of Social Democracy (PDSR) is polishing up its image as he leads a push for acceptance from governments and business, particularly in the United States.

Iliescu is in the U.S. this week for the second time in a month, and takes with him proof of a break with extreme allies.

It is Iliescu's drive for U.S. investment and ties to NATO that led his PDSR to sever links last week with the small Greater Romania Party (PRM), which taps veins of nationalism and anti-Semitism always just below the surface in Romania.

Greater Romania president Corneliu Vadim Tudor used his newspaper for unprecedented attacks on Iliescu, saying he was selling out Romania with his drive for western acceptance.

"Comrade Iliescu, you subordinated the country to the Jews. The Jews brought you in power, you stay with the Jews," Greater Romania's weekly newspaper said recently.

Such language is Tudor's stock-in-trade, but has never before been directed at Iliescu, who remains the strongest figure in Romania almost six years after he emerged from the communist party in the 1989 revolution to replace dictator Nicolae Ceauşescu.

It was the excuse the PDSR needed to cut Greater Romania out of a 10-month coalition which also includes the hard-line National Unity Party and neo-communist Socialist Labour Party.

"The PRM has been not only a troublesome partner but also a continuous discredit to Romania's image abroad, because of its leader's outbursts, Ziua Newspaper quoted Iliescu saying.

Tudor's attacks embarrassed Iliescu while he was in the United States late last month for his first official meeting with President Bill Clinton. It may be no coincidence Greater Romania was expelled two days before Iliescu returned to the United States for a week of political and business meetings.

Washington's ambassador to Bucharest, Alfred Moses, has been an outspoken critic of Prime Minister Nicolae Vacaroiu's accommodation with xenophobic and anti-Semitic groups.

A day before Greater Romania was dumped, Moses predicted it, saying: "We will not bemoan that development if it occurs."

With the weight of U.S. military cooperation and more importantly the promise of badly needed U.S. investment behind him, Moses comments unusually freely on Romanian politics.

"We don't pick coalition partners but we have expressed in the past and continue to believe that Romania is best served by a centrist coalition," Moses said last week.

"Centrist right, centrist left, that's up to the Romanian people. But we don't think that extremist views are in the best interests of the future partnership between Romania and the West. Our view on that has not changed," he said.

The neo-communists may follow Greater Romania out of the coalition and the National Unity Party, which holds several key cabinet posts, has moderated its rhetoric.

Analysts say Iliescu's ruling party, facing a divided opposition, can survive, if not thrive, until elections in late 1996 when the fruits of lower inflation, privatisation and more foreign investment may be more evident.

A SUMMONS TO COTROCENI

While still in the press conference, I received word that President Iliescu wanted to see me at Cotroceni. On my arrival I was immediately escorted to Iliescu's second-floor office. President Iliescu and Diplomatic Adviser Chebeleu were waiting for me. Iliescu and I again sat side by side, coatless, on a gold velveteen divan. He began by telling me about his renewed efforts to streamline approval of foreign investment. I listened with interest but was skeptical that anything positive would emerge from his declaration. I remained convinced that the Romanian bureaucracy would find ways to block President Iliescu's good intentions. However, the meeting gave me the opportunity to raise other issues, such as our two countries' cooperating in the intelligence field, and the need for Romania to stop shooting itself in the foot by adopting laws such as the proposed amendments to the penal code. The amendment would impose stiff criminal sanctions for defamation and slander, with even stiffer jail sentences for journalists, and would outlaw the singing of foreign anthems and the displaying of foreign flags in Romania.

My previous proposal to Chamber of Deputies President Nastase on the amendment of the penal code had not been enacted. In Washington President Iliescu had assured me that "we will find a way to solve this problem."

Now back in Bucharest, he was less sure, saying that Nastase had met with a delegation of journalists and was trying to reach agreement. There was no mention of flags and anthems or the dropping of criminal sanctions for slander and defamation, a step backward from his Washington assurances. I also reminded him of the discussion at the Washington Holocaust Museum about obtaining lists (fonts) from the National Archives. He promised to look into it when he returned from Houston.

Meanwhile, on the good news, bad news front, Parliament agreed to drop penalties on journalists for slander and defamation by dropping the specific reference to journalists, but increased the maximum jail sentence from two years to three. This would take some sting out of the amendments, at least for journalists, but it would have been far better if slander and defamation were dealt with civilly, not criminally. I made this point to Nastase. He agreed, but I did not get the feeling he was solidly behind the idea. The same thing for foreign flags and anthems. The provision outlawing the flying of foreign flags and the singing of foreign anthems was still in the draft bill. (I thought I had gotten rid of this months ago, but in Romania putting something in the closet does not mean it stays there.)

A month later, on November 1, I received a letter from Nastase telling me that the proposed penal code would make flying foreign flags and singing foreign anthems a crime only if done in a public gathering with intent to abrogate the Romanian constitution, which declared Romania a unitary, indivisible, state. In other words, the amendments to the penal code were for show—to placate Romania's nationalists. They would never be applied.

In September President Iliescu invited me to a book-signing party for his new book on his trip to Washington in which he summarized his fall meetings in the United States. The event was designed to promote improved Romanian-American relations and help Iliescu politically. It was interesting to see who attended and who did not. Among the NATO ambassadors, only the Canadian and Portuguese showed up, plus the new Turkish ambassador, who had not yet presented his credentials. The British, French, and German envoys were absent. Looking around, I saw the Russian and Ukrainian ambassadors, both listening attentively to President Iliescu's speech and my follow-on remarks, no doubt preparing to report home on the state of American-Romanian relations and its implications for Romania's eventual admission into NATO. I ended my comments with a reference to the flying of the Romanian flag along with those of the sixteen NATO members at the Supreme Allied Commander Atlantic (SACLANT) conference in Norfolk, Virginia, in 1995 and the hope of the United States that Romania's flag would some day officially fly alongside those of other NATO members in Brussels.

THINGS ARE LOOKING UP

From time to time, the sun did shine in Bucharest. McDonald's had opened its first Golden Arches in Bucharest in June, small and medium-sized businesses were growing, privatizations moved ahead, albeit in fits and starts, and Romanians for the first time in decades were beginning to see better times ahead. One small example was a new shopping arcade in the metro station underneath University Circle in downtown Bucharest. It had been a hellhole cluttered with debris, water dripping from the cement ceiling, a dark spot at night and dimly lit in the day, a reminder of Ceauşescu-inspired gloom. In the summer of 1995 it had been completely renovated with fashionable boutiques and fast-food outlets built by private investors. Nevertheless, Romanian cleaning ladies still wet-mopped the floors, which was both time-consuming and inefficient. Needed were people sweeping litter into boxes at the end of hand-held poles, as was done in American shopping centers. Two people with poles and litter boxes could do more than ten cleaning ladies with wet mops. When I returned three weeks later, two smartly dressed men were sweeping litter into pole-held boxes.

In April I had visited a porcelain factory on the outskirts of Piteşti that was equally impressive. Privately owned, it made money exporting porcelain dinnerware to Western Europe, adopting for each country its most popular design—for Italy a floral pattern, for Germany something plainer. The production line used modern equipment purchased after the revolution from Germany. Plans were in place to modernize the entire factory. Liking what I saw, I bought china sets for each of our four children to be used strictly for company.

One of my dreams was that private interests in Romania would sometime in the future redevelop the Lipscani district (the rundown former financial center in Bucharest) into a modern inner-city arcade. Built in the early 1900s, Lipscani was a long-neglected architectural gem. I talked to architects and real estate developers about turning the district into a major tourist attraction with pedestrian walk zones, restaurants, and shops along the lines of similar developments in Bratislava, Vienna, Munich, and other European cities. Government money would be needed to clean up the exterior of the distinguished buildings, install better street lights, enact zoning laws to preserve the exterior of the buildings, and close narrow streets to vehicular traffic. Once this was done, greed would take over and good things would happen. There was money to be made by risk takers with imagination. In this vein, I convinced the Kuwaiti businessman Fathi Taher, then living in Bucharest, to buy the centuries-old Hanul Iui Manuc Inn, which anchored the Lipscani district, and to invest in other upgrades in the area. My dream came true a decade later. Lipscani is today a Bucharest hot spot.

ANOTHER PIECE OF THE PUZZLE: THE ARMS PROLIFERATION CONTROL AGENCY

Romania was anxious to become a member of the Arms Proliferation Control Agency (APCA; the successor organization to Combatant Command, or COCOM), but was behind other countries in Central Europe in applying for membership. The reason was straightforward: it had been selling weapons to pariah states such as Iran, Iraq, Sudan, and Libya, all the while officially denying that such sales had taken place. Romania received an official invitation from the State Department to begin negotiations on a confidential agreement as the first step to becoming a member of the APCA. The Romanians dragged their feet.

Romania's eligibility for the APCA was on my agenda throughout 1995. Romania continued to sell military components to both Iraq and Iran. When I confronted Foreign Minister Meleşcanu, Diplomatic Adviser Chebeleu, and Mircea Geoana, Romania's ambassador to the United States, with the facts at lunch at my residence, they denied it, but the facts were the facts. I was not free to give them names and other specifics, but the facts were known, at least within the Romanian Defense Ministry. The director of international trade in Romtehnica (an RA) and the commercial attaché in the Romanian embassy in Iraq were both involved. The sales to Iraq involved components that could be used to assemble missiles, and the Iranian sales included missile components for the A-6 missile that Iran purchased from the former Soviet Union.

On December 13 a U.S. government group came to Bucharest to look at Romania's sophisticated weaponry capability. There were valid complaints that the Romanians were holding back on information sharing. General Dumitru Popa, in command of the Defense Ministry's industrial companies, was the culprit. He was dismissed after the 1996 elections.

TONY RODHAM'S ROMANIAN DEAL

That fall I found myself in a tricky spot that I should have been smarter in heading off. Earlier in the fall, during President Iliescu's Washington visit, after President Clinton introduced Iliescu to the press at the entrance to the West Wing of the White House he pulled out a small piece of paper, looked at it, and asked me if I knew anything about the Romanian-made Aro, an off-road vehicle. I said no, but if there were a problem, I would take a look.

That afternoon I received a call from Tony Rodham, Hillary Rodham Clinton's brother, who was staying at the White House. He caught up with me the next night at the Romanian ambassador's residence and explained that he and his business associates were interested in selling the Aro in the United States. A day or two later he came to my Washington office with two loose-leaf notebooks. I looked at them briefly, discarded the promotional material, and held on to the financial and other papers.

When I returned to Bucharest a few days later, I learned that an American lawyer in Romania had informed the U.S. embassy that his law firm had withdrawn as counsel for Rodham and his partners, after determining that they were making false representations about their venture's financial condition. The lawyer later gave me a notebook purporting to show that Rodham's financial statements were false, and that his two associates had been collecting prospective dealer deposits in Florida and were not placing them in escrow, as required by state law. I promptly informed Romanian officials that the U.S. government was not connected in any way with Mr. Rodham's endeavors, nor was President Clinton.

Unfortunately, this was not the end of the matter. Once I had the supposedly incriminating notebook I was required by law to inform the U.S. Department of Justice. This was not a happy thought, for I realized that if the press got hold of the story, it could result in a full-blown attack on President Clinton and the first lady. I had gone through a similar episode fifteen years before concerning President Carter and his brother Billy. After further thought, I decided my first stop should be the office of White House counsel, where I met with Judge Abner Mikva, the president's counsel and a former chief judge of the U.S. Court of Appeals for the District of Columbia Circuit. Without a moment's hesitation, Judge Mikva agreed that the material should be sent to the U.S. attorney's office in Miami. Not unexpectedly, a few weeks later I received a call from the Criminal Division of the Department of Justice asking me to meet at the department. I had little to say. I had only met Rodham once. I knew no incriminating facts, and had it not been for the notebook given to me by the lawyer in Bucharest, I would not have thought further about the matter. Certainly, President Clinton had not asked me to do anything improper, nor did Tony Rodham. As far as I knew, the matter ended there. I was later told by President Clinton's personal lawyer that when Judge Mikva told the president about our conversation, he was upset, but on further reflection realized I had protected him by keeping the matter within official channels and away from the press.

NOVEMBER 4: A SAD DAY IN JERUSALEM

It was a clear, crisp November evening in Bucharest. I was attending a glittering formal affair in progress in the Marble Hall at the Palace of the National Military Circle, an ornate building on Calea Victoriei in downtown Bucharest, when our embassy resident security officer told me that Prime Minister Yitzhak Rabin had been assassinated in Tel Aviv. I was shaken. I had known Rabin for thirty-five years. I immediately left the ball. Back at the residence, I called Carol and spoke with a close friend in Jerusalem, who, as it turned out, had had lunch with Rabin earlier in the day. He confirmed the terrible news. Rabin's death was a great loss for Israel and the peace process. He, and perhaps he alone, had the military credibility and the high confidence of the Israeli public needed to conclude peace with the Palestinians.

Two days later, I flew with President Iliescu and Foreign Minister Meleşcanu on the president's private plane to Tel Aviv for Rabin's funeral. Iliescu beckoned me to sit next to him to discuss the standby loan. Again, negotiations had broken down. I told him to expect a call from the IMF's managing director, Camdessus, informing him that the IMF would not extend the present agreement, but would move promptly to negotiate a new standby loan. This would result in a major delay. President Iliescu reacted emotionally, claiming that Romania was being treated unfairly, citing Hungary's 9 percent budget deficit to buttress his case. There was some truth in this, but in the end Romania needed the IMF. To go it alone, as President Iliescu threatened, would be to replay Ceauşescu's disastrous decision to eliminate Romania's foreign debt. Later that same day on the flight back to Romania, I recounted to Foreign Minister Meleşcanu my discussion with Iliescu, and he agreed that Romania had no option but to reach agreement with the IMF.

Once we arrived in Israel, everything moved with "Israeli precision." The helicopter on which we were to fly to Jerusalem was full, but our Israeli guide shrugged her shoulders and said, "There will be another," and indeed there was. When we arrived in Jerusalem, there was no transportation to take us to President Ezer Weizman's residence, but after a few minutes a bus miraculously appeared and quickly filled up with foreign representatives, and off we went to President Weizman's residence.

Some thousand foreign officials lingered about the residence. President Weizman milled with the crowd, many of whom did not recognize him. He had no identification badge, and no aides to direct people. Still, it worked. There were mini-summits all around—the Hungarian and Slovak prime ministers conferred in one corner, British Prime Minister John Major and Prince Charles in another, King Hussein of Jordan in still another, and so it went. From President Weizman's residence we rode by minibus to Mt. Herzl— the "Arlington National Cemetery" of Israel, named for Theodor Herzl, the founder of the modern Zionist movement—for the funeral ceremony and burial. There were a few more minor protocol slip-ups. There was no seat for President Iliescu; he had decided at the last minute to make the trip. An

Israeli officer simply grabbed a chair and put President Iliescu's name on it and told him to sit in the front row next to Prime Minister Viktor Chernomyrdin of Russia. I had no official position but was seated next to Meleşcanu in the third row. I saw lots of American friends as well as Israelis. The entire U.S cabinet was there. Jordan's King Hussein delivered the most impressive speech, President Clinton's speech was the best drafted, and Yitzhak Rabin's granddaughter gave the most moving talk. The whole ceremony was enormously impressive. At about 4 p.m. we got back on the bus, this time for the trip to Ben Gurion Airport and the flight to Bucharest. As we approached the airport, our Israeli guide suggested that we call ahead to tell the Romanian pilots we were coming. We did, and the bus took us directly to the Tarom plane; fifteen minutes later we were in the air, on our way back to frigid Bucharest, having left an eighty-degree Jerusalem, sunny but in mourning, for cloudy, cold Bucharest.

When I returned to Bucharest, I looked at the USAID FY1996 budget for Romania. It was an improvement over the budget for 1995 in that it reduced the number of contractors by about a third, but it was still too broad in scope and did not shift the principal responsibility for implementation to the Romanians. It was like a community chest in the United States, dribbling out small bits of money here and there without first identifying which areas had the greatest need, were consistent with U.S. interests, would achieve maximum impact using Romanians to train Romanians, and were not making grants to institutions that would lop off big chunks in administrative costs.

THE RESURRECTION OF ION DIACONESCU

In November the NATO ambassadors' lunch rotation returned to the German embassy. It was my turn to be rapporteur. The major developments: the election of Ion Diaconescu as head of PNT-CD (the previous party leader, Coposu, died two days later) and the potential pollution from a Bulgarian nuclear plant that had recently resumed operations and was similar in design to the failed Russian plant in Chernobyl. So there was good reason for concern but nothing to be done by NATO ambassadors eating lunch in Bucharest other than shake our heads and hope for the best.

When I met with Diaconescu a few days later, I realized that his views were close to those of Coposu, but he was not as stern or as self-righteous. Clearly, PNT-CD had a generational problem. The old guard led by Diaconescu had no experience governing, and in any event they were too old to take on the rigors of public office. I predicted that they would likely hold on to leadership until after the 1996 elections, but then the party would need new blood or would face a major challenge four years later (2000) in the next national elections. In 1996 Diaconescu stuck with Emil Constantinescu as the party's choice to run against Iliescu for president. After the PNT-CD won the 1996 elections, it tried to find qualified people to govern, but for the most part failed. It awarded key ministries to members of the Social Democratic Party (PD), its coalition partner, but even this was not enough to stave off defeat at the polls. PNT-CD did not receive enough votes in the 2000 elections to be represented in Parliament and the party ceased to be a force in Romanian political life.

ONWARD WITH IMF AND WORLD BANK NEGOTIATIONS

Throughout the fall, the IMF was increasingly concerned about Romania's economic performance. It painted a gloomy short-run picture predicting Romania's budget deficit would far exceed 3 percent of GDP, which meant foreign exchange would continue to be tightly regulated by the National Bank of Romania to protect the leu and Romania would need to borrow money in international markets to finance its budget deficit and pay for petroleum imports, both short-term initiatives that did not deal with the underlying structural problems.

In December the Romanians reluctantly agreed to the IMF's final terms for the standby loan, after which the foreign exchange market operated in sync with the official National Bank of Romania rate. The National Bank of Romania was still looking for ways to build the central bank's foreign reserves by year-end. It quickly closed two Swiss Bank–managed loans of $50 million and a Citibank-managed $110 million eighteen-month loan. The interest rate on the Citibank loan was high, 2.25 percentage points above the LIBOR rate, but Romania had no choice. Governor Isarescu now realized that Romania should have reached agreement with the IMF and the World Bank in the summer, when Romania's economy was stronger. I had urged him to do this at the time, but the Romanian negotiators dragged their feet and it was now December. At Governor Isarescu's request, we sent Jed Smith, a U.S. Treasury expert on government syndications, to Romania to advise the central bank on international bond financing, a market it was looking to tap in the first half of 1996.

DEFENSE MINISTER TINCA, BELL HELICOPTER, AND THE APCA

The December streets of Bucharest were covered with snow and stalled traffic when I was summoned without warning to the Defense Ministry for a meeting with Defense Minister Tinca about Romania's proposed purchase of Bell AH-1 Cobra helicopters and its eligibility for the APCA.

With nine minutes to go, sirens blaring and blue lights flashing, my driver managed to weave around traffic, up one-way streets the wrong way, down the wrong side of two major boulevards, to get me to the Defense Ministry building exactly on time. I bolted up the white marble steps to the second floor and was immediately ushered into Defense Minister Tinca's huge, ornate office. My first question to Tinca was how the government of Romania would pay for the ninety-six Cobras it wanted to co-produce with Bell. The price tag was more than the Romanian military's entire budget. If sales were financed externally, it would require a government guarantee. Twenty percent of the procurement price had to be paid in 1998, and based on what I knew, the Romanian government would not have the money. Tinca was not fazed. "We expect major improvement in the economy over the next five years."

The discussion then turned to Romania's desire to join the APCA. It was already too late for Romania to be a founding member, and unless it acknowledged its past sales to Iraq and Iran and bound itself not to sell military or dual-use items to those countries in the future, it was not going to make it. Tinca continued to claim that no such sales had been made, to which I replied this was not credible. I did not accuse him of lying, only of being misinformed. He asked for details, and, of course, that was the rub. I thought to myself, "Sooner rather than later we are going to have to come up with the facts and force Romanians to confess." We also went over Romania's offer to send an engineering battalion to Bosnia: this would put a strain on Romania's military budget and oblige Romania to recall part of its medical battalion then in Angola. I suggested that he not tie the two together, which would make it look like Romania was giving with one hand and taking with the other, but applauded the decision to help in Bosnia.

ONE WIN FOR AMERICAN BUSINESS

Aircraft sales are big business, and American manufacturers (Boeing, McDonnell Douglas, and Lockheed) were in fierce competition with manufacturers from around the world. In December 1995 Boeing was the successful bidder over European competition for the sale of eight 737s, intermediate-range planes, to Tarom. It was an important sale that had looked doubtful earlier in the year, but in the end the Romanian government came through with sovereign guarantees. Immediately after the revolution, Tarom had bought three planes from Airbus, an international European consortium. On April 1, 1995, one of the planes crashed shortly after taking off from Bucharest's airport on a flight to Brussels. Petre Roman was prime minister when the Airbuses were purchased. In his student days, he had lived in France and had close French connections. Now the Americans were back on top. In time Tarom's international fleet became 100 percent Boeing. I celebrated the Tarom contract at a dinner for Boeing officials at my residence. Boeing later acquired McDonnell Douglas and Lockheed stopped manufacturing civilian aircraft, leaving Boeing as the only U.S. manufacturer of commercial passenger aircraft.

THE DEMISE OF BANCA DACIA FELIX AND SEVER MUREŞAN

The Banca Dacia Felix situation continued to spiral downward. In late 1995 the National Bank of Romania took over supervision of the bank and pumped money into it to keep it afloat. Three former directors, including Mureşan, "borrowed" hundreds of millions of dollars from the bank. Mureşan's story was that he borrowed only $80 million for his own account. The other $200 million he received represented loans he took over to clean up the bank's balance sheet. National Bank of Romania Governor Isarescu had a different story. Mureşan had borrowed $180 million from Dacia Felix to invest abroad. This was illegal under Romanian law. One story was that the money was sitting in a "Luxembourg account." Later Mureşan claimed he had invested the funds in Italian bonds. With the demise of Dacia Felix, another short-lived Romanian high-flyer hit the dust, and the bank headed for liquidation. Mureşan was gone from Dacia Felix but not from Romania. He was arrested after the fall elections on orders of the newly elected president, Emil Constantinescu.

FOLLOW-UP MEETING WITH OPPOSITION LEADER EMIL CONSTANTINESCU

Before year-end I met for the second time with Emil Constantinescu, the PNT-CD candidate for president. He still struck me as a *Luftmensch*, a head-in-the-clouds person with little practical experience, but I thought he would be a serious opponent to President Iliescu. Even if not a hard-nosed politician, he was likable and politically "clean." Romanian pundits were saying that President Iliescu would "eat him alive." I was not so sure. PSM had just announced that it was leaving the parliamentary coalition with PDSR. This meant that two of the three extremist parties were now out of the parliamentary alliance: Romania Mare (PRM) and the Socialist Party of Romania (PSM). As for the remaining coalition partner, the Romanian National Unity Party (PUNR), Georghe Funar, recently reelected president by his party's congress, was attacking President Iliescu daily in the press. Hardly a strong political alliance. I thought PUNR would run its own candidates in the elections, and if PDSR emerged with a plurality of the votes, it would form a government with parties other than PUNR. Constantinescu told me that PNT-CD would not try to bring down the now-minority government with a vote of no confidence before the elections. The same day as our meeting, Constantinescu publicly announced that PNT-CD was training 15,000 people to work in the government after the elections. This was wholly fanciful, but revealed PNT-CD's utter lack of experience in governing. In fact, when PNT-CD formed a government after the 1996 elections, no one from its ranks, with the exception of Prime Minister Victor Ciorbea, Bucharest's mayor, had previous government experience or training.

HIGH AND LOW FINANCE

In some countries an ambassador's job includes the prosaic one of bill collecting from the host country, a chore that fell to me from time to time. In late 1995 Romania was behind in paying a bimonthly installment on Tarom's indebtedness to Boeing for the 737s the airline had purchased. Tarom's debt was guaranteed by the U.S. Export-Import Bank, which in turn was backed by the sovereign guarantee of the government of Romania. On December 1 I spoke directly to Finance Minister Florin Georgescu, who promised to let me know later that day when payment would be made. I insisted on immediate payment. Late payment would have had a snowball effect on other big-ticket items. EXIM Bank was holding up its guarantee of Romanian government indebtedness for the purchase of Lockheed radar units until payment was received on the Tarom indebtedness. Once the rails were greased, the train moved quickly. Georgescu called back an hour later to tell me that he had transferred leu to the National Bank of Romania to pay the current installment, and National Bank of Romania Governor Isarescu had promised to make payment the same day. True to his word, I received a call later that day confirming that the National Bank of Romania had wired the funds to EXIM Bank in Washington. (My American counterparts in Paris and London did not have to concern themselves with bill collecting.)

When Nicolae Vacaroiu became prime minister in 1992, Romania's foreign reserves were a paltry $30 million. By the time I arrived in Bucharest two years later, they had grown to $700 million, still a very small number. (As of December 2017, they were over $30 billion.) By late 1995 Romania's economy had progressed to the point where National Bank of Romania Governor Isarescu and others, under pressure from the IMF, began to think about allowing the leu to float freely on the foreign exchange market. As a preliminary step, the IMF required the government to move ahead with bank privatization, raise heavily subsidized energy prices to at least 80 percent of world market prices, and test the euro and yen bond markets for floating Romanian debt. Heavily subsidized energy prices were dependent on an overvalued leu to hold down the cost of imported oil and gas. In late 1995 Citibank formed a syndicate to sell a $110 million Romanian bond offering, and in the spring of 1996 the Japanese holding company Nomura Group did the same for a ¥497 million bond offering.

With improved credit ratings, over the next twelve months the National Bank of Romania borrowed $610 million in the bond market and close to 800 million in yen. Romania used U.S. dollars and Japanese yen to pay for imports and boost the economy. American firms such as McDonnell Douglas, Philip Morris, Colgate-Palmolive, and Delta Airlines were seeking to exchange leu earned in Romania for dollars, but the Romanian government put pressure on the National Bank of Romania to keep the exchange rate below 3,000 leu to the dollar. At this price, banks were not selling dollars, instead speculating on a devaluation of the leu. Exports were down, which meant dollars were not flowing into the country, and the National Bank of Romania was reluctant to put the hard currency it borrowed into the Romanian banking system. In short, Romania's foreign borrowing was supporting consumer spending, not restructuring the economy and building infrastructure. Sooner rather than later Romania would have to pay the piper.

END-OF-YEAR POLITICAL CRYSTAL BALL

I was constantly looking for opportunities to meet with leaders of the political opposition. As the American ambassador, I dealt primarily with President Iliescu, his ministers, their staffs, and Romania's parliamentary leaders, Senate President Gherman and Chamber of Deputies President Nastase. The Romanian press was quick to pick up on my frequent meetings with President Iliescu, my accompanying him on his two trips to the United States, and his efforts to portray our closeness. I liked Iliescu and encouraged the importance he attached to Romania's relations with the United States. He represented stability at a time when Romania might otherwise have slipped into political chaos. I was also persuaded that, despite his two earlier reversions to communist strong-arm tactics when he brought the miners to Bucharest, he was genuinely committed to move Romania to full democracy and a market economy. However, I also knew that in time Iliescu would be gone and the political opposition would be in power. It is ever thus in a democracy.

In addition to my two meetings with Emil Constantinescu, who had lost the presidential election two years before to Iliescu, I also met on several occasions with the venerable Christian Democratic leader, Corneliu Coposu, and later with his successor, Ion Diaconescu, as well as with Senator Radu Vasile, PNT-CD's secretary general. I attended the pre-election Christian Democratic convention walking arm in arm with Vasile, shaking hands, nodding and greeting. When Vasile introduced me to the delegates en masse, I was greeted with thunderous applause, which surprised me. I also developed a good relationship with the leaders of the Democratic Union of Hungarians in Romania (UDMR) and most of the smaller political parties, as well as with Petre Roman, the PD leader.

In our last meeting Petre Roman exuded his usual confidence and claimed that despite the polls predicting a 10 percent share, PD would get 20 percent of the vote in the following year's elections. (In the event PD's share was 12 percent.) He also told me "confidentially" that he planned to run for president against Iliescu and Constantinescu. If, as was likely, neither of the two got a majority of the votes, he would be the kingmaker, throwing his votes in the runoff to the higher bidder. He did, and he came in third. He knew he had little chance of winning the presidency, but running for president would help his party in the parliamentary elections. Being realistic, he planned to file for a parliament seat in case he lost in the presidential race. He ran for the Senate, was elected, and became president of the Senate from 1996 to 1998 (he served as foreign minister from 1998 to 2000). Roman was wholly a mentee of President Iliescu, who had plucked him out of nowhere to be his prime minister. As Roman saw it, PDSR had more qualified people and on this score would be a better coalition partner than PNT-CD, but the latter was more "democratic." His party, PD, ended up forming a government with PNT-CD, UDMR holding one ministry.

MY SECOND ANNUAL CHRISTMAS PARTY

Carol and three of our four children arrived in Bucharest on December 12 for the pre-holiday season. We planned to fly to Israel on December 17 for the family dedication of a building in Jerusalem named for my parents. But before leaving Bucharest, Carol and I hosted the annual Christmas party for the embassy staff. Carol, our three children, and I stood in the receiving line for close to an hour, a herculean task for Carol. Yet she seemed to gain strength each day she was in Romania. The Christmas party was even better than the previous year's. We had two choral groups, one Jewish and the other an American-trained church choir. No doubt this was the first time Hanukkah songs were sung at the embassy Christmas party, but the embassy staff applauded enthusiastically.

SUMMING UP: MY NON-PAPER ON U.S.-ROMANIAN RELATIONS

Late December was a good time to sum up events of the past year and look ahead to 1996. I drafted a non-paper for President Iliescu containing my thoughts regarding our countries' bilateral relationship, focusing on the following:

- 1996 as the year for Romania to build closer ties with Western political and economic structures and to strengthen the United States-Romania bilateral relationship

- Improvement of United States–Romania bilateral relations in 1995, highlighted by President Iliescu's trips to Washington, New York, and Houston and improvements in Romania's military

- Notable participation by Romania in UN peacekeeping missions

- Need for Romania to meet criteria for membership in APCA

- Need for Romania to meet the IMF's criteria for the standby loan and the World Bank's requirements for the FESAL

- Basic treaties with Hungary and Ukraine concluded

- Romania's bid for NATO membership

- Emphasis on Romania's need to carry out economic reform (privatization, petroleum, and bank privatization bills in Parliament, and accelerated American investment)

- Recommendations as to procedures to enhance election standards in the upcoming Romanian national elections

- Deals pending with Bell Helicopter and Lockheed Martin

Foreign Minister Meleşcanu gave my non-paper to President Iliescu and to Mircea Geoana, who was slated to take up his post as Romania's ambassador in Washington in January. At a lunch in late December at my residence—attended also by Foreign Minister Meleşcanu and Diplomatic Adviser Chebeleu—Geoana came across as serious and determined to make his mark. He did not defer to others, including his boss, the foreign minister.

AULD LANG SYNE

My last official meeting to close out the year was with President Iliescu at Cotroceni. He agreed it had been a good year for U.S.-Romanian relations. I gave him pictures of his Oval Office meeting with President Clinton, including a photo of the two presidents signed by President Clinton. I also delivered a letter from President Clinton, drafted by the National Security Council's Dan Fried and me as a follow-up to the Oval Office meeting. President Iliescu also had before him a copy of my end-of-year non-paper, which he had read and commented on quite graciously. The only point on which we differed was permanent MFN status. The non-paper struck a cautious note on MFN, whereas President Iliescu wanted to plunge ahead. He turned out to be right. On armaments sales to Iran and Iraq, President Iliescu took the now-familiar Romania position that more details were needed. It was hard to tell whether this was a ruse on his part or whether he did not know what was going on. He agreed that Romania's economic situation would be challenging, particularly during the winter months. The polls showed that President Iliescu and PDSR's popularity were down, reflecting the bad economic scene and squabbling within the PDSR over much-needed economic reform, a harbinger of things to come in the year ahead.

My sense of things at the end of the year was that Romania lagged behind its neighbors politically and economically in rebuilding the country. But there were positive signs that gave me hope. The fall Parliament session had been productive. A good copyright law had been passed by both chambers, and the petroleum law was close to adoption. The objectionable amendments to the penal code were *not* adopted—a definite plus! Looking ahead, for the PDSR to remain in power with President Iliescu as head of the government, the party should engineer changes that would be viewed as welcome, such as finding centrist coalition partners. A repetition of the old, however comforting it was for some, would not carry the day.

PART THREE

Romania's Democracy in Action

1996

A New Year, Step-by-Step

WINTER 1996

A HARBINGER OF THINGS TO COME

The January NATO ambassadors' monthly lunch was at my residence with President Iliescu as the guest. Most of the NATO ambassadors were anti-Iliescu to the point that one of them, the Spanish ambassador, called me a few days before the lunch to tell me that the "group" had requested that Iliescu not bring press or photographers. The first one was easy. The lunches were not open to the press. But there was no reason President Iliescu could not bring his photographer or anyone else he wanted. Romania was his country, not ours. Nevertheless, he showed up without press or photographers, accompanied only by his diplomatic adviser, Traian Chebeleu, who called me that morning to ask if he could attend. Iliescu did a masterful job, outlining Romania's position on current foreign policy issues—NATO, EU, the basic treaties with Hungary and Ukraine, and his assessment of developments in Russia. He answered questions without a hostile edge, and most of the ambassadors gave him high marks. In truth, most of them had never met President Iliescu. Now they had, and it had given them something to report back home.

DIPLOMAT OF THE YEAR

Little in Romania was straightforward. Invariably, there were twists, hairpin bends, and sometimes pretzel-like curves. This was such an occasion. In early January I received a congratulatory letter from the director of *Nine O'Clock*, Romania's only daily English newspaper, informing me that I had been chosen "Diplomat of the Year," and that I would receive the award later that month. A few days later, the editor, Radu Bogdan, invited me to lunch at an upscale Bucharest restaurant. When we sat down at the large center table with a white linen tablecloth and fresh flowers, I understood why he had invited me. With some hesitation, Bogdan told me that this year there would be two "Diplomats of the Year," the French ambassador, Bernard Boyer, and myself. He did not explain why two rather than one were chosen or why Boyer had been selected just the previous week. I later learned the reason. Bogdan was trying to start a French-language edition of *Nine O'Clock* and was hoping to get the backing of the French government. I commended Bogdan on his wise choice of Boyer.

ECONOMIC REFORM ON THE MENU

The economic scene in early 1996 was dominated by the tug of war between economic reform and the incumbent government's desire to hold on to power. For the incumbents, this meant slowing down economic reform and loosening the fiscal purse strings. On the political side, the opposition party, PNT-CD, had elected Radu Vasile as its secretary general. Vasile was not an ideologue in the Coposu mold, or even a "believer," like the PNT-CD's Emil Constantinescu and Coposu's successor, Ion Diaconescu. (Vasile became prime minister in 1998 after President Constantinescu dismissed his first prime minister, Victor Ciorbea.) Vasile was pro-American, and we met often. I enlisted his support on everything from the Mass Privatization Program (MPP) to the Hungarian-Romanian Basic Treaty. Vasile liked to please, and I gave him every opportunity.

A LAVISH AFFAIR

On January 15 President Ion Iliescu hosted the annual big party for diplomats. Once again, it was a lavish affair at Cotroceni. Indeed, it was unnecessarily lavish, but the Romanians thought it in keeping with their self-image. Arriving ambassadors were escorted up the long marble stairway, past the "praetorian guard," and into an elegant chamber marred by tacky photographs mounted on display poster boards similar to those seen in public libraries in the United States. Once the fifty or more ambassadors were lined up in order of seniority, the procession moved to a small theater, where we waited for Iliescu to appear, along with the Iraqi ambassador, third in line of seniority behind the ambassador from Zaire (who was without a suit) and the Lebanese ambassador, who was out of country. After President Iliescu said the expected welcoming words, the Iraqi ambassador offered a noncontroversial reply, congratulating Romania on its economic reforms and strong support for peace. After the speeches, music was to follow, but the musicians were missing. They showed up half an hour later, by which time the diplomats had moved to another salon for drinks and food. Iliescu joined us and immediately sought me out so the television crew in attendance could film the two of us in conversation on the evening news as further proof of the close relationship between the United States and Romania.

FESAL IS SIGNED; REFORM SLOWS DOWN

January saw, finally, the signing of the World Bank's Final Enterprise Structural Adjustment Loan (FESAL). This should have been the signal for the State Ownership Fund (SOF) to recruit strategic investors, primarily foreign, to privatize 900 companies. The economic section in our embassy put the likely number at closer to 100. I thought the lower figure was too optimistic, which regrettably proved to be the case. Our economic section, led by our senior Foreign Service officer, Richard Rorvig, was usually right, but the SOF found a way to confound just about everyone. The SOF raised the asking price for the 900 companies to 125 percent of their appraised values and ceased selling shares to foreigners under the installment method. This all but killed interest on the part of foreign strategic investors in acquiring to-be-privatized Romanian companies.

Economic reform, such as it was, slowed even more later in the year. Romania had made little progress in restructuring state-owned money losers, including the eight key *régies autonomes* (RAs), which was a condition for disbursement of the second tranche of the FESAL. This meant the disbursement would be deferred until the second quarter of 1997, when a new government would be in place. Moreover, further disbursements under the IMF standby loan were unlikely to be made until the National Bank of Romania opened the foreign exchange market. The government of Romania was propping up the leu in the lead-up to the elections. This was bad economics and proved to be bad politics as well. With little moving on the economic front, Romanians were likely to vote for change.

THE HUNGARIAN-ROMANIAN BASIC TREATY

In early 1996 agreement on the Hungarian-Romanian Basic Treaty remained elusive, largely due to problems on the Hungarian side.

The holdup in Romania was the negative precedent set by the Hungarian-Slovakian Basic Treaty (signed but not ratified), which lacked the proposed Romanian treaty language clarifying that Council of Europe Recommendation 1201 did not call for group rights or territorial autonomy.

Also, in the Hungarian-Slovakian treaty, the clarifying language regarding group rights was in a side memorandum, which posed a problem for Slovakia's combative prime minister, Vladimir Meçiar, a former professional boxer. For many months he lacked the parliamentary majority needed for ratification. Ethnic resentments have a long half-life in Eastern Europe, and anti-Hungarian sentiment in Slovakia was no exception. It began in the pre–World War I period, when Slovakia was part of the Austro-Hungarian Empire, and intensified later, when Hitler ordered the eastern portion of Slovakia ceded to Hungary.

Until the Slovak Parliament ratified the treaty with Hungary, Hungary was not going to move on the treaty with Romania. Sadly, our embassy in Budapest was not fully aware of the Slovak angle and its reporting blamed Romania for the holdup. When our ambassador to Hungary, Donald Blinken, visited me in Bucharest in February, I arranged for him to meet with President Iliescu to gain greater insight into the complex historical background and the present state of negotiations.

PROMOTING AMERICAN INVESTMENT IN ROMANIA

From the day I arrived as ambassador, I tried to promote American investment in Romania. This was consistent with U.S. policy. The difficulty lay primarily with Romania's inability or, more accurately, unwillingness to streamline its approval procedures, simplify privatization, establish a strong independent judiciary, and generally put in place a legal and financial structure to attract foreign investors.

The petroleum sector was a good example. With oil production, refineries, and downstream petrochemical facilities in place, Romania should have been attractive to American oil and chemical companies. The petroleum conference in Houston that former president Bush had organized in October 1995 was followed in February by a U.S. Department of Energy oil and gas mission to Romania that included ten major American energy companies. The result was the same in both cases: initial interest and even enthusiasm that waned when hardheaded and experienced American businessmen compared opportunities in Romania with prospects elsewhere.

Other industries came to the same conclusion regarding investment in Romania. At one time or another I met with representatives from Amoco, Atchison Casting, General Electric, Westinghouse, Crane, Case Industries, Exxon, General Motors, Tenneco, AT&T, and a slew of other American companies, but with few exceptions these companies ended up going elsewhere. American companies came to Romania, looked around, saw things they liked, heard encouraging talk from the Romanian side, but nothing happened. This was true for scores of American companies. The SOF was not selling money-making companies, and the Romanian government was not helping.

Another failure was when Hugh Aiken, the CEO of Atchison Casting, of Kansas City, made efforts to purchase IMGB, a large foundry in Bucharest, in early 1996. This would have been good for Atchison and good for IMGB. Atchison would have brought capital and technology upgrades to the IMGB facility, which employed 3,500 workers, but the SOF made it clear it would not sell IMGB to a foreign company, preferring that it remain in Romanian hands—preserving national pride, but dooming IMGB to a slow death.

I visited numerous factories throughout Romania—detergent plants in Timişoara, western Romania; a bread factory in Bucharest; oil refineries; petrochemical plants in Ploieşti, northeast of Bucharest; the Dacia automobile factory near Piteşti, northwest of Bucharest; truck, helicopter, and tractor plants in Braşov, in the foothills of the Carpathian Mountains; a rig manufacturer near Constanta, on the Black Sea; a steel mill in Galati, northeast Romania; an aluminum plant in Slatina, southwestern Romania; and extracted metal facilities elsewhere. The story was always the same—antiquated facilities starved for capital, bloated workforces, and multilayered management that added up to enormous waste and high costs. In sum, inability to compete with Western companies.

Even on the few occasions when structural roadblocks were overcome, other problems lay in store. For example, no sooner was the Procter & Gamble plant in Timişoara up and running than counterfeit packaging hit the market. The packaging was virtually indistinguishable from the real thing. The fake detergent inside, manufactured in Romania, was a mixture of an inferior agent and inert material. The Romania police were alerted. The fake packaging was being imported from Turkey and later was stopped at the border. The police also located the manufacturer of the inert material and put a stop to it. Claude Papas, P&G's general manager in Romania, aptly observed that operating in Romania presented problems not encountered in the United States—just one more obstacle in attracting American investors.

A short time later, Tenneco, another large U.S. company, had a meeting at Cotroceni—complete with a lunch hosted by President Iliescu for Tenneco's CEO, Dana Mead—to celebrate the groundbreaking for Tenneco's wood products operation in western Transylvania. But two years later, Tenneco withdrew, citing numerous delays and obstacles.

High-level business meetings were not uncommon. John McDonnell, the

CEO of McDonnell Douglas, came to Bucharest in the first half of 1996 for two days expecting to sell three MD-11 jet airliners to Tarom. He thought he had a deal and expected to pick up a down payment of $450,000 at a breakfast at my residence. I explained the obvious: promises were not the same as money. The price tag for the MD-11s was over $300 million and would cost Tarom $16 million each year, more than it was paying for its two Airbuses. McDonnell offered to take the Airbuses in exchange. Moreover, the MD-11s were dual passenger-cargo planes that would have boosted Tarom's ambition to become a major transatlantic cargo carrier. I accompanied John to a lunch at Cotroceni hosted by President Iliescu, where the champagne bubbles evaporated along with McDonnell Douglas's dreams. Romania lacked the financial resources to pull the trigger on major deals. In 1997, with Emil Constantinescu president and a center-right, more business-friendly government in power, Congressman Tom Lantos brought a group of American business representatives to Romania to look at investment opportunities, but again there were no takers.

A LOOK AT AMERICAN TECHNICAL ASSISTANCE

The United States offered Romania myriad forms of technical assistance, but never knew whether and when Romania would accept the aid offered. For example, in early 1996 USAID engaged the U.S.-based corporation Bechtel to study Romania's electric power generation, distribution, and sale, over which the state electric company, RENEL, had a monopoly. The ending of RENEL's monopoly would open up the three channels and free the Romanian government's budget from the huge cost of subsidizing energy prices. The study released in March 1996 recommended incorporating the three channels separately and then privatizing them. The recommendation was received with acclaim, followed by the usual inaction. The same was true for the petroleum industry. Bechtel recommended that the government close two large refineries in Ploiești and two smaller ones elsewhere. The first recommendation was politically impossible, as it would have put 30,000 to 40,000 people out of work in the lead-up to national elections, but the more modest proposal had the same fate.

On another occasion, in late spring, USAID sent a Treasury Department consultant to Bucharest to advise the Finance Ministry on short-term fund-raising. The expert was convinced that if the government of Romania auctioned treasury paper rather than selling it at fixed prices to favored banks, as it had been doing, it would get better prices and attract more leu-denominated foreign investments. This could only happen if the paper were auctioned in a manner similar to U.S. Treasury note sales. For reasons best known to the Romanian Finance Ministry, it rejected our expert's advice.

The National Bank of Romania also needed help, particularly in drafting procedures for bank supervision and on a proposed Eurobond offering, the first since the fall of communism. This time the outcome was more positive. National Bank of Romania Governor Isarescu told me that no one at the bank had experience with bond offerings; in his words, "We are not even beginners." This opened the door for Merrill Lynch to take the lead with a U.S Treasury expert sent to assist. The Eurobond offering became a turf war between Governor Isarescu and Finance Minister Georgescu as to which entity would issue the bonds, the National Bank of Romania or the government of Romania (meaning the Finance Ministry). Our expert did a masterful job walking the Finance Ministry and the National Bank of Romania through the labyrinth of obstacles bearing on the success or failure of a public debt offering. In the end, the bonds were issued in the name of the government of Romania, making the indebtedness sovereign debt, thereby lowering the cost to Romania.

My concern regarding the breadth of USAID programs in Romania in the more mundane areas of health, democracy building, civil participation, education, and welfare was reinforced by a report written by Tom Carothers of the Carnegie Foundation that was published in January 1996. In "Assessing Democracy Assistance: The Case of Romania," he pointed out that the agency's programs in Eastern Europe were directed from on high in Washington with little local input and were implemented through private volunteers and independent contractors, again without needed local involvement. The examples he cited were two USAID hospital programs in Romania, one directed toward cost accounting and the other to train birth control practitioners. Both programs lacked Romanian government support and the money ended up being wasted. The same was true for a $1 million program to write standards for hospital accreditation that were never adopted and ended up as an expensive stack of paper.

In time, we managed to change USAID's methodology and programs in Romania. We started training Romanians to save energy by using profit incentives rather than relying on U.S. experts to come to Romania to advise on energy saving. On the democracy front, we convinced USAID to close down "feel good" projects such as enhancing professionalism in the print media. There was little we could do to raise professional standards in the press. Moreover, we had no legitimate interest in supporting dozens of Romanian newspapers, most of which would have folded without our support. They lacked readership and had little impact on the Romanian public's views.

Modernizing Romania's customs service, however, was not a "feel-good" project. The temptation for border officials to dispense favors in exchange for money could be irresistible and was as old as border crossings themselves. Romania was not an exception. No doubt there are corrupt customs services elsewhere, but the customs service in Romania was widely known to be corrupt and inefficient. It had neither trained personnel nor the modern equipment needed to do the job. Until Romania's border security met EU standards, Romania was not going to be admitted to the EU. Again, the U.S. government stepped in, trained Romanian customs officials, and supported Romania's plans to build a modern customs training center outside Bucharest. We also assisted with training and technical enhancements, and slowly things turned for the better. Upgraded customs facilities were needed at all heavily trafficked border crossings. I visited most of them, talked to the officers, and strongly encouraged the Romanian government to upgrade its customs service and enhance border security.

MINNOWS, ANTS, FUEL, AND SERBIA

Serbia's complicity in the Bosnian civil war resulted in a United Nations embargo on the export of fuel and most other goods to Serbia, excluding medical supplies. As expected, fuel prices in Serbia skyrocketed and there was a breakdown in the embargo. At one point, the Danube River was a

principal conduit for fuel reaching Serbia in small boats from Romania—
called the "minnow trade." Romania had strong historical ties to Serbia
but was nevertheless bound by the international sanctions to which it gave
lip service but which it never wholeheartedly embraced. Pressure from the
United States and the EU eventually closed down the minnow trade, but
not the "ant trade," trucks with nearly empty fuel tanks that refueled on
the Romanian side of the border and then crossed into Serbia. There were
a dozen or so refueling stations in operation. Romania could have closed
them down if it had wanted to. I urged the U.S. Serbia Army Mission
team in Bucharest to step up the pressure, and it did—but then came the
"fly trade," refueling of Serbian planes at Timişoara airport in western Romania. Several flights a week arrived from Belgrade with only one or two
passengers. The planes landed with just enough fuel to touch down, fill up,
and fly back to Serbia.

The border between Serbia and Romania remained porous, but Romania's close relations with Serbia sometimes yielded valuable nuggets of intelligence. For example, when President Iliescu returned to Bucharest in May
1996 from his meeting with President Slobodan Milošević in Belgrade, he
confided to me that Milošević would agree to autonomy for Muslim Kosovo
but not its unification with Muslim Albania. Kosovo had historic importance for Serbia: the Battle of Kosovo in 1389 marked the day when Serbia
lost its independence to the Ottoman Turks, and the name had remained an
important symbol of Serb nationalism. President Iliescu's report turned out
to be accurate. Two years later, NATO bombed Belgrade continuously for
seventy-eight days, from March to June 1999, until Serbia agreed to Kosovo's de facto secession. The United States and most EU countries recognized
Kosovo's declaration of independence from Serbia in 2008, but Serbia and
Russia did not.

AMERICAN TOP BRASS IN BUCHAREST

On February 7, Romania pulled the brass ring when General John Shalikashvili, chairman of the U.S. Joint Chiefs of Staff, the top U.S. military officer,
made a two-day visit to Bucharest. "Shali" was a model chairman of the Joint

Chiefs, self-confident without being arrogant, even courtly, but every inch a soldier. He knew the military backward and forward and was articulate, direct, and in all respects impressive. The themes he returned to throughout his stay in Romania were NATO and Bosnia. His message was that NATO expansion would proceed in a deliberate way—Russia had no veto—the expansion would be based on individual merit—there would be no blocs—it was for NATO to build a special relationship with Russia—the military situation in Bosnia was going well—Russian troops served under U.S. command in Bosnia as part of a joint NATO force. Conclusion: Bosnia would hold together—the future would be all right—NATO forces would start to withdraw from Bosnia within a year, after which remaining sanctions would be lifted and the peace process implemented.

As for the Romanian military, Shali pushed hard for multiyear planning. The U.S. military operates on a two-year budget cycle and five-year planning. The Romanians had no multiyear budgeting or planning. Time and again Shali emphasized "training, training, training . . . more important than equipment." Interoperability meant operating procedures, joint exercises, command and control with common communications systems. Interoperability for air traffic control and air defense needed a common radar network. Ground forces were the largest element and the most important in any country's military. Shali offered to send a U.S. mobile training team to work with unit commanders in Romania. Until then, U.S. training of Romanian troops had been in the United States as part of the IMET program, not in Romania.

Shali, his staff, and I met in Defense Minister Georghe Tinca's office along with the Romanian military's chief of staff, General Dumitru Cioflina. Tinca quickly covered the delivery of the four C-130s, plus Romania's purchase of five Lockheed radar systems and plans to purchase radar sensors from Lockheed. He also mentioned the possibility of purchasing F-16s "in the future." (This occurred in 2013, when Romania purchased twelve used F-16 military aircraft from Portugal; three years later it announced its intention to purchase an additional twenty from the United States.) Tinca also made a pitch for the United States to use Romanian air facilities in Timişoara as a NATO base, an offer frequently made and never accepted. But Tinca was not the first or the last Romanian defense minister to dangle a carrot in the hope of establishing a NATO military presence in Romania. (Giant oaks from acorns grow. In late 2016 NATO's deputy secretary general, Sergio Balanzino, announced that NATO planned to increase its presence in the Black Sea region with a Romanian-led multinational framework brigade on land and additional NATO forces in the air and on the sea—all Romania-based.) The visit had its ceremonial side. Shali was accorded full military honors on entering the Defense Ministry building. Upon leaving, he and General Cioflina had their pictures taken saluting a fourteen-foot snowman and graciously invited me to join them.

I have rarely been as cold as I was when I accompanied Shali to review a Romanian engineering brigade slated to go to Bosnia. The soldiers were assembled on an open snow-covered field, with the temperature far below freezing, which felt even colder with a strong wind blowing. The Romanian soldiers wore Afghan hats, Shali was wearing his less protective regular army hat, but this son of a Baltimore hat manufacturer was totally unprepared for the cold.

The real test of strength came that night at a dinner at the Cercul Militar National, an ornate building on downtown Bucharest's central boulevard, Calea Victoriei. It began at 8 p.m. and went on until midnight, by which time we had listened to nine musical ensembles, plus twenty-five individual performances. The six-course dinner, complete with toasts and speeches, became an endurance test made more difficult by the absence of heat in the large marble hall. When I began to feel sorry for myself, I thought of Shali and his team, who had only just arrived in Bucharest that afternoon from Washington.

A RIGHT TURN

An inflection point in my ambassadorship came with a speech I delivered at Babeș-Bolyai University in Cluj on February 22. Before my speech in Cluj, in every meeting with important Romanians I had laid out the steps Romania needed to take to improve its standing in the West and to be eligible for membership in Western alliances. Despite some negative chattering in the extremist press, I remained popular with most Romanians. This continued after my Cluj speech, but the role of the PUNR, PRM, and PSM in Romanian politics had taken on a new prominence that continued throughout the remainder of 1996, by which time PRM and PSM were no longer part of PDSR's voting coalition in Parliament.

I delivered the speech in a grand paneled hall with the university's faculty assembled on raised wooden tiers in front of me and the audience behind me. The rector of the university stood by my side. The long speech was intended to be a major statement, and it was greeted with loud and sustained applause. The speech called on Romania to take concrete steps to strengthen democratic values and modernize its economy. I also urged Romania to lay aside old conflicts and grievances, conclude basic treaties with Hungary and Ukraine, and move forward on the path to membership in the Western family of nations. Last, I said that Romanians should reject extremist parties: "It is up to the Romanian people to decide which parties are extremist, but there have been extremist statements from leaders of PRM, PSM and PUNR, and as a result the three parties are considered extremist in the West." Largely overlooked were my concluding words: "Together we shall overcome the difficult hurdles that lie ahead until Romania takes its proper place among the Western family of nations. I have faith that Romania will succeed." I had been saying the same thing in every press conference and interview and in most official statements for the past fifteen months, but my speech seemed to come like a bolt out of the blue for the three voting coalition partners.

Three months later, in May, when I gave a radio interview on PRO-FM, a popular radio station in Bucharest, the questions were familiar, but now included some concerning my previous statement in Cluj about extremist parties. When the interviewer asked me to name extremists, I gave the same answer I had in Cluj. It was up to the Romanian people to determine which parties were extremist. By now this was old news, and there was no reaction in the press or elsewhere. My repeated reference in interviews, speeches, and public statements on the desirability of a centrist coalition government had an effect: all political parties in the 1996 elections referred to themselves as centrist.

A FIGHT OVER SERPENT ISLAND

Ukraine's ambassador to Romania, Oleksandr Chaly, praised my speech in Cluj, particularly the part urging Romania to conclude basic treaties with Hungary and Ukraine. He then tried to persuade me to take Ukraine's side in the negotiations—a strange notion. Ukraine had recently upped the ante by insisting on an explicit statement in the Romania-Ukraine treaty that Romania had no claims to Serpent Island and that it recognized Ukraine's de jure ownership of the island. In return, Ukraine would agree to abide by the "gentleman's agreement" reached by the Soviet Union and Romania in the early 1960s that the Soviet Union would not exploit the Black Sea south of Serpent Island. Ukraine had recently begun exploring for oil and gas in the Delphin Block, southeast of the island, claiming it was outside the boundaries of the "gentleman's agreement." Romania disputed this. Geography was on Romania's side. This was the beginning of protracted negotiation that, happily, ended in a ratified treaty in June 1997.

THE COBRA DEAL

Bell Helicopter's president, Lloyd Shoppa, came to Romania in late February 1996, and for a time the Cobra deal looked likely. Bell had a well-deserved reputation for high-tech excellence, and if it invested in an assembly plant in Brașov, IAR-Brașov, it would be lending its prestige to a Romania that sorely needed it. Bell held 62 percent of the world helicopter market, and if it established a plant in Romania, it would be the first Western high-tech company to undertake major manufacturing in Romania. As Shoppa put it, "If Romania can prove that it is capable of manufacturing state-of-the-art aircraft, it will go a long way toward qualifying Romania to manufacture other high-quality products."

Engine production would be in a separate facility. I visited Turbomecanica, an *régie autonome* in Bucharest, built in the 1970s to manufacture the Puma helicopter engine and a fixed-wing aircraft engine under license from Rolls Royce. The technology was now out of date and the plant was operating hand-to-mouth doing repair work and manufacturing spare parts. In January, Pratt & Whitney of Canada had made an offer to buy a 51 percent interest in Turbomecanica, but the offer was turned down because Pratt & Whitney did not intend to manufacture engines, only parts. This would have ended Turbomecanica's engine manufacturing capability, built up over twenty years. The company's management hoped to attract offers from Rolls Royce (United Kingdom) or Allied Signal (United States), but none came. This left the Cobra deal the only one on the table. If it went ahead, Turbomecanica would manufacture the T-700 engine for the Cobra under license from General Electric.

I was convinced that the Cobra deal made sense. Most of the economic benefits would have stayed in Romania in the form of payments to the government for the Braşov facility, which would assemble the airframes, and to Turbomecanica, which would manufacture the engines. Textron, Bell Helicopter's parent company, was willing to put a civilian helicopter product line in the Braşov plant as well as other metalworking products. This would have been a complete package. Later Bell offered to buy a minimum of 51 percent of IAR-Braşov and use the facility as its manufacturing base in Europe. Both Prime Minister Vacaroiu and Defense Minister Tinca supported Bell's proposal. Vacaroiu, an economist, immediately understood that for Bell to buy 51 percent of IAR-Braşov, Romania needed to enter into a firm contract to buy the Cobras in order for Bell to finance production between then and 1999, when the first Cobras would be delivered. The front-end money, approximately $30 million, would come from the SOF and Romanian Defense Ministry's R&D fund. The SOF had the money, having just sold a large combine factory in Bucharest to Fiat. It could work.

Later, President Iliescu gave his blessing to the Bell deal, and for a time Bell's management and I were optimistic, but the $30 million down payment continued to be the sticking point. Tinca claimed that the Defense Ministry did not have $30 million in its budget and could not find it elsewhere. With a straight face he suggested that Bell should accept approval of the deal by the Romanian Parliament in lieu of cash. Nice try, but that was not the way business worked. Negotiations continued. I urged both sides to reach an agreement—in effect, cheerleading for U.S. business. This meant tracking down Shoppa by telephone as he traveled around the world and importuning Defense Minister Tinca and Finance Minister Georgescu to come up with innovative ways to finance the front-end payment. As usual, the SOF and its president, Emil Dima, were sphinxlike in their silence.

 **10**

Washington Pays Attention

SPRING 1996

THE CALL OF THE COUNTRYSIDE

In spring, the Romanian countryside was a lush green. Roads were being re-paired after the long winter. Tree trunks lining the road were freshly painted white, adding brightness to the scene. Villages untouched by Ceauşescu's socialist building mania had preserved their historic authenticity. A typical Romanian village consisted of brightly colored one-story wooden houses on the two sides of a paved road facing each other with abandoned cars and farm machinery scattered about. Farther back from the paved road were even more modest homes on unpaved, often muddy, rutted lanes. Living conditions could be harsh; many homes were without indoor plumbing or running water.

BELA MARKO

I met with Bela Marko, the leader of the Democratic Union of Hungarians in Romania (UDMR), in April 1996. By that time he was more moderate than he had been when we met the previous year. We discussed aligning his ethnic Hungarian party with PDSR or PNT-CD in order to end its isolation and give it greater political clout. Since 93 percent of the Romanian electorate was ethnically Romanian, UDMR on its own could not achieve much. I again pointed out that extremist Hungarian rhetoric on the part of UDMR produced a similar extremist outcry on the ethnic Romanian side, represented by the Romanian National Unity Party (PUNR). Marko was quoted in the papers the next day condemning a party member for extremist language, so maybe the message got across.

The Hungarian problem was less a case of actual grievance and more one of political rhetoric designed to appeal to the faithful. Max Van der Stoel, the Organization for Security and Cooperation in Europe high commissioner for national minorities, had stated in a private conversation with me that there was no meaningful discrimination against ethnic Hungarians in Romania. In a second meeting in early 1996, Van der Stoel told me that the Romanian education law required university entrance examinations to be taken in Romanian for courses taught in Romanian, but that law had not been applied to ethnic Hungarians and had been suspended by Secretary General Hrebenciuc. When I asked Van der Stoel where else in Europe university applicants could take entrance examinations in a language other than the national language, he paused before saying, "Perhaps in Finland entrance examinations can be taken in Swedish for one or two courses." The fact that the law in Romania was more liberal than in any other country in Europe did not stop ethnic Hungarians from complaining about "cultural genocide."

THE MARCH NATO AMBASSADORS' LUNCH

The NATO ambassadors' spring lunch was at the residence of the Netherlands ambassador, Monique Frank. Oliviu Gherman, president of the Senate, was our guest. With great solemnity, an all-but-tearful Gherman told the NATO ambassadors that if the PDSR executive committee, which was meeting in an hour, did not vote to expel Romania Mare (PRM) from the PDSR-led coalition, he would resign from PDSR. The sentiment was sincere, but the drama was manufactured; there was no doubt that PDSR would do exactly that. This was six months after President Iliescu's trip to Washington and after Iliescu had made the decision to break with the crypto-fascist PRM and later with the crypto-communist PSD. Gherman was hardly the captain standing on the burning bridge while his ship went down. He knew the decision to expel PRM had already been made, so the emotion was for our benefit and for his own image polishing. Most of the NATO ambassadors were indifferent or uninterested in Romania's journey westward. For them, Bucharest was just another post. Their governments did not expect them to perform miracles in Romania and they were not looking for a chance to do so. Only the British and German ambassadors were reflective, well informed, and truly committed to furthering relations and moving Romania in the right direction.

GRADUATING ROMANIA TO PERMANENT MFN STATUS

At a spring meeting at the State Department in Washington, it was agreed to take another look at getting permanent MFN status for Romania through Congress. Dan Fried, director for Eastern Europe at the National Security Council, was opposed unless we received something in return from the Romanians, in particular, positive movement on human rights. Dick Schifter of the National Security Council and the rest of us at the meeting—including the State Department officials Deputy Assistant Secretary Marshal Adair, Director of the Office of North Central European Affairs Jonathan Rickert, and Terry Snell, the head of the Office of Eastern European Affairs—agreed that the Jackson-Vanik Amendment only dealt with freedom of emigration, not ethnic relations, and that Romania's performance on human rights, by all objective standards, had been good. Moreover, from the U.S. standpoint, we needed to bring Romania closer to us. Treating it like a misbehaving stepchild only reinforced Romania's feelings that it would never be accepted by the West. In the end, Dan went along.

After that, legislation for graduating Romania to permanent MFN status began to move in Congress. Senators Hank Brown (R-Colo.), Charles Grassley (R-Iowa), Max Baucus (D-Mont.), and Paul Simon (D-Ill.) introduced a bill in the Senate making MFN for Romania permanent, and a companion bill was introduced in the House by Phil Crane (R-Ill.) and Barbara Kennelly (D-Conn.). Much of the work was done by Ambassador Geoana and his Romanian embassy staff in Washington. Hank Brown was a late convert to graduation, but he took the lead. He had pushed early admission to NATO for the "Vişegrad Four" (Poland, Czechoslovakia, Hungary, and Slovakia), putting Romania behind, but after visiting Bucharest a few months before he came away favorably impressed and put Romania up with the frontrunners. In the House, my good friend Congressman Tom Lantos lent his support, as did Deputy National Security Adviser Sandy Berger, speaking for the White House.

The only serious opposition came, as expected, from Congressman David Funderburk (D-N.C.) and, somewhat surprisingly, from Congressman Chris Smith (R-N.J.), who had previously indicated his support. Funderburk's opposition was predictable; he did not want Iliescu and his party, PDSR, to claim credit for MFN graduation, particularly with national elections scheduled for November. Funderburk strongly supported PNT-CD and wanted to deny the PDSR credit for permanent MFN status. To counter this, I met with the leaders of the principal opposition parties in Bucharest and obtained their full support for MFN graduation, thus making MFN graduation a nonpartisan issue in the fall elections. It also defanged Funderburk's opposition to MFN graduation on Romanian political grounds.

Congressman Tom Lantos was Romania's most effective champion. Born in Hungary, a Jewish activist, and the first and only Holocaust survivor to serve in Congress, Tom had enormous credibility on the Hill, especially on issues involving Central Europe. He became Romania's champion in the debate on Romanian MFN status on the House floor, overshadowing Congressman David Funderburk, who spoke against permanent MFN status for Romania but had little credibility on either side of the aisle.

RADU VASILE

In April, Senator Radu Vasile, secretary general of PNT-CD, arranged for me to meet with the PNT-CD's leadership to enlist its support for signing basic treaties with Hungary and Ukraine and to explain to them the economic reform agenda we were supporting along with the IMF and World Bank.

Senator Vasile was portrayed in the Romanian press as the favorite to be prime minister in a future PNT-CD-led government—but he never impressed me as serious or hard-working. After the election, President Emil Constantinescu and the PNT-CD leader, Ion Diaconescu, initially gave the prime minister job to Victor Ciorbea, but after two years of indecision on Ciorbea's part, Constantinescu turned to Vasile, who served as prime minister for less than two years before being replaced by the governor of Romania's national bank, Mugur Isarescu.

Senator Vasile was also close to French ambassador Bernard Boyer, who told Vasile that France would support Romania's entry into NATO only if Romania favored French business interests. Actually, Boyer put it more crudely, telling Vasile "not to give everything to the Americans." Boyer never stopped undermining the United States. He had a Gaullist mentality, telling the Israeli ambassador, Avi Milo, "I have no objection to Jews having full rights in France." At the time, Boyer's daughter was living in Washington, and I thought maybe I should tell him I had no objection to his daughter, a French citizen, having full rights in the United States, where she lived with her husband and children.

COBRAS, CONTINUED

The Bell Helicopter deal moved slowly throughout 1996. The Romanians had not decided on weaponry or avionics for the Cobra, but if, as expected, they asked for attack missiles, this would require approval in Washington. Defense Secretary William Perry in his meeting with President Iliescu at the Pentagon the previous September had indicated this would not be a problem. The price tag was an even greater obstacle. The package of ninety-six Cobras Romania wanted would cost some $1 billion with $200 million to be paid in 1998. This was about 25 percent of the Romanian defense budget, and it would be hard for Romania to come up with the cash. I planned to meet with Defense Minister Tinca to learn how the Romanians expected to pay.

MOVING THE AMERICAN INTERNATIONAL
SCHOOL OF BUCHAREST

In most foreign capitals, there is an American school that educates American and other foreign national children using English as the language of instruction. Traditionally, the deputy chief of mission (DCM) in the American embassy is the chairman of the board of the American school. Michael Einik came to Bucharest in the summer of 1995 to take up the DCM post after the departure of Jonathan Rickert. Under Mike's leadership, in 1996 we arranged to move the American International School of Bucharest from an overcrowded location in downtown Bucharest to a new campus near Baneasa Airport, the Bucharest airport for domestic flights.

Fathi Taher, the Kuwaiti businessman I had enlisted to help restore the Lipscani district in downtown Bucharest, had assembled a large tract of land on which he planned to build 400 residential units as part of a planned community. I had done major real estate deals in the United States, so this one was right up my alley. Fathi, Mike, and I put together a proposal whereby Fathi would deliver, at no charge to the United States, a finished school in return for the school's leasing the property with an option to purchase it at a nominal price at the end of twenty to twenty-five years. This would give Fathi what he was looking for, financing, and he could include the cost of the school in the purchase price of the residences, meaning that the school rent would be less than the amount needed to amortize the loan. Fathi rightly concluded that the school would be a major attraction for families with school-age children and thus would boost residential sales. Mike worked out the details after I left Bucharest. I later visited the school. It was truly a gem. The campus was designed by Colden Florance, an architect in Washington with a sterling reputation, who was awarded the contract by Fathi on the basis of merit. As of 2018 the K–12 school has more than 800 students enrolled for the fall term.

A TALE OF TWO ROMANIAN SPORTS HEROES

Two of Romania' most beloved heroes came to worldwide prominence and popularity via the world of sports. One was the Olympic gymnast Nadia Comaneci, the fourteen-year-old phenomenon who in 1976 scored the first perfect 10 in Olympic history. She went on to score six additional 10s in the 1976 Olympics and won the all-around individual gymnast title, as well as three gold medals, capturing the hearts and souls of Romania and everyone else. The other was Romania's bad boy, the ill-tempered, clownish Ilie Nastase, who despite his court antics had won the U.S. Open, had become the number-one-ranked player in the world in 1973–74, and had gone on to earn more than 100 Association of Tennis Professionals titles in his career, one of five players in history to do so.

Cut to April 1996. Nadia, now thirty-four, had retired from competition but was still a major personality in Romania. She was regal and lovely. She came to my residence on April 26 for a reception the day before her wedding to U.S. Olympic gold medalist Bart Conner. It was a beautiful day. There were 150 guests, mostly Nadia and Bart's American friends. One of the guests whispered to me, "It reminds me of the Hamptons." The wedding the next day, April 27, was a media event staged by Nadia and Bart. The American sports media were there in full force.

Ilie Nastase was authentically Romanian and his fellow countrymen loved him. In 1995 he had returned to Romania and gone into politics. President Iliescu selected him to be PDSR's candidate for mayor of Bucharest. Initially, he was way ahead in the polls based on name recognition and fame, but in the June 1996 election he lost badly to Romania's future prime minister, Victor Ciorbea, a former Ceaușescu prosecutor who by the time of the elections had become a Christian Democrat.

During the campaign, the politically naïve Nastase was hurt by his vulgar language and vituperative outbursts. He tried to cover his lack of experience by announcing he would rely on experts to advise him. Ciorbea's answer was, "I am the expert. Why vote for somebody who knows nothing and is primarily a showboat."

After the election, Ilie became my doubles partner. Not surprisingly, he carried me. Having the former world champion as my partner meant I never lost a set!

ROMANIAN NATIONAL ARCHIVES, ROUND 2

In April 1996, Paul Shapiro and Radu Ioanid of the Holocaust Museum came to Bucharest to examine various Romanian archives. The principal difficulty was obtaining files from the renamed Romanian National Archives. Congressman Ben Gilman (R-N.Y.), chairman of the House International Relations Committee, had threatened to hold up graduation of Romania's MFN status to permanent until the problem was solved. I asked Diplomatic Adviser Traian Chebeleu at Cotroceni and Secretary General Viorel Hrebenciuc for help. "Mr. Fix-It" did his magic. Within the hour, Hrebenciuc called back to tell me that Prime Minister Vacaroiu would immediately issue a government decree that would "take care of the problem." Chebeleu also pitched in, joining me at a meeting with the director of the National Archives. True to Hrebenciuc's word, Vacaroiu signed an order instructing the National Archives to give the Holocaust Museum access to all government files pertaining to Jewish individual and communal property, including the fonts. Paul and Radu were satisfied and communicated this to Congressman Gilman's office, thereby removing a major obstacle on the road to Romania's attaining permanent MFN status. A year later Radu was still complaining that the military archives were dragging their feet on some 220 rolls of microfilm. I immediately met with General Dumitru Cioflina, Romania's military chief of staff, who solved the problem. There was blame on both sides. Radu tended to see the worst in his Romanian counterparts, and the Romanians had no incentive, other than pressure from our embassy, to respond to the Holocaust Museum's quite considerable requests.

BUCHAREST TO WASHINGTON: PAY MORE ATTENTION TO ROMANIA!

By late spring, matters were adrift in Bucharest. The basic treaties with Hungary and Ukraine were stuck in bilateral negotiations with little progress being made, each side expecting the other to cave in. The basic treaty with Hungary was on hold until Slovakia's Parliament ratified Slovakia's bilateral treaty with Hungary. Ukraine was not prepared to move on the Molotov-

Ribbentrop Pact issue before Russia acted. Economic reform was entangled with electoral politics, and the RASDAQ build-out was beset with technical problems that would take time to solve. Moreover, it was increasingly clear to me that Romania was not going to be included in the first round of NATO enlargement, and that would diminish the importance of the United States in Romania's eyes—and lessen our chances of persuading Romania to do the things it needed to do in its own interest.

With these thoughts in mind I drafted a memorandum, dated May 3, with the concurrence of John Kornblum, Richard Holbrooke's successor as assistant secretary of state for European and Canadian affairs, and Marshall Adair, Kornblum's deputy, recommending that Secretary Christopher invite Foreign Minister Meleşcanu to meet with him in Washington to discuss NATO enlargement. I traveled to Washington in early May to deliver the draft memo in person. It read in part:

Romania is nervous about NATO enlargement. If Hungary is admitted and Romania left out, the GOR is fearful that this will cause a rise in extremist sentiments within the country, recreate the geopolitical chessboard that resulted in the two great tragedies of this century, and foster the perception that Romania is again being abandoned by the West. In Romanian eyes, the result will be a division of Catholic West from Orthodox East along the traditional political fault line of Central Europe. If this happens, Romanians' post-revolution mantra of joyous welcome, "We have been waiting 50 years for the Americans," could turn into a cry of disillusionment.

Romanians are unabashedly pro-American—over 90 percent consider Romania's relationship with the United States its most important. This is reinforced by Romania's historic fear of Russia; a Romania left outside of NATO will fuel this concern. Germany's historic arc of interest does not include Romania, and France is seen as too weak and otherwise distracted to be a reliable partner. For these reasons, Romania looks to the United States to boost its ties to the West.

Politically and economically, Romania has made considerable progress in the last year. Following President Iliescu's Oval Office visit in September, the government coalition shed its two extremist parties—one left, the other right. Several thousand companies will be privatized this year. By year-end, more than 50 percent of Romania's GDP will come from the private sector.

Romania is an active and enthusiastic participant in Partnership for Peace; bilaterally, the Mil-to-Mil program is among our most robust. Romania is a member of the Australia Group and a founding member of the Wassenaar Arrangement. Cooperation in the intelligence field is expanding; Romania is becoming a reliable and helpful provider.

Romania favors the United States for military procurement. It has contracted to buy five Lockheed air control and defense radar systems at a cost of $80 million and has signed a letter of intent to purchase ninety-six Cobra helicopters at an estimated cost of $1 billion. The Cobras will be co-produced at the IAR plant in Brașov. The engines, expected to be General Electric T-700s, will also be co-produced in Romania. A French company (Puma) has been actively seeking the helicopter business. Romania's Defense Minister Georghe Tinca has made it clear that the decision to buy the Cobra shows the importance Romania attaches to its relationship with the United States.

Romania knows that U.S. resources are limited and does not expect major financial assistance, but does seek high-level American recognition of Romania's desire to move closer to the United States and, more important, is looking to the United States to keep the door open for Romania to join NATO. It recognizes that other countries such as Poland and the Czech Republic are likely to be admitted first. The sensitive issue is Hungary.

We need to manage the bilateral relationship in a way that will encourage Romania's pro-Western reforms and continuing close ties to the United States without producing false expectations that Romania will be admitted to NATO in the first round. The challenge for us is to keep the NATO race open, assisting those behind such as Romania to catch up so that at the end of the day all aspirants will have a fair chance for inclusion, creating a stable and united bloc of new NATO nations across Central Europe.

The memo was well received at State. Upon my return to Bucharest, on May 14, I was able to deliver Warren Christopher's letter inviting Foreign Minister Teodor Meleşcanu to Washington in July.

There was still a lot of jockeying on our side on NATO enlargement. Ralph Johnson, our ambassador in Bratislava, the capital of Slovakia, wanted the American ambassadors in Central Europe to meet with representatives from the EU to discuss the lead-up to NATO and how to handle the situation in countries that did not get into NATO in the first round. I nixed it. A conference along the lines Ralph proposed would end up being a beauty contest, with each ambassador championing his or her country. I thought: Decisions on NATO enlargement will be made in Washington on largely political grounds, without a strict grading system based on merit. At this point, the less said the better, certainly in Bucharest and probably in other capitals as well.

A TRIP TO ORADEA

On a clear April morning, I flew to Oradea, in western Transylvania. The city dated from the Middle Ages and still retained a strong Hungarian identity. It was one of the most beautiful cities in Romania, and much of the old city remained. On my agenda was a visit to a modern Coca-Cola plant on the outskirts of town. Built in 1993, the plant employed over 300 workers and used only Romanian raw materials even for bottle caps, labels, and packaging. However, the emotional highlight was the next stop on my agenda, a brief visit to the Oradea synagogue. When we entered the building, a choir of twenty-five young people sang Hebrew songs. It was obvious from their faces that many of them were one-half or one-quarter Jewish by birth. None of the choir members could read or speak Hebrew and this made their singing even more remarkable for me. Somehow, the congregation functioned without a rabbi, serving primarily as a meeting place for Oradea's dwindling Jewish community.

The next stop was a sharp contrast with the small synagogue: an enormous Baptist church built after the revolution, where some 600 youngsters filled the church. They sang beautifully, but again there was an odd side to the music:

they sang Negro spirituals. The choir director told us he was from Mississippi, and presumably he had convinced the choir members that the deeply
spiritual songs they were singing grew out of our Southern religious heritage
in the United States. I was seated on a raised platform in the front of the
church enjoying the hymns when I was peremptorily instructed to get up to
speak. Without too much fumbling, I thanked the choir for its performance
and congratulated the congregation for its profession of faith. As I looked at
the young believers with their radiant faces and sincere fervor, I could not
help but think about the 200,000 Transylvanian Jews who had been deported
in cattle cars to Auschwitz by the Nazis with the complicity of their fellow
Transylvanians, and of the decimation of the Jewish community of Oradea
during the Hungarian occupation in the early 1940s. Then the lines from
Milton's Sonnet 19, on blindness, came into my mind: "They also serve who
only stand and wait." I told the audience that to "stand and wait" was sublime
as an article of faith, but waiting—my not-very-subtle reference to singing
hymns—was not a substitute for doing what was right and just. That night our
consul general, who had been seated next to me in church, told her daughter
in Colorado about my speech in highly effusive words, to which her daughter
rightly responded, "What do you expect, Mother, he is a trial lawyer."

In the afternoon we flew from Oradea to Sibiu, founded in the sixteenth
century as a German Saxon city, nestled in the southeast corner of Transylvania. Most of its ethnic Germans left in the late 1960s, when Ceaușescu
made a deal with the Federal Republic of Germany to send Romania's ethnic
Germans to the fatherland in return for a head tax of $10,000 per person.
For Romania's ethnic Germans, the term "fatherland"—*Vaterland*—had real
meaning. Sibiu had three large open markets surrounded by late eighteenth-
and nineteenth-century buildings badly in need of repair. The magnificent
Lutheran Cathedral of Saint Mary dated back to the 1500s. During the
Counterreformation, it became a Catholic Church but later reverted to the
Lutheran community. The old Saxon wall surrounding the city had been pre-
served, as had many period buildings.

A visit to the local synagogue in Sibiu was an emotional letdown after the
moving experience in Oradea. Oradea had 40,000 Jews before the war. Most
of them had been transported to and killed at Auschwitz. Sibiu had a little
over 1,000 before the war. The community now numbered about 70.

VIRGIL MAGUREANU'S SRI

American intelligence services regularly inquired of the SRI (Romanian Internal Security Service) about Hezbollah, a Lebanon-based Shiite terrorist organization, and Iraqi and Iranian activities in Romania. When not looking for soft targets in country, all three groups were using Romania either as a staging platform for missions elsewhere or as a safe haven for rest and recovery for its operatives. SRI Director Virgil Magureanu pledged cooperation with our intelligence services, but the SRI's capabilities were limited. Under Ceaușescu, the Securitate, the SRI's infamous and loathed predecessor, had used primarily strong-arm tactics against its countrymen, gathering useless data on ordinary citizens, tapping their phones, and eavesdropping on private conversations—all rudimentary stuff in a thuggish police state. A sophisticated intelligence service relies on analysis, backed by a coherent strategy and well-conceived and executed operations to address threats to national security. The SRI lacked these tools and skills. Surveillance was the most we could hope for from the Romanians, and possibly information on the Hezbollah structure in Romania and elsewhere, but we never received the latter.

SRI Director Magureanu always played the sphinx, but that did not stop me from working with him. He was anxious to visit CIA headquarters in Langley, Virginia, and in return wanted the CIA director, George Tenet, to visit Bucharest, a carrot I dangled in exchange for hard information on what the North Koreans, Iranians, Iraqis, Hezbollah, and others were up to in Bucharest and assistance on counterterrorism. The most we got from Magureanu was a list of personnel in the North Korean embassy in Bucharest, some of whom were undoubtedly engaged in intelligence. Not enough. The game continued.

 **11**

A Visit from Hillary Clinton

SUMMER 1996

A DAY IN IASI

My official trips out of Bucharest fell into a pattern: an early morning flight, arrival ceremony at the destination airport hosted by local dignitaries, a police-escorted drive into the city, meetings with the prefect, mayor, and city council members. My trip to Iasi in June was no exception. Iasi has a famous history. For one thing, it was the jumping-off point for the German Wehrmacht's invasion of the Soviet Union in July 1941. Centuries before it had been the historic capital of the principalities of Wallachia and Moldavia. It is less than ten miles from Romania's border with Ukraine. When I visited the border crossing, Romanian soldiers were on the lookout for drugs, weapons, and nuclear material. The drugs came chiefly from Afghanistan, the nuclear material from Ukraine, and weapons from just about anywhere.

As always, the lunch in Iasi was too long and too elaborate. After the fourth course I was able to make a getaway for the synagogue in the center of town. When I arrived, I was an hour late, reminding me of my last visit to the synagogue with Rabbi Rosen, in 1984. The synagogue was as I remembered it, only a bit shabbier and the congregation a few years older and a tad smaller in numbers. A speech, handshakes, and hugs, and then out the door for meetings and speeches, first with the city council, then at the University of Iasi, where I addressed the school's senate. My speeches, too, had become routine and did not require preparation or even much forethought. I always invited questions, most of which were predictable and easy to answer.

On this occasion, however, I was asked by an Orthodox priest who headed the university's theology department whether "private enterprise was undermining traditional values," a great question that is frequently posed by theologians and non-religious thinkers alike in the United States. It deserved a serious answer. The priest's question allowed me to offer a heartfelt message about the need for religion to fulfill people's innermost spiritual needs; otherwise it will wither, as it has in much of Western Europe. (My Washington training came in handy: Use the question to deliver your message, not necessarily answer the question.)

Later that day at a press conference I was asked whether I thought that Romania was complicit in the Holocaust. This, too, was a question frequently asked. Romanians generally discounted or rejected Romanian complicity in the Holocaust, putting the blame on Germans or Hungarians. Romanians are not the only ones to put the blame on others, and in Romania's case the historical record shows that this was partly true. But it could not be denied that hundreds of thousands of Jews were killed in Romania by Romanians in Transnistria, or were shipped from Transylvania in cattle cars to Auschwitz. My frequently repeated Holocaust message was not what Romanians wanted to hear, but the facts were the facts. As for acknowledging the terrible truth, Romanians would do well to emulate today's Germans in facing their past, instead of blaming their neighbors.

LOCAL ELECTIONS IN JUNE

Chamber of Deputies President Adrian Nastase had confided to me that he saw tough sledding ahead for PDSR in upcoming local elections in June, to be followed by general elections in November. He was genuinely pessimistic.

Local elections were held on June 2. The ruling PDSR lost badly. Victor Ciorbea trounced Ilie Nastase in the mayoralty race in Bucharest. Similar results occurred throughout the country. Most Romanian pundits predicted that President Iliescu would still win the presidential race in November, but I was becoming increasingly convinced that Iliescu would also lose. He was listening to a small cadre of loyalists and his campaign seemed rudderless. When he arrived in a town or village to speak during the campaign, nothing had been prepared for him. He was on his own, falling back on tired slogans that might have worked in the past but were no longer relevant. In the television debates leading up to the election, he again had no help. His diplomatic adviser, Traian Chebeleu, gave him some talking points, but he did not use them. His opponent, Emil Constantinescu, proudly proclaimed his Romanian Orthodox beliefs, forcing President Iliescu to mumble that he was a "free thinker," reminding listeners of his communist past.

A year before the election the signs had been the other way: Iliescu had seemed unbeatable. But in the ensuing year he had done little to help himself. It was his election to lose, and he lost it. Instead of moving toward the middle, picking up votes from the opposition, he spouted nationalist rhetoric, waving the anti-Hungarian "bloody shirt," and scared peasants saying that if the opposition won the election, they would lose their farms to former landowners. None of this worked. He should have come out as a reform president running against Parliament, corruption, and those standing in the way of economic progress. Instead, he wrapped himself in a quasi-socialist blanket and surrounded himself with yes-men. Even the business community of Iliescu insiders abandoned him; only George Paunescu was left. The others ran away.

I met with Victor Ciorbea immediately after he won the mayoral election. We had lunch in a small private room in a Bucharest restaurant near my residence. Not only was he now the mayor of Romania's capital and largest city, but in my mind he was a possible future prime minister in a PNT-CD–led government if, as I expected, it won the elections in November. Mayor Ciorbea struck me as well intentioned but naïve and lacking the requisite political tools to be an effective political leader.

A day or two later I visited Ciorbea in his mayoral office. When I arrived in mid-afternoon, he was just starting lunch. He worked eighteen-hour days and, when not dining at my residence, which he frequently did, ate at odd hours. We discussed a proposal whereby USAID would provide school bathroom facilities for some 8,000 students in Bucharest. The program succeeded. Early on, Ciorbea took my side publicly in the brouhaha over the International Republican Institute's leaving Romania, and our close association continued for the remainder of my time in Romania.

ILIESCU'S INTERMINISTERIAL COMMITTEE
AND THE INSCRUTABLE MR. DIMA

On June 20, 1996, an interministerial committee established by President Iliescu to promote U.S. investment in Romania held its first meeting in the main conference room of the Foreign Ministry. The session was chaired by Foreign Minister Meleşcanu, who was his usual gracious self, explaining that his "orders" from President Iliescu were to expedite direct American investment in Romania. In response, I named six American companies that were interested in investing: Westinghouse, Amoco, Western Union, Johnson & Johnson, Barrington Associates, and TransChem. Of these, only the TransChem deal materialized. Two years later, TransChem aggregated some 150,000 hectares of agricultural land for irrigation, mechanized farming, planting of hybrid seed, application of fertilizer, and other upgrades along the lines of Western-style agriculture. By then I had returned to Washington. The project was a total bust. It had not produced the bountiful crops promised by its U.S. sponsor. Before I left Romania, I learned that TransChem had had a similar failure in Ukraine. After hearing this and closely analyzing TransChem's proposal, I withdrew our support. (Unfortunately, the project went ahead.)

We had three or four follow-up meetings with Meleşcanu. The results were always the same. Meleşcanu and others would assure us of results, but nothing happened. At each turn, the answer was the same. Whether the government of Romania was incompetent or dissembling, I never knew. Were President Iliescu, Minister Meleşcanu, and the others just going through the motions for show, or was the bureaucracy incapable or unwilling to deliver? One problem was that the sale of state-owned enterprises (SOEs) to foreign investors was the province of the State Ownership Fund (SOF) and its head, Emil Dima. Until December 1996 Dima was a power unto himself, answerable solely to Parliament, which really meant to no one.

Dima looked like a communist apparatchik from central casting: rumpled suit and workingman's jacket. He would go unnoticed in a crowd of workers leaving a factory at the end of the day. He was unpretentious, but, as Winston Churchill might have said, "He had little to be pretentious about." He was a crafty politician, always two steps ahead of the pack. I was told that President Iliescu had tried to fire him, but Dima's supporters in Parliament made him untouchable. No one had any illusions about how he got his support (one hand washed the other). He intended to remain where he was as long as he could. Once again, the impenetrable veil surrounding Romanian decision-making prevented us from learning what was really happening.

THE LEGEND OF DRACULA

Rank has its privileges. The National Bank of Romania owned a dacha on the shores of Lake Snagov, a forty-minute drive from Bucharest. On June 20, National Bank of Romania Governor Mugur Isarescu invited me and the embassy economic counselor to visit the dacha that came with an American-made speed boat, which our host captained in expert fashion, giving Richard Rorvig, our economic counselor, and me a tour of the lake complete with a stop at a small rocky island with a thirteenth-century church. The tiny church's chief attraction, we were told, was the entombed body of Vlad the Impaler, aka Dracula.

A few prominent Romanians owned dachas on the lake, including Prime Minister Vacaroiu; Gheorghe Hagi, Romania's most famous football player, who modestly placed his initials on the roof of his house; Razvan Temeșan, the head of Bancorex, Romania's largest bank; and one or two others whom Isarescu termed "nouveau riche." But ordinary Romanians were there, too, such as simple fishermen with modest cottages. The lake was neither clean nor scenic, but Romanians took pride in it and in its history.

MAYOR CIORBEA WELCOMES
HILLARY CLINTON TO BUCHAREST

The NATO lunch in June 1996 was hosted by the Turkish ambassador, and our guest was Victor Ciorbea, the mayor of Bucharest, newly elected in the local elections that had just taken place. Ciorbea, then in his forties with a high forehead and coal black hair, and wearing horn-rimmed glasses, was intense but honest to the core. He had been a forceful prosecutor under Ceaușescu but saw the light and became a Christian Democrat after the revolution. His stated goal was to clean up the city in the next 120 days, thereby demonstrating that PNT-CD could deliver services. When he talked about his efforts to clean up Bucharest, I mentioned that First Lady Hillary Clinton would be visiting in early July and would be staying at the Majestic Hotel, with a magnificent view across a courtyard to Calea Victoriei, Bucharest's most prominent boulevard. The problem was that the courtyard was filled with rubbish. Mayor Ciorbea got the message and immediately had the courtyard cleaned up.

Several weeks in advance of Hillary's trip the State Department sent a cable requiring U.S. ambassadors in the four Central European countries she intended to visit to propose a schedule for her twenty-four-hour visit. We responded the next day proposing visits to an orphanage, an AIDS clinic, a walking tour of Revolution Square (scene of Ceaușescu's last speech, in 1989, and his abrupt departure from Bucharest), a meeting with representatives of women's groups, a major speech focusing on children's issues, a tour of the Village Museum close to my residence, and meetings with President Iliescu and others. This became Hillary's agenda. Although not explicitly told, we assumed that Hillary's Central Europe tour was aimed at attracting the ethnic vote in the United States in advance of the U.S. presidential election in November.

In late June the embassy learned that the U.S.-based Jehovah's Witnesses were planning an international conference in Bucharest in July, shortly after Hillary's visit. The announcement was met with derision by the Romanian Orthodox Church, which denounced Jehovah's Witnesses as "criminals and Antichrists." The embassy was not asked to help with the conference, and we assumed that despite the Romanian Orthodox Church's opposition, the conference would go ahead. The Romanian Ministry of Cults had sanctioned the conference a year before. However, in late June Secretary General Hrebenciuc announced that the government was canceling the conference. The ostensible reason was lack of hotel rooms and other facilities to accommodate the visitors, but no one believed it, least of all Romanians. The real reason was that a few days before Patriarch Teoctist had issued a pastoral letter condemning the conference.

There was little we at the embassy could do beyond making sure that Hillary, who was scheduled to arrive in a few days, would not become embroiled in the dispute surrounding the conference. A week before, the head of her advance team and I visited the Orthodox Church near Revolution Square, where she was scheduled to speak, to assess the situation. What we saw were posters denouncing Jehovah's Witnesses in defamatory language. We immediately canceled Hillary's visit to the church—a logical step taken so she would not become embroiled in the dispute surrounding the conference.

Visits by first ladies or presidents of the United States consume a lot of embassy time. In Hillary's case, security details and logistics meant a walk-through of every step of her visit with her advance team. Every stage of Hillary's visit was painstakingly choreographed. The main emphasis was on photo ops. There would be little that was spontaneous or natural. The White House staff was primarily interested in how it would play back home. No one asked how to use the trip to help our country's larger interest in Romania or in the region. By the time Hillary arrived on July 1, her traveling party exceeded ninety. Added to this was a special armored vehicle flown into Romania on June 30, courtesy of the U.S. Secret Service. This was a pale forerunner of the president's visit a year later, when he arrived with a full entourage of hundreds of high-level government officials, staff, press corps, and security on *Air Force One* plus a backup 747 and a C-130 transport carrying armored limousines.

On the security front, I wanted to avoid the excesses displayed by Romania's security services when the Bushes visited in April 1995. The caravan security detail for the Bushes had donned ski masks and busted the sideview mirrors of cars that did not pull off the road fast enough for the Bush cavalcade to speed by.

In addition to the usual responsibilities an ambassador has when a high-ranking government official visits, in this case I had the added responsibility of bringing Senate President Gherman, Chamber of Deputies President Nastase, and Mayor Ciorbea of Bucharest together for the welcoming ceremony in front of the Senate building. It was a turf battle with serious domestic political ramifications, with Gherman insisting that anything that took place within the perimeters of the Senate building was his fiefdom. The other side of the line belonged to Mayor Ciorbea; poor Chamber of Deputies President Adrian Nastase and his wife, Dana, were turfless. A compromise worthy of King Solomon was struck. Gherman and Nastase together with their wives would greet Hillary at the steps of the Senate and then escort her to a memorial stone in front of the building, where she would lay a wreath in memory of those persons killed in Revolution Square in December 1989. I would then escort her across the square to a line just beyond the Senate building perimeter, where I would introduce her to Mayor Ciorbea and his wife.

We were hoping for a crowd of several thousand. Earlier in the day I held a press conference in which I ran through Hillary's schedule, mentioning at least four times that she wanted to meet and greet children and their families in Revolution Square at 1 p.m. on July 1. The press, radio, and television had carried the announcement all week. In the end, over 5,000 people showed up, a respectable but not more turnout. (A year later over 500,000 people jammed into Revolution Square to hear President Clinton.)

Her visit produced lots of challenges, not just for us, but for Romanian officials as well. In addition to the jockeying that went on among the Romanian politicians themselves as to who would stand where, a more delicate problem was the unpredictable public: PDSR leader Gherman and Nastase were likely to be met with boos in Christian Democratic Bucharest. Mayor Ciorbea would most likely be cheered. Hillary, a political veteran, could no doubt handle the situation with aplomb, but it was awkward nonetheless.

On July 1, I greeted Hillary on her arrival at Otopeni Airport. Still on board the plane she was in a bit of a snit, but once we arrived at Revolution Square she hit all of her marks, receiving flowers from the Ghermans and Nastases, greeting the Ciorbeas, and walking the rope line extending her hand to the 5,000 smiling, enthusiastic Romanians there to greet her. She placed a candle on the cement slab commemorating those killed in the revolution, after which she was given a Romanian flag with the hammer and sickle cut out, a symbol of the revolution. She turned to the cameras holding the

flag in front of her, which was the picture on the front pages of U.S. newspapers the next day. As far as the White House staff was concerned, mission
accomplished.

After the square, it was the usual—a pediatric AIDS clinic; a school
named for her, with her sitting on the floor reading a book to the children—
all captured on television. Then on to the Odeon Theater, where she delivered
a superb speech, the occasion being the graduation of 100 nurses who had
finished a course sponsored by Baylor University in Texas and Humana Inc.
After an hour or so of down time, she greeted the embassy staff with a pep
talk and lots of picture taking. The evening concluded with a meeting at Cotroceni; President Iliescu greeted Hillary on the steps of the palace, a Romanian custom when greeting dignitaries.

The next event was bizarre but benign. President Iliescu escorted Hillary through one chamber, then into a second, where ten chairs were set in a
small horseshoe with Hillary and President Iliescu seated at the closed end.
The meeting was scheduled to last fifteen minutes, but dragged on and on
as President Iliescu delivered a forty-minute soliloquy. I sat there trying to
figure out whether he was nervous or concerned that if Hillary had the opportunity to speak, she might say something uncomplimentary about Romania.
President Iliescu delivered a history lesson of the region. There was nothing
offensive in his remarks, and, much to my surprise, Hillary told me later she
enjoyed listening to him—maybe because it gave her time to rest and mentally
regroup. After brief handshakes with Senate President Gherman, Chamber
of Deputies President Nastase, and Prime Minister Vacaroiu we moved into
a large reception hall where 150 people had been waiting for an hour. There
were the usual "pull-asides"—"important" people brought by attendants to
talk one-on-one with Hillary—followed by a private showing of Salvador
Dali's drawings in the museum section of the palace.

Once back in the car, she seemed to be on a high, sensing correctly that
it was a good day for her and probably glad it was over. Back at the hotel, a
gaggle of press waited to interview her. She immediately perked up and said,
"Okay, Al, let's go schmooze the press." As we crossed the courtyard, Hillary
graciously said to the Reuters correspondent, "You know Ambassador Moses,
don't you?" whereupon the Reuters writer immediately said, "Of course, we
know Ambassador Moses; he is the best ambassador you have anywhere"—an

unsupportable exaggeration. Upon hearing this, Hillary turned to me and said, "Great! I am going to bed."

The next morning we drove from the hotel to Elisabeta Palace and the adjoining Village Museum, where Hillary viewed two or three village houses, replicas or reconstructions of period homes. Romanian "museum actors" wearing historical period dress complemented the scene. One woman sat on a front porch weaving, a musician played wood flutes, a woman painted hollow eggs in traditional Romanian native colors. (The following year President Clinton also visited the village—and bought everything he saw!)

At Elisabeta Palace, Hillary met with fifteen NGO representatives. To a person, they were upbeat about life in Romania—it almost seemed like a set-up. As Hillary exited the palace, there was time for group pictures with the embassy staff, followed by "Three cheers for Mrs. Clinton!" As we got into the car to go to the airport, she gave me a note that had been handed to her by a man standing next to the car window holding his young daughter, who had no fingers. The note asked for medical help for the daughter. Handing the note to me, Hillary said, "I know I should not take these things, but how can I turn down someone who needs help?" She was right. Our superb consul general, Susan Jacobs, and I were able to arrange for the girl to be operated on at a Methodist hospital in North Carolina, where surgeons transplanted toes onto her hands, giving her some dexterity. Back in Washington, I tried to give Hillary credit for helping the child, but she seemed uninterested and never spoke of it again.

Once on the tarmac at the airport, she whispered, "God bless you" and, kissing me on both cheeks, boarded the plane. Next stop: Poland.

Later that day the embassy was flooded with questions from the press about why Hillary did not visit the Orthodox church in Revolution Square. Our response did not mention that church by name but extolled the notion of the free exercise of religion.

Despite the flap over the church, Hillary's whirlwind trip was a huge success.

RUN-UP TO THE ELECTIONS AND JULY FOURTH ADDRESS

In early July, Ion Diaconescu, Coposu's successor as leader of PNT-CD, and PNT-CD stalwart Ion Ratiu came to the embassy for a two-hour "chat." Diaconescu understood that Romania's problems were largely economic: he grasped that the money Romania had borrowed abroad had gone into consumption, not production—in other words, pump priming in the run-up to the elections—rather than infrastructure. Diaconescu explained that much of the corruption that Constantinescu and others in the opposition talked about came down to well-connected people taking advantage of opportunities after the revolution. Much of this happened when Petre Roman was prime minister. One would think this disqualified Roman and his party, the Democratic Party (PD), as a coalition partner for PNT-CD, but in politics, practicality rules. Diaconescu understood this. PNT-CD was prepared to overlook Roman's past transgressions in favor of a broad-based coalition with PD. Roman for his part was eager to defeat President Iliescu, his former political partner and mentor.

My thoughts about the election were reinforced a few days later at our annual July Fourth party. We were honored to have President Iliescu with us—he did not usually attend national day celebrations, so his attendance was a news story. He was there principally to demonstrate his close connection to the United States. There was nothing objectionable or unseemly about it, but United States–Romania relations were not the top issue for Romanian voters. For them, as it had been for candidate Bill Clinton in 1992, "It's the economy, stupid." Romanians wanted jobs and improved living conditions and they wanted to bury the memory of Nicolae Ceauşescu. President Iliescu said all the right things, but the spark was gone. I thought to myself that unless he gets it back and looks and acts like a winner, he is going to lose the election. Most people, including those in the political opposition, thought President Iliescu was a sure winner. I saw it differently.

The real highlight of the July Fourth party was the performance by the entire forty-three-piece U.S. Air Force Band, Europe. Thank you, General Fogleman! They gave two other performances in Bucharest, both public performances for large audiences who wanted to hear American music.

GETTING TO KNOW ROMANIA'S ORPHANS

For many Americans, the name Romania conjured up, first, the name Dracula, and, after 1989, Romanian orphans and street children. "Orphans" was an inexact term that included children whose parents were alive but who had abandoned them, often for economic reasons. "Orphans" also included children of unwed parents trapped by the former communist regime, which had banned birth control in an effort to increase the population. By the time I arrived as ambassador, there were over 100,000 children in orphanages, thousands more living in substandard conditions. Evangelical Christians in the United States came to post-Ceaușescu Romania by the hundreds to adopt orphans, but the state intervened to discourage them, seeing it as a black mark against Romania and possibly harmful to the children. The whole situation with Romanian orphans became an international cause célèbre. The EU later joined in opposing adoptions. American couples, many of them evangelical Christians, who came to Romania expecting to return home with a child (sometimes seen on a previous visit) were heartbroken, but there was little the embassy could do to help. Together with other embassy staff I regularly visited Romania's orphanages. The children were well cared for and, for the most part, seemed happy. But that did not tell the whole story: once the children reached the age of eighteen, they had to leave the orphanage, unprepared for work other than low-paying jobs, and even those lucky enough to find work had great difficulty adjusting to life on their own.

On one occasion, I spent a day at Casa de Esperanza, a Catholic orphanage near the Black Sea for HIV-positive children. These were children born to mothers infected with the virus. The orphanage had been founded by a monastic order from Texas and was largely supported by private American donations. Since the orphanage's founding, twelve of the children had died. Their memories were commemorated by pictures in a small chapel. The children lived in families of six with their own "parent," the children sleeping on stacked bunk beds in a small room with an adjoining living room and separate small eating area. The children were amazingly cheerful, all of them dressed beautifully for the visit of the Americans, including not only our embassy staff but a half dozen or so members of the crew of the USS *Briscoe*, a Navy destroyer. Included among the visitors was the ship's woman physician. The

Briscoe was in port after participating in naval exercises with Romania in the Black Sea. It was a sight to behold. The *Briscoe's* chief petty officer sat on the floor playing with the children. Even the toughest old salt was putty in the hands of appealing children! Earlier in the summer, the Alabama National Guard had put in thousands of hours fixing up the orphanage, laying cement walks, installing new screens, painting the building, grading the grounds, and building playhouses and slides for the children. One of the playhouses was a ship where the children could crawl in and out. I was immensely proud to be part of a culture that gives and keeps giving. Our military was part of this, but so, too, were the hundreds of Christian missions and other volunteer organizations that cared for others.

Another trip was to Casa de Copii, an orphanage for girls in a poor neighborhood of Bucharest. Some seventy-five girls, ages five to eighteen, were housed in a dormitory-style building that, despite the crowded conditions, had a warm, even homey, feeling. The girls had been abandoned or semi-abandoned by their parents. The girls danced and sang for the American visitors and seemed in good spirits. The real problem, as the director explained, was that once the girls left the orphanage, few of them went to university; most had to find their way on their own without families, halfway houses, or other institutions to help them find jobs or places to live. A chilling prospect.

When I was ambassador, there were also about 2,500 street children in Bucharest. It was estimated that 600 of them had no homes whatsoever; others floated in and out, living in the streets during the day but returning home at night. I visited the two largest centers for street children. Both were maintained by a Swiss foundation, Terre des Hommes, which cared for youngsters ages three to eighteen. The children were attractive and friendly. They craved affection and took pride in their lives, now that they were off the streets. One fellow about sixteen years old told me proudly that he was "not going to go back to stealing," that he wanted to go to college and learn to be a welder. Another told me he hoped to become a carpenter. Many of them spoke good English, learned from watching television.

Underlying the problem of Romania's street children was the country's grinding poverty. Too many families simply could not feed, clothe, and house their children. In 1997 Traian Basescu, the minister of transportation (later prime minister), decided to clean up Bucharest's largest railway station, Gara de Nord, which had become a major gathering place for street children, who stole, assaulted passengers, and offered sexual favors of every variety. Basescu gave them uniforms and put them to work cleaning the station. A success story.

NATO EXPANSION WITHOUT ROMANIA

By the summer of 1996, it was clear that Romania was not going to get into NATO in the first round. Poland, the Czech Republic, and Hungary would be admitted with no room left for Romania, regardless of how hard it tried. The previous summer, Sandy Berger had hinted this to me when he said that President Iliescu's visit with President Clinton in the Oval Office "may take the edge off Romania's disappointment if it does not get into NATO in the first round." Romania lacked clout in the U.S. Congress and retained its negative image from the Ceaușescu days, reinforced by the absence of Western-style political leaders. I thought this might change with a new coalition government after the elections in 1996, but Romania was also behind its neighbors economically, and it would not catch up until it quickened the pace of economic reform.

This caused me to start thinking about a special status for Romania in its bilateral relationship with the United States if, as I expected, it was not included in the first round of countries admitted to NATO. We emphasized to Romanian officials—subtly, I hope—that whatever happened, Romania would continue to be represented in NATO's North Atlantic Cooperation Council, would have a representative at Supreme Headquarters Allied Forces Europe, and would participate in joint task force planning and exercises as well as in a stepped-up Partnership for Peace. All it would lack was the Article 5 guarantee of NATO defense of Romania's borders against foreign invasion. This was a remote risk, certainly in 1996.

SCRUM IN WASHINGTON OVER THE BASIC TREATY

In mid-July, Foreign Minister Teodor Meleşcanu came to Washington to meet with Secretary of State Warren Christopher, who said nice things about the briefing papers we prepared for him and then greeted Teodor warmly, introducing him to the press with positive words. As expected, Secretary Christopher reassured Meleşcanu that Romania was a strong contender for NATO membership but then added there was no assurance this would happen or in what order. For Meleşcanu, this was the encouragement he was looking for with some positive quotes from Secretary Christopher he could use with the Romanian press.

Meleşcanu also had good meetings on the Hill, particularly with Senator Richard Lugar (R-Ind.), the chairman of the Subcommittee on European Affairs of the Senate Committee on Foreign Relations, who was supportive of Romania's NATO aspirations. But the real breakthrough came later at lunch at State hosted by Undersecretary Peter Tarnoff, who on cue raised the issue of the Hungarian-Romanian Basic Treaty, having been briefed by us earlier that morning. Meleşcanu had assured me a few days before that the proposal he advanced to the Hungarians (accepting Council of Europe Recommendation 1201 but with the clarifying language regarding group rights and territorial autonomy in the treaty text) had the blessing of the government of Romania and that if Hungary accepted it in its present form, the government of Romania would sign the basic treaty before the general elections in November. At lunch, Meleşcanu gave the same assurance to Under Secretary Tarnoff.

The ball was now in our court. We called Hungary's deputy foreign minister, Ferenc Somogyi, in Budapest, telling him that if Hungary accepted Meleşcanu's proposal, the Romanian government would sign the treaty with no further negotiation. Minister Somogyi was ecstatic, saying if this was really the Romanian position, Hungary would accept it and that László Kovács, Hungary's foreign minister, would write a letter to Minister Meleşcanu confirming Hungary's acceptance. My next call was to Meleşcanu, who, after speaking with Kovács, stated that the deal was done.

TEXTRON'S CEO

In August 1996 Jim Hardymon, the CEO of Textron, Bell's parent, joined me at the residence for breakfast along with a government of Romania team composed of Defense Minister Tinca, Finance Minister Georgescu, Chamber of Deputies President Adrian Nastase, and Dima's number two at the SOF, Mihu. The Romanians assured Hardymon the Cobra deal would go forward. When I asked Mihu whether Dima was on board, Nastase spoke up saying, "Dima will not be a problem." That was wishful thinking. There was still a lot to do. Once Textron gave its approval, Bell had to negotiate with the SOF on the purchase of a 51 percent interest in IAR-Brașov, the Defense Ministry had to agree on the configuration of the Cobra, and the parties had to agree on price. Bell still had to decide on the product lines it would manufacture in Brașov, and the government of Romania had to give its sovereign guarantee for payment of the Cobras. A deal was signed in May 1997, but it later came undone after IMF objections and a lack of support on the part of my successor.

MR. FIX-IT'S EXIT

When I saw Secretary General Hrebenciuc in August after PDSR's poor performance in the local elections, he told me he expected to be dumped by the party and by President Iliescu as PDSR campaign chairman for the general elections in the fall. He was right. Hrebenciuc's star had faded. There is always a price to be paid for election defeats, and usually it is the campaign manager who takes the hit. Hrebenciuc was also singled out in the press for corruption. He was an operator for sure—and corrupt, maybe—but as far as I knew, no one had the goods on him. Whatever his faults, Hrebenciuc was perceptive. After the local elections, he told me that regardless of who won the general elections in the fall, the real winner would be Romanian democracy. In that judgment, he was absolutely right.

By late August 1996, Hrebenciuc was also out as secretary general of the government. Mr. Fix-It was now gone from government. He had told me in June that he was under attack within the party as a result of PDSR's poor showing in the local elections. Now that the opposition press was calling him corrupt, his value to the government as a "doer" was outweighed by his liability to PDSR at a time when its image had been damaged by accusations of corruption.

President Iliescu tried to distance himself from these charges by calling on PDSR to clean up its act and drop those accused of corruption and by surrounding himself with so-called "experts" not tainted by corruption in foreign policy and economics. Foreign Minister Meleşcanu was first on the short list of such experts. A superb diplomat, he was asked by President Iliescu to head his reelection campaign in the fall. Meleşcanu knew he was not a political guru, but could not refuse a direct request from President Iliescu. If Iliescu won, Meleşcanu would continue as foreign minister, but there is no such thing as a personal obligation in politics. If President Iliescu lost or a PDSR coalition government was formed after the elections and one of the coalition parties insisted on the Foreign Ministry portfolio, it would be "bye-bye Teodor."

Foreign Minister Meleşcanu asked me to speak with President Iliescu and persuade him not to bring him into the campaign. I did not speak with President Iliescu directly—this would have been a leap, even for me—but I did pass the word along to Traian Chebeleu, his diplomatic adviser, and in the end Iliescu wisely dropped the idea. I also met with Adrian Nastase, who spoke bravely, but was not optimistic. The Christian Democrats would form the next government, probably with PD, and although Nastase said that he was "certain" Iliescu would be reelected, this, too, looked increasingly doubtful. The country wanted change and was likely to vote out the old crowd, without knowing what the new one would do.

OFF TO NATO HEADQUARTERS IN BRUSSELS

In September our political counselor, Bob Whitehead, and I visited NATO headquarters in Brussels. We were told by NATO's top military command that Romania's performance in the Partnership for Peace was as good as or better than that of any other NATO aspirant. We heard the same from other NATO officials, including Chris Donnelly, NATO's special adviser for Eastern and Central Europe. Chris was full of ideas about what Romania should do to enhance its readiness for NATO. At my request he agreed to come to Bucharest to present his ideas, such as professionalizing the Romanian intelligence services, training parliamentary committees on military planning oversight, and bringing in Western experts to work with Romanians in implementing their new air control capability using the five Lockheed radar systems that the Romanian military was due to receive later this year.

At about this time, a distinguished German military expert confided to me that Germany was committed to its "near abroad," Poland, and was not going to spend its political capital championing Romania. Iliescu and his crowd were simply not accepted in Bonn as eligible partners for NATO. The same was true in the United Kingdom. In a frank moment, Chris Crabbie, the United Kingdom's ambassador to Romania, told me that Prime Minister John Major, Defense Minister Malcolm Rifkind, and the professionals in the Foreign Office were not supporting Romania. He was very direct in saying that what Romania lacked was a champion to advance its NATO cause, and this had to be either the United States or France—the same thinking as in Romania.

There was also constant jockeying for position among the NATO aspirants themselves. Poland's ambassador to Romania, Bogumil Luft, regularly denied the assurances Poland's defense minister gave the U.S. government that it was in favor of expanding the number of countries admitted to NATO to include Romania. He claimed that Romania was behind the others, and if invited to join NATO, it would seek to export its "state-controlled doctrines in the economic field." This was hogwash, but clear evidence that Poland was distancing itself from a Romania that it saw as a competitor in the race to enter NATO.

Our first morning in Brussels Bob and I received word that the Supreme Allied Commander Europe (SACEUR), the American general George A. Joulwan, had returned unexpectedly from Bosnia and was available to meet with us. General Joulwan exuded energy and, although claiming to be "only a simple soldier," was impressive in every respect. A former West Point football star, he wore two hats, commander of U.S. Forces Europe and Supreme Allied Commander Europe, the titles General Dwight D. Eisenhower once held. Joulwan had nothing but praise for Romania's military, its accomplishments in the Partnership for Peace, the reorganization of its military along Western lines, civilian control, and general adaptability to NATO thinking. This was a message repeated by others at NATO.

As NATO commander, General Joulwan's principal focus was on Bosnia, where a 54,000 International Peace Keeping Force (IFOR) was serving under his command. The real question was what would happen after IFOR left. General Joulwan was hopeful, but not optimistic, that the Bosnia Muslims, Croatia, and Serbia would support the tripartite institutions created under the Dayton Accords, including the tri-headed presidency, and in time would conclude that the people of Bosnia had more to gain preserving unity than going their separate ways with renewed fighting.

INTRIGUE

In late August a Romanian Internal Security (SRI) operative walked into the American embassy offering to disclose SRI secrets in return for money. The initial introduction to the embassy had been made by the SRI officer's girlfriend, a suspicious omen. The chief of station—a declared CIA agent—was out of country. In his absence, CIA headquarters in Langley, Virginia, proposed that an undisclosed CIA officer meet with the defector, and sent along a list of suggested questions. I nixed this. I had no confidence that the defector had anything worthwhile to tell us, and there was at least the possibility that we were being set up. I decided that any further discussion would have to await the return of the chief of station. This made our undisclosed CIA agent unhappy, but so be it. I was not going to allow an undeclared embassy staff member to become identified with the CIA, particularly when the benefits were likely to be minimal. Furthermore, by disclosing his identity we would jeopardize other embassy staff members, who would be suspected of being CIA agents.

When the chief of station returned, he met with the defector in a third country. To no one's surprise, the defector wanted money to keep his "girlfriend" happy. He had nothing of value to tell us. I kept telling the folks in Langley that there was very little the SRI could do that would hurt us. Better for us to concentrate on what they could do to help us in Iran, Iraq, and elsewhere.

ROMA LIFE

Another weekend routine, weather permitting, was for me to head out of Bucharest with embassy friends and bicycle twenty-five miles or so into the country. We rode on largely unpaved village roads where several feet of water accumulated in low spots after a heavy rain. One reward for our efforts was to see Roma, or Gypsy, life outside Bucharest. We passed through farming communities where the work was largely done by hand, or, for the lucky few, by horse. We frequently encountered brightly colored horse-drawn carts with uniformly friendly Roma families inside. The village dogs were better behaved than their canine cousins who roamed wild in Bucharest. Some of the villages had electricity, others not. What struck me most was the number of new houses being built. Some were gaudy mansions reputedly owned by "gypsy princes" who worked their trade—various types of scams—in Western Europe, principally Germany, and then returned home with their "earnings."

On one of my late summer rides through the Romanian countryside, I saw Roma caravans—horse- or mule-drawn wooden carts laden with family possessions under a tarp, an occasional metal bucket hanging by the side, and the parents sitting in the front, children hanging out the back. The occupants from one caravan were hard at work making camp, erecting wooden tent poles for their somber black tents. I spied an occasional youngster or single woman walking alone, gazing at the horizon, possibly dreaming of another life or what might lie beyond the drudgery of the nomadic Roma existence.

Romania was a country of contrasts—rich and poor, urban and rural, educated and uneducated—but nothing in Romania equaled the contrast between a Roma caravan of horse-drawn wooden carts covered with black tarps and the amazing replica outside Bucharest of the "Dallas Hotel" from the American television series *Dallas*. Parked in front of the South Fork replica was an American white stretch limousine owned by J.R. in the television series. Here was fake American opulence on display for Romanians to gape at and to pay their hard-earned money to enter "South Fork" for a closer look. American television was enormously popular in Romania, and *Dallas* caught the imagination (and maybe aspirations) of Romanians just as it did its American viewers.

Run-up to the General Election

FALL 1996

THE PERFORMING ARTS

Romania has a long-standing theater, music, and opera tradition. The Romanian National Opera, in Bucharest, performed five nights a week from September through June and was a major element in the city's cultural life. When the opera house in Bucharest opened in 1953, Stalin attended the opening performance. The exterior was in the dull gray communist style—a flat cement facade and square columns—but the interior was a gem, beautifully decorated and conveying a sense of intimacy. I attended the opera whenever I could. Ticket prices were absurdly low, around $3 a seat. One of my favorite operas was Verdi's *Nabucco*, also a great favorite in Romania. It is a story of the Babylonian conquest of Jerusalem and the exile of the Jews to Babylon, where the king sets them free after recovering from an illness. As with most operas, the story line in *Nabucco* was a distinct second to the music, which, as in Verdi's other works, was dramatic, rising in tempo to a grand crescendo. The theatrical performance was distinctly uneven, but the chorus was excellent, as were the staging and costumes.

THE IMPORTANCE OF GETTING OUT AND ABOUT

Most of my time in Romania was consumed with official business, but week-ends were free, and when I could I traveled around the country with embassy colleagues—skiing in the Carpathians, mountain-climbing when weather permitted, taking snowy rides in the winter, and swimming in the Black Sea in the summer.

On an occasional Sunday with embassy friends I headed for Azuga, a small resort in the foothills of the Carpathian Mountains. On one occasion in the fall of 1996, a heavy mist on the trail blocked the mountain view. I encountered a fellow hiker in his early twenties who climbed with enthusiasm from Azuga but then turned the wrong way and was headed back to Azuga. I steered him in the right direction but then lost sight of him in the mist. The foliage had started to turn soft yellow, not the fiery red of maple trees common in New England. The panorama was breathtaking, but fleeting. In another week or two it would be gone.

Another common drive from Bucharest was to Constanta, on the Black Sea, and back to Bucharest. Each time, I was struck by the beautiful rolling countryside, much of it unmarred by industrial development. The villages were picturesque, even bucolic, with haystacks behind houses and the occasional cow grazing in front. A paved road ran through each village, but side roads—lanes really—had not changed for centuries. They were muddy in the rainy season, frozen in the winter, and, at their best, barely navigable by car. In the fall the countryside was covered with wilted sunflowers, wheat stubble, and dried cornstalks. Farmers were working, mostly with horse-drawn carts—even on Sundays. The occasional mechanized farm equipment, largely of Romanian manufacture, looked ancient, held together by goodness knows what.

Nicolae Ceauşescu was Romania's replica of the "czar of all the Russias," answering to no one other than his equally despotic wife, Elena. In "appreciation" for his leadership, the "people" (the communist government) built villas for him in all forty-one Romanian *judets* (counties). After his overthrow, ownership of the villas passed to "the new select," one of whom was Bancorex, a state-owned bank that financed Romania's import-export trade. It owned a magnificent villa a few miles from Braşov, a former Saxon city about a three-hour drive north of Bucharest. One fall weekend when Carol was in Bucharest for a spell, she and I, joined by other embassy couples and their children, rented the villa for the weekend. We took long walks in the foothills of the Carpathian Mountains and visited Brașov with its faded German-style town square. German colonists known as the Transylvanian Saxons had played a decisive role in Brașov's development. A few years after I returned home permanently, the square was completely restored and became a major tourist attraction. Even before the restoration, the square served as a reminder of the vibrant life of centuries-old ethnic German communities in Romania.

Even on weekdays when I was not tied down with work, I would travel outside Bucharest to see what was happening. During my three years in Romania I managed to visit most of the country—big cities, small villages, painted churches in the north and customs stations in the south, automobile plants in Pitești and industrial plants and other sites throughout the country—and to talk with religious leaders, prefects, mayors, and ordinary people doing their job or just trying to survive under difficult economic conditions. These talks reinforced for me the commonality of humanity. Despite our differences in language, culture, religion, and level of material wellbeing, we are one with the same impulses, hopes, ambitions, and dreams.

One of my trips was to Pitești, an industrial city of 200,000 about an hour and a half west of Bucharest where USAID was sponsoring a public administration assistance program. The mayor of Pitești, Tudor Pendiuc, in 1996 was a forty-two-year-old mathematician studying for a doctorate in international relations. My initial welcoming in front of Pitești's city hall was nothing short of grand. After the usual round of handshakes, I walked toward city hall but stopped short as down the concrete steps came "His Honor the mayor," wearing a Romanian tricolor sash. After the customary embraces, the two of us headed to the new "VIP Center," where we were supposed to cut the inaugural ribbon before entering the building—perhaps not the first time the ribbon was cut. As was typical in Romania, the mayor's scissors did not work, so rather than cut the ribbon we ducked under it.

The highlight of the Pitești trip was our visit to Oltchim S.A. in Râmnicu Vâlcea, about an hour's drive from Pitești, an enormous refinery and petrochemical plant, the largest in Romania—a dinosaur kept alive by massive infusions of government money. There I witnessed an emergency evacuation drill. About 100 spectators gathered on the roof to watch the response to a simulated major earthquake, supposedly registering 7.8 on the Richter scale. According to the simulation, the earthquake caused several small fires and a chlorine leak in one of the plants. In response to this imagined emergency, a carnival unfolded. One hundred or more women dressed in white nurse's uniforms emerged from one building and marched toward the chlorine plant. Meanwhile a billowy chute extending from the third story of the adjacent building was inflated, and for the next twenty-five minutes a single man jumped from a third-floor window onto the cushion of air below, ran back into the building, up the three flights of stairs, and again jumped out the window onto the inflated platform. At the same time someone was supposed to descend in an emergency chute, but despite the chute being extended from a fourth-floor window to the ground, nobody slid down. A rope pulley that extended from the roof of the building got better use: a man was actually evacuated in what looked like a big golf bag.

Simultaneously, two antiquated fire trucks rolled out of a garage and proceeded slowly to the scene of the supposed fire. Next, two helicopters appeared, one circling the complex, the other landing at a helicopter pad and simulating the evacuation of the wounded. Then an empty train arrived from Râmnicu Vâlcea's railroad station equipped to evacuate 1,000 workers—all of whom continued to labor away inside the building throughout the simulated emergency. On cue, gendarmes appeared to guard against looters. The high point of the exercise was the appearance of a dog wearing a gas mask and pulling a stretcher on wheels. Lo and behold, someone was actually placed on the stretcher, and the dog proudly pranced off followed by loud applause. It was a marvelous spectacle reminiscent of my father's homemade silent movies.

After the exercise, we trudged down from the roof into an overheated meeting room on the ground floor, supposedly to critique the exercise. I was foolish enough to expect comments from various experts, but I had forgotten Romanian etiquette. Four or five Romanians dutifully stood up and extolled the exercise. Two non-Romanians also spoke. One was an army officer from the Republic of Macedonia, who gave a fifteen-minute political speech in Macedonian; the other, a representative of Moldova, speaking Romanian, uttered a few polite words.

Still in a daze from this surreal exercise, I moved on to the nearby Dacia

(Romanian automobile brand) plant, which was typical of Romania's antediluvian heavy industry. Situated in an enormous complex on a large tract of land outside Piteşti, it produced about 85,000 cars a year, of which 70 percent were sold in Romania, where the brand had a captive market. The rest were sold in South America and South Africa and in less advanced economies elsewhere. Under the communists, the factory produced two models, which, like Henry Ford's Model T, came in any color you wanted, as long as it was black. The price in Romania was about $4,000, a third the price of the nearest competitor. Despite the poor quality of the Dacia, a Romanian had to wait three to four months for delivery. The manufacturing operation was at least thirty years behind the West and was performed largely by hand. The car body, engine, and frame had not changed in design for thirty years.

Official luncheons in Romania are a Bacchic feast. The lunch that followed the Dacia factory tour took place in the Bratianu family ancestral home, a nineteenth-century Romanian manor house that was unmatched elsewhere in the country. It was built of stone with three levels, including a large wine cellar. Ion Bratianu had founded the National Liberal Party in the 1850s, and successive generations of Bratianus headed the party until the communist takeover. His son, also named Ion, was prime minister during World War I and represented Romania in the peace treaty negotiations in Paris. The last Bratianu, Georghe, the leader of the National Liberal Party, died under clouded circumstances in 1953 in the communist jail in Sighet.

The most memorable thing about the lunch was its duration. At 4:00 p.m., with no end to the revelry in sight, I rallied our embassy team and headed for the exit—but not before the local troupe of musicians played "Hava Nagila" and we danced the hora with the prefect, mayor, vice mayor, and nearby Oltchim S.A. management. Not to be outdone, when we were halfway out the door, the director of the nearby Dacia factory promised me immortality, which in Romanian means someone with no authority offering to name a street for you in Bucharest. I was often "immortalized" in this way, but no street was ever named for me.

On the weekends when I was not traveling, my residence was open to embassy staff to swim in the indoor pool, built in 1947 by the former communist leader Ana Pauker, to entertain visitors, and to enjoy an occasional en masse Sunday night dinner cooked by me with lots of help from others. Sarah Solberg, one of our senior staff and a former university English professor, even whipped us into shape to perform *King Lear* in its entirety. Guess who played the aged, befuddled king?

THE END OF THE COALITION GOVERNMENT

On September 2 the Social Democratic Party of Romania, PDSR, announced that it was terminating its coalition with the Romanian National Unity Party, PUNR, the last of the extremist parties and the only one in the government coalition. The other two, PRM and PSM, had voted with the PDSR-PUNR coalition in Parliament. The final break came as a result of a personal attack on President Iliescu by Gheorghe Funar, PUNR's titular chair, over the Hungarian-Romanian Basic Treaty. Funar claimed that the treaty would cause Romania to disappear by the year 2000, which was utter nonsense. On the contrary, it was PUNR that disappeared as the Romanian political scene moved closer to the center. I privately took comfort from the fact that seven months after my speech in Cluj, the government was no longer tied to the extremists—Romania was one step closer to joining NATO.

HUNGARIAN-ROMANIAN BASIC TREATY: A DONE DEAL

The meeting on July 18 at State with U.S. Under Secretary Tarnoff and Foreign Minister Meleşcanu yielded a treaty in September. I managed on the margins to draft the treaty language resolving the differences between Hungary and Romania. This led to the signing of the basic treaty in advance of Romania's national elections. I gave much of the credit to President Iliescu, who took a political risk in signing the treaty before national elections, thereby running the risk that PUNR or other political forces would accuse him of weakness in yielding to Hungarian pressure.

The Hungarian-Romanian Basic Treaty was signed in Timişoara, Romania, on September 16, with cheers in official Washington, where Don Blinken, our ambassador in Hungary, met with Deputy National Security Adviser Sandy Berger. Sandy suggested that the two of us write an op-ed piece for the *Washington Post* giving credit to NATO enlargement as the underlying motivation for Romania's and Hungary's signing of the treaty. I wrote a draft that Don signed off on and sent to State for review. The final version approved by State was published in the *Washington Post* on September 19. As Sandy hoped, it garnered attention and advanced the argument in the United States for NATO enlargement.

NATO TALK

At the NATO ambassadors' lunch in September, our guest was Robert E. Hunter, the U.S. ambassador to NATO, who was visiting Bucharest as part of his tour of capitals of NATO aspirant countries. Bob was an old friend from the Carter White House, where he had the Middle East portfolio under Zbigniew Brzezinski in the office of the national security adviser. Bob delivered a brilliant exposition of the NATO enlargement process and his view of how Romania fitted in. He was careful not to give the impression that Romania would be in the first wave. This gave me the opportunity to persuade Christopher Crabbie, the new British ambassador, to join in my funnel approach, meaning we needed to put Romania in the funnel leading to NATO membership without fixing the date of entry or giving Romania a false impression of its place in the order of entrants.

WHAT BEING JEWISH MEANS TO ME

In the 1990s the American Jewish Committee began running a series of pieces in the *New York Times* entitled "What Being Jewish Means to Me." In early September David Harris, AJC's executive director, asked me as AJC's former president and now American ambassador to Romania to write a piece to appear during the Jewish High Holy Days in late September. This was easy for me, but I did not expect the positive reaction the piece received. Years later people told me how deeply they were moved by my words—music to my ears.

I had the good fortune of being raised in a traditional Jewish home where the Sabbath was a day of rest, the holidays were days of joy, and the dietary laws were strictly observed. This set me apart from my

friends and neighbors. In my early years religious observance inter-
fered with my favorite pastime, playing baseball. The highlight of my
week was seeing how many innings of baseball I could get in before my
father dragged me off to synagogue. But by my late teens, I took great
pride in being a Jew who knew Hebrew, could recite the traditional
prayers from memory, and was a wiz at Jewish Trivial Pursuit. The rise
of Hitler, the devastation of European Jewry and the creation of the
State of Israel etched in my heart a sense of Jewish peoplehood that
would later take me around the world in support of endangered Jewish
communities. During my lifetime, I have seen enormous changes in
the Jewish world. While external threats to the Jewish people have
diminished, Jewish continuity in the United States is being questioned
as never before. Young Jews ask me, "Why be Jewish? In America
today you can affirm your identity as a Jew or ignore it." The level
of acceptance in our country makes both options acceptable. Being
Jewish then is increasingly a matter of choice.

To their question I answer: Judaism has a 3,000-year-old tradition of infusing the spiritual into our everyday lives, not for personal
gain, but to uplift the lot of mankind through adherence to ethical
and moral principles, and to preserve through this common endeavor
a sense of connectedness with a people. This, the essence of our cov-
enant, gives us tools to deal with the disparate and often confusing
aspects of modern life.

For me this has meant combining my career as a lawyer in private
practice with communal and public service as an officer in the Navy,
later as special assistant in the Carter White House, then as president
of the American Jewish Committee, and now as United States ambassador to Romania, a country I first came to know through helping
Jews and others escape from behind the Iron Curtain. In all these
endeavors I have been inspired by the teachings of the Torah and the
Talmud: each of us has an obligation to work to make people's lives
better.

CURTAIN UP ON RASDAQ

The RASDAQ, Romania's first stock exchange, opened for business in October, but work had been ongoing since January to get it, and the whole capital markets program, off the ground. Romania's privatization could only work if there was a market for publicly owned shares—a stock exchange. Two years before, the United States had offered to build the RASDAQ, the Romanian version of the U.S. NASDAQ (originally, National Association of Securities Dealers Automated Quotations). To proceed, we enlisted the Romanian National Securities Commission, the Romanian counterpart to our SEC, which would oversee the operation of the RASDAQ.

Back in January, well in advance of the RASDAQ's opening in October, I went to the Romanian National Securities Commission (CNVM) headquarters to discuss the planned exchange with the regulators. The CNVM was housed on the third floor of a walk-up building built in the Ceaușescu era; it looked more like a public housing project in Chicago than a national securities regulator's headquarters. Inside the walls were dull brown, the paint chipped, the secondhand furnishings badly worn. We met the five commissioners, all former academics, who were seated at a long table wearing heavy jackets to protect them from the cold in an unheated building. Emitting frosty breaths, each of the commissioners mumbled something positive, pledging his/her support for the RASDAQ. The meeting was largely a formality. The CNVM was a neglected stepchild with no political clout and little in the way of enforcement powers to regulate Romania's securities markets.

The RASDAQ build-out was actually honchoed by Sarah Ackerson, a securities market expert on loan from the SEC, aided by four contractors and their respective teams, who were responsible for share registration, market structure, coordination of Romanian securities regulators, and the setup of investment funds. There was a lot to do. I met regularly with Sarah and the four U.S. teams. The principal problem was coordinating American efforts with the broker-dealer group in Romania headed by George Paunescu, the omnipresent Romanian businessman.

Paunescu, a formidable figure with his fingers in lots of pies (he had bought the Intercontinental and Lido hotels), wanted to control the entire capital markets program. This was okay with me, provided he made the capital markets program work. With his many interests, he needed to delegate respon-sibility, something he resisted. We also had trouble coordinating with other countries' donor groups, the Canadians, the British Know-How Fund, and the EU's PHARE. Despite the obvious need to work together, these groups often got in each other's way. Delays on the part of the Romanian government were a bigger problem, leading me to ask Finance Minister Georgescu to intervene at the National Agency for Privatization (NAP), which was hold-ing up share registration. This went on for months. I also met with Prime Minister Vacaroiu to enlist his support for the capital markets program. To my surprise, he pitched in and helped us get around bureaucratic roadblocks at the NAP and elsewhere.

Slowly, slowly, the pieces fell into place. The redoubtable George Pau-nescu negotiated a lease at the newly built Bucharest World Trade Center, a half mile north of my residence, for the entire capital markets program. This included the depository and share registry as well as the mainframe computer to handle RASDAQ trades. After I persuaded Finance Minister Georgescu and Economic Reform Minister Coşea to drop a proposed government deci-sion that would have crippled the share registry in its infancy, the NAP even-tually delivered the critical shareholder lists.

We had a demonstration opening of the RASDAQ on September 27. President Iliescu purchased the first share, and Foreign Minister Georgescu was the seller in the mock transaction. The two of them moved through RASDAQ offices in the World Trade Center turning on computer switches as they moved from room to room. President Iliescu made a major political event out of it, spending about an hour discussing computers, capital markets, and privatization, all filmed by public and private television. Then Chamber of Deputies President Nastase showed up, thereby confirming the political message that Iliescu intended to send. Romania had moved away from com-munism to a capital market economy to complement its political democracy. In a word, Romania was increasingly Western. There were odd moments when the camera picked up someone scratching his head or making a facial grimace that brought chuckles from people watching on a large screen in the next room. Television in Romania was still in its early stage of development, more like home movies than professional American commercial programming.

When the RASDAQ officially opened for business on October 25, only six companies' shares were traded and there were just four active brokers, but at least it was open. After that, whenever there was an internal RASDAQ problem, I turned to George Paunescu. He had all the trappings of a mafioso—a wood-paneled office, bodyguards, and hushed conversations that always bespoke "confidences." However, the bottom line was that Paunescu did what he had said he would do, and that was good enough for me.

For someone who has not lived in Romania and worked with the government, it would be hard to understand the ever-present bureaucratic knots that had to be untied to make progress. A week after the RASDAQ opened, I was back in Economic Reform Minister Coșea's office. At first he agreed to sign a letter instructing the NAP to transfer its remaining stockholder lists to the RASDAQ registry. Then he got cold feet, and I spent the rest of the day trying to put steel in his spine. Finally, I told Coșea that if there were further delays, I would send our consultants home and not waste U.S. taxpayer money on a RASDAQ that as of that day had only six companies out of 3,200 eligible to trade. Without our consultants, the Romanians could not run the RASDAQ, and I had no intention of spending taxpayer money supporting a market with only six companies. Coșea signed the letter, and thereafter the number of companies on the RASDAQ jumped from six to more than 1,200.

PREJUDICE COMES IN MANY FORMS

Oliviu Gherman, president of the Senate, had a manner of speaking that conveyed gravity but sometimes verged on pomposity. He spoke slowly, with a heavy overlay of sincerity, but the effect on the listener was a strong urge to help him get his words out. He was a respected academic, but he surprised me with a comment he made when we were discussing the bank privatization bill. He assured me there would be no limitation on foreign ownership of privatized banks and then added, "I am not worried about European or American investors, only Asian." This was followed by a verbal barrage about the "yellow peril."

Like most people, Romanians have deep-seated prejudices that can come to the fore when least expected. This was the case with Gherman, whose education and status did not immunize him against prejudices. I would later hear similar outbursts from future president Constantinescu about "American Negroes." Although anti-Semitism was never far below the surface in Romania, I was usually spared its expression. But the Roma—Central Europe's Gypsies—got the worst of it. They were often blamed for petty crimes or worse, moving about in clusters without regard to territorial demarcations or international borders. When settled, they lived in "shantytowns" that most closely resembled American junkyards. From time to time the government talked about improving the lives of the Roma and settling them permanently, but in a country strapped for cash the Roma always seemed to be at the back of the queue. Perhaps most of the Roma preferred to remain seminomadic, true to tradition.

Romanians' animus toward Asians was again in evidence when I attended a reception in the Chinese embassy in honor of that country's national day, September 30. Missing were the luminaries—no President Iliescu, no one from the Foreign Ministry, only Prime Minister Vacaroiu, who had visited China earlier that year. The rest of the government had declined the invitation.

PROGRESS ON THE ROMANIAN-UKRAINIAN FRIENDSHIP TREATY

Ukraine's ambassador to Romania, Oleksandr Chaly, was "certain" that Romania would be among the first countries admitted to NATO. He therefore wanted Romania to conclude a treaty with Ukraine so as to avoid Ukraine's having a "loose cannon on its doorstep." He was equally adamant that Romania needed the treaty to get into NATO. Whether his reasons were valid or not, he was enormously helpful, as explained later, in pushing Ukraine and steering me through the intricacies of political life in Kiev.

In October Chaly returned from Kiev brimming with optimism. He was confident that Ukraine was prepared to resolve the Molotov-Ribbentrop issue using the verbal formula we previously discussed, which was that the parties would condemn "all secret pacts entered into with totalitarian powers." As for Serpent Island, Chaly thought Ukraine would agree to defer the issue, leaving it to future negotiations or ultimate resort to the International Court of Justice at The Hague. In the meantime, Ukraine would desist from exploration in the Delphin Block, the area in the Black Sea in dispute. This turned out to be the basis of the Romanian-Ukrainian friendship treaty signed on June 2, 1997.

OCTOBER ECONOMIC OUTLOOK

At the NATO lunch in late October, Mugur Isarescu, the governor of the National Bank of Romania, gave a fact-filled presentation on the state of the economy. He predicted inflation in 1996 at about 36 percent, GDP would increase slightly over 4 percent, with an 8 percent increase in industrial production. Mugur said that the current account deficit would be about $1 billion, or between 3.2 and 3.8 percent of GDP. (This would bust the IMF standby loan. The actual figures turned out to be far worse, with a budget deficit of 8 percent and a current account deficit of $1.9 billion.) Isarescu had the same priorities as the United States: reach agreement with the IMF on a macro stabilization plan to give confidence to external markets, negotiate sector loans with the World Bank, especially for energy, move ahead with privatization, and encourage foreign investment to sustain growth.

Given the need for large imports of machinery and other equipment to modernize Romania's industry and to meet consumer demand, export revenues alone could not generate the hard funds needed. Here is where direct foreign investment was needed. Romania faced a critical need for foreign currency. The government of Romania had paid lip service to attracting foreign investment, but in practice, the bureaucracy had frozen out foreign direct investment. Even after the elections in November 1996, which brought in a new PNT-CD-led government, Isarescu confided to me that he did not expect the new government would have the political courage to make the hard fiscal and monetary decisions needed. (In 1999 Isarescu became prime minister and imposed the needed reforms.)

THE C-130S FLY IN

Romania's Armed Forces Day on October 25 was celebrated at a ceremony at Bucharest's Otopeni Airport with the arrival of the first two of the four C-130 (Hercules) aircraft from the United States. Romania was getting the C-130B, a model built in the 1960s but upgraded, still operational and would continue to be for at least another decade. Four C-130s might not seem like much, but for the Romanian Air Force, which had not received upgrades for over a decade, it was a major step forward. There were the usual speeches, but the real show came when an Orthodox priest with a strong right arm and an appropriate blessing heaved holy water up fifteen feet, landing miraculously on the nose of each plane.

THE ROMANIAN HORSE RACE

By the fall I was all but certain that the November 1996 elections would result in a new government coalition headed by PNT-CD. I reached out to the frontrunners, first to Emil Constantinescu, whom I expected to be the next president, and a few days later to the two candidates for prime minister, Victor Ciorbea and Radu Vasile. Other PNT-CD candidates for important ministries were Ulm Spineanu and Senator Mircea Ciumara. Spineanu was vice president of one of the private ownership funds. When he arrived in my office along with his wife, on October 21, he had just returned from two weeks in Washington, where he claimed he received a commitment from a "group of American banks" to extend $4 billion to $5 billion in credits to the "new" government. This was preposterous, even by Romanian standards. He told me "in confidence" that he was being considered by PNT-CD to be prime minis-ter but preferred the economic reform portfolio, without, however, expressing any understanding of what that job entailed. To prove his credentials, halfway through the meeting he and his wife pulled out a long trail of computer print-outs and proceeded to explain that the printouts contained his economic plan for the new government. They were the same mumbo-jumbo as the "economic plan" he described to me orally when he had first entered my office. As he was talking, I thought, "Where are the twelve thousand people Constantinescu said were training to take over the government?" After listening to Spineanu, I realized how unprepared the Christian Democrats were to assume the reins of government.

Senator Ciumara was different from Spineanu. If Spineanu was outspoken and ambitious in seeking the prime ministership or, more realistically, the Economic Reform Ministry, Ciumara was modest and soft-spoken. A former economics professor, he was hoping to become finance minister. He said all the right things—the importance of American investment, speeding up reform, electing a strong centrist coalition government that would make tough decisions in its first 100 days. But neither Spineanu nor Ciumara had a grip on what needed to be done. They spoke in generalities. The more forthright leaders of PNT-CD admitted that no one in the party had experience in governing and that they would need help. It was the Democratic Party (PD) that would help, with three key ministers who had government experience.

In October 1996 the PNT-CD leader, Emil Constantinescu, came to my office and stayed for over two hours. I had the impression that he was still caught up in the past. He kept repeating his three campaign pledges, one of which was to prosecute those guilty of corruption; the last thing Romania needed was a witch hunt. The other two planks were that when he became president, he would ride in an ordinary car and live in an ordinary apartment and would ask Parliament to increase wages for pensioners by $18 a month. By the time we met, he had dropped his previous campaign pledge, "to bring back the king," which polls showed most Romanians opposed. Constantinescu's campaign pledges were entombed in a lengthy document entitled "Contract with Romania," a title he borrowed from his American political mentor, Newt Gingrich (R-Ga.), who headed the Republican Party's 1994 congressional campaign, during which he promoted his "Contract with America." Constantinescu's presidential campaign that fall proved to be humdrum, but votes for "not Iliescu" would be enough to elect Constantinescu.

An hour into our conversation, I urged him to focus on the future of Romania under his leadership. He understood the country's economic problems and talked about a government coalition composed of the Democratic Party (PD), Democratic Union of Hungarians in Romania (UDMR), and the Democratic Liberal Party (PDL). The government would be headed by Radu Vasile as prime minister. The next day, October 10, the Romanian newspapers carried a press interview with Constantinescu in which he referred to his meeting with me and stated that he told me that PNT-CD would not form a coalition government with PDSR, something that had not come up in our discussion. This was the first and only time a Romanian political leader purported to disclose publicly what was said in a private meeting with me. I attributed it to Constantinescu's inexperience.

To add to election hype, a letter appeared in *Romania Libera* on October 31, a couple of days before the general elections, presumably written by a Romanian living in Canada, in which he accused me of accepting a $20 million bribe from President Iliescu to support him in the elections, part of which I had then given to President Clinton's campaign in the United States. The charge showed an active imagination—but what happened to the rest of the money? The writer referred to me as an "honorable person" who would surely denounce President Iliescu as the KGB (former Soviet Union security agency) agent he really was.

Romanians often tend to credit foreigners with more knowledge about internal Romanian affairs than they possess themselves. In late October, a few weeks before the general election, Diplomatic Adviser Traian Chebeleu asked me how I saw the election turning out, as if I knew more about the Romanian electorate than he, President Iliescu's close confidant. When I demurred, he told me that Bernard Boyer, the French ambassador, had told him that PNT-CD and UDMR would form the next government. It was amazing that one of Iliescu's principal advisers would ask the French ambassador and me, the American ambassador, about the outcome of the upcoming election in Romania—I could not imagine a similar inquiry in the United States! When the conversation turned to the urgent need for economic reform, Chebeleu said that it was not clear to him just what this meant. He then asked pointedly, "Does this mean supporting American investment in Romania?" He and others in Romania never understood that American policy on NATO expansion was not tied to American investment in Romania. The French tied the two together and pushed the point hard on behalf of French companies looking to do business in Romania. The cultural gap between ourselves and Romania was enormous and proved difficult to close.

Christine Spolar, the *Washington Post* correspondent for Eastern Europe, stationed in Warsaw, came to Bucharest in November to cover the elections. Like many Western journalists, she was skeptical about Romania's economy, asking why it had not caught up with Poland and other countries in the region. She identified strongly with Poland, the country where she was posted. She failed to take into account that Poland's economy was far ahead of Romania's when the Berlin Wall came down. In the intervening seven years, Romania had progressed at about the same pace as Poland, which meant it was still behind, but the gap was the same. Spolar spent the day talking to people at PNT-CD headquarters, hearing only one side of the story but, nevertheless, rightfully questioning the basis for President Iliescu's popularity and why the polls showed him the likely winner, but this soon changed.

With the opposition gaining in the polls, Prime Minister Vacaroiu was dispatched by President Iliescu to convince the diplomatic corps that, despite the election polls, PDSR would win the election. The time-honored way to do this in Romania was to invite whomever you wanted to convince to lunch. True to tradition, in late October Vacaroiu hosted a long lunch for European, North American, and a few Asian ambassadors, a "modified G24," at which he tried to put the best face he could on things, particularly the economy. A professional economist, he reeled off the numbers, putting a positive spin on them: inflation this year would be 35 percent, about the same as last year; GDP would be up 4 percent, and the budget deficit would be 3.5 percent. In answering questions, he defended the past and gave a rosy picture of the future. He projected that the next government would be a coalition of PDSR and PNT-CD and would hold about 75 percent of the seats in Parliament. Strangely enough, I was the only one who challenged him, pointing out that the perception in the West was that Romania remained behind its neighbors and needed to accelerate economic reform to catch up. Most of the other ambassadors in private had been critical of the government, but in Vacaroiu's presence they clammed up. After lunch a few of them thanked me for speaking up, even though I had worked more closely than they with President Iliescu and his PDSR government.

THE VOTING BEGINS

In the first round of the presidential election on November 3, President Iliescu ran about five percentage points ahead of Constantinescu. Petre Roman, of the Democratic Party, ran a distant third, with 20 percent of the vote to Constantinescu's 28 percent and Iliescu's 33 percent. Even before the election, I thought Iliescu no longer had his old bounce and seemed to be going through the motions. In the parliamentary elections, PNT-CD was the clear winner, with 32 percent of the vote to PDSR's 24 percent, followed by PD with 14 percent and UDMR with 7 percent. PRM and PUNR barely squeaked into Parliament, each receiving about 3 percent of the vote. PSM fell below the parliamentary cutoff and would not be in the next Parliament. Romania had matured as a democracy. The elections took place without major incidents. Foreign election observers could now pack up and go home with the expectation that they would not need to return.

Despite the United States' strict neutrality in the elections, two Romanian newspapers, *Romania Libera* and *Ziua*, accused President Clinton and me of supporting President Iliescu and the PDSR, publishing my correspondence with the International Republican Institute's Lorne Craner. Most of the barbs were directed at me, with the added spin that in return for my not allowing IRI to use U.S. government money to help the political opposition in Romania, the PDSR made "a secret pact" with me to return Jewish property after the elections. The correspondence came from Craner, or possibly from Congressman Funderburk's office. One pays a price for high visibility in Romania, with a little bit extra for being Jewish.

WINNERS AND LOSERS

A few days after the first round of voting, I had lunch with the PD leader, Petre Roman, at his favorite Bucharest restaurant, La Premiera. Although he received only 20 percent of the vote in the presidential race, he was now the kingmaker. He told me he would throw his votes to Constantinescu in the runoff. In return PD would get three key ministries—Foreign Affairs, Defense, and Transportation. Roman also reported that he would be president of the Senate, where he expected to continue to lead PD, but others in the party were ambitious and would try to knock him off. (Traian Basescu did this a few years later.) Last, he confirmed that both Talpes and Magureanu would stay on as the directors of SIE and SRI, respectively.

Although well past his prime, the venerable Ion Diaconescu, then eighty, was now the head of PNT-CD. I found him courteous and straightforward. Our most memorable meeting was at PNT-CD headquarters, an ancient building in downtown Bucharest, a day or two after the first round of the elections. He wanted my thoughts on who should be prime minister and head other ministries. Waiting outside the room were petitioners seeking ministerial positions. The scene would not have been out of place in the Ottoman Grand Vizier's royal court, or in Tammany Hall. A nervous Ulm Spineanu told me that he would most likely be minister of economic reform, but had not been officially offered the job. Later, at lunch, another petitioner told me that Emil Constantinescu was supporting him for the same job. Intraparty rivalries were keen and the fight for spoils fierce. For the position of prime minister, I suggested to Diaconescu that he take a close look at Victor Ciorbea, the only Christian Democratic leader who had government and administrative experience.

Both Ciorbea and Spineanu got the jobs they wanted. Ciorbea became prime minister and Spineanu minister of economic reform. A month later I met with Diaconescu, now president of the Chamber of Deputies, in his new palatial office. Even with his new title, the eighty-year-old Diaconescu, imprisoned for seventeen years by the communists, could most charitably be described as disheveled. He sat in an ornate presidential office with twenty-foot-high marble ceilings and inlaid wood paneling on the walls—with one of his shoes tied with a string. When I asked him whether he ever imagined he would one day sit in such a grand office, he replied, "I didn't, and I don't want it now." He claimed not to like the office or the job and made no secret of his intention to resign as president of the Chamber of Deputies in a year or two. He claimed he did not have the energy to be both president of PNT-CD and president of the Chamber. He was a wise man who had earned the respect and support of his party and seemed bemused by all the political wrangling going on around him. First, who would be prime minister? Now that this was settled, a fight had broken out over the allocation of prefecteurs in the forty-two Romanian *judets*, after which the coalition parties would likely squabble over sixty-five state secretaries, positions below ministerial level. I suspected he was happier out of power than in power as the leader of a fractious group, but in reality there was nobody to take his place.

Radu Vasile lost out in the shuffle for ministers, but as a leading member of PNT-CD, he continued to be a political player. He confided to me that he intended to wait to see how Ciorbea fared as prime minister. If he failed, Vasile would put his hat in the ring to be his successor. (This happened in 1998.)

THE RUNOFF ELECTION

President Iliescu won a plurality of the votes in the first round of the presidential election, but in the runoff two weeks later, on November 17, he lost to Constantinescu, who received 32 percent of the vote to Iliescu's 28 percent, largely because of PD's support. In return, as Roman had told me at lunch a week before, PD got three important ministries and Roman was president of the Senate (first in line of succession to the president). PNT-CD held all but one (it went to UDMR) of the rest of the ministries, including the prime ministership.

My fellow NATO ambassadors were not the only ones fooled by the election results. Petre Datculescu, Romania's foremost political pollster, who had correctly forecast the parliamentary elections two weeks before, predicted two days before the runoff that President Iliescu would win with 52 to 53 percent of the vote. I disagreed, whereupon Datculescu stuck out his hand insisting we make a handshake bet. I took his hand and said, "It's a deal." He promised to call me after the polls closed on election night to tell me, "I was right, you were wrong." He never called.

ELECTORAL POSTMORTEM

Two days after the runoff I went to Cotroceni for a farewell meeting with President Iliescu. He was upstairs in a small meeting room. The retinue of guards and petty officials was gone. Iliescu looked well, his face a bit thin, but with good color. He proceeded to lambaste Petre Roman as "egotistical and therefore unreliable" (he was not entirely wrong on this). He characterized the incoming president, Constantinescu, as politically naïve, possessing no previous political experience, "not even as a member of Parliament." He said nice things about my role in strengthening the bilateral relationship and talked wistfully and a bit forlornly about his future role as "simply a member of the Senate." He had not met with President-elect Constantinescu since the elections and there were no plans for them to meet, but Iliescu hoped to find an opportunity to impart some advice, particularly on foreign policy, hoping that Constantinescu would continue the close Romanian-American relationship that "the two of us have established."

LOOKING BACK AND AHEAD

By the time of the runoff election, most of the issues that President Clinton and President Iliescu had discussed in the Oval Office the year before had been accomplished. Romania had permanent MFN status, the Hungarian-Romanian Basic Treaty had been signed, and the government of Romania had shed its three extremist parties and Romania would now have a new centrist coalition government. Democracy had taken root, and the election campaign had been tame by comparison with previous elections.

The one remaining problem—and it was a big one—was the economy. Like National Bank Governor Isarescu, I wondered whether the new government would be strong enough to take the draconian steps needed to free up the foreign exchange market and accelerate privatization.

MEETING THE NEW FOREIGN MINISTER

At the first NATO ambassadors' lunch after the elections, the new PD foreign minister, Adrian Severin, was our guest. He covered familiar ground about improving Romania's standing in Eastern Europe to enhance Romania's case for NATO membership, a shift from the previous government's policy of continually knocking on NATO member doors begging to be let in. As he saw it, the best way for Romania to build its case was to demonstrate its contribution as a stabilizing force in the region with emphasis on the tragic consequences of dismemberment of the former Yugoslavia. He speculated that if things continued to unravel in Belarus and Moldova, both of which were ruled by strongly pro-Russian presidents, Romania's importance to the West would increase. This was all right as strategy but did nothing to advance Romania's readiness to meet the criteria NATO laid down for new members.

Severin answered questions candidly, but when asked what Romania would do if it did not get into NATO in the first wave, he answered that the psychological impact would be enormous and difficult, but Romania had no alternative but to stay on a Western course and that if Romania was not in the first wave, the government needed to prevent a negative backlash against the West and a boost for extremism. He was certainly right on the latter point. We needed to keep Romania in the funnel leading to NATO membership, regardless of which countries were admitted in the first wave, but Severin took a lot of heat within Romania when he repeated his answer in public.

I would later meet frequently with Severin in "four eyes only" meetings. He was a great interlocutor—imaginative, creative, and reliable. Initially, my principal objective was to persuade Severin to keep Mircea Geoana as Romania's ambassador in Washington. He was doing a good job, but was vulnerable, having been appointed by former president Iliescu, which raised questions about his loyalty to the new government. Geoana was smart enough to head this off by calling President Constantinescu immediately after the election to tell him that the results were "the best thing that ever happened to Romania." Constantinescu bought in to this and stuck with Geoana, but others in PNT-CD were less certain. Foreign Minister Severin, who was not a Christian Democrat, supported Geoana and he remained ambassador.

ESTABLISHING A NEW RELATIONSHIP

President-elect Constantinescu had been urged by Ambassador Geoana and Vice President Albert Gore, with whom he met in Lisbon a few days after the election, to work closely with me, but Constantinescu had doubts, largely because in his view and that of some of his inner circle, I had worked too closely with President Iliescu. They didn't understand the difference between my working with Iliescu as the president of Romania and supporting him politically, which I had never done. President Constantinescu and I later worked closely together. He was always open and friendly. We regularly exchanged kisses on both cheeks, the traditional Romanian greeting between friends.

MY OPTIMISTIC OUTLOOK

The December NATO ambassadors' lunch, the last for the year, was at our embassy. Among those present, only I had predicted that Constantinescu would win. When he did, it came as a complete surprise to my colleagues, especially Bernard Boyer, the French ambassador, who knew I had worked closely with Iliescu and therefore assumed I would favor him in the election and expect him to win.

As the year ended I was optimistic. I thought that the new government, with closer ties to the West and no baggage from the Ceaușescu era, could move ahead rapidly to accelerate economic reform, conclude the friendship treaty with Ukraine, spur foreign investment, and change the dialogue from old ways to new ways, in the spirit of Robert Browning's line in his poem, "Rabbi Ben Ezra": "The best is yet to be."

PART FOUR

Changing of the Guard in Romania

1997

 **13**

New Faces, Old Story Lines

WINTER 1997

When I returned to Bucharest in early January 1997, my desk was piled high with unopened Romanian-style Christmas cards, artistic, many quite beautiful. The list of senders signaled a changing of the political guard. Only a few greetings were from members of the former government—Ion Iliescu, Teodor Meleşcanu, and a handful of others with whom I had worked closely. But nearly everyone in the new government sent a card: President Emil Constantinescu, Prime Minister Victor Ciorbea, and most other ministers. The year before I had received holiday wishes from few in the opposition—Senator Radu Vasile and one or two others—but the wheel had turned. Romanians are more formal than Americans. Their Christmas cards were greetings to the office, not the person.

Bucharest in the first weeks of January looked gloomily surreal, with heavy mist, snow on the ground, and long shadows in the early morning and again at dusk. The ever-present smog added to the gloom, presenting a landscape fit for a mystery thriller. Two weeks later the sun was shining, the feeling of depression had lifted, and Romanians returned to the streets, walking briskly with smiles on their faces.

It was a new year with a new Romanian government, so our guest at our first NATO ambassadors' lunch of the year, at the French embassy, was President Constantinescu, whose party had won the November election. Over the years the NATO lunches had evolved into an intramural sport, with ambassadors vying to outshine each other with witticisms or comments rarely intended to inform. This time the French ambassador, Bernard Boyer, declared, "Mr. President, feel free to speak in French, a language we all understand." Of course Boyer knew that I did not speak French. But Constantinescu was not taken in and declared without a smile, "I shall speak in Romanian." I silently applauded.

The only news was President Constantinescu's announcement that General Dumitru Cioflina was out as military chief of staff. Cioflina was popular in Romania and was considered by our military to be a good soldier and leader. His principal limitation was that he did not speak English. His replacement, a one-star general, Constantin Degeratu, some twenty years his junior, had studied in the United Kingdom and was fluent in English. For NATO aspirants such as Romania, the ability to speak English was important. I was later told that Cioflina had been dismissed because of "his business dealings" but had been offered the position of head of the Romanian Military Academy to save face. Like so many things in Romania, the matter was forgotten and no charges were brought. The action also marked the thinking of the new defense minister, Victor Babiuc, in replacing the military top brass with younger, English-speaking officers. The change raised no concern for us. Degeratu was known to be solidly pro-American.

A NEW PRESIDENT TAKES CHARGE, WITH HELP FROM AN OLD FRIEND

Once he became president, Constantinescu realized that he lacked political experience and needed help. He turned to his former academic colleague, Zoe Petre, a professor of ancient history at Bucharest University, for help. Some fifteen years Constantinescu's senior, Zoe assumed major responsibilities at Cotroceni, writing Constantinescu's speeches and in general advising him on policy issues. A mother figure and confidante, she was usually at Constantinescu's side offering encouragement and reassurance. She was pro-American, worldly, and wise. When I had doubts about raising an issue with President Constantinescu, I would run it by Zoe to get her reaction and advice. She was also a frequent guest at my residence for lunch. When the conversation was not about Romanian politics and Cotroceni decisionmaking, we discussed Roman history and the remains of Roman camps still visible on the western shore of the Black Sea.

U.S. SUPPORT FOR THE NEW GOVERNMENT

Once the new government was in place, the United States began a three-week training course for police officers. I spoke at the opening ceremony. The trainees were forty-five police officers at the deputy chief level. It was an impressive group, all wearing ties and jackets. Romania's military and police have historically been all male. Now there were four women deputy chief police officers in the course.

We also arranged, at Cotroceni's request, for Denis Clift, who seventeen years before had been foreign policy adviser to Vice President Walter Mondale in the White House, to come to Bucharest for six weeks to establish a national security council modeled on the U.S. National Security Council, with its office at Cotroceni, again copying the American model of having NSC officials housed in the White House complex. The structure was put in place at Cotroceni and was still functioning in 2017. In a similar vein, the United States built a secure communications system to allow President Constantinescu to communicate with his intelligence network wherever he was, including outside Romania.

Legal training took place in both the criminal and civil justice systems. Regarding the former, the United States set up a financial crime training group in Bucharest to work with the police, banks, and the Finance Ministry to help detect and root out this growing problem in international finance. The United States also sent a legal team to Bucharest to train the Romanian judiciary and lawyers on bankruptcy proceedings. When the American team arrived, there were more than 3,000 bankruptcy petitions on file. U.S. assistance for Romania also included grants to upgrade steel processing at Romania's huge steel plate facility in Galati, close to the border with Ukraine. I had previously visited the plate plant in 1984, and even then the plant was out of date, having been built in 1974 with Soviet technology. The signing of the steel assistance agreement took place in the U.S. embassy and was witnessed by a group of plant managers, a gap-toothed, no-neck, purple-suited entourage so familiar to me from the past.

To ease the burden of Romanian workers displaced by privatization and market forces, we brought U.S. factory worker teams to Romania to retrain displaced workers at the community and factory level and to help laid off workers find jobs in the newly emerging economy and, if necessary, to relocate them. Culturally, this ran against the Romanian grain. Moving from one part of the country to another in search of work was not the Romanian way of doing things. For Romanians, the village where you were born and raised was where you remained. To move meant leaving family and friends, an act of disloyalty, but old ways needed to change if Romania was to move ahead.

We also had a U.S. Treasury advisory team in Romania that produced tangible results. It drafted a new Romanian external debt law and put in place the mechanism for auctioning government paper. The Finance Ministry adopted our recommendations, scheduling external debt for auction and issuing debt instruments with terms negotiated by the National Bank of Romania as agent for the Finance Ministry. We encouraged the principal investment banking firms doing business with Central Europe, including Merrill Lynch, CS First Boston, J. P. Morgan, and Deutsche Bank, to underwrite Romanian debt.

The United States also brought to Bucharest a three-person bank supervision team to work with the National Bank of Romania. This was after Parliament passed the bank privatization bill we had recommended, meaning that Romania's five state-owned banks would be privatized. We also recommended measures to ensure bank safety and soundness and compliance with government regulations after privatization. To complete the necessary reform, the Parliament passed legislation making the National Bank of Romania— Romania's equivalent of our Federal Reserve Bank—truly independent, with sole responsibility for issuing official Romanian government financial reports, promoting economic growth, and supervising Romania's banks. Romania was finally shedding its communist past and adopting Western economic norms.

THE NEXT MILE ON THE NATO ROAD

On January 9 Walter Slocombe, U.S. under secretary of defense for policy, arrived in Bucharest for a two-day visit. A foreign policy and defense expert with years of government service in Washington, he would be the highest-ranking American official to visit Bucharest in the lead-up to the decision in the spring of 1997 on NATO enlargement. I knew Walt from Washington. He had had a brilliant academic career that included his being a Rhodes scholar. He came to Romania as an enthusiast for NATO enlargement. By the time he left, on January 10, he was an enthusiast for Romania's joining NATO in the first wave, saying, "Romania is on the right road to NATO entry and will receive an invitation for entry in the first group." This was all well and good, but I knew—and I suspect Walt knew—the decision would not be made by the Pentagon or the Department of State but by the President of the United States and his national security team.

Walt's visit was important. He had also been the first high-level foreign official to come to Bucharest for bilateral meetings after the Romanian election. Others followed: A month later the United Kingdom's foreign minister, Malcolm Rifkind, arrived, followed by President Jacques Chirac of France and, later, Foreign Minister Klaus Kinkel of Germany.

The symbolism of these high-level European visits was not lost on the Romanians, who correctly perceived that Romania still did not have top ranking in Washington among NATO aspirants. Prior to the election, former president Iliescu's government suffered from Western Europeans' doubts about the democratic bona fides of post-Ceauşescu Romania. By contrast, the new Christian Democratic government had excellent relations with its sister party in Germany and the Conservative Party in the United Kingdom. It also had the benefit of Petre Roman's ties to the socialists in France and Spain. Walt was quick to pick up on this in meetings, advising Romania that its case for NATO membership ran through European capitals, not just Washington.

In his meeting with Walt, Romania's new defense minister, Victor Babiuc, described Romania's defense procurement plans as directed primarily toward meeting NATO interoperability standards (thus adhering to precatory words from U.S. Defense Secretary William Perry). The expected cost was between $2 billion and $3 billion, plus another $1 billion or more for the Cobras. We already knew that Michel Camdessus, the managing director of the IMF, had told President Emil Constantinescu in December that Romania could not afford the Cobras. Camdessus was French, and France's helicopter manufacturer Puma was Cobra's principal competitor, making Camdessus's advice suspect in the minds of Romanians. The government of Romania continued to support the Cobra, despite Camdessus's advice, but in 1998 gave up on the Cobra purchase.

Walt also met with Prime Minister Ciorbea, who impressed him positively, and President Constantinescu, who disappointed him. Constantinescu blamed the United States for fifty years of communism in Romania: he stated that there were only 800 communists in Romania at the time of the 1946 elections, as compared to over 1 million members of the National Peasants Party. "Because of Soviet chicanery," he said, "the communists seized control of the country." The Soviet Union had a large military presence in Romania at the time. "Romania has been waiting ever since for the Americans," he continued, "and now if Romania does not get into NATO in the first group, Romanians will again see it as American 'treachery.'" President Constantinescu also complained that the "United States did nothing to help me in the election." Of course, we did nothing to help him, or anyone else, but as President Constantinescu saw it, he was the good guy and Iliescu the bad guy, which in his eyes meant that it was our moral duty to help him.

President Constantinescu was fast becoming a historical revisionist, a trait often found in Romania. For example, when he met with Vice President Albert Gore in Lisbon on the margins of the Organization for Security and Cooperation in Europe summit in December 1996, he claimed that the November election was the first democratic election in Romania in over sixty years. I suppose he considered the elections in 1992 not democratic because he lost. He also took credit for the smooth transfer of government power following the recent elections without so much as a nod in the direction of Iliescu and the former government. After all, they gave up power gracefully without a whimper.

Prior to Slocombe's exchange with Constantinescu, we had thought about setting up a meeting for President Constantinescu with President Clinton in Washington. After hearing Constantinescu's anti-American diatribe, Walt and his entourage discouraged a White House meeting. For all the talk about democracy, the new crowd showed alarming signs of adopting the philosophy that the ends justify the means. The government wasted no time kicking out the professional staff at the Romanian national television station, RTV, and putting in its place its political supporters, in violation of the Romanian law governing national television. I also learned that my correspondence with the International Republican Institute had been brought from Washington to Bucharest by the new spokesperson in the Foreign Ministry, who was also the author of wild accusations that appeared in the press, written under a pseudonym, about President Clinton's and my role in the Romanian elections.

I hosted an official dinner for Walt at my residence for nineteen guests that included five ministers. During dinner Foreign Minister Severin told me he was having difficulty with President Constantinescu, the two of them vying for primacy in foreign policy. The difficulty reflected President Constantinescu's unhappiness as a Christian Democrat with the Democratic Party's (PD) presence in government. Severin was a member of the PD. The coalition was a necessary compromise, but ideologically—and for Constantinescu, morally—there was a world of difference between his beliefs and those of the PD. The conflict between the two would continue.

Despite the good press the new government received in the West, it was clear to me that Romania would not be in the first wave of NATO expansion. Deputy Secretary of State Strobe Talbott had met in January with Germany's foreign minister, Kinkel, in Washington, where they talked about three or four countries in the first wave. It seemed likely that the fourth country—after Poland, the Czech Republic, and Hungary—would be Slovenia, not Romania. There was still time before the decision would be made, but Romania's chances were slim to none. The number of countries in the first wave would be limited to avoid a major struggle in the U.S. Senate. The thinking in Washington was that it was better to go with the thin edge of the wedge, wait a while, then bring in the rest.

SLINGSHOT MATCH AT THE PDSR CORRAL

Dan Fried, the National Security Council's senior director for Eastern Europe, accompanied Walt to Bucharest. Soon after he arrived, Dan and I visited former president Ion Iliescu at the Social Democratic Party of Ro-

mania (PDSR) headquarters. It was a surreal experience. Iliescu was late, so
for thirty minutes or so we sat around with other party members—Adrian
Nastase, Oliviu Gherman, Teodor Meleşcanu, and Viorel Hrebenciuc—not
knowing whether or when Iliescu would appear. It was like old home week
with the Romanians lambasting the new government, citing its neglect of
U.S. relations, with Nastase harping on economic issues and the threat to
the social fabric from recent price increases. I disagreed. In my view, the
new government would have to stumble badly before PDSR would return
to power.

When Iliescu finally arrived, he seemed more vibrant and feisty than he
had been during the election campaign. Rather than showing bitterness at the
election outcome, he extolled the virtues of defeat, claiming it was good to be
"back with the people" and away from the "insularity of government." He was
right about this, but he always had a feel for real life. Not so for some of the
others, particularly Nastase, who missed the prestige accorded him when he
was president of the Chamber of Deputies.

On January 10, Fried and I met with prominent representatives of the Romanian media, one of whom had become the spokesman for Prime Minister
Ciorbea. The other media people, all of whom had voted for the opposition in
the recent election, had already changed their minds and were now criticizing
the new government, citing the illegal firings at RTV, the government's failure to explain the need for recent price increases, and questions about Foreign
Minister Severin's integrity. The media seemed to be as critical of the new
crowd as they had been of the old.

The Iliescu meeting had a long shelf life in the Romanian press. After the
meeting, a PDSR spokesperson put out a press release claiming that Fried
had delivered a private message of greetings from President Clinton to Iliescu in which he praised him for his service as president and credited him
with advancing Romania's chances of being in the first group of countries
to join NATO. Not to be outdone, the Romanian press compounded the
misinformation by reporting that Dan had said this directly to the press. I
put out a press statement denying the existence of a message from President
Clinton and the press statement attributed to Fried. This provoked an angry
telephone call from the former foreign minister, Teodor Meleşcanu, in which
he complained that this was the first time the American embassy had gone

to the trouble of correcting misinformation by a political party. Later in the day I received an unsigned fax from Iliescu's press person, complaining that we should have set the ground rules for Fried's visit in advance. I faxed back, stating that there were no ground rules because there was no message from President Clinton, and I criticized PDSR's efforts to turn a simple courtesy call into something more.

PDSR looked even sillier a few days later when one of the Bucharest newspapers published an interview with former president Iliescu in which he stated that Fried had not brought a message from President Clinton and in other respects repudiated the PDSR press release. It was a strange way for a major political party to behave, but at least its leader was honest. I never asked what happened to the spokesperson.

Iliescu's denial did not stop the rumor mill. President Constantinescu himself asked me a day or two later about the "secret message" from President Clinton to Iliescu, and a day or so after that two of my fellow NATO ambassadors asked me for details about the message Fried brought from President Clinton.

OPENING UP THE SRI

A major breakthrough, and a break with the past, was signaled by reforms at the Romanian Internal Security Service (SRI). On January 28 SRI Director Virgil Magureanu invited me to a private dinner at a small villa on the outskirts of Bucharest, part of SRI's substantial empire. The service also controlled its own food supply: hothouse vegetables (including vine-ripe tomatoes), its own beef herd, and poultry farms. The Danube delta was also SRI territory, with a private yacht and guest houses. Magureanu was a political survivor who had linked up with Iliescu before 1989 to plot Ceaușescu's overthrow, only to abandon the effort when the military did not join in. He had supported Ion Iliescu in the 1992 election but actively worked behind the scenes to defeat him in the 1996 election. He was always shrouded in mystery. In our conversation that night, however, he was right on target: economic reform was key to Romania's future. By comparison, Romania's immediate entry into NATO was not nearly as important. We both agreed that if the Romanian economy performed as it should, the political situation would take care of itself, and in the long run Romania would be part of the West. A stagnant or underperforming economy would create problems for Romania, regardless of whether it was in or out of NATO.

That was the chitchat portion of the evening. The real issue was my offer to Magureanu for the CIA to train mid-level SRI analysts. Magureanu's aides had parried the question. The dinner gave me the opening to ask Magureanu directly. He said yes, and the deal was closed. No more Tweedledum, Tweedledee. For the first time, the CIA would have a direct link with Romania's Internal Security Service.

JOGGING WITH THE MARINES

My routine on Sunday mornings was to jog five to six miles with the embassy's Marine detachment. Our route started at my residence, headed north from there, continued to the northern outskirts of Bucharest, and then headed south to the Dambovita River in the center of town. Running at my slow pace was not much exercise for the Marines, and at the end of each run they turned around and repeated the course, adding another five or six miles before ending up at my residence for breakfast, which I cooked. A typical breakfast for the Marines consisted of waffles, toast, juice, and four or five eggs per Marine. Their appetites were gargantuan, matching their esprit de corps, with the gunnery sergeant in command.

THE DIPLOMATS' NEW YEAR'S PARTY

January 16 was the date set for Romania's new president, Emil Constantinescu, to perform the annual Romanian rite of greeting the foreign diplomatic corps at Cotroceni. This year the ceremony was different. The "praetorian guard" was still there, but the reception took place in a single room with President Constantinescu greeting each ambassador separately. Then, as we stood together in a line facing him, he delivered a thirty-minute speech, which was translated from Romanian into English and French. It was a statesmanlike address, devoid of Romanian political jargon and striking the right tone. But the real historical precedent was performed by the doyen: the Zairean ambassador finally showed up wearing a suit. He delivered a short address in French that was not translated, I assumed, because it was not considered important. The other change was culinary: the lavish hors d'oeuvres of the past were gone; in their place were ladyfingers washed down with a choice of Coca-Cola, bubbly water, or lemonade, a fitting demonstration of matching one's money to one's mouth, in this case, unfortunately, our mouths.

MAKING THE ROUNDS

I called on all the new ministers. Most of them had no previous government experience and were reluctant to engage in conversation beyond the usual pleasantries. The exceptions were at the Ministries of Defense, Foreign Affairs, and Transportation, where PD ministers Babiuc, Severin, and Basescu, respectively, had served in Petre Roman's government from 1991 to 1992.

However, the most amusing meeting was with Dinu Gavrilescu, minister of agriculture. When I introduced myself, he sat starry-eyed, explaining over and over the significance of his meeting with the American ambassador, something he claimed he never dreamt of before the elections when he had been a mere agriculture researcher. The flattery soon turned toward the surreal. Gavrilescu did not speak English, and his interpreter was not up to the task of conveying his sentiments in English. When I asked about his predictions for the winter wheat crop, he gave me a questioning look, clearly indicating he did not know what I was talking about.

CHANGING OF THE GUARD AT THE STATE DEPARTMENT AND ROMANIA'S NATO CHANCES

John Kornblum, one of the State Department's senior career officers, was Dick Holbrooke's successor as assistant secretary of state for European Affairs. He came to Bucharest on February 1 to meet the new government at a dinner at my residence with Prime Minister Ciorbea, Foreign Minister Severin, and others. On the critical issue of NATO, John was more optimistic than I about Romania's chances, or maybe he was just being polite. He put the odds at better than fifty-fifty. My estimate was close to zero. The idea of NATO enlargement itself was still a controversial issue in the United States, and the longer the list of new members, the harder the path would be. I could not see the Clinton administration seeking Senate ratification for five new members, the number needed if Romania were included. Despite Romania's progress and the boost given to its chances by the recent elections, Romania was still seen in Washington as "less like us than the three leading contenders," Poland, the Czech Republic, and Hungary, or Slovenia, then in fourth place.

Support for Romania's accession was also lacking among important NATO members, notably Germany and the United Kingdom. British Foreign Minister Malcolm Rifkind had said, following a recent trip to Romania, "NATO should enlarge naturally, not by announcing waves or groups." By "naturally" he meant geographically. For Romania this meant a long wait. Chancellor Helmut Kohl of Germany had given a flat no, banging his fists on the table, when recently asked about Romania's entering NATO. The British could not see beyond Poland, the Czech Republic, and Hungary. Denmark and Norway linked Romania's entry to the admission of the Baltic states, and as they would not be in the first wave, neither would Romania.

Another reason Germany looked with disdain on Romania was the large number of Roma who had migrated to Germany since 1989 and were implicated in organized crime and acts of brutality. At the same time, the Germans shared our view that no one knew what would happen in post-Yeltsin Russia: a strong, missile-bound, xenophobic government could try to put a stop to NATO enlargement, even though we would continue to say publicly that Russia did not have a veto over NATO membership. This argued in favor of moving ahead without waiting decades.

Meanwhile, we were doing positive things for Romania in Washington. First, my special assistant, Mihai Carp, and I drafted a lengthy piece for Congressman Tom Lantos (D-Calif.) to insert in the *Congressional Record* covering his two days in Romania. The message was unabashedly positive. In late January Nicholas Burns, the State Department spokesman, commenting in a press conference on Assistant Secretary Kornblum's upcoming visit to Bucharest, made a positive reference to Romania, repeating the now familiar line that Romania was a serious contender for early admission to NATO. Added to this were two good pieces on Romania that appeared in mid-April in the *International Herald Tribune*: in one article, the Paris-based columnist William Pfaff argued for Romania's entrance into NATO, citing the Hungarian-Romanian rapprochement as the principal reason, and in another article, Peter S. Green and Justin Keay touted the investment potential in Romania, citing the establishment of the RASDAQ, which, according to them, was set up "with help from USAID"—a bit of an understatement—to augment Romania's new market economy.

These were all positives for Romania, but the general sentiment in the United States had not changed. For example, in February Tom Carothers, vice president of the Carnegie Endowment in Washington, came to Romania for ten days. On a merit scale of 1 to 100, he put Romania's chances in the low 50s (up from the low 30s two years earlier); for Poland and the Czech Republic, it was in the low 70s. Tom rightly saw the new regime in Romania as a boost for Romania, but it was still a long shot. Tom, too, had been attacked by the International Republican Institute (IRI) because of his criticism of its political meddling in Romania and elsewhere.

THE CONTINUING BELL SAGA

Prime Minister Ciorbea announced in late January that he would sign a letter of intent for the sovereign guarantee by the government of Romania for the purchase of the ninety-six Cobras. Ulm Spineanu, minister of economic reform, was present for the announcement and joined in the rousing chorus. A few days later I delivered the draft letter of intent to Prime Minister Ciorbea's office and picked up the signed copy the next day. This happened exactly as planned, in stark contrast with the frustrations I had encountered in trying to get Ciorbea's predecessor, Prime Minister Vacaroiu, to sign.

For a time the Bell deal looked like it would happen; the two sides appointed negotiating teams for the purchase of the IAR-Brașov plant. Bell got into the spirit and made generous donations to American NGOs working with Romanian children, which was duly noted and applauded in the Romanian press. Prime Minister Ciorbea continued to advocate for the Bell deal and brushed aside pressure from the German-French consortium.

The remaining stumbling block was financing. It was clear that the money had to come from the Ministry of Defense budget. However, the ministry was looking to increase its budget by only 0.5 percent per year for the next three years, and this would not cover the front-end cost of the Cobras. The balance would have to be borrowed externally, which presented a new set of problems.

In early March Bell put a $50 million offer on the table to buy a 75 percent interest in IAR-Braşov. Economic Reform Minister Spineanu was overjoyed and immediately accepted the offer. In my judgment, it was more than Bell needed to pay, but if the deal went ahead, the difference was not significant. The next hurdle was to arrange for financing to carry the project until the government of Romania took delivery and paid for the first Cobras. The cumulative predelivery costs would be close to $400 million.

The Ministry of Defense pushed for an increase in its budget from the previous year's 2.2 percent of GDP to 3 percent for FY1997. Countering this, the IMF's managing director, Michel Camdessus, lobbied the U.S. Treasury Department and others in Washington to support the IMF's view that Romania's economic reform was more important than an increase in its military spending, and that the two were incompatible. This might have been true, but the Romanian military was not buying the IMF line. Like defense officials elsewhere, the Romanian military wanted to spend more, not less, and the government of Romania was apprehensive that if the military budget remained at 2.2 percent of GDP, it would count against Romania at the upcoming June Madrid NATO summit. The size of the military budget had a big impact on the Cobra deal. It would be hard to tell Romania not to spend more on defense while at the same time pushing the Romanian government to purchase ninety-six Cobras at a cost of $1.5 billion, even if most of the bill's impact would be deferred to later years.

French President Jacques Chirac's visit to Romania in February had a negative impact on the Bell deal. I was not surprised. After President Chirac left, I mentioned my concerns to Prime Minister Ciorbea. He confessed that he had succumbed to French pressure during Chirac's visit and agreed that the Romanian government would seriously consider a French counter-offer before signing a contract with Bell. Prime Minister Ciorbea put on his Romanian negotiator's hat and asked whether Bell would agree to the French supplying civilian helicopters, thereby splitting the baby. Bell's answer was no. The French civilian helicopter was an old model that the French had been unable to sell elsewhere. From Bell's standpoint, even though it would not object to IAR-Braşov's honoring the contract it had earlier signed to manufacture the French model, this was not a viable solution going forward. After considerable discussion, Prime Minister Ciorbea assured me that Bell would get the deal: the Romanian government would "find something else for the French."

I frequently hosted dinners for Bell's president, Lloyd Shoppa, attended by Prime Minister Ciorbea, Economic Reform Minister Spineanu, and others. The dinners were always upbeat, with resounding expressions of confidence on the part of all present. But bonhomie by itself was not enough. The elephant in the room was always who was going to pay, how much, and when.

The IMF was concerned that this year's (1997) Cobra cost, $105 million, would, together with other nonbudgeted costs, increase the deficit to 6.5 percent of GDP. Moreover, the borrowings would bust the IMF's imposed lid of $3.2 billion on external borrowing. The Bell program was not the IMF's only concern. An array of other expenses were not in Romania's budget, such as the Romanian government's continuing to subsidize home heating and gas prices and the failure of RENEL, the Romanian government–owned electric company, to cut off power to nonpaying industrial users, thereby adding to RENEL's off-budget losses.

TWO HEADLINE ARRESTS

A short time after the new government took office, it announced the arrest of George H. W. Bush's erstwhile host, Sever Mureşan, and Miron Cosma, the notorious boss of the miners in the Jiu Valley who had led the raids in Bucharest in 1990 and 1991. The 1991 raid had brought down the Romanian government. Mureşan had supported Emil Constantinescu in the elections and placed himself in a prominent spot at Constantinescu's appearance in December in Alba Iulia, hoping, no doubt, to gain reflected glory and to be perceived as influential at Cotroceni. President Constantinescu later told me that he personally decided Mureşan should be the first person arrested to demonstrate that his new government's campaign against corruption was not politically directed. After Mureşan's arrest, President Constantinescu received a letter from Mureşan's mother pleading for his release, citing his support for Constantinescu in the elections.

Mureşan took a gamble in returning to Romania after the elections rather than remaining in Dijon, France, where he owned a house. He must have thought that his support for President Constantinescu would protect him. Rumors of corruption were rife. Mureşan was accused of taking several hundred thousand dollars from Banca Dacia Felix with the whereabouts of the money unknown. One rumor was that it was in Mafia hands in Italy. I wondered at the time how long Mureşan would remain in jail; in the end he was never brought to trial, and a few months later he was released.

The arrest of the miners' leader, Cosma, was a different story and was far more than political payback. He had a long history of bullying and thuggery, engaging in strong-arm tactics while surrounded by an entourage of bodyguards. Ceauşescu used to send ex-convicts to work in the coal mines in the Jiu Valley, and the union itself was heavily infiltrated by the Securitate. Ceauşescu used the miners as political goons. Cosma had a political change of heart before the 1996 elections and supported Petre Roman, whose government had fallen in 1991 after the second miners' raid. The press still criticized Roman for his role in bringing the miners to Bucharest, first in 1990 and then in 1991, to quash antigovernment student demonstrations.

After he was no longer prime minister, Roman blamed President Iliescu, saying that the miners had come to Bucharest in June 1990 at Iliescu's request. The plan, Roman claimed, was for Iliescu to use the miners as a show of force, to thank them for their support, and then tell them that Romania was now a democracy and that there should be no violence. Instead, Iliescu told them to "clean up the city." Following two days of widespread rioting and hooliganism, much of which was directed against political opposition headquarters and the private homes of opposition political leaders as well as students, including some brutal beatings, the miners were herded into one of Bucharest's large exhibition halls, where Iliescu was supposed to remonstrate with them for the violence. But when he was greeted by wildly cheering miners, he dropped the criticism and thanked them. I had trouble separating fact from fiction. Roman, like Iliescu, was afraid in 1990 that the government would be toppled by street demonstrators. The police were outnumbered and the military was unreliable. This left it to the miners to do the government's dirty work. The Roman government succeeded in quelling the demonstrations, but ended up paying a political price for the violence. So, too, Iliescu.

A U.S. CONGRESSMAN RETURNS TO HIS ROOTS

Members of Congress like to travel abroad. Maybe it is a break from the Washington scene, or perhaps it gives them a chance to spend a few days without having to answer constituent calls and mail. Whatever the reason, our embassy was besieged by congressional delegations. Unfortunately, the occasional delegation displayed more enthusiasm than knowledge. Some members of Congress possessed little knowledge of the country they were visiting, its problems and aspirations.

This was not the case with Congressman Tom Lantos, who visited Bucharest in February 1997. A Jew born in Budapest, Tom survived the Holocaust and enrolled at the University of Budapest. An essay he wrote on Franklin D. Roosevelt won him a scholarship to study in the United States, where he became a naturalized U.S. citizen in 1953. He earned his B.A. and M.A. degrees from the University of Washington and a Ph.D. in economics from the University of California, Berkeley. A decade later he was a professor of economics at San Francisco State University. In 1978 he went to Washington to work as an adviser to Senator Joe Biden (D-Del.). In 1980 he was elected to Congress, where he was still serving his country twenty-seven years later.

Congressman Lantos took an interest in Romania for the right reasons. He knew its history, politics, and leadership. He was a strong champion of human rights and an outspoken and effective advocate for integrating the former communist countries in Eastern Europe into the West. He had taken the lead in support of the legislation granting Romania permanent MFN status. Tom was a personal friend as well as an important American political leader. I wanted to make sure his visit went well. I checked with Zoe Petre at Cotroceni before asking President Constantinescu to host a dinner for Tom and his wife, Annette. President Constantinescu agreed. Tom and Annette arrived a few days later. He was immediately interviewed on PRO-TV's *Face to Face*. Articulate and forceful throughout his stay, Tom stressed the significance of the recent elections in advancing Romania's stature in the West, the benefit of having included the ethnic Hungarian party UDMR in the government (it got one ministry), and his unqualified support for Romania to be included with Poland, the Czech Republic, Hungary, and Slovenia in NATO accession talks.

President Constantinescu asked me to brief him in advance of the Lantoses' visit. Mihai Carp, my special assistant, and I explained that the congressman was a strong voice in Congress on behalf of Romania and that he should be commended for his past support of Romania and encouraged to continue his support.

Tom's first meeting with President Constantinescu did not go well. He dominated the conversation and at one point seemed to be lecturing President Constantinescu on the importance of lowering Romania's expectations of being included in the first NATO wave. The example he gave, neither apt nor immodest, was his recent congressional campaign, where he had predicted he might win 51 percent of the vote but ended up with 72 percent. "Had I predicted I would get 72 percent of the vote," he instructed Constantinescu, "I would have been setting myself up for possible disappointment." President Constantinescu listened politely. By then he had become accustomed to Americans telling him what to do. We as a people are not shy about sharing our views with foreigners, even on occasions such as this, telling a foreign head of state what was in his best interests when we were his guests, as if we Americans know better than foreign leaders how to run their countries.

Other meetings for Tom followed with Prime Minister Ciorbea and his ministers. In each meeting, Tom performed marvelously, but I was still concerned about an upcoming dinner with President Constantinescu, to be attended only by Constantinescu, Zoe Petre, the two Lantoses, and me. On the drive to dinner at a government guest house on the outskirts of Bucharest, I suggested to Tom that he encourage President Constantinescu to do most of the speaking. After all, he was the president of Romania and we were his guests. Annette immediately piped up, saying "Tomas, you should remember to be quiet and let the president speak." Like most good husbands, "Tomas" listened to his wife, and the dinner was a great success. Given the opportunity, Constantinescu spoke volumes, always on point and interesting. On the drive back to my residence, Tom could not stop praising Constantinescu, going so far as to call him "Romania's shining light."

TRANSYLVANIA: A GLISTENING LAND OF PAINFUL MEMORIES

On a beautiful, clear February Sunday morning, Susan Jacobs, our consul general, my special assistant, Mihai Carp, and I flew in a U.S. military plane from Bucharest to Baia Mare, the capital of Maramureş, a *judet* (county) in northwest Romania. The two-day visit began with the usual police escort and greetings by local dignitaries. Baia Mare still had a functioning synagogue, a handsome building used for religious services by the hundred or so remaining Jews. The president of the congregation, a strikingly handsome eighty-eight-year-old gentleman, was invited by the mayor to join us at lunch, an elaborate affair that began with a prayer by the Orthodox archbishop followed by words of welcome from the local dignitaries, each of whom spoke, a formality in a part of the world where such things still matter, and then a performance by an eight-piece musical ensemble wearing native costumes. It was a reminder of what had once existed but now seemed dated.

Inhabitants of Maramureş rightly prided themselves on the *judet*'s natural beauty, which we witnessed firsthand on the forty-five-mile drive from Baia Mare through the Carpathian Mountains to Sighet, a city of some 40,000 nestled on the Tisza River, separating northern Romania from Ukraine. The newly fallen snow on the mountains glistened in the sunshine.

The Nobel laureate Elie Wiesel was born in Sighet in the late 1920s. More than half of its inhabitants were Jewish, mostly Satmar Hasidim (ultra-Orthodox). Descendants of those not killed in the Holocaust now live in Brooklyn and Monsey, New York. The enormous Jewish cemetery in Sighet contains the remains of thousands—centuries—of Satmars, many with the surname Teitelbaum. Joel Teitelbaum, the founder and rebbe of the Satmar Dynasty, was born in Sighet and died in Brooklyn in 1979. Sighet's most famous son, Wiesel was Jewishly religious but not Satmar. His family home was still there in the center of town with a plaque identifying the house as Wiesel's birthplace. In the afternoon I visited the one remaining synagogue in Sighet. Only seventy-five Jews remained out of the more than 14,000 who lived in Sighet before the war. There were not enough Jews to maintain the main sanctuary, so afternoon services were held in a small adjoining room.

Sighet was known in Romania for a reason other than being Elie Wiesel's birthplace. For seventeen years it was the site of the prison where prominent political leaders were jailed by the communists and where Iuliu Maniu, the leader of the National Peasant Party, and Gheorghe Bratianu, the leader of the National Liberal Party, died under mysterious circumstances. Ana Blandiana, one of Romania's leading dissidents under the communists and the former wife of Mihai Botez, who was Romania's ambassador to the United States (1994–95), led an international campaign to preserve the jail as a memorial to those who perished there. The project was supported by the Council of Europe. A heroic figure, Ana accompanied us throughout the day. She gave a moving talk at the prison, after which I talked about the evils of fascism and communism, and stressed the importance of preserving memorials to victims of totalitarianism to both sanctify their memories and safeguard future generations from its recurrence.

From the prison we walked to the adjoining cemetery, where probably the remains of Maniu, Bratianu, and others killed by the communists were buried, and from there to the memorial to Sighet's Jews who never returned from Auschwitz.

The Tisza River, which now forms part of the border between Romania and Ukraine, was part of Czechoslovakia before the war. Hamlets across the river had once been suburbs of Sighet, but Soviet troops sealed the border in 1945, separating families for the next fifty years. Tragically, children who left their homes in the morning to go to school across the border never returned to their homes. They grew up, married, and became parents and grandparents without ever seeing their relatives a few miles away.

Romanian hospitality was on full display when we left Sighet. As we departed, we were met by the director of the local hospital, his mother, sisters, and assorted relatives, all in local dress, who greeted us with hugs, kisses, and tuica (plum brandy) to fortify us against the bitter cold. Our hosts insisted that we accept beautiful handwoven woolen blankets and with nary a pause shoved us into open wagons with wooden seats draped with woolen covers for a horse-drawn wagon ride to the "Merry Cemetery" in Sapanța, a half mile away. Even with blankets and tuica, the cold was bone-chilling. People came out to greet us as we trundled down the main street of the village. The spirit was more like Fourth of July in a midwestern town than a cold February morning in a Romanian village.

The cemetery has to be seen to be believed. Grave markers are made of wood, brightly painted with an Orthodox cross on top, and below an artist's rendition of the life of the deceased together with a legend telling how each person had lived and died: "He drove too fast," "He drank too much," or "He loved life but not his family." Deceased farmers are shown tending their flock; women, baking or sewing. The spirit is uplifting. We were told that thousands of tourists came each year to see the Merry Cemetery, designated by the Romanian government as an outdoor museum. A few years ago an article in the *Wall Street Journal* described the cemetery in Sapanța as the world's most unusual cemetery. The cemetery church is also unusual. As the priest explained, the liturgy is part Romanian Orthodox, part Roman Catholic. The church's interior is stark white plaster, unlike the dark, ornate frescoes usually found in Romania's Orthodox churches.

From the cemetery we moved on foot or, more accurately, on ice to a small house where the mayor of Sapanța lived with his mother. Forty or more people sat on benches at three small tables in what I assume was the family's living room. The mayor's mother had prepared the traditional Romanian cornmeal porridge called *mamaliga*, with melted cheese, not my favorite food. Next on the menu was bucketloads of fried fish, a local delicacy from a nearby stream. Their appearance was unappetizing, but the fish were delicious. In any event, eating was not optional, nor was drinking tuica. In a word, hospitality in Sapanța was overwhelming and apparently genuine, not a show put on for the American ambassador. I suspect that if I were to return unannounced and unknown, the reception would be just as warm, if perhaps more modest. The "locals" make their living from tourism; as their financial resources were limited, they offered friendship.

TWO ROMANIAN HEROES FROM THE HOLOCAUST

A week after our trip to Transylvania, I spoke briefly at a ceremony at the Israeli embassy at which Gabriela Strauss-Tiron and the Pop family received the "Righteous Person" award from Yad Vashem, the Holocaust memorial in Jerusalem. They were honored for saving Jews from being deported to concentration camps and almost certain death. I spoke extemporaneously, but the Israeli embassy recorded my remarks:

Thank you Mr. Ambassador, Senator Radu Vasile, friends of Israel, friends of Romania, the Pop family, and all that have gathered here today. This is a joyous occasion, a time for us to acknowledge and pay tribute to those who risked their lives to help others. I have been present at occasions like this elsewhere. In Japan, where the person honored was a Japanese foreign service officer who issued visas to Lithuanian Jews in Vilna, claiming they were Japanese citizens and therefore under the protection of the Japanese government. And I was present in the Israeli embassy in Washington with the great Polish Catholic hero, Jan Karski, who brought the message to President Roosevelt in 1942 that millions of Jews in Central Europe were being killed by Nazi Germany. But I've never been present for an occasion in Central Europe honoring those who saved Jews during the Holocaust. It is therefore especially meaningful for me to be here today, because we are on the very soil where the tragedies took place, in a part of the world that witnessed the destruction of six million Jews and millions of other innocent people, who died as a result of the despotism of fascism. We are also in a land that suffered under communism. Millions of people in the world died under the oppression of communism.

. . .

What struck me on previous occasions, and strikes me now, is that we frail human beings seldom display courage in the face of oppression. What is almost as shocking as the number of persons who were killed as a result of oppression is the few who stood up and displayed personal courage at great risk to themselves to save others. And that is why it is important that while we do not forget those who perished, we never forget those who saved others. Gabriela Strauss-Tiron and the Pop family are not only heroes of the Holocaust, they are heroes of humanity. All of us at some time or another have asked ourselves in the stillness of the night, would we have had the courage to do what they did? We don't know; we can only hope that we, too, would have stood up and done what was right, despite the risks to ourselves. It is only by such acts of courage that we redeem our nobleness as human beings. My congratulations to you and my thanks for all that you did.

On a Sunday evening in February I attended *The Emperor of Atlantis oder Der Tod Dankt Ab* (The Emperor of Atlantis or Death Abdicates), an opera written in 1943 by Viktor Ullmann, a famous Jewish composer, with a libretto by Peter Kien. They collaborated on the work while imprisoned in Theresienstadt, a Nazi concentration camp in Czechoslovakia. It was a full house, with President and Mrs. Constantinescu in attendance. Ullmann wrote the opera on orders from the Nazi SS to be performed by Jewish prisoners to persuade a Red Cross delegation visiting the camp that its Jewish inmates were well treated. On seeing the final rehearsal, the SS canceled the performance, realizing that the Emperor depicted in the opera, on whose orders a character called the Angel of Death refused to kill the innocent, was in reality Hitler. Soon after, Ullmann and his would-be performers were shipped to Auschwitz and killed.

Rachel Worby, the wife of the former governor of West Virginia, conducted the all-Romanian orchestra and cast.

AWARD DAY (AGES FOUR TO SEVEN)

The next morning, I gave awards at the American School to two first-graders who had won a worldwide poster contest sponsored by the U.S. State Department. There were 100 children, ranging in ages from pre-K through second grade. They talked about safety, the theme for the posters. One little girl said, "You should not pour water in an electric outlet"; another, "Don't jump over fire;" and, of course, one offered "Don't get in a car with a stranger." The children were spontaneous and uninhibited. The teachers and children had been born in different countries, mostly in Romania but also elsewhere. Their diverse origins evidently represented Europe, Asia, and Africa. When the school was founded, there was a special English-language program (taught by a Yugoslav) for those who could not speak English when they first arrived in school. (Now, twenty years later, these children are adults making their way in Romania, a country different from the one they knew as youngsters.)

THE NEW ECONOMIC PROGRAM

On February 18, in a three-hour speech that was broadcast on television, Prime Minister Ciorbea announced the government's ambitious new economic reform program: The budget deficit was capped at 4.5 percent of GDP. The government would sell at auction its remaining interests in 2,700 companies still to be privatized under the Mass Privatization Program (MPP), two large oil refineries were to be closed, and the remaining large state-owned money-losers were to be liquidated by April 30. Similar ambitious measures were slated for the agriculture sector, including the privatization of large still state-owned farms and the government-owned intermediaries, including Romcereal, which controlled Romania's grain trading. The government would stop subsidizing farm credit programs, funded through Banca Agricola. Prices would be liberalized, import tariffs for agricultural products would be sharply reduced or eliminated, and a voucher program would be adopted to enable private farmers to acquire feed and fertilizer without resort to Romcereal. A large social support program was proposed to protect children, pensioners, and those who became unemployed, all at a cost of about 10 percent of the national budget. Inflation was expected to reach at least 100 percent in the coming year, before leveling off at an annual rate of about 30 percent. In the short term, the living standard of the average Romanian would decrease 2 percent or more. This was bitter medicine, and Prime Minister Ciorbea acknowledged that the economy would not recover before the spring or summer of 1998 at the earliest. The question was whether the government would have the courage to implement such measures and whether the populace would be willing to endure the cost.

In response to Ciorbea's speech to the nation, I immediately arranged to meet with Sorin Dimitriu, the new head of the State Ownership Fund (SOF), to offer to send to Romania a long-term U.S. economic adviser to work directly with him to push the government's privatization plan. I had made the same proposal a year before to Emil Dinu, Dimitriu's predecessor, without receiving a response.

The goal was to have someone full-time at the SOF by mid-1997 to work directly with Dimitriu, and later to add three other full-time U.S. technical advisers to assist with auctions and negotiated sales and to give advice on the packaging and presentation of companies to be sold to strategic investors. Only part of our package was accepted by the SOF. The total program would have cost tens of millions of dollars, and we ended up sending a smaller team of five to help the SOF accelerate privatization.

The business mood in Romania turned upbeat after Ciorbea's speech. The U.S. restaurant franchise McDonald's opened thirteen restaurants and planned to double the number by the end of the year. American investment portfolio managers began arriving in Bucharest, hoping for first-mover opportunities in Romania. Despite the rhetoric and announced plans, I remained skeptical. The road ahead was uncertain. It would be a difficult year for Romania, and I did not see a near-term turnaround. The pieces were not in place to fill the promises Ciorbea had made.

Mugur Isarescu, the governor of the National Bank of Romania, had the same concerns as I. Nevertheless, he tried to persuade the American Chamber of Commerce that things would be better. In his speech to the Chamber a few days after Ciorbea announced the government's new economic plan, he said that GDP had increased 5 percent the previous year, although the real figure was smaller. Even if he had been right, that increase was not sustainable. Imports were up, but exports were down, and Romania could not continue to fund its current account deficit by borrowing money abroad. The result would be ruinous with runaway inflation. Governor Isarescu's answer was to seek increased direct foreign investment in export-producing manufacturing plants. This was sound in theory, but it was the product of hope over experience. Where were the investment opportunities, and who would invest in the uncertain business climate that still existed in Romania?

Despite my private doubts, I invited a group of American businesspeople to my residence for lunch—representatives of Tenneco, Procter & Gamble, IBM, AirTouch, R. J. Reynolds, Nabisco, and General Electric. All were optimistic. Tenneco would move ahead with its $50 million wood processing plant east of Timişoara. (It later withdrew.) Procter & Gamble's detergent plant in Timişoara was scheduled to open in May. John Pepper, P&G's CEO, would be in Romania for the opening. IBM had $60 million of sales in Romania in 1996 and was hoping to increase revenues in 1997 with a contract to install a computer and cell phone system for the government of Romania, a smaller version of the system it installed for the U.S. government in Washington, plus computer upgrades for the Romanian Customs Service. None of this materialized; Romania did not have the money.

In mid-February John McDonnell, McDonnell Douglas's chairman, came to Bucharest for a day of meetings and lunch at my residence with Prime Minister Ciorbea, Economic Reform Minister Spineanu, and Minister of Industry and Trade Calin Popescu Tariceanu, plus a high-level Tarom official, followed by a meeting with Defense Minister Babiuc. McDonnell made an attractive offer to Tarom: three new MD-11s, long-range cargo-passenger planes, which would cost Romania a total of $350 million to $400 million. In return McDonnell would give Romania a credit of $62 million for its two Airbuses and commit to $105 million in offset purchases in Romania, plus build a new hangar for the MD-11s at Otopeni. At the end of twelve years, McDonnell would repurchase the MD-11s for 45 percent of their original cost. The deal would require a guarantee from the Romanian government.

After much urging on my part, Finance Minister Ciumara agreed to support a government guarantee covering the purchase price of the three MD-11s. This left the decision to Transportation Minister Traian Basescu, who after first telling me he would support the purchase refused to back the deal. This ended the negotiations. Basescu later told me that he had decided Tarom should "defer" its decision to purchase long-range aircraft and concentrate on its European routes by modernizing its in-country fleet of planes. For its European routes Basescu's pilot friends at Tarom wanted an all-Boeing fleet, and they got it. McDonnell was left out in the cold.

After selling $80 million worth of radar equipment in 1996 for Romania's regional air control system, Lockheed Martin continued to look for Romanian business. At the end of March, Norman Augustine, Lockheed Martin's CEO, joined me for dinner at my residence. The guests included Prime Minister Ciorbea, Foreign Minister Severin, and Defense Minister Babiuc, together with General Degeratu, the new army chief of staff, and the deputy defense minister, General Zaharia. The next day the same ministers, plus President Constantinescu, gathered again. Norm was understated but highly effective. He radiated confidence and integrity. An engineer by training, he had spent most of his career working for air space companies, beginning with Douglas Aircraft, then Martin-Marietta. He now headed Lockheed Martin, America's largest defense contractor.

Norm quickly adopted my suggestion that Lockheed Martin present itself in Romania as more than an "arms merchant." If it was selling without creating jobs in country, Romania could not pay the freight. Lockheed wisely decided to open an office in Bucharest and seek investment opportunities. In his meetings, Norm touched lightly on NATO enlargement, making the point that even large businesses such as Lockheed Martin had little influence on American government policy, but as an individual he thought now was the time to push for NATO enlargement, not knowing what the future might bring in Russia. Lockheed Martin agreed to support Romania's NATO bid in Washington, but, he added, Romania was at a disadvantage compared to Poland and Hungary, which had strong lobbies in Washington. In our meeting at the Defense Ministry, General Zaharia talked about Romania's acquiring F-16s, F-22s, and the to-be-built F-35, a Joint Strike Fighter next-generation American military plane. As it was, Romania was having trouble paying for the refitting of its old Soviet MiG-21s by Elbit Systems Ltd., an Israeli defense electronics company, let alone thinking about buying or leasing F-16s or later-generation aircraft. (In 2016 Romania acquired a small fleet of F-16s.)

LAST MILE ON THE ROAD TO NATO ENLARGEMENT

A few days after French President Chirac's February visit to Bucharest, Foreign Minister Severin briefed the NATO and EU ambassadors: France, he said, had made Romania's early entry into NATO a precondition for France's agreeing to NATO enlargement. French ambassador Bernard Boyer took exception to the foreign minister's remark, stating that France had only offered to be Romania's advocate, not to make Romania's entry into NATO a precondition for enlargement. In the process, Boyer delivered what amounted to an anti-American diatribe, stating that heretofore Romania had only listened to its "rich uncle," leaving France in a lower position in the NATO pecking order. Now, with the visit of President Chirac, France had raised its relationship with Romania to a new level, or perhaps a higher level than Romania's relationship with the United States. Severin shot back that France's position had changed, not Romania's, and that Romania would continue to seek close relations with all NATO members. I did not solicit the opinions of my fellow ambassadors, but I thought Bernard's performance was pitiable. He was like a stepchild, complaining that he was less loved than his siblings.

In late March a dejected Foreign Minister Severin returned from two days of meetings in Bonn to report that Germany's foreign minister, Klaus Kinkel, had told him that Germany favored a three-country package to start NATO enlargement, which left Romania out.

Later, Kinkel delivered the same message to Eric Edelman, one of Deputy Secretary Talbott's top staff members at the State Department, telling him that he was impressed by what he had seen and heard in Bucharest but that it was too late for Romania to get into NATO in this round, and that although Romania deserved a respectful hearing, Germany had not changed its mind.

14

More Peace and More Business

SPRING 1997

BUILDING BRIDGES OVER TROUBLED WATERS:
THE ROMANIA-UKRAINE FRIENDSHIP TREATY

Oleksandr Chaly, Ukraine's energetic ambassador to Romania, never missed an opportunity to talk to me about prospects for a treaty between his country and Romania. As he described the situation, the points of contention were the Molotov-Ribbentrop Pact, the renunciation of territorial claims by Romania, the rights of Romanian language speakers in Ukraine, and the delimitation of territorial waters in the Black Sea. I continued to think the differences were bridgeable. I offered the services of American experts to advise both sides on historical precedents for solving the delimitation of territorial waters issue. I was convinced that the presence of third-party experts would make it easier for the two sides to compromise, but I never heard back from Chaly.

A short time later I checked with State Secretary Dumitru Ceausu, Romania's chief negotiator (state secretary was a title below minister). Ceausu, an experienced Foreign Ministry official, was also optimistic. As he saw it, the differences between the two sides had narrowed. Romania had dropped its insistence on including a condemnation of the Molotov-Ribbentrop Pact, which left the territorial waters dispute the major remaining issue. State Secretary Ceausu was confident that if the issues were submitted to the International Court of Justice (ICJ) at The Hague, Romania would prevail. Meanwhile, our "third-party" strategy seemed to be working. Ambassador Chaly was the first to tell me that our pressure on Romania was producing positive results, and two days later State Secretary Ceausu used almost the exact same words, thanking me for putting pressure on Ukraine.

William Miller, the U.S. ambassador in Kiev, came to Bucharest in late January to help with the Ukraine negotiations. Miller had an illustrious career in academia and public service. By the time he returned to Kiev, he and I had boiled the issues down to the territorial question, and if the parties could not resolve that issue, either country could refer the matter to the ICJ for resolution. We further proposed that no reference be made in the treaty to Serpent Island, the disputed spot of land in the Black Sea, but the treaty would reaffirm the Helsinki Final Act of 1975 and its provisions on postwar boundaries. By implication, Serpent Island would remain part of Ukraine.

After that, the Romania-Ukraine friendship treaty negotiations plodded along. President Constantinescu helped by giving Romania's chief negotiator, State Secretary Ceausu, wide latitude, reserving only the issue of territorial waters in the Black Sea. I followed up with a meeting with Chaly, who at my urging recommended to his government in Kiev that it agree to submit the issue to the ICJ.

In early February I received a phone call from Ambassador Miller in Kiev. He confirmed that the Romanian side had conceded on virtually every issue, including dropping the reference to the Molotov-Ribbentrop Pact, Romania's claims to the navigational channel in the estuary to the Black Sea, and its previous position that Serpent Island not be taken into consideration in delimiting the territorial waters. In return, Ukraine gave up nothing and did not agree to submit the delimitation issue to the ICJ. Ukraine was taking the position that both parties would have to agree to submit the issue to the ICJ, that no referral could be made for five years, and until then Ukraine would be free to exploit the area in contention. This would leave Romania with an empty declaration that if the parties could not agree on the zone, the ICJ would decide, but only if both countries agreed to the referral. Later Miller reported that he thought Ukraine would agree to a two-year limit for negotiations on the delimitation issue, after which, failing agreement, either side could refer the issue to the ICJ.

The next day Foreign Minister Severin asked me to come to the Foreign Ministry to discuss the Ukraine negotiations. He was afraid that Ceausu had gotten the short end of the stick the previous week in Kiev, and indeed he had. We agreed that I would raise the outstanding issues with Ambassador Chaly, who was coming to my residence for lunch that day. As it turned out, Chaly was quite forthcoming. He indicated that Ukraine would agree to a two-year time limit, after which either country could refer the delimitation matter to the ICJ. He also indicated that Ukraine might be flexible on Serpent Island and, importantly, agreed that Romanian flag vessels would have the right of free passage through Ukrainian waters leading to the Black Sea.

The next step was for Deputy Foreign Minister Victor Buteyko, Ukraine's negotiator, to come to Bucharest to wrap up the treaty, after which Foreign Minister Severin and his Ukrainian counterpart, Foreign Minister Hennadiy Udovenko, would initial the documents in advance of the two presidents signing the treaty. If Ukraine agreed to the terms I discussed with Ambassador Chaly, the treaty was done. I told Chaly that without agreement along these lines, Romania might end up initialing the treaty, or even signing it, but would not submit it to Parliament for ratification, which would render it without legal effect. Chaly recognized the problem and said he would get back to me after he received instructions from Kiev. Immediately after lunch I returned to the Romanian Foreign Ministry to report to Severin on my talk with Chaly. He seemed relieved and was even happier later in the day when I called to tell him that U.S. Secretary of State Madeleine Albright had agreed to meet with him in Washington on April 21.

I spent much of the next two days on the phone with Foreign Minister Severin and Ambassador Chaly going over the open points in the negotiations. Chaly planned to return to Kiev in a day or two and wanted me to accompany him. Severin also pushed for me to go to Kiev, as had Bill Miller. I stayed put, but gave an entire day at the end of March to the negotiations. I met first with the Romanian negotiator, State Secretary Ceausu, then with Severin at the Romanian Foreign Ministry, and later with Chaly at my residence. Each side had its negotiating tactics, but the basic reason for the failure to reach agreement was that neither side trusted the other. For its part,

Ukraine had concluded that Romania needed the treaty more than Ukraine did, in order to get into NATO. This was true up to a point, but if Romania did not get into NATO, Ukraine would have lost the opportunity to settle its border dispute with Romania. None of the points of disagreement was major, but previously settled issues kept reappearing.

The Chilija River, a distributary branch of the Danube leading to the Black Sea that was controlled by Ukraine, was such an issue. Romania wanted the right of free navigation on the Chilija, which Ukraine was willing to give, but only if Romania agreed to grant Ukraine the right of free navigation on the other navigable arm of the Danube, the Sulina, which traversed only Romanian territory. Although the Sulina was not the main natural channel running to the Black Sea, Romania kept it open by dredging. Romania charged fees to ships using the Sulina to cover the cost of dredging and would not agree to free passage for ships flying the Ukrainian flag.

As for delimiting the economic zone in the Black Sea, Ukraine had taken the position that the two-year period for negotiation would not begin until the two countries had concluded a border treaty, which was likely to take another two years, delaying referral of the delimitation issue to the ICJ for at least four years. Ukraine also wanted Romania specifically to acknowledge the binding effect of a 1948 protocol between Romania and the Soviet Union, which forced Romania to cede Serpent Island to the Soviet Union. This was political anathema for Romania; it proposed a formulation that would confirm the sanctity of Ukraine's borders on the date it declared its independence from the Soviet Union as set forth in then-existing protocols, which would include the 1948 protocol by implication. None of the issues seemed insurmountable to me. Three days later I flew to Kiev to try to settle matters.

My mission to Kiev began on a creaky Soviet-era plane that Ambassador Chaly, who came to the airport to say good-bye, shamefacedly termed "very old." Disembarking in Kiev two hours later, I immediately knew I was in the former Soviet Union. Even Bucharest's Otopeni Airport looked modern by comparison to the one in Kiev. An old tram car pulled by a tractor took us from the plane to the arrival lounge, a bare metal building where I joined about ten people in line for passport stamping, with an ever larger group huddled in a corner filling out papers. When I finally got to the passport control booth, my diplomatic passport in hand, a Ukrainian family of ten pushed ahead of me—husband and wife, grandmother, children, assorted friends, stray animals, and bundles wrapped in paper and held together with string and masking tape. Fortunately, I was rescued at the other end of the passageway by a political officer from the American embassy, who escorted me to Ambassador Miller's residence.

Dinner was at a Ukrainian military base in honor of U.S. General George Joulwan, who was his usual ebullient self, matching the Ukrainian defense minister toast for toast. Dinner started at eight thirty and mercifully ended a little after ten—only to be followed by an hour and a half of music. I was prepared for the violins but not for the Italian arias or for a Ukrainian baritone's heavily accented rendition of "New York, New York."

The next day began with my meeting the director and head of the Foreign Strategy Department of the National Security Studies Institute, Ukraine's foremost think-tank. This was an opportunity for me to lay out my vision of a future trilateral relationship among Poland, Ukraine, and Romania, an idea I had previously raised with President Constantinescu and he had enthusiastically endorsed. It called for (1) more border crossings (which had been stagnant since Ukraine's independence from the USSR), (2) open skies (air space) among the three countries, (3) enlargement of Romania's regional air space capability to include Ukraine, (4) scientific exchanges, (5) improved rail transport, (6) an increase in the number of consulates representing each of the three countries in the other, and (7) general expansion of contacts.

Volodymyr Chumak, the director of the institute, seemed taken with the idea of a trilateral relationship. The only reservation he voiced was one that I had anticipated: What will Russia think? The same question came up when I first raised the idea at the U.S. State Department. My answer was that Russia should be kept fully informed; the negotiations should be open and transparent with a Russian observer invited to attend the trilateral meetings. In time the trilateral configuration could be enlarged to include Russia in a quadrilateral group. (Despite President Constantinescu's strong endorsement, the idea died after I left Bucharest.)

As I always do when visiting a new city, I went to the Jewish community building in Kiev, where I found Rabbi Jacob Shteyerman, a recent arrival from Brooklyn, in charge. He was as American as I: remove the black coat, hat, and beard, and he could have been selling securities on Wall Street.

Six years earlier, in 1991, when Ukraine gained its independence, the Jewish community in Kiev barely existed. One synagogue remained open. This was in accordance with the communist practice of keeping one synagogue open in large cities to show to foreign visitors. Only old people attended services. The young were discouraged from participating in Jewish life. Now there were 600 Jewish youngsters enrolled in Kiev's Jewish day school and another 250 in the Jewish kindergarten. I met the *shochet*, the ritual slaughterer, who was from B'nai Barak, Israel. This year (1999) the Jewish community in Kiev baked thirteen tons of matzoh for the Jews of Ukraine to celebrate Passover.

In Kiev, my principal meetings were with Foreign Minister Hennadiy Udovenko; Deputy Foreign Minister Buteyko, Udovenko's deputy and Ukraine's chief negotiator on the treaty with Romania; Volodymyr Horbulyn, the president's national security adviser; and Volodymyr Ogryzko, the director of the foreign policy department in President Leonid Kuchma's office. I initially intended to limit my involvement on the treaty to matters of process and timing—the need to conclude the treaty within weeks, not months. However, at lunch with Deputy Foreign Minister Buteyko, I was drawn into a discussion on the specific issues and ended up proposing bridging language. As for process, I urged Ukraine to respond quickly to the proposals that Foreign Minister Severin had recently put on the table and requested that Ambassador Chaly in Bucharest be authorized to negotiate any remaining issues. Foreign Ministers Udovenko and Severin would then meet to finalize the treaty and to initial it. Horbulyn, Kuchma's national security adviser and also his close political confidant, understood immediately the importance of concluding the treaty quickly. As he put it, the negotiators were beginning to "hate each other."

Negotiations of this sort run their course, and there comes a time to bring the process to a conclusion. The two sides were now at that point. If the negotiations dragged on, they would be overtaken by NATO's decision in Madrid in July. If Romania was not invited to begin NATO accession talks, the enthusiasm and motivation in Bucharest for reaching agreement with Ukraine would fade, and the opportunity would be lost for years. Now was the time to wrap things up.

I was successful in nudging the Ukrainian side to accept Romania's good faith, but Deputy Foreign Minister Buteyko, in particular, was fed up with the Romanians. I listened patiently to his recitation of grievances and then finally said, "If you're going to dwell on the past, you will never have a treaty. Past difficulties are best forgotten in the interest of reaching agreement." Eventually, Buteyko accepted this, and we took up the issues one by one. He accepted language in the treaty that referred to the 1961 treaty between Romania and the Soviet Union without insisting on a specific reference to the 1948 protocol (recognizing the Soviet Union's ownership of Serpent Island). In exchange, Foreign Minister Severin would send a note, withdrawing the note Romania sent on August 1, 1991, that claimed Romanian ownership of Serpent Island. I convinced Buteyko that Romania's position on free navigation on the Chilija, which formed part of the Romanian-Ukrainian border, was reasonable and should be accepted by Ukraine without insisting on free navigation on the Sulina, which ran wholly through Romanian territory. He agreed and also accepted a two-year limitation on negotiations for delimiting territorial waters in the Black Sea, after which either side could refer the issue to the ICJ. Other points of compromise were discussed, and in the end I came away feeling the deal was done.

Before returning to Romania, I drove from downtown Kiev to the outskirts of the city to say the kaddish, the Jewish memorial prayer, at Babi Yar, the ravine where 36,000 Jews were shot by the Nazis in 1941 on the eve of Yom Kippur. The deep ravine ran about a mile and a half down to the Dnieper River. A simple menorah-shaped monument was erected in 1991 commemorating the horror. A larger Soviet memorial, about a quarter of a mile away, had been erected in memory of an even larger number of non-Jews who were slaughtered by the Nazis at Babi Yar.

The next day I traveled by car from Kiev to Kishinev, the capital of Moldova, through rich chernozem (black soil) farmland, rolling low hills, and fields plowed by ancient machinery left over from communist times. (Moldova, formerly Bessarabia, had been part of Romania from 1920 to 1939.) Ukraine had not privatized its farms. Large cooperative and state-owned farms were dominant. Principal roads in Ukraine were good. For example, the road from Kiev to the Moldova border was four lanes most of the way, with few cars on it. Unlike in Romania, Ukrainian villages were not built along the road but were set back several miles. This made the drive less picturesque. Moreover, the highway, built in communist times, did not follow historic routes through villages. From what I saw, Ukraine's villages were far less colorful than their Romanian counterparts. The architecture showed little of the fancy paintwork, often whimsical, that marked Romanian villages. Along the way hundreds of new houses were being constructed like the housing outside Bucharest for the nouveau riche—persons who prospered after the fall of communism through prior connections or corruption. Of the three cities, Kiev was more modern than decrepit Bucharest or drab Kishinev. In Kiev, I had expected to see old ladies with babushkas and long dresses. Instead, I saw young women wearing miniskirts. Except for public transportation, which still used ancient Soviet-made buses and trolleys, everything was up to date. The only things missing were Western-style retail stores. In other words, Kiev, like other cities in Central and Eastern Europe, was complicated—showing progress in some areas, not in others.

Four hours after leaving Kiev I was in Kishinev, where, as in Kiev, I witnessed a renaissance of Jewish life in a city that before World War II was predominantly Jewish and had been the scene of pogroms in 1903 and 1905. In 1997 the city had only 30,000 Jews left. As in Kiev, one synagogue in Kishinev remained open under the communists. Jewish education was forbidden, and Jewish community life did not exist. Now there were 250 Jews enrolled in Kishinev's Jewish day school, over 100 attending Saturday services, and the community hoped to raise $3 million to rebuild its famous yeshiva, which had once housed 1,000 students but had been abandoned under the communists, who had used it for a print shop. In Kiev I saw a dozen teenage boys studying Talmud, and in Kishinev I heard two youngsters preparing for their bar mitzvahs. Jewish life was being reborn across the former Soviet Union, rekindled in the souls of young Jews who five years before had barely known they were Jewish.

The U.S. embassy in Kishinev was embarrassingly small. We had taken over a dilapidated former private residence and converted it into a functioning chancery. The ever-watchful Russians put their embassy across the street and reportedly had cameras trained on the entrance to our chancery. The U.S. ambassador's residence was similarly modest, as was the German ambassador's residence close by. Across the street were dilapidated houses with chickens in the yards producing the expected morning cacophony.

That evening at dinner at the American ambassador's residence, a former

KGB (Soviet secret service) agent who had been in Bucharest when Ceauşescu was in power told me the Soviets shed no tears when Ceauşescu fell. This was certainly true for President Mikhail Gorbachev. In 1987 he had met Ceauşescu first in Moscow and then in Bucharest, where, after delivering a major address, he was greeted by silence. Ceauşescu then spoke and received thunderous applause, all prearranged by Ceauşescu's lackeys. The experience did not endear Romania or Ceauşescu to Gorbachev.

Moldova was beset by huge problems. It declared independence in 1991 and immediately found itself locked in a war with the rump state Moldova Republic of Transnistria and its largely Russian-origin population of about 600,000. Moldova proper was about 60 percent Romanian, with the balance of the population made up of Russians, Ukrainians, and a group in the south speaking a Turkic language that even the Turkish ambassador could not understand. The Transnistria sector was heavily industrialized by the Soviets, but Moldova to the west of the Nistria River remained agricultural. Now that Moldova had gained its independence, its leaders struggled with the enormous problems inherent in creating a new nation with an inadequate economic base and no reason to exist other than being the product of the dismemberment of the former Soviet Union. Moldova by whatever name was never an independent country. Its leaders regarded Romania as the "great power," an anomaly for Romania. Listening to the Moldovans at dinner reminded me of a conversation I had had years before with a group of lawyers in Bangor, Maine. One of them, a Yale University law graduate, had been invited by his alma mater to talk to law students about "small town law practice." Hearing this, one of the other lawyers in the room spoke up: "In Dover Foxcroft, where I live, we consider Bangor the big city." Moldova's political leaders felt the same way about Romania.

After I returned to Bucharest, Ambassador Chaly endorsed the proposals I had put on the table in Kiev, and the Romanian side also agreed. After more than a year of negotiations, the deal was done. President Constantinescu rightly took credit for the success, and on June 2 the treaty was signed in Bucharest by the two presidents, Constantinescu and Kuchma. Both Ambassador Chaly and Foreign Minister Severin invited me to attend the signing ceremony, but I decided not to go. Other members of the diplomatic corps had not been invited, and my presence would have highlighted the American role in the treaty negotiations, something I wanted to avoid. When I told this to Ambassador Chaly, he kindly told me that I would be with him in spirit, a nice tribute from a thoughtful colleague.

A ROMANIAN ATTEMPT AT CHURCH ACCORD

Another effort at bridge building and laying to rest ancient animosities had been undertaken a month before by Foreign Minister Severin when he took off for a four-day visit to Italy, where he was to sign a commercial agreement between Romania and Italy and then visit the Vatican. He was hoping to put together a concordat between the Uniate Church and the Romanian Orthodox Church. If he succeeded, it would be a major achievement burnished by a visit of the pope to Romania at the invitation of the Romanian Orthodox patriarch. Attempting to deal with church matters to reverse hundreds of years of discord proved more difficult than an optimistic Severin had envisaged. Both sides remained obdurate, and Severin finally conceded defeat, but he earned an "A" for trying.

RISKY AMERICAN BUSINESS

In the spring of 1997, TransChem, owned by the Kaplan family of Florida, made a big push for a major deal with the Romanian Agriculture Ministry: the purchase of 800,000 hectares (more than 3,000 square miles) of farmland and the supply of irrigation infrastructure, feed, fertilizer, and supervisory staff. I took a close look at the deal. The government of Romania would be required to issue its sovereign guarantee for the cost of equipment TransChem would purchase in the United States as well as the costs TransChem would incur in Romania. TransChem planned to purchase the equipment wholesale in the United States and charge the government of Romania the retail price, pocketing the difference, a profit of some $20 million, which it would then use to pay for the feed, fertilizer, and irrigation equipment it was billing to Romania. TransChem in effect would be playing with the Romanian government's money, and when the debt was repaid, TransChem would pocket the difference between the wholesale and retail price of the equipment plus one-half of the value of the increased productivity from the project. This was a sweet deal for TransChem but not for Romania. Seeing the handwriting on the wall, our embassy withdrew its support to avoid being blamed later. After I left Romania, TransChem persevered and won the contract. Predictably, the result was a total disaster.

IMPROVING USAID PROGRAMS

In late April I spoke for about an hour at the USAID regional representatives' conference in Bucharest, stressing my pet theme: the United States should fund fewer programs, all narrowly focused on U.S. policy interests with a multiplier effect and strong Romanian government support. To be effective, these programs needed in-country political support. Otherwise, most of the money would be wasted. I pushed for a larger commitment by USAID to technical assistance for the State Ownership Fund (SOF) to boost the Romanian government's economic reform program. There was general agreement with an occasional demurral by the purists who wanted to separate USAID from our country's broader policy interests. In other words, they wanted USAID to fund exclusively development projects like those in Africa and South America, involving aid grants that had ended up with little to show for them in Romania. In Central and Eastern Europe, as I saw it, the emphasis should be on economic reform. A growing economy would take care of the rest.

HOLBROOKE REDUX

In early May Dick Holbrooke returned to Bucharest for a four-hour whirlwind visit. He was no longer in government but juggled his Washington influence as a former assistant secretary of state with his business interests on behalf of the Swiss bank CS First Boston. His bank was seeking to be appointed a consultant to the Communications Ministry on the privatization of Romtelecom, the Romanian government-owned telephone monopoly. Dick admitted

he knew nothing about Romtelecom or privatizations, but as usual managed
not to fall from grace or dangle on the edge of defeat. Without making any
blatant misstatements, he puffed up his influence in Washington and offered
to be personally involved in Romania's efforts to get into NATO, provided CS
First Boston was retained by the Romanian government to advise the Communications Ministry. Just what he would do in Washington was left unsaid.
If Dick skated on thin ice in his first meeting with Prime Minister Ciorbea,
Finance Minister Ciumara, and Economic Reform Minister Spineanu, he
fell through it in a later meeting with President Constantinescu. After continually mispronouncing Constantinescu's name, he wisely stuck with "Mr.
President," claiming credit for NATO enlargement and stating he had been a
steadfast supporter of Romania's admission to NATO, neither of which was
exactly true. Not to be outdone, President Constantinescu claimed credit for
the treaty with Ukraine. With it all, Dick did no harm for CS First Boston
or the U.S. government. In fact, his presence may have helped on both fronts,
particularly when he put the blame (unfairly) for Romania's NATO difficulties on Congress, not the administration. He knew, but was too politically
savvy to say, that the Clinton administration was reluctant to go to the Senate
with five new NATO members and had cut the number to three, excluding
Romania.

CYPRUS CALLING?

In May I had told the White House and State Department that I intended
to end my service as ambassador in July to return to Carol and Washington.
Meanwhile, the flare-up of tensions on Cyprus between Greek and Turkish
Cypriots led to renewed efforts in Washington to end the internecine conflict.
There was talk that President Clinton might be planning to appoint a special
presidential envoy to act as his representative to both sides in the conflict.
Assistant Secretary of State Marc Grossman had proposed my name to Secretary of State Albright to be the special presidential envoy, and I had expressed
to Marc my strong interest in being considered for the job, which would be
based in Washington.

One evening in mid-May, two messages were waiting for me when I returned from a dinner at Cotroceni with President Constantinescu, one from the White House and the other from Deputy Secretary of State Strobe Talbott. I immediately thought the White House was calling to offer me the special presidential envoy position, and that Strobe was calling for the same reason. I was wrong on both counts. The call from the White House was to ask me if I would be willing to serve as ambassador until the fall. President Clinton had selected my successor, a Maryland state legislator, but the security background check and other procedures were likely to drag on through the summer. I was noncommittal but said I would cooperate and that if an emergency arose, I would return to Bucharest.

As for Strobe's call, he wanted to talk about the recent visit by German Foreign Minister Klaus Kinkel to Washington, where the two sides discussed NATO enlargement. As an aside, Strobe asked me about my relations with the International Republican Institute (IRI) and said that Senator John McCain (R-Ariz.) had raised the issue in a recent talk with him. I went through the story of IRI's involvement in Romanian politics in 1996 and the ensuing campaign by IRI Director Lorne Craner to discredit me. Strobe listened patiently but without comment.

Senator McCain was important to the administration: he backed it on the Chemical Weapons Convention and the administration wanted to stay in his good graces. I had been told that his objection to my appointment to the Cyprus post had held it up. Whether the White House intended to work the matter out with Senator McCain or appoint someone else for the post was not clear. As it turned out, the Cyprus post went to Dick Holbrooke, who had been looking for a way to get back into the game at State, and on June 5 President Clinton named him his special presidential envoy for Cyprus. (In 1999 when Holbrooke was appointed U.S. ambassador to the UN, I was named special presidential envoy for the Cyprus conflict.)

BUSINESS CAN BE TRICKY IN ROMANIA

On occasion, an American businessman came to Bucharest to look at a specific investment prospect. One of them was Jay Pritzker, the CEO of Hyatt Corporation and a legendary American business leader and philanthropist. He was interested in acquiring the Bucharest Hotel. He and his Israeli associates presented a written proposal to Economic Reform Minister Spineanu, who at first was enthusiastic but then, as was all too often the case, cooled on the deal. After much back and forth, Pritzker and his group walked away, frustrated by indecision on the Romanian side. Others who came with investment interests were John Reed, CEO of Citibank; Ed Bavaria, deputy president of McDonnell Douglas; and top officials from Continental Can and Coca-Cola. All were attracted by reports of the new business-friendly government in Romania. Business-friendly, yes, but efficient or decisive, no.

As matters dragged on, most American companies lost interest. Procter & Gamble was an exception. John Pepper returned to Romania in May for the opening of the renovated P&G plant in Timişoara. Both President Constantinescu and Prime Minister Ciorbea met with him to demonstrate the great importance they attached to American investment. In return P&G did all the right things. Its detergent plant in Timişoara was state of the art. P&G brought in its standard packaging and material handling equipment to make the plant a modern Western manufacturing facility. John Pepper spoke at the dedication, which was big news in Romania. Later the same day he spoke at Timişoara University, where he announced that P&G would award twenty scholarships to university students.

Amoco looked seriously at a secondary recovery project in Romania and hoped to negotiate an agreement by the end of the year to buy a 50 percent interest in several Romanian gas fields, invest millions of dollars in secondary recovery, increase production by about 15 percent, and receive in payment one-half of the value of the increased production. Amoco's total investment would have been close to $1 billion. In effect, Amoco was monetizing Romania's gas in the ground against a future payout stream. This would have modernized gas production in Romania, but the cost to the country would have been high. The negotiations stalled, and after waiting a year or two for an answer, Amoco withdrew.

Sadly, neither President Constantinescu nor Prime Minister Ciorbea was adept in maneuvering through Romania's bureaucratic maze. Neither had previous government experience. By temperament, Prime Minister Ciorbea found it difficult to act decisively—which, to business leaders' ears meant "Do nothing." President Constantinescu, with all his good intentions, was at heart a geology professor, not a businessman.

SPLITTING THE BABY

By cultural disposition, Romanians prefer to avoid confrontation. Side-stepping and compromise were traditional Romanian answers to conflicts, both military and economic. In the spring of 1997 TransChem and Valmont Industries, both American firms in the agricultural sector, found themselves competing for the same agricultural project worth about $140 million. Valmont signed a deal with the government of Romania to sell agricultural equipment to the latter as part of the new government's program to modernize Romanian agriculture. No sooner had the deal been signed than TransChem, already heavily involved in promoting its own agricultural deal, showed up with a competing bid for the equipment contract. To complicate matters further, both companies were financed by New York–based Citibank, and debt-imposed limits by the IMF and the World Bank did not leave room for both deals.

At the request of the Romanian government, representatives from the two companies and I went to Cotroceni to confer with President Constantinescu and Prime Minister Ciorbea. In typical fashion, Ciorbea suggested that the deal be split between TransChem and Valmont with each company having the benefit of government guarantees of about $80 million. This did not please Valmont, whose chief operating officer criticized me for my role as mediator, even though the idea of my involvement had come from Citibank's representative in Bucharest, who said he was speaking for both Valmont and TransChem. When I pointed out to Valmont's representative that they should have closed the deal with the Romanian government before TransChem arrived on the scene, he agreed, but it was now too late. I was skeptical of the TransChem deal and now had an unhappy Valmont on my hands. But an ambassador's role is not to choose sides between American companies. In the end, both companies were unhappy.

PROGRESS BY THE ROMANIAN MILITARY

The Romanian army's new chief of staff, Major General Constantin De-geratu, now with two stars on his shoulders, made an official visit to the United States at the invitation of the U.S. military chief of staff, General John Shalikashvili. I had set up the visit at a meeting at the Pentagon in February. By May, Major General Degeratu looked and acted like a military leader. Although of medium height, he had assumed a commanding presence and spoke with authority. At my residence for breakfast in Bucharest before leaving for Washington, he told me he was looking for U.S. help to reorganize Romania's navy and air force, both of which, like the Romanian army, were now headed by younger officers. The United States made this happen. The Romanian military was ahead of the country's economy in reforming, and arguably was the best in Central Europe.

MEET THE PRESS, ROMANIAN STYLE

Mihai Bacanu, the editor and principal owner of the Bucharest daily newspaper *Romania Libera*, had been my bête noire during the election campaign in the fall of 1996, when I was attacked by the paper for being too close to President Iliescu and for having closed down IRI's attempt to help PNT-CD in the election. In May, six months after the elections, Bacanu invited me to lunch. As we were getting up from the lunch table, he asked me to do a long interview for his paper, to be published as a main-spread article. I may have missed the boat by not schmoozing the Romanian press when I first arrived in country. I held lots of press conferences but I did not work the press one on one. Each journalist had ties to this or that political faction or personality. In Bacanu's case, he was close to the writer and former dissident Ana Blandiana, President Constantinescu, and now Prime Minister Ciorbea, in that order. Suddenly, I was in the good graces of *Romania Libera*, even though my views had not changed since I first arrived in country.

THE GENERAL AND THE CANTOR

In mid-May, General George A. Joulwan hosted a major USEUCOM (United States European Command) conference in Stuttgart, Germany. Although I arrived late, after 8:00 p.m., I was still in time to catch the tail end of the reception for American ambassadors in Central and Eastern Europe. There were about forty of us in the room, but only one counted, General Joulwan, Supreme Allied Commander Europe and commander in chief of the United States European Command. George was a personality who had to be seen and heard to be appreciated. He always appeared in the role of the quarterback and coach in the last thirty seconds of a close football game. Wherever he went, there were only two people present, General Joulwan and the rest. Unfortunately, he was continually butting heads with the brass in the Pentagon and officials elsewhere, including the White House, but from what I saw, he was usually right. He had a clear view of NATO enlargement and had none of the timidity of the policymakers in Washington. He wanted to expand NATO rapidly by bringing in five countries, including Romania, in the first wave. He assured me that this would present no problem on the military side, but not so with policy circles in Washington.

When I arrived back in Bucharest the next day, I attended a late lunch at the Israeli embassy to honor my friend Yossi Malovany, the esteemed cantor of the Fifth Avenue Synagogue in New York. Yossi and I talked about the great composers of Jewish liturgical music—the nineteenth-century Viennese Salomon Sulzer, Berlin's Louis Lewandowski, and other Central and Eastern European greats. In his rich tenor voice, Yossi sang compositions by each. I then asked him how he sang "Unetaneh Tokef," the cantorial centerpiece of the Rosh Hashanah (New Year) and Yom Kippur (Day of Atonement) service. He answered, "I sing it like a simple Jew." For a moment I thought I was listening to General Joulwan, who liked to refer to himself as "just a simple soldier." The similarity did not end there. Both Joulwan and Malavani had adequate egos, and deservedly so—one a great general, the other a great cantor, each of whom thought of himself as carrying on the noble traditions of his profession.

BUKOVINA AND THE PAINTED CHURCHES

It was a beautiful day in May for a one-hour flight to Suceava, a major city in Bukovina that for two centuries had been the capital of the Principality of Moldavia. Accompanying me on the plane were my sister Amalie; my special assistant, Mihai Carp; U.S. Warrant Officer Keith Reigart; and a Romanian military colonel. Vasile Ilie, the prefect of Suceava, met us at the airport carrying the traditional gifts of flowers for the women, bread and salt for the rest of us, with kisses on both cheeks for men and women alike. The ride to Suceava was the usual high-speed, sirens blaring, heart-pounding adventure. At city hall we were greeted by the mayor and various local dignitaries, who were eager to tell us about their *judet*: Suceava is the second largest county in Romania, with a population of 700,000. Despite significant unemployment (10 percent) almost double the national average and insignificant foreign investment, we were told a happy citizenry comprising various nationalities lived in peace and harmony. Even the PDSR opposition leader talked positively about Suceava, going so far as to applaud the new government's economic reform program. These bucolic tales had become all too familiar. Nevertheless, there was no denying the beauty of Suceava, which constituted Romania's remaining share of a once united Bukovina that was divided by the 1939 Molotov-Ribbentrop Pact, Northern Bukovina (with its large Ruthenian population) going to the Soviet Union, now part of Ukraine.

After the welcoming ceremony, we were herded into Suceava Fortress, supposedly built by Michael the Brave after he briefly unified Romania in the sixteenth century, defeating the Turks and everyone else who stood in his way.

Next stop was Siret, on the Ukraine border, where we met first with local town officials, followed by an impromptu tour of a carpet factory, the largest employer in the region, with over 1,100 workers. The factory operated at about 70 percent of capacity. With no export sales and a large, stagnant inventory, it was having a rough time. Completed in 1982, it was modern with imported high-quality looms and a highly skilled workforce. The large factory floor—I estimated 400,000 to 500,000 square feet—was well maintained with white painted walls and clear glass skylights. The factory could just as well have been in the United States, but situated where it was, it suffered the ills that beset the Romanian economy.

Next we went to the ancient city of Rădăuți, where we met with about twenty representatives of the Jewish community, four of whom claimed to be presidents of this community or that. Before the war, there were seventy synagogues and 10,000 Jews in Rădăuți, of which only about 2,000 returned from deportation to Transnistria. Following the Molotov-Ribbentrop Pact in 1939, Soviet troops briefly occupied Suceava. Apparently, the Soviet occupation was enough for Marshal Ion Antonescu to accuse the region's Jews of being Soviet fifth columnists, with predictable tragic results. After Nazi troops invaded the Soviet Union in July 1940, Soviet troops withdrew from Suceava, and Antonescu promptly ordered that Suceava's Jews be deported to Transnistria, where most of them perished. Virtually all of those who later returned to Rădăuți eventually emigrated to Israel. Today there were only thirty-five Jews in Rădăuți—around seventy if you count intermarrieds. It was a struggle for them to maintain the one remaining synagogue, a beautiful Austrian-style building badly in need of repair, but nevertheless still functioning, where I said the afternoon prayers with a few old-timers joining in.

By way of contrast, our next stop was Sucevița Monastery, a Romanian Orthodox monastery built in 1585 about five and a half miles south of Rădăuți. The father superior accompanied us as we walked around the painted church, completed in six years. The artists used a pigment that has miraculously withstood the trials of centuries of harsh weather. I was told that an expert from DuPont had examined the paint but was unable to discover the secret of its durability. The murals depicted scenes from the Bible, some Old Testament, others New, but the most striking image was a forty-one-rung ladder reaching into heaven with the angels on one side exhorting those attempting to ascend. Most climbers, not being able to adhere to the forty-one virtues leading to heaven, fell into the netherworld.

The last stop was at the nearby Romanian Orthodox Putna Monastery, attributed to Prince Stephen the Great, who, legend has it, shot an arrow from a surrounding hill to mark the place where the monastery was to stand. The father superior who welcomed us was enormously kind and spiritual. He joined us for dinner and for breakfast the next morning. He had been elected father superior five years before, when he was just thirty-two. His fellow monks chose wisely. He was intelligent, open, a splendid conversationalist, and remarkably worldly. The Romanian Orthodox Church would be well served if it were some day to elect him its patriarch. The food, all grown at the monastery, was unusual and tasty. No meat was served (maybe because no kosher meat was available for me, an observant Jew), but the vegetable dishes and fish more than satisfied appetite and spirit.

Following breakfast the next morning, the father superior escorted us to our waiting cars. Kisses on both cheeks were only a prelude to a five-minute plea by the father superior first for Christian fellowship, then to preserve Romania from its Slavic neighbors, and last the familiar words about NATO. Even the clergy was singing the NATO chant! The scene was surreal in seeming violation of Jesus' injunction to render unto God what was God's and unto Caesar what was Caesar's. Here a Romanian Orthodox priest and an American ambassador stood in a four-handed handshake, eyes meeting, a small number of Americans and Romanians surrounding us, and the father superior, in his soft Romanian, translated by my special assistant, Mihai Carp, making the oft-repeated plea for understanding of Romania's unique place in Europe.

THE BELL COBRA DEAL AND NATO MEMBERSHIP

On May 21, Webb Joiner, Bell Helicopter's chairman, was my guest at a lunch that included Prime Minister Ciorbea, Foreign Minister Severin, General Zaharia of the Romanian army, the Merrill Lynch team, and assorted others. Not unexpectedly, much of the conversation was taken up by Prime Minister Ciorbea's plea for NATO membership. I tried as best I could to make the case that the upcoming decision in July in Madrid would not be nearly as critical for Romania as most Romanians thought. Sooner or later Romania would get into NATO, and in the meantime, the important thing was for Romania to continue its economic reform and enhance its military interoperability.

From lunch we headed to the World Trade Center, a mile from the residence, for the opening of the SOF's new offices, complete with glass-encased displays of scores of Romanian companies that the SOF was trying to privatize. It was a major press event with all major Romanian media present. President Constantinescu and the head of the SOF, Sorin Dimitriu, cut the ribbon, followed by a rush of others—including Prime Minister Ciorbea,

Economic Reform Minister Spineanu, and Sorin Dimitriu's identical twin, Andrei, who headed the National Agency for Privatization (NAP)—to tour the new SOF offices.

Bell's signing of the agreement with the SOF and the Ministry of Defense followed, after which I spoke, as did Bell's chairman, Webb Joiner, and the SOF's Dimitriu. Unfortunately, immediately after I spoke I had to leave to give a speech at a Merrill Lynch symposium and missed the rest of the program. But the opening of the SOF's office and the Bell signing were front-page news the next day.

No sooner was the Bell agreement signed than Michel Camdessus, the managing director of the IMF, sent a letter to Prime Minister Ciorbea objecting to the deal. When Ciorbea came to my house for lunch the next day, he showed me Camdessus's letter and asked me to draft a reply. Mircea Costa, the deputy head of the SOF, had assured me that he had taken care of the IMF objection when Camdessus first raised it back in December. Costa thought he had persuaded the IMF that the proposed financing would not violate the conditions of the IMF standby agreement.

A week later we received U.S. Commerce Secretary William M. Daley's letter to Prime Minister Ciorbea strongly supporting the Bell deal. Daley stated, "This letter represents the official position of the United States Government," a sentence I added to an earlier draft to dispel doubts in Romania as to whether the U.S. Treasury and State Departments supported the deal. The letter concluded with language urging the government of Romania to work with the IMF "to bring this important sale and investment to fruition."

The Romanian side was convinced that Camdessus was wearing his French, not IMF, hat, trying to kill the Bell deal in order to help Eurocopter. True or not, the IMF had legitimate grounds to question aspects of the Bell deal, particularly the proposed use of *régies autonomes* to finance the purchase, a clear violation of the IMF standby agreement. The reply we drafted for Prime Minister Ciorbea made a strong affirmative case for the Cobra program. On the merits, it should have gone forward, but the Romanians had a way of knuckling under to pressure and they eventually did in this case.

DECISION TIME FOR NATO

In May the U.K.'s foreign minister, Robin Cook, met in Washington with our foreign policy team, Secretary of State Albright, Defense Secretary Cohen, National Security Adviser Berger, and Deputy Secretary of State Talbott. It was increasingly clear that Poland, the Czech Republic, and Hungary would be the only countries invited in Madrid to join NATO. Romania's name only came up in the context of what to do when it was not included. As I had been told many times, the decision in Washington would be heavily influenced by the administration's judgment of the Senate's appetite for NATO enlargement, not just the relative merits of the aspirants.

QUESTIONING PRIME MINISTER CIORBEA

At the NATO ambassadors' lunch in May, our guest, Prime Minister Ciorbea, made a positive impression. The ambassadors fell over each other with praise. Without seeking to sound a discordant note, I picked up on a question Ciorbea had asked about what he should say to the Romanian people in a television broadcast scheduled for the following week. He recited a litany of government accomplishments. All of this was fine, but the average Romanian was hurting: incomes were down and prices were up. I asked the prime minister to visualize a cartoon with him telling the Romanian people everything was fine while family members listening said to each other, "If everything is so fine, why does it hurt so much?" Economic reform was being carried out on the backs of the Romanian people, and unless Prime Minister Ciorbea acknowledged this in his television talk, he would be missing an opportunity to let the Romanian people know the government understood they were the ones making the sacrifice and that without their steadfastness and support, economic reform would fail. Public opinion everywhere is fickle. My last comment was that once public opinion turned against the government, all the king's horses and all the king's men could not put the government together again. A year later, with the economy still faltering, Ciorbea was dismissed from office along with Finance Minister Ciumara and Economic Reform Minister Spineanu. In 2000 Ion Iliescu and PDSR returned to power, in part because the new government elected in 1996 had failed to enlist the Romanian public's support for its economic reform program.

ANOTHER VISIT BY CONGRESSMAN LANTOS

Tom and Annette Lantos returned to Bucharest in late May, this time with twelve businessmen, which complicated logistics. Tom asked for the sun and the moon—lunch with Prime Minister Ciorbea, a separate meeting with President Constantinescu, and an invitation for his entourage to a state dinner President Constantinescu was giving in honor of President Árpád Göncz of Hungary. Tom brought a letter from President Clinton that he intended to deliver to the two presidents, Constantinescu and Göncz, before dinner, which would have been awkward at best. True, Congressman Lantos had led the battle in Congress for permanent MFN status for Romania the previous July, and was surely entitled to gratitude for his advocacy, but as far as I knew, he played no role in the Hungarian-Romanian Basic Treaty, and that was the event being celebrated at President Constantinescu's dinner for President Göncz. Tom, Annette, and a Lantos granddaughter flew to Bucharest in a private plane along with the others whom he invited to join him. He insisted that the entire group attend all meetings—first with the prime minister, then a lunch the prime minister was hosting for President Göncz, and finally the state dinner at Cotroceni. The only time the entourage would be missing was a private meeting Congressman Lantos and I had with President Constantinescu an hour before the state dinner.

Tom, never at a loss for words, went a bit far at dinner. With 150 guests and press looking on, he invited Prime Minister Ciorbea to come to Washington to open a photo exhibit that Annette Lantos and others were putting on in the Rotunda of the Capitol. Prime Minister Ciorbea accepted the invitation without knowing whether he would be in Washington for other reasons. If not, he would not show up at the photo exhibit.

In his meeting with President Constantinescu, Tom talked about a "recent" meeting he had had with President Clinton, the president's principal foreign advisers, and congressional leadership. Actually, the meeting had taken place in February. Worse yet, he was repeating words he had spoken about the same meeting when he met President Constantinescu in Bucharest in February. President Constantinescu remembered the conversation and asked Tom when the meeting occurred. Somewhat flustered, Tom said, "a few weeks ago," but both knew he was trying to sell the same blanket a second time. At the state dinner, Tom read the letter from President Clinton, which was fine, but then with his customary rhetorical flourish made much of the signature, "Bill Clinton," pointing out the difference between the familiar and the more formal "William Jefferson Clinton," implying that the former was a sign of special friendship. The press made fun of this the next day, pointing out that the letter said nothing, and that the signature, "Bill Clinton," did not make up for the lack of substance. As Congressman Lantos and most everyone else knew, President Clinton usually signed letters, autographs, and most everything else "Bill Clinton."

Despite these gaffes, Tom's visit was a success. He did not change the landscape or bring Romania closer to NATO, but he extended the hand of America's friendship and support, which were much appreciated.

ROMANIA'S NATO HOPES DASHED

At the NATO foreign ministers' meeting in Sintra, Portugal, in late May, the United States torpedoed Romania's hopes to be in the first wave of entrants to NATO. With no forewarning to our embassy or anyone else, Secretary of State Albright dropped the bomb on Romania's NATO ambitions. In her remarks, she made it clear that the United States was supporting only Poland, the Czech Republic, and Hungary, referring rather dismissively to the applications of the other candidates. She characterized the three selected countries as fully prepared to contribute to the alliance's defense and as mature democracies with flourishing market economies. The facts were different. Neither the Czechs nor the Hungarians had an effective military, and what they possessed in the way of military capability was inferior to Romania's military. Unlike the situation in Romania, where the military was held in high esteem, the militaries in the Czech Republic and Hungary had been badly compromised by the communists, and there was little public support for them in either country. As for democracy, it was as well rooted in Romania as in its three neighbors. Only the economy in Romania was behind, but even that was now on the right road with the new government.

In a night letter to President Clinton a few days later, Secretary Albright explained that her "preemptive" strike in Sintra was to head off a possible European consensus around five rather than three countries. The additional two were Romania and Slovenia. France supported Romania's candidacy, even though it knew it would not succeed. There were nine votes in favor of five countries, including Romania and Slovenia, and five abstentions, including Germany and the United Kingdom. Only Iceland joined the United States in holding the line at three. Germany announced it was in favor of the smaller number but would not block Romania's entry if the other NATO members were in favor. With the United States on record opposing Romania, this was an easy call for Germany. U.K. Foreign Secretary Robin Cook did not take a stand one way or the other.

The next day I called on President Constantinescu at Cotroceni to deliver a letter I had drafted for President Clinton to send him in which he congratulated Romania on the upcoming signing of its treaty with Ukraine. I also wanted to tell him in person that I would be departing Bucharest in July. He entered the room a half hour late and was obviously unhappy, almost to the point of being unfriendly—there was none of the usual exchange of kisses on both cheeks. Given what had happened at Sintra, President Constantinescu's mood was understandable. He might well have asked me, "What did Romania ever do to Iceland?"

President Constantinescu carefully read the letter from President Clinton, which concluded with a paragraph stating that the United States congratulated Romania on its courageous economic development program and fully supported Romania's efforts to integrate into the European-Atlantic community. Had I been forewarned about Sintra, I might have drafted a softer message to retain credibility. The one bright spot was that President Constantinescu agreed that he would submit the Ukraine treaty to Parliament as soon as it was signed. He then started in on Secretary of State Albright, stating that she was the principal obstacle to Romania's NATO quest, not the White House nor the Pentagon. Fortunately, he ran out of time and we agreed to meet next over the weekend. Later that day I received a call from Cotroceni announcing that the president would like to see me the next day.

We met for the better part of an hour. He was more friendly than the day before, but by the time the meeting ended, the somber mood had returned. President Constantinescu and the government had raised NATO expectations so high in Romania that it was difficult for them to climb down. He told me he responded to comments from the press yesterday, stating that Secretary Albright's assessment in her Sintra remarks was entirely correct: Romania was behind the other three countries because of the failure of President Iliescu's government to move forward with economic reform. This was the obvious way out for the present government. President Constantinescu asked me to deliver a message to Secretary Albright explaining the significance of the Romania-Ukraine treaty, the responsibility he, President Constantinescu, took in going ahead with the treaty, the importance of Romania to NATO's southern flank in the event that Turkey turned in a fundamentalist direction, and the strong support in Romania both for entry into NATO and for the government's economic reform program. As I sat listening, I realized once again that none of these points had made a difference in the outcome; the decision had been made on the basis of the administration's assessment of the political risks in seeking Senate ratification for a larger enlargement than three countries. Then Deputy National Security Adviser Berger had told me this two years before—the administration was not going to risk defeat on NATO enlargement. This had been clear from the outset and had been reinforced every step since, including the meeting Secretary Albright had had with Foreign Minister Severin in Washington in April.

In our conversations, President Constantinescu made it clear that he was still hoping for a positive sign from the United States at the July NATO summit meeting in Madrid to give him political cover, such as mentioning Romania as one of the countries to begin accession talks a few years down the road, or setting a date for the next round of accession talks.

He maintained that without such cover, the United States would be seen in Romania as blocking its NATO entry with no meaningful second prize. If that happened, the United States would again be viewed as abandoning Romania as it had, in their eyes, fifty years before at Yalta. I weighed in by cable to Washington, urging that we come up with a plan to salvage the bilateral relationship and preserve the special status of the United States in Romania. There was much back and forth on this but little in the way of concrete suggestions from Washington.

A few weeks later, on a flight from Frankfurt to Washington, Ron Asmus, a deputy assistant secretary of state and a special adviser to Deputy Secretary Strobe Talbott, and I came up with the idea of a "strategic partnership" between the United States and Romania that became the centerpiece of our bilateral relationship and has remained so ever since. Ron and I then set about selling the idea in Washington. I immediately met with Secretary Albright. She liked the idea.

I was trying to get many pieces of the bilateral relationship in place in Washington before I returned to Bucharest. Now that the NATO decision was made, we needed to find other ways to solidify Romania's role as a stabilizing force in the region and position the United States as Romania's principal supporter in the next round of NATO enlargement. To this end, I drafted a letter for Secretary Albright to send to President Constantinescu reassuring him that the door to NATO membership remained open for Romania and giving her blessing to a later meeting in Washington between Prime Minister Ciorbea and Vice President Gore. Six weeks later, President Clinton gave a speech in Bucharest in which he announced the "strategic partnership" between the United States and Romania.

15

A Bountiful Harvest

SUMMER 1997

A TALE OF TWO RABBIS

In June I attended a lunch in Bucharest at the Romanian Academy in honor of Rabbi Alexandru Şafran (age eighty-six), the former chief rabbi of Romania and later chief rabbi of Geneva, Switzerland. The occasion was the induction of Rabbi Şafran into membership in the Academy, the most prestigious intellectual institution in the country. He had been elected by his fellow rabbis as chief rabbi of Romania in 1940 at the age of twenty-eight. He survived the war years, largely due to the skill of Wilhelm Filderman, the head of the Romanian Jewish community, who had gone to school with Marshal Ion Antonescu and had maintained a relationship with him to the end, including throughout the war. At Antonescu's trial, Filderman testified on his behalf, pointing to things Antonescu had done to protect Romania's Jews. In truth, despite his relationship with Filderman, Antonescu was not a friend of the Jews. In addition to the deportation of the Jews in Bukovina to Transnistria, he ordered Jews in Romania to wear yellow stars. For a time, Jews were made to serve in forced-labor battalions and Jewish businesses were closed, a decision Antonescu reversed when he realized the negative effect this was having on the Romanian economy.

The communists expelled Rabbi Şafran from Romania in 1947 after which, under communist orders, Moses Rosen took over as chief rabbi. According to Şafran, Rosen was not an ordained rabbi, only a teacher in a small Bucharest synagogue in Falticeni. However, Moshe Arad, a Falticeni native who was Israel's ambassador to the United States from 1987 to 1990, told me Rosen had been his rabbi in Falticeni.

The two rabbis could not have been less alike. Şafran was physically small and delicate, a Jewish scholar, modest, yet worldly. Rosen was far more theatrical, a large man physically and in personality. He had a commanding presence and was a superb organizer. He was also a lawyer by training, and although I had previously heard that there was some question about his ordination, I was told he received his rabbinical stature through study in Vienna. Whatever the truth may be, he performed an enormous service for the Jewish community during the communist period.

SPECIAL PRESIDENTIAL ENVOY TO CYPRUS

In June I took a trip to Washington to check up on Carol's health. While I was there, National Security Adviser Sandy Berger called me to tell me President Clinton had decided to appoint Dick Holbrooke as his special presidential envoy for Cyprus, which I already knew from State Department sources. I thought I had been derailed by Senator McCain's intervention, but this may not have been the real story. Sandy made light of the McCain matter, saying that he had received a "call from John," but implied that Senator McCain's intervention was not the desideratum. One thing for sure: Dick was anxious to be back in the swim and may have pushed his way through, still basking in the glory of the Dayton Accords that ended the war in Bosnia.

At my request, Sandy arranged for me to meet with Senator McCain a few days later. The two of us met alone at the senator's office, neither of us giving much ground. He took me to task for a sentence in one of my letters to Lorne Craner, the director of the International Republican Institute (IRI), in which I had likened the IRI's support in 1996 for the loser in the 1992 Romanian elections to helping weaker teams in the NBA and NFL player drafts. I explained that the reference was an effort by me to relate to people younger than I, which he partially accepted. The rest of the time we talked about IRI activities in Mongolia, Albania, and Bulgaria, four or five years before, and my consistent support for democratic and economic reform in Romania. The meeting ended with his saying, "You have made some very persuasive arguments, and I would like to think about it." In the end, the matter simply died a natural death. There was nothing further to be done by Senator McCain or me.

QUELLING THE NATO BACKLASH

Back in Bucharest, to quell the furor over the NATO decision at Sintra, I agreed to an interview on the Romanian television station PRO-TV to explain the U.S. decision. It would be filmed and shown on the evening news with subtitles in Romanian. PRO-TV had close to 60 percent of the Romanian viewing public and was by far the most influential media voice in Romania. I was told the interview went well and my words may have helped dampen the uproar.

A proposed last-minute visit by Prime Minister Ciorbea to Washington in mid-June took on added significance after the Sintra decision. President Constantinescu saw Prime Minister Ciorbea's visit as Romania's last chance to appeal the decision at Sintra before the NATO summit meeting in Madrid in the second week of July, where the book on NATO membership would be closed. A bit of power playing followed. Constantinescu wanted my assurances that if Ciorbea went to Washington, he would be able to meet with Vice President Gore and possibly with Secretary of State Albright. I explained that the meeting with the vice president was possible only if we had assurances that Ciorbea would not publicly criticize our decision at Sintra. Both Constantinescu and Ciorbea stated explicitly that they understood and accepted the ground rules. My final word to Ciorbea before he got on the plane to New York on June 17 was to tell him that Romania's best approach in Washington would be to show it was a reliable, mature partner and that this would not happen if the Romanians were seen to be whining and asking for things they were not going to get. In addition to my assurances, Deputy Secretary of State

Talbott "called in" Romania's ambassador, Mircea Geoana, and delivered the same message.

PRESIDENT CLINTON IS COMING TO BUCHAREST!

On June 18, I received a late-night call from Sandy Berger asking whether there would be any negative "visuals" if President Clinton visited Bucharest immediately after the Madrid summit. A few minutes later I got a call from Dan Fried, the National Security Council's senior director for Eastern Europe. Anxious about being left out of the loop, he asked me whether I had spoken with Sandy, and I confirmed I had. The next day I took up the idea of a presidential visit with President Constantinescu and Foreign Minister Severin. Both were enthusiastic. The Romanian public may not have liked the U.S. decision at Sintra, but the United States and President Clinton were enormously popular in Romania. A visit by the American president was sure to be a historic event. Romanians still talked about President Nixon's visit in 1969 when two million Romanians lined the streets of Bucharest to greet him, an outpouring of popular support for the West and an expression of anti-communist feeling. The situation today would not be as dramatic, but the government of Romania was certain to go out of its way to make President Clinton's visit a success. I reported this to Sandy, who replied that Bucharest was on the schedule.

Later in June, I called President Constantinescu from Targu Mureş in Transylvania. I was spending a day with local officials visiting factories and taking a look at a synagogue I had first seen twenty years before as part of Rabbi Rosen's Hanukkah tour. I told President Constantinescu that it was official: President Clinton would be in Bucharest on July 11. Constantinescu was thrilled: the presidents of the United States and Romania side by side for a photo op in Bucharest. Meanwhile, in Washington, I heard from the State Department that Prime Minister Ciorbea kept pushing for wholly unrealistic financial and military assistance to compensate for its non-selection to be in the first wave of NATO enlargement. The next day I sent a cable to Deputy Secretary of State Talbott suggesting it was time to cut off Romania's importuning. President Clinton's visit was more than the Romanians had a right to expect. Talbott agreed.

In late June we started preparing for President Clinton's visit. The White House approved the schedule we recommended, including his speaking in University Square. Briefing papers were prepared, including a draft of the president's speech. The draft went from the embassy to the president's speech-writers, then to National Security Adviser Berger for final review and back to us. Everything was on schedule.

Next arrived the advance team headed by Nick Friendly, a gem of a guy and far less demanding than Mrs. Clinton's advance team. At one point I mentioned to Nick what a pleasure it was to work with him, to which he responded, "After you've gone to Cleveland for the fourth time in the same campaign, an eight-hour stopover in Bucharest is a piece of cake." We quickly decided President Clinton would not deliver his speech from the balcony in University Square where President Constantinescu spoke on election night in 1996, as this would be seen by Romanians as a tilt in President Constanti-nescu's political favor. President Clinton would speak from a raised platform in the square.

To make sure the public would show up for the speech, we arranged for a band to play in the square several hours before the president spoke. Xerox would distribute 20,000 handbills urging people to attend, and we arranged for Coca-Cola and Pepsi to hand out free drinks. When I mentioned this to President Constantinescu, he was shaken, blurting out, "Romanians are not like your Negroes in the South. They won't show up for free drinks." Zoe Petre went even further, expressing her concern that by offering free drinks and "fun," we would be getting a "lot of Gypsies." Political correctness had not reached Romania.

An arithmetic guessing game followed. The day before President Clinton arrived, President Constantinescu and Zoe Petre told me there would be a crowd of 60,000: "Twenty thousand will come to see President Constanti-nescu, 20,000 will come to see the U.S. president, 10,000 will come to show solidarity with the Romanian government, and another 10,000 will come for whatever reason"—including, they supposed, "free drinks and fun."

When I was not working on President Clinton's pending visit, I drafted a long article explaining Romania's NATO aspirations and its qualifications for future consideration for membership two years hence, in 1999. The article was published in the fall 1997 issue of the *SAIS Review of International Affairs* (published by the Johns Hopkins School of Advanced International Studies).

GOOD-BYE TO A NATO COLLEAGUE

It was customary for NATO ambassadors to give a dinner in honor of departing colleagues. The dinner on June 19 in honor of the departing Greek ambassador, Christos Alexandris, the longest-serving NATO ambassador in Romania, was livelier than normal. Christos was a delightful interlocutor; his only fault was a lack of self-restraint. This dinner was his swan song. He extolled the virtues of each of his fellow ambassadors with historical references, not all of which were apt or appropriate, spoken in four languages, and ended by his singing an aria from a German opera with words added in tribute to our host, the German ambassador.

SENATOR ROBERT DOLE IS COMING TO BUCHAREST, TOO!

Despite losing the 1996 election to President Clinton, Robert Dole was an enormously popular figure in the United States and well known abroad, including in Romania. He came to Romania on June 22. It was not clear why he decided to make the trip, but come he did, on the private plane of businessman and professional sportsman Ion Tiriac, for a two-day visit. Before leaving Washington, he spoke with President Clinton about Romania but, bucking the custom, did not check in with the State Department. After he arrived, the press gave him every opportunity to criticize the U.S. administration and the U.S. president, but he did neither. Everywhere he went, Senator Dole was greeted as a celebrity. There was an honor guard to greet him at the airport and to see him off on his departure. At Cotroceni, where he met with President Constantinescu, the president was waiting at the bottom of the steps to welcome him and escorted him to his car when he left.

In his two days in Romania, in addition to his meetings with President Constantinescu, who hosted a private lunch in his honor at Cotroceni, he had dinner with Senate President Petre Roman, Foreign Minister Severin, and Justice Minister Valeriu Stoica at Roman's villa on Lake Snagov. The following morning he went to Parliament for a breakfast hosted by the new president of the Chamber of Deputies, Ion Diaconescu. From there he went to the Senate, still located in the former Communist Party headquarters (the Senate is now in the colossal building Ceauşescu built), to address a joint meeting of the Foreign Affairs, Military, and Human Rights Committees of the Senate.

The meeting at the Senate was quite a show. Senate President Roman chaired the meeting, with Senator Dole and me flanking him, facing about thirty assembled senators. After a perfunctory introduction by Roman, Senator Dole spoke briefly about Romania and NATO enlargement. Without criticizing the U.S. administration, he spoke in favor of Romania's joining NATO now. Senate President Roman then called for questions, whereupon Senator Dole interrupted him to ask whether he was going to introduce me. Although Roman can be charming, particularly when talking one on one, he often lacked graciousness. This was such an occasion. He replied dismissively, "Everyone knows Ambassador Moses," which drew a questioning look from Senator Dole, as if to say, "That's not the way we do things." Senator Roman had displayed a similar lack of graciousness by not meeting Senator Dole when he arrived nor escorting him on leaving, an oversight not typical of Romanians.

The meeting was an opportunity for speech-making. Romanian politicians were rarely edifying when speaking, and this occasion was not different. The rambling speeches included one by the extremist Senator Corneliu Vadim Tudor (PRM), who, with his customary flowery oratory, driveled on and on, his comments largely incomprehensible. The real drama came later, when the session was over. I had spotted Senator Tudor when we entered the hall and had whispered to Senator Dole, "See that guy? He is a fascist." Senator Dole whispered back, "I don't want to have anything to do with him." As we were leaving the hall, Tudor, with his photographer in tow, pushed his way through the crowd to give Senator Dole a book he had written, the gesture to be captured on film by his photographer and to appear the next day in Tudor's newspaper, *Romania Mare*. I stuck close to Senator Dole, running interference so that the photographer could not get the shot he wanted of the two senators only. I knew Tudor would not want my picture in *Romania Mare* standing next to Senator Dole.

A press conference followed, which lasted about thirty minutes. The press made a good showing in terms of numbers, but only five journalists spoke up, the same one asking the first and last questions. The Romanian press was not prepared to interact robustly with big-name foreigners, a holdover from the Ceaușescu era of tight press control.

In his meetings, Senator Dole spoke with a raspy voice, frequently resorting to humor, rarely making a major mistake, but displaying only a limited knowledge of the issues. He would pick up a comment or two from others as he went along, but did not pretend to know more than he did. When we were alone, he was direct and amazingly frank in talking about the recent U.S. presidential election—he said he had lost the middle ground because of pressure from "right-wing extremists," in particular, on the abortion issue. President George H. W. Bush had told me the same thing about his campaign in 1992. Senator Dole described his own political views as moderate and talked about various persons he had considered as his potential vice presidential running mate. One possibility had been Governor Tom Ridge of Pennsylvania, whom Senator Dole viewed as a coming political star. He had served in the U.S. Army in Vietnam, and his father was a union leader. But he decided Governor Ridge did not have enough political experience to help the ticket. He then switched to Governor Christine Whitman of New Jersey, whom he liked, but she was not acceptable to the party's right wing. His last personal comment was about Senator Jesse Helms (R-N.C.) whom he called an example of the old obstructionist breed "that is fortunately disappearing in the Senate," and went on to describe the difficulties he had encountered after the 1994 midterm elections in dealing with new members of Congress who were "undisciplined and refused to follow party leadership."

Senator Dole in person was not different from the man you saw on television. He spoke in phrases, not sentences. His thoughts were not expressed clearly or consistently, and he frequently had trouble answering questions, either because he did not remember the question or had trouble staying on track. Still, he was enormously likable and, as my grandmother would say, "a real mensch."

INTRAMURAL SKIRMISHES WITHIN THE RULING COALITION

During their trip to Washington, Prime Minister Ciorbea and Deputy Defense Minister Constantin Dudu Ionescu of the PNT-CD met with Deputy Secretary of State Talbott to talk about NATO. At their meeting, Ionescu asked Strobe's staff to use him, Ionescu, as a back channel to the Romanian government rather than going through Ambassador Mircea Geoana—who, he explained, was "not one of our people," meaning he was not a member of PNT-CD. When Talbott met with the Romanian delegation a second time at the request of the Romanians, he told them, "We communicate with the Romanian government through our embassy in Bucharest, and we expect your government to communicate with us through your ambassador in Washington. If the Romanian government does not have full confidence in its ambassador, it should choose someone else, but we will not back-channel." Ambassador Geoana had done a splendid job in Washington on behalf of Romania, first in persuading Congress to grant Romania permanent MFN status and then in elevating Romania's status in official Washington, but he was continually undercut by the Romanian émigré community in the United States, which was led by people with a strong Christian Democratic Party view of Romanian political life. In trying to bypass Geoana, Ionescu was also bypassing the Romanian Foreign Ministry, headed by Severin, a member of PD. By continuing on this course, PNT-CD caused increased tension within the governing coalition.

As soon as Prime Minister Ciorbea returned to Bucharest, he asked to meet with me to get my feedback on the reaction in Washington to his visit. I answered honestly, pointing out the negative effect of the incessant pleading for this or that by him and his delegation. Prime Minister Ciorbea was crestfallen. He had hoped to hear good things. He tried to emphasize the positive by saying that at least he was able to deliver a message more moderate than Foreign Minister Severin's—a sharp criticism of our Sintra announcement. This was another example of intramural squabbling. He also told me that when he was in Washington, the IMF all but "ordered" him to drop the Bell deal.

Foreign Minister Severin called late the same night for a private talk. He was preoccupied with his power struggle with President Constantinescu and now Prime Minister Ciorbea. Under the Romanian constitution, the Romanian president's foreign policy powers were limited to signing (not negotiating) treaties, appointing the foreign minister and ambassadors, and accepting the credentials of foreign diplomats. Ignoring these limitations, President Constantinescu sought to carve out a wider role for himself, in part to prevent Foreign Minister Severin and PD from directing Romania's foreign policy. President Iliescu had done the same with a more compliant foreign minister, Teodor Meleșcanu. Severin was in a difficult position. Without Prime Minister Ciorbea's support, there was little he could do to restrain President Constantinescu. After the 1996 election, PD won the battle on the coalition agreement, receiving three plum ministries—Defense, Foreign Affairs, and Transportation—but Severin's wings were being clipped by President Constantinescu. A day or two before my call from Severin, President Constantinescu had stated publicly that he was the foreign policy "originator," and that the Foreign Ministry's role was to carry out his policies. All of this understandably rankled Severin. The matter came to a head when Gilda Lazar, the Foreign Ministry spokesperson, in a taped telephone conversation with a reporter from the Romanian newspaper *Zuiz*, criticized Prime Minister Ciorbea's visit to Washington. Lazar was giving voice to Severin's thinking, now no longer concealed from Constantinescu or Prime Minister Ciorbea. In response, Ciorbea called for Lazar's dismissal, which Severin ignored. The coalition was not likely to break up, as both PD and PNT-CD needed the other to govern, so an uneasy modus vivendi prevailed. By the time the 2000 elections rolled around, both PNT-CD and PD were politically eclipsed.

A WHIRLWIND MONTH

July would witness another big July Fourth celebration, my farewells, and President Clinton's visit, the highlight of my tour as ambassador. The embassy's July Fourth celebration would be my last as host. I believed I had done all I could in Romania as ambassador and that Romania would stay the course to recovery with or without me. I planned to leave when President Clinton departed on July 11.

MY LAST JULY FOURTH CELEBRATION IN
BUCHAREST, AND FAREWELLS

For a time I was concerned that the American position on Romania's entry into NATO would put a damper on our July Fourth celebration, but exactly the opposite took place. We had almost 3,000 guests. The entire government came, including Prime Minister Ciorbea, speaking in President Constantinescu's absence (he was in Turkey). So, too, did both former president Ion Iliescu and Adrian Nastase, chairman of the Social Democratic Party of Romania. To my surprise, Patriarch Teoctist also came, his first July Fourth party. My welcoming remarks were greeted with huge applause. There seemed to be agreement across political lines that I had been a strong positive force for Romania.

At one point, President Iliescu took me aside, interrupting a discussion I was having with Prime Minister Ciorbea, to tell me I had fallen into a trap by agreeing for President Clinton to speak at University Square. For former president Iliescu and his Social Democratic Party, the square was identified with the anti-government demonstrations in 1990 and 1991, which Iliescu characterized as fascist, monarchist, and anti-American. (Iliescu was to repeat this outburst when he met with President Clinton the following week, leading Clinton to comment to me in an aside, "Iliescu was quite excited, wasn't he?")

Most observers thought the Bucharest demonstrations in the early 1990s were anti-communist, not anti-American. The truth lay in between. The demonstrators were calling for the replacement of President Iliescu, Prime Minister Roman, and others in power, all labeled "crypto-communists," and for the return of King Michael. For many on the political right, King Michael was the symbol of government legitimacy, and the Christian Democrats seized on this. Now that Constantinescu was president, restoration of the monarchy was no longer an issue. Before 1992 and the second miners' raid, President Constantinescu had been a political unknown as rector of Bucharest University, but after Corneliu Coposu, the leader of the Christian Democrats, died in 1995, he inherited Coposu's mantle. Now that he was president, he faced many of the same problems that had plagued former president Iliescu: how to deal with an overstaffed, not very competent bureaucracy afraid to make decisions. For all the talk of economic reform, the hard decisions still lay ahead. Industry was still in the hands of large state-owned companies and *régies autonomes*.

After the July Fourth party, I walked a mile or so that night from my residence to Herastrau Park for a fireworks display that had been arranged by Bill Conover, a U.S. businessman living in Bucharest. There was a huge crowd, numbering in the tens of thousands. The fireworks were spectacular. The crowd applauded the United States whenever the country's name was mentioned, which seemed to confirm our continued popularity despite the NATO decision. So did the pervasiveness of American music and movies in the local culture and the dominance of English as the second language among school-age Romanians. All this confirmed for me that, for Romanians, America remained the land of the free, the shining city on the hill.

In early July the Canadian ambassador, Gilles Duguay, hosted the dinner for the departing NATO member country ambassador; this time it was for me. Duguay was a jolly fellow and a marvelous host. He brought in two musicians from Kishinev, who played an assortment of Romanian, American, and other songs. We were seated at three tables rather than the customary one long one, so the conversation was less stilted. France's ambassador, Bernard Boyer, as the senior NATO ambassador, gave me the traditional silver plate signed by all the NATO ambassadors and made a friendly, warm speech to which I responded in the same spirit, ending with my giving him a red, white, and blue hat—American, not the French tricolor—after which I donned a stiff French officer's hat, complete with gold braid à la *Beau Geste*.

The next night Foreign Minister Severin held a dinner in my honor, a lovely event hosted by a warm and talented friend.

More going-away parties followed. Mike and Sarah Einik hosted a dinner with the embassy's country team, and the following evening the Jordanian ambassador presided over a lavish affair at the Elite Restaurant, owned by Fathi Tahir, who no doubt was the real host. The Israeli ambassador sat at one table, the Palestinian at another, the Tunisian ambassador at a third, and the Egyptian ambassador sat with me and the Jordanian ambassador at the head table. "Only in Romania!"

At a farewell lunch at the American Chamber of Commerce, David Garner of Citibank said kind words and presented me with a framed certificate. Next up was Claude Papas, general manager of Procter & Gamble, who gave me a carton of detergent labeled "Moses Power" and a written testimonial citing my assistance to P&G and other American businesses. It was all quite convivial.

The last going-away affair was a dinner given by Ukraine's ambassador to Romania, Oleksandr Chaly, who was ebullient, as always. He was a good friend and deserved much of the credit for the Romania-Ukraine agreement, which was ratified a few days later by the two countries' parliaments.

Last on the list of good-byes was the embassy family picnic on July 5. Deputy Chief of Mission Mike Einik presented me with a picture of our embassy signed by the embassy staff together with the traditional gift of an American flag that had flown over our embassy. It was an emotional time for me and others. We had become a close family. It was hard to say good-bye.

I also wanted to say farewell to good friends with whom I had worked for three years. Former president Iliescu was at the top of the list. His office at PDSR headquarters was across the street from my residence. Iliescu greeted me warmly, wearing an open shirt and jacket, looking not in the least presidential, but it became increasingly clear that he was living in the past. He still thought in terms of class conflict, mixing his familiar diatribes with observations about governing. For example, he criticized the new government for not using experienced people at the top, relying instead on party loyalists with no experience, a charge that was sadly true. He again raised the issue of University Square, harking back to the early 1990s when students and others had sought to bring down his government. He called President Constantinescu "at best an opportunist" and compared Constantinescu's career with his own: having broken with Ceauşescu in 1971, he was expelled from the Communist Central Committee and was sent first to Timişoara and then to Iaşi as prefect, after which he spent five years working as a hydro engineer and later as director of a technical printing house in Bucharest. Yet, he commented ruefully, he had been branded a crypto-communist and Constantinescu a democratic reformer. Despite President Iliescu's negatives, he regained the presidency in 2000 after Constantinescu wisely decided not to run for reelction and the PNT-CD had fallen from favor, having failed to live up to its promises during the 1996 campaign.

Next was a farewell call on Prime Minister Ciorbea. Rather than discuss important things, he asked me what he should wear when he greeted

President Clinton at the airport. Like many newly elected Romanian officials, when he came into office seven months earlier, his wardrobe was threadbare. Now he wore spiffy clothes, yet his unease remained. I told him the suit he was wearing was fine. I used the rest of the meeting to make a plea for American businesses: Bell, Westinghouse, Case, and Hyatt. Prime Minister Ciorbea gave the usual assurances, but I was not convinced.

Next came Foreign Minister Severin. Our meeting was cordial, but not productive. It was all but impossible for Severin to be direct and brief. I suggested that he not dwell on the past in the meeting he would be having the next day with Secretary Albright, but to present himself as a serious interlocutor dealing with our common interests in the region. He then proceeded to tell me that at Madrid he "apologized to Secretary Albright for being so nasty in promoting Romania's efforts to get into NATO." Ambassador Geoana had also tried after Sintra to persuade Severin to drop the rhetorical gamesmanship and to stick to two or three issues that could be productively explored in the thirty to forty minutes that he would have with Secretary Albright.

Before my meeting with Severin, Ambassador Geoana gave me the talking points that Zoe Petre had prepared for President Constantinescu to use in his meeting with President Clinton. They contained the usual Romanian bluster, such as references to Romania's strategic importance to the United States, noxious flattery, an example being a reference to President Clinton as the man who brought peace and stability to a united Europe, and Romania's sensitivity to what it perceived as a lack of respect. In this regard, Constantinescu intended to push for a state visit in the fall, rather than the working visit that had been discussed. Constantinescu had considerable charm and would present his points well, but if he stuck to his script, he would lose the opportunity to make a convincing case for Romania based on Romania's commendable recovery from the Ceaușescu nightmare and its plans for continued progress, particularly in developing a sustainable private economy.

I also said my good-byes to most of the embassy staff, going from office to office to exchange hugs. It was hard to leave, but the time had come to move on.

LAST-MINUTE MANEUVERS BEFORE
NATO'S MADRID SUMMIT

On July 7, the day before the Madrid Summit was to convene on July 8, I received a call from John Kornblum, our assistant secretary of state for European and Canadian affairs. He was calling on behalf of Secretary Albright and National Security Adviser Berger requesting that I meet with President Constantinescu to ask him to put out a statement making it clear that Romania was not insisting on first-round accession if that would sabotage enlargement. The French were still playing their Romania card, threatening to hold things up and giving the United States fits. President Constantinescu agreed and an hour later read to me the statement he intended to give in response to a question from a Rompress reporter. (This was the usual way for a head of state to get out a short statement. The press asks and the president responds. President Carter did this.) The answer was the text I had suggested, stating in effect that Romania supported enlargement starting immediately and that Romania would abide by the consensus decision which it nevertheless hoped would be favorable to Romania. There was no reference to a future date when it was certain that Romanian would join, or even a suggestion that the consensus should include Romania in the first round. Problem solved.

The same day, July 7, I had lunch with Mircea Geoana, Romania's ambassador to the United States, who was in Bucharest for Clinton's visit. He expected to be fired by President Constantinescu, probably sometime this fall, after President Constantinescu's visit to Washington. I was convinced that he had done an outstanding job as ambassador, and it would be a mistake to drop him. The only strike against him was that he had been appointed by former president Iliescu and former foreign minister Meleşcanu—in the case of diplomatic appointments that is often enough to justify recall. He also told me, and I believed him, that Foreign Minister Severin was touting "a moral foreign policy"—a term Severin intended to mean that Romania should reward its friends, France and Germany, and by implication punish the United States for not supporting Romania at Madrid. Geoana asked, rightly: Whoever heard of a "moral" foreign policy? Certainly not Romania or Severin. I suggested to President Clinton that he put in a good word for Geoana when he met with President Constantinescu. He did, and Geoana kept his job.

THE BIG DAY

On July 11, the Marines showed up at my residence at 7 a.m. for our last run, after which I hurried off to PRO-TV to tape an interview that would be shown the day after President Clinton's speech. I referred to the speech, quoting a line or two to capture the essence of it, and the warm reception President Clinton received, all in the past tense for the next day's TV viewers.

The weather was perfect. President Clinton's planes, flying from Warsaw, arrived early. It was a magnificent sight as two 747s with "United States of America" in huge letters painted in blue on white fuselages against the background of the blue sky slowly descended. I stood on the airport's apron as *Air Force One* taxied up to the VIP building. After everyone but the president descended, President Clinton came down the metal stairs. He greeted me warmly, after which I introduced him to the Romanian delegation: Prime Minister Ciorbea, Foreign Minister Severin, Defense Minister Babiuc, Zoe Petre, and Ambassador Geoana. President Clinton's official delegation included Secretary of State Albright, National Security Adviser Berger, Deputy Secretary of State Talbott, and various White House aides and security.

Clinton entered his armored limousine, parked at planeside, and off we went to Cotroceni. Enormous crowds lined the streets. Seated next to me, Secretary Albright looked out and commented on how shabby the people looked compared to the crowds she had seen the previous day in Poland. Once at Cotroceni, President Constantinescu greeted President Clinton, after which the two presidents reviewed an honor guard drawn up in their hot wool uniforms, high black boots and plumed hats. Then the two presidents rode together up the circular drive to the palace.

Although it was not on the official schedule, President Constantinescu insisted on a ten-minute tête-à-tête with President Clinton, having previously agreed at the White House advance team's request that the bilateral meeting would include the official delegations. The larger meeting itself did not cover new ground. Only the two presidents spoke: President Clinton stressed the importance of Romania's continuing its economic reform, acknowledging that it would be difficult in the short run. He compared Romania's situation to Poland's of a few years ago, then added that he was amazed at the transformation that had taken place in Poland.

As for NATO, the important thing, Clinton said, was for Romania to keep its spirits up. The decision at Madrid was not a negative vote on Romania. We wanted to help Romania get into NATO but the United States thought that a smaller number of countries would make it easier to begin the enlargement process. Other NATO members thought it would be better to bring in five countries and then shut the door. This would have excluded the three Baltic states, Slovakia, and Bulgaria. (This was a masterful reformulation, putting the onus on unnamed NATO members who wanted to stop enlargement at five countries, which would have excluded the five others.) The United States' long-term objective, he said, was to integrate Europe both economically and militarily. "All this will not be done in the three and a half years left in my term," he said wistfully. But he expressed the hope that before he left office systems would be in place to ensure the future, saying, "Romania is a profound part of that and we want to be supportive over the long pull."

He also referred briefly to the Bell deal, calling it a good project, and mentioned the strategic partnership between our two countries as a program to build a relationship of support that would lead to a continuing evolution in a positive direction. He congratulated Romania for its participation in the Partnership for Peace and for its peacekeeping in Bosnia and Albania. Returning to NATO, he referred to the language in the Madrid communiqué that called for a review in two years, stating that if Romania continued on its present path, "No one will have a stronger case."

President Constantinescu in his remarks dwelled on Romania's regional role, its strong pro-American sentiments, and the potential threat from "national communism." He expressed his concern about the future of Ukraine, referring to Ukrainian President Leonid Kuchma's comments to him about the upcoming Ukrainian parliamentary elections in March 1998: Kuchma feared that the eastern part of the country would vote pro-Russia (which in fact happened in succeeding elections). He also took credit for the recently signed Romania-Ukraine treaty. The bilateral meeting lasted approximately 50 minutes, after which both delegations proceeded to a larger hall where 150 or so people were gathered to greet the two presidents.

Before the two presidents entered the larger hall, Secretary Albright and I worked the room. I introduced her to Romanian officials and the diplomatic corps. The two presidents were then announced, and after some brief remarks,

President Constantinescu steered President Clinton around the room, giving everyone an opportunity to shake his hand and exchange a few words with him. There was food and drink, but neither president stopped long enough to enjoy either. President Clinton departed on schedule for two hours of down time at my residence—a miracle I was able to perform by uttering the magic words "The Secret Service says you need to leave."

Secretary Albright and I then headed to a bilateral meeting with Foreign Minister Severin at the Foreign Ministry. Like President Constantinescu at Cotroceni, Foreign Minister Severin whisked Madeleine away for a tête-à-tête in his office. Only this time Ambassador Geoana made sure that the two would not be alone for long. He escorted Deputy Secretary of State Talbott and me up the stairs to the second floor while the two principals rode on the elevator. The three of us sat across the room, talking in low voices, causing Madeleine to ask, "What are you going to do—sit over there and whisper?" So we joined her. The first issue on her agenda was Romania's sale of A-6 missile parts to Iran, the subject of a formal complaint I had delivered to Foreign Minister Severin a few weeks before. She then congratulated Romania on its recent political and military progress, calling attention to Romania's need to be completely integrated in a unified Europe. She pointed to Romania's importance, like Poland's, anchoring a strategic part of Europe. She stressed that NATO was initially a military alliance but now had both economic and political components.

Foreign Minister Severin said that although Romania itself was not threatened, the region was not secure. Relations with Hungary were most important for Romania, and the two countries had now overcome their past differences. Severin went on to say that Poland and Romania could form a vital link to Ukraine, allowing the three countries to work together in combatting illegal emigration, drugs, nuclear proliferation, and organized crime. He referred to Romania's relations with Russia as "cool": there was no basic treaty; Russia's attitude was "take it or leave it." He concluded by stating that Romania would like to coordinate foreign policy issues with the United States.

In her reply, Secretary Albright made it clear that our strategic partnership with Romania would not be a security umbrella, nor would there be any new money. The partnership, though important, should not be viewed by Romania as a substitute for NATO, but rather as a consultative mechanism looking at a broad range of issues. The only reason for not supporting Romania for NATO accession now was that Romania's reforms had been "short-lived." She added, "Everything has been done right, but it must be irrevocable." Privatization was critical if Romania was going to remain economically stable. "There must be a good climate for foreign investment." Here she strongly supported Bell, Tenneco, and Westinghouse by name. Reading from cue cards, she ticked off Romania's adhering to the IMF standby agreement, returning Jewish and other communal properties, and ensuring religious freedom, saying that some religious groups in Romania had been harassed, most recently in Moldavia. She concluded by saying that this was one of the most interesting discussions that she had had and she was looking forward to more.

The next stop was the residence, to reassemble the U.S. group for the drive to University Square and President Clinton's speech. Crowds had poured into the streets and were already lined three or four deep along Calea Victoriei and on Bulevardul Republicii, leading to the square. Secretary Albright and I arrived together, followed a few minutes later by the two presidents, who were greeted by shouts of "Emil! Emil! Emil!" and "Clinton! Clinton! Clinton!" By this time, the crowd was immense. The Secret Service estimated that 500,000 people were jammed into the square and up the avenue for another half mile. President Constantinescu paraded around like a prize fighter. President Clinton was more reserved but obviously was enjoying the show. President Constantinescu spoke first, and too long, sounding more like a professor than a politician. President Clinton was then introduced by a young girl who had just graduated from the American School in Bucharest and was heading to Wellesley College, Hillary Clinton's alma mater, on a full scholarship. President Clinton's superb speech, interrupted by frequent applause, was translated sentence by sentence into Romanian by my special assistant and close friend, Mihai Carp, whose voice was as good as the president's.

> Thank you. Mr. President, thank you for your wonderful welcome. And to the young student who just spoke, Simida Munteanu, if she is a representative of the youth of Romania, the future of this nation is in good hands.
>
> I am proud to be the first American President to visit a free Romania. I am proud to stand in University Square, where so many have

sacrificed for freedom. Most of all, I am proud to see in this vast crowd the face of a new Romania, moving beyond the past to build a bright future of possibility for all your people. Congratulations!

America knows that Romania's destiny lies in an undivided, democratic, peaceful Europe, where every nation is free, and every free nation is the partner of the United States. To all the people of Romania who love freedom so dearly: I come to Romania because of all you have already done. I come because I know what you still can do. I come because of all that we must do together to achieve your destiny in the family of freedom.

No people—no people have suffered more under Communist repression, no people paid a higher price for the simple right to live in freedom. No people faced greater challenges in the struggle to start anew. But though your path has been steep and hard, you are going forward. And for that, we salute you.

In America—in America, we have seen your spirit, your endurance, your determination symbolized by the feat of one of your young Romanian athletes. At the end of the New York marathon last fall, a runner named Anuta Catuna came from behind to close the lead and earn her way to victory in one of America's most prized races. Like her, Romania has set its sights on the long run. And like her, the Romanian people have won the world's respect for moving so far, so fast, and for believing in yourselves and your future. Like her marathon race, the marathon of freedom is not a sprint; it takes steady and persistent commitment to stay the course. After more than 200 years, America now knows the journey of democracy is never over; it must be traveled every single day.

But what progress you have made. You have launched bold economic reforms to give your people the chance to make the most of their own lives. In the short term I know there are costs to this market reform. But in the long term, the rewards are far greater, in better jobs, new opportunities, more trade and investment from around the world for your people. And in recent years, we have learned from other nations' experience that those who reform the fastest make the most progress for their people.

Romania has been making up for lost time, and the whole world is taking notice.

You have turned old grievances to new friendships, within your borders and beyond. You have forged landmark treaties with Hungary and Ukraine. You have brought ethnic Hungarians into democratic government for the first time. You are giving minorities a greater stake in your common future. Together you are doing something that people all over the world must do; you are reaching across the lines that divide you to build one Romania. And for that, I salute you.

You have shown the way of responsible leadership here in your own region. In Bosnia, it was Romanian engineers who repaired the first train crossing the Sava River so that critical aid could reach the Bosnian people after years of deprivation. In Albania, Romania's peacekeeping battalion has played a key role in promoting stability and securing free elections. Your nation, at its own initiative and its own expense, has helped your faltering neighbors get their feet back on the ground. And for that the world salutes you. Of course, there is more work to do. I come here to say that America will do that work with you.

The values that govern Romania today, liberty, openness, tolerance, free markets, these are values shared by the community of democracies Romania is joining. The community includes security cooperation through the Partnership for Peace. It includes strong ties of trade and investment. It includes institutions like the European Union. And, of course, it includes NATO.*

I welcome Romania's deep desire to contribute even more fully to Europe's security and strength. I welcome your desire to join NATO. I want that, too—for Europe, for America, and for you. And I say to you today, stay the course, and Romania will cross that milestone.

To all nations who embrace democracy and reform and wish to share the responsibilities of membership, I reaffirm from this plaza of freedom: the door to NATO is open. It will stay open, and we will help you to walk through it.

*The next three paragraphs were added by National Security Adviser Sandy Berger and me before the president's text went final.

NATO has committed to review aspiring members in 1999. Romania is one of the strongest candidates. And if you stay the course and manifest the love of liberty we all see here today, there can be no stronger candidate. Stay the course. Stay the course. The future is yours.

Thank you.

In the meantime, your President and I have agreed to establish a strategic partnership between our nations, a partnership important to America because Romania is important to America, important in your own right, important as a model in this difficult part of the world. Romania can show the people of this region and, indeed, people throughout the world that there is a better way than fighting and division and repression. It is cooperation and freedom and peace.

Mr. President, citizens of Romania, my visit has been brief, but our friendship will endure the test of time. As long as you proceed down democracy's road, America will walk by your side.

The great Romanian-born playwright Ionesco once said, "There has always been at every living moment of culture a will to renewal." Here in Bucharest, I see that will to renewal all around. I am reminded of the words of your hymn, once forbidden but never forgotten: "Wake Up, Romania." You have shown the world, and you have shown me here today, that Romania has awakened, awakened to democracy, awakened to freedom, awakened to security, awakened to your destiny. And because of you, the world has awakened to Romania. May the light of your freedom shine forever, and may God bless the Romanian people and the future of our two peoples together.

Thank you and God bless you.

On hearing President Clinton's strong endorsement for Romania's joining NATO, the U.S. State Department attendees were taken aback, but the president's words were effective. His assurances of future United States support persuaded Romania that the United States remained a true friend and Romania's best hope for being invited into NATO. President Constantinescu and Zoe Petre's crowd estimates had been way off base: not 60,000 but 500,000 came, and for one reason only—to see and hear the president of the United States. After addressing this enormous crowd, President Clinton was in high spirits. He invited me to join him in his limousine. Large crowds hugged our route the rest of the day. Before going to the residence to meet and greet the American embassy staff, President Clinton stopped briefly at the Peasants Museum housed inside a late-nineteenth-century brick building. I had thought we were going to the more open Village Museum that Hillary visited the year before. It afforded much better "visuals." Pressed by his staff, he agreed to a short stop at the Peasants Museum before heading to the Village Museum, where he climbed in and out of four or five nineteenth-century peasant cottages, asking questions at each step. He was enormously curious about everything and engaged like no one I had ever seen. He could not resist shopping, making three or four purchases in the Village Museum's gift shop and loading up his staff with his purchases.

Back at the residence, he and I were whisked onto the terrace accompanied by presidential music and a formal announcement—"The president of the United States, William Jefferson Clinton, and the American ambassador to Romania, Alfred H. Moses"—to greet the embassy staff and families. I spoke briefly, referring to the previous visits of President Bush and Senator Dole and how pleased we were to welcome the winner of the last two presidential elections. President Clinton, still in high spirits, talked about America's role as the only superpower in the world and the need for our country to remain engaged in Europe and elsewhere in the world. He ended his speech asking the American staff to help him persuade the American public and Congress to fund "American diplomacy," and then worked the rope line, shaking hands, exchanging comments, and posing for pictures, including one with the six-year-old daughter of the embassy valet; she gave the president a turtle wrapped in paper which she assured him was not alive.

President Clinton's trip was the culmination of my service as ambassador. I would leave Romania with him on the presidential plane. I was now physically welded to President Clinton, which meant I could not give proper good-byes to staff and friends. I did manage to shake hands with each member of the embassy's Marine guard, who were standing at attention, some of them crying, and posed for a picture with them in their dress uniforms together with President Clinton. The president and I also said good-bye to the household staff and posed for another group picture.

As we were driving from place to place, President Clinton opened the discussion of NATO by asking me whether I agreed with the decision at Madrid, to which I replied that I had told Strobe Talbott a month before that I thought Romania was two years away. In the interim, we should work to tee up Romania for the next round. Clinton explained that he had decided not to support Romania for NATO expansion, preferring, as he put it, to wait two years, when the Romanian economy would start to recover. "There will then be another two years before Romania formally enters NATO, which should be enough time for the Romanian economy to improve to the point where Romania can spend five percent of GDP on its military." Three percent was the NATO standard. He thought Romania was on the downslope of a J-curve. Once the economy bottomed out and started to pick up, Romania would be able to shoulder the cost of NATO membership. In the meantime, it needed to accelerate economic reform. I agreed, not just because he said it, but because he was right.

President Clinton also talked about his daughter, Chelsea, who was headed for Stanford University in California. Her ambition at the time was to become a physician. The president was surprised that she had chosen Stanford over Yale, where six of her closest friends from high school were going, or Harvard. Chelsea, and Chelsea alone, had made the decision, the president said, after she had meticulously considered every angle. The fact that she was going to California seemed to please the president, who commented that in the past she had been reluctant to be far away, fearing that something might happen to him. Now she was a grown-up and soon would be out on her own. Seeing his daughter off to college was a watershed event for the president, as it is for all parents.

On arriving at the airport, President Clinton was greeted by the official Romanian delegation that had welcomed him on his arrival that morning. As I was about to board the plane to return with the president to Washington, our senior embassy staff arrived in time for hugs and kisses, an emotional time for me as I climbed aboard *Air Force One* for the flight to Copenhagen and, the next day, to Washington. That flight ended my service as American ambassador to Romania.

I returned to Bucharest the following November to be the guest of honor at the Marine Ball and thereafter from time to time for consultations, most importantly in December 2000, following Iliescu's reelection as president. The State Department dispatched me to Bucharest to deliver confidential messages to incoming President Iliescu and Prime Minister Nastase, which helped persuade them to reappoint Mugur Isarescu as governor of the National Bank of Romania. I was also invited by private citizen Bill Clinton to accompany him and Chelsea Clinton on a visit to Romania in May 2005 that included a friendly meeting with President Basescu at Cotroceni.

Once back in Washington, I resumed my career as a partner in the law firm of Covington & Burling and, along with Carol, welcomed a growing brood of grandchildren that numbered eleven by the time Carol died of ovarian cancer in February 2004.

Epilogue

Romanian History in the Making

On November 23, 2002, standing under an umbrella in a Bucharest downpour, President George W. Bush welcomed Romania into NATO. Standing next to the U.S. president was Ion Iliescu, who had been reelected Romania's president for the third time in 2000. In the audience was Emil Constantinescu, Romania's former president, now retired. Romania had come a long way since Christmas Day, 1989, when the country's communist dictator, Nicolae Ceauşescu was executed. The country's democratic institutions were now firmly in place, its economy had seen three years of growth, and per capita income had recovered from the Ceauşescu era. Finally, Romania's "NATO chant" had been heard. It was a full member of the Western alliance, protected by Article 5 of the North Atlantic Treaty and the United States' nuclear umbrella. Romania had stayed the course and the naysayers were in retreat. In 2007 Romania was admitted to the European Union.

The Romanians, an ancient, often maligned people, had long lived on the periphery of Europe, overshadowed or overwhelmed by the great events that took place around them. Now, in the twenty-first century, Romania was an integral part of Europe and a strategic partner of the United States.

Romania's fate could have been different. After the fall of Ceauşescu, Romania's future hung in the balance. There were those within and outside Romania who would have moved the country in a different direction, forsaken democracy, and turned Romania inward and away from the West. To paraphrase Tweedledee, "That which might have been, could have been, but as it was, it wasn't." Why? Principal credit goes to former presidents Ion Iliescu and Emil Constantinescu and to the Romanian people. Iliescu and Constantinescu were very different in background, political beliefs, and even in temperament, and yet they shared a common vision of Romania's future. Both of them were firmly committed to a Romania that was free, independent, and closely allied with the West. Each of them moved from an ideological-bound past to recognition of the legitimacy of competing ideas. For Iliescu, it meant leaving communism behind. For Constantinescu, it meant moving beyond a Christian Democratic ideology that was largely mired in the past.

Romania is not a poster child. Its faults and weaknesses are there for all to see, but in a world that is increasingly divided and less sure of its future, Romania has firmly planted itself on the side of freedom and democracy.

Some words about former presidents Iliescu and Constantinescu bear repeating. Iliescu was an important, if controversial, figure in Romanian history. Constantinescu was less significant, but had a positive influence on the course of Romanian history.

Iliescu assumed power the day Nicolae Ceauşescu fled Bucharest, serving first as head of the National Salvation Front and then as president of Romania, from May 1990 to December 1996. He returned as president in December 2000. Barred by the constitution from running for reelection, his political career came to an end at the close of his four-year term in 2004. For much of this time, Iliescu dominated the Romanian political scene and changed the course of Romanian history.

I last saw him in the summer of 2016, when he was eighty-six. He told me he was writing his memoirs, beginning with his days in the communist youth movement. He had passed into history and was no longer a political player.

The Iliescu of yesteryear had many virtues—courage, integrity, humility, and a genuine commitment to build a democratic, egalitarian Romania. Therein lay the problem: Could Romania be both democratic and egalitarian? One or the other had to give and Iliescu did not want Romania to return to its pre–World War II days of gross inequality. His mission, as he saw it, was to protect Romania's workers. He had a visceral distrust of "rich people" and would shrug his shoulders when I said (which I frequently did), "Mr. President, you can't have a prosperous country without rich people." It was this conflict and the two miners' raids that prevented him from being enshrined in Romania's pantheon of heroes.

The son of a railway worker, he was born in 1930 into a family of Communist Party sympathizers. At a time when there were few communists in Romania, he rose rapidly in the party hierarchy until 1971, when he openly criticized Ceaușescu's totalitarian ways. After this his trajectory went the other way. He was serially demoted, ending in 1984 as director of an obscure technical publishing house in Bucharest. By then he was a known party dissident who advocated a more open Romania along the lines of Gorbachev's later perestroika in the Soviet Union and Janos Kadar's "goulash communism" in Hungary.

The group of intellectuals and others who gathered to establish a new political order after Ceaușescu fled lacked experience in governing and quickly turned to Iliescu for leadership. He immediately assumed the dominant role in what became the National Salvation Party and thereafter as president of Romania for ten of the next fourteen years. Initially he was looked upon by many Romanians as the savior of their country, but then things turned ugly.

The opposition parties never accepted Iliescu's legitimacy, claiming that he was a "crypto-communist." Iliescu compounded his problems in a divided country by his complicity in bringing miners to Bucharest in June 1990 to end the occupation of University Square by protesting students. Fifteen months later, the miners returned to Bucharest, leading to the resignation of Prime Minister Petre Roman. The two actions by the miners discredited Iliescu abroad and with many at home. Iliescu justified these actions by the miners claiming that the protesters were seeking to restore fascism, a baseless claim.

President Iliescu was basically pro-reform and anti-corruption. He did not seek personal gain—unusual in Romania—and continued to live modestly with his equally modest wife, Nina, a scientific researcher, in an apartment building with four other units. Ironically, some opposition leaders criticized Iliescu's stated desire to "die a poor man" and accused him of "stupidity."

To be sure, President Iliescu's pro-reform policies were not without contradictions. He had run for president in 1992 promising voters to build a "social market economy," a fuzzy term that combined private property and free enterprise with state regulation to prevent extreme inequality. When he first assumed power in 1989, Iliescu had no practical alternative but to keep the old political and economic bureaucracy in office. There were no others qualified to do the job. In 1996, seven years later, the same people held the majority of positions in Romania's bureaucracy, many of them remaining in place during Constantinescu's four-year presidency.

After the initial wave of privatizations in the early 1990s, the pace of privatization slowed. Caught in a political vise between his pro-reform, pro-Western policies and his fear of rapid change and inequality, President Iliescu failed to win over the political opposition and alienated key parts of his political base, leading to his defeat in late 1996 by Constantinescu.

President Constantinescu had a different set of problems. In carrying out his right-of-center policies, he did not have to deal with the same inherent contradictions as Iliescu, but he lacked political experience and probably political shrewdness. Initially he tried to succeed politically by emphasizing his conviction that he was morally right in his political beliefs—only to have to backtrack when his campaign promises were rejected by the public or proved to be hollow campaign rhetoric. For example, part of Constantinescu's "Contract with Romania" was to bring back King Michael I, but when the polls showed that only 20 percent of Romanians favored the restoration of the monarchy, Constantinescu dropped his pledge. Likewise, during the 1996 campaign, Constantinescu repeatedly stated that his party had 12,000 people in training ready to take over the reins of government. When it turned out there was no one in training, he, like Iliescu, was stuck with the bureaucracy inherited from communist days.

Perhaps Constantinescu's greatest contribution to Romania's place in history was his election as president and the smooth transition from Iliescu to him, ushering in a tradition of peaceful transitions of power in a country with a long prior history of totalitarian rule and political violence.

When Constantinescu left office, Romania's economy had grown from the bottom up, private enterprise had taken hold. Despite some bumps in the road along the way, the country was on the road to economic expansion and relative prosperity. Most important: both Iliescu and Constantinescu remained true to their commitment to build a Western-style democracy in Romania and to make Romania a permanent member of the Western family of nations. Post-Ceauşescu Romania did not turn back the political clock to the pre-communist era. It did not restore the monarchy, and after the elections in 2000, none of the pre–World War II political parties has been represented in Parliament. In that sense Romania has looked ahead, not back.

If Presidents Iliescu and Constantinescu deserve credit, so, too, does the United States. Following the fall of communism in Eastern Europe, our country leapt into action. It was a shining moment for the United States. Looking only at Romania, we gave of ourselves to rebuild a nation devastated by communism. Our embassy staff in Bucharest was part of that effort. Ultimately the triumph was not ours, it was Romania's triumph. But in a larger sense, it was a triumph for human welfare and individual freedom.

Romania suffered much under fascism and communism. After Ceauşescu was gone, Romanians wanted democracy and a free economy. In the ensuing twenty-nine years, Romania has not deviated from this path and is not likely to do so in the foreseeable future. Some may say Romania had no choice; it had to rejoin the West. Most things are clear in hindsight, but in December 1989 Romania's fate was unknown. After Ceauşescu fell, the United States alone had the credibility, resources, and goodwill to take Romania by the hand. In the words of President Clinton: "As long as you proceed down democracy's long road, America will be by your side." In so doing, we helped to preserve the post–World War II order. It remains to be seen whether seventy-three years after the end of World War II our country will preserve that order or undermine it.

I had the good fortune to be the American ambassador to Romania at a time that allowed me to be more than a witness to history. For a brief moment in a far-away country, I helped make it.

Glossary of People and Places

ACHESON, DEAN GOODERHAM: U.S. Secretary of State, 1949–53; senior partner in the Washington, D.C., law firm of Covington & Burling, the author's law firm at the time he was appointed ambassador

ACKERSON, SARAH: USAID project leader for RASDAQ

ADAIR, MARSHALL P.: U.S. Deputy Assistant Secretary of State for Eastern Europe, Balkan and Nordic Affairs

AIKEN, HUGH: CEO, Atchison Casting Corporation

ALBRIGHT, MADELEINE: U.S. Secretary of State, 1997–2001

ALEXANDRIS, CHRISTOS: Greek ambassador to Romania, 1992–97

ANDREI, STEFAN: Romanian Foreign Minister, 1978–85

ANGHELESCU, GHEORGHE: Admiral, Commander of the Romanian Military Navy, 1990–97

ANTONESCU, ION: Marshal, Romanian army; Romanian Prime Minister, 1940–44

ASMUS, RONALD D.: U.S. Deputy Assistant Secretary of State for European Affairs, 1997–2000

ATHENEE PALACE HOTEL: Historic hotel in Bucharest, remodeled as Hilton International 1995–97

AUGUSTINE, NORMAN R.: CEO, Lockheed Martin Corporation, 1995–97

BABEŞ-BOLYAI UNIVERSITY: Largest university in Romania, located in Cluj

BABIUC, VICTOR: Romanian Minister of National Defense, 1996–2000

BACHE, ANDREW: U.K. ambassador to Romania, 1992–96

BAKER, JAMES A.: U.S. Secretary of State, 1989–92

BALANZINO, SERGIO: Italian, Deputy Secretary General of NATO, 1994

BALE, PETER: Reuters journalist in Bucharest during the author's tenure

BANCA DACIA FELIX: Romanian bank in Cluj, taken over by an Israeli group in 1997; entered bankruptcy in 2000

BACANU, MIHAI: Editor-in-chief of *Romania Libera*, Bucharest newspaper

BARNES, HARRY G., JR.: U.S. ambassador to Romania, 1974–77; Chairman and Trustee of the Romanian American Enterprise Fund, 1996–2010

BASESCU, TRAIAN: Romanian Minister of Transport, 1996–2000; President of Romania, 2004–14

BAUCUS, MAX: U.S. senator, Montana (Dem.), 1978–2014

BAVARIA, ED: Deputy President of Douglas Aircraft Co. (division of McDonnell Douglas)

BECK, ERNEST: *Wall Street Journal Europe* reporter

BEGIN, MENACHEM: Israeli Prime Minister, 1977–83

BERGER, SAMUEL ("SANDY") R.: U.S. Deputy National Security Adviser, 1993–97; U.S. National Security Adviser, 1997–2001

BIDEN, JOSEPH: U.S. senator, Delaware (Dem.), 1973–2009; U.S. Vice President, 2009–17

BLANDIANA, ANA: Romanian poet, essayist, and human rights advocate

BLINKEN, DONALD: U.S. ambassador to Hungary, 1994–97

BOGDAN, CORNELIU: Romanian ambassador to the United States, 1967–76

BOTEZ, MAGDA: Wife of Mihai Botez

BOTEZ, MIHAI: Romanian ambassador to the United Nations, 1992–94, and to the United States, 1994–95

BOYD, ALBERTA ("BERT"): Wife of Frank Boyd Jr.

BOYD, FRANK, JR.: U.S. Army colonel and U.S. military attaché, Bucharest, 1993–96

BOYER, BERNARD: French ambassador to Romania, 1993–97

BRATIANU, GHEORGHE: Son of Ion, died in Sighet Prison, 1953

BRATIANU, ION I. C.: Five-time Romanian Prime Minister, 1909–27; led Romanian delegation to Paris Peace Conference after World War I

BREZHNEV, LEONID: General Secretary of the Central Committee, Communist Party, Soviet Union, 1964-82

BRODY, KENNETH D.: President and Chairman, Export-Import Bank, 1993–95

BRONFMAN, EDGAR M.: President, World Jewish Congress, 1981–2007

BROWN, GEORGE HANKS ("HANK"): U.S. senator, Colorado (Rep.), 1991–97

BROWN, RONALD H.: U.S. Secretary of Commerce, 1993–96

BRUCAN, SILVIU: Romanian ambassador to the United States, 1955; Romanian ambassador to the United Nations, 1959–62

BRZEZINSKI, ZBIGNIEW: U.S. National Security Adviser, 1977–81

BURG, AVRAHAM ("AVRUM"): Chairman, Jewish Agency, 1995–99; Speaker of Israeli Knesset, 1999–2003

BURNS, NICHOLAS: U.S. ambassador to Greece, 1997–2001; U.S. ambassador to NATO, 2001–05; Under Secretary of State for Political Affairs, 2005–08

BUSH, BARBARA: First Lady of the United States, 1989–93

BUSH, GEORGE H. W.: President of the United States, 1989–93

BUTEYKO, ANTON: Ukraine First Deputy Minister of Foreign Affairs, 1995–98; later ambassador to the United States

BUYER, STEPHEN E.: U.S. congressman, Indiana (Rep.), 1993-2011

CAJAL, DR. NICOLAE: President, Romanian Jewish Federation, 1994–2004

CALCIU-DUMITREASA, FATHER GHEORGHE: Romanian Orthodox priest and dissident imprisoned by communist regime; later served as a priest in Holy Cross Romanian Orthodox Church in Virginia

CAMDESSUS, MICHEL: Managing Director, International Monetary Fund, 1987–2000

CAROL I, KING (AND QUEEN ELIZABETH): Romanian ruler, 1866–1914

CAROL II, KING (AND PRINCESS HELEN OF GREECE): Romanian ruler, 1930–40

CAROTHERS, THOMAS: Vice President for Studies, Carnegie Endowment for International Peace

CARP, MIHAI: Special Assistant to American ambassador to Romania, 1995–97

CARSON, JOHNNIE: U.S. ambassador to Uganda, 1991–94; U.S. ambassador to Zimbabwe; 1997–97; U.S. ambassador to Kenya, 1999–2003; Assistant Secretary of State for Bureau of African Affairs, 2009–13

CARTER, BILLY: Younger brother of President Jimmy Carter

CARTER, JIMMY: President of the United States, 1977–81

CASA DE ESPERANZA: Orphanage for HIV-positive children, Bucharest

CEAUȘESCU, ELENA: Wife of Romanian president Nicolae Ceausescu

CEAUȘESCU, NICOLAE: General Secretary, Romanian Communist Party, 1965–89; President of Romania, 1974–89

CEAUSU, DUMITRU: Romanian State Secretary, 1993–97; UN Committee on Economic, Social and Cultural Rights, 1997–2004

CEMETERY, MERRY (SAPANȚA): Picturesque cemetery in northern Romania

CHALY, OLEKSANDR: Ukraine ambassador to Romania, 1995–98

CHEBELEU, TRAIAN: Spokesman for and diplomatic adviser to Romanian President Iliescu

CHENEY, RICHARD: Vice President of the United States, 2001–09

CHERNOMYRDIN, VIKTOR: Prime Minister of Russia, 1992–98

CHIRAC, JACQUES: President of France, 1995–2007

CHIUZBAIAN, GAVRIL IOSIF: Romanian Justice Minister, 1994–96

CHORAL SYNAGOGUE: Historic seat of the chief rabbi of Romania, Bucharest

CHRISTOPHER, WARREN: U.S. Secretary of State, 1993–97

CHUMAK, VOLODYMYR: Head of Department of Foreign Policy, Ukraine National Institute of Strategic Studies, Kiev

CIOFLINA, DUMITRU: Chief of the Romanian Army General Staff, 1991–96

CIORBEA, VICTOR: Prime Minister of Romania, 1996–98

CIUMARA, MIRCEA: Finance Minister of Romania, 1996–97

CLIFT, DENIS: National Security Adviser to Vice President Walter Mondale, 1977–81

CLINTON, CHELSEA: Daughter of President and Mrs. Clinton

CLINTON, HILLARY: First Lady of the United States, 1993–2001; U.S. Secretary of State, 2009–2013

CLINTON, WILLIAM JEFFERSON: President of the United States, 1993–2001

CODREANU, CORNELIU: Founder and leader of the Romanian Iron Guard

COHEN, WILLIAM S.: U.S. Secretary of Defense, 1997–2001

COMANECI, NADIA: Romanian gymnast and five-time Olympic gold medalist

CONNER, BART: American gymnast and two-time Olympic gold medalist

CONOVER, BILL: American businessman in Romania

CONSTANTINESCU, EMIL: President of Romania, 1996–2000

COOK, ROBIN: U.K. Shadow Foreign Secretary, 1994–97; Secretary of State for Foreign and Commonwealth Affairs, 1997–2001

COOPER, JEROME GARY: U.S. ambassador to Jamaica, 1994–97

COPOSU, CORNELIU: Founding leader of Romanian Christian Democratic National Peasants' Party, 1989–95

COŞEA, MIRCEA: Romania Minister of Economic Reform, 1993–96

COSMA, MIRON: Labor union head of Jiu Valley coal miners

CRABBIE, CHRISTOPHER: U.K. ambassador to Romania, 1996–2000

CRANE, PHILIP M.: U.S. congressman, Illinois (Rep.), 1969–2005

CRANER, LORNE: President, International Republican Institute, 1993–2001

CUTLER, LLOYD: White House Counsel, 1979–81, 1994

CUZA, ALEXANDRU ION: First prince of united Romania

D'AMATO, ALFONSE M. ("AL"): U.S. senator, New York (Rep.), 1981–99

DALEY, WILLIAM M.: U.S. Secretary of Commerce, 1997–2000

DANFORTH, JOHN: U.S. senator, Missouri (Rep.), 1976–95

DASCHLE, THOMAS: U.S. senator, South Dakota (Dem.), 1987–2005

DATCULESCU, PETRE: Romanian political pollster

DAVIS, JOHN: U.S. ambassador to Romania, 1992–94

DEGERATU, GENERAL CONSTANTIN: Deputy Chief of Operations Division of the Romanian Army General Staff, 1995–97; Chief of Romanian Army General Staff, 1997–2000

DIACONESCU, ION: Co-founded Christian-Democratic National Peasants' Party, 1989; Speaker, Chamber of Deputies, 1996–2000

DIEHL, JACKSON: Journalist and editor, the *Washington Post*

DIMA, EMIL: President, Romanian State Ownership Fund, 1993–96

DIMITRIU, SORIN: Director, Romanian State Ownership Fund, 1997–99

DINE, THOMAS A.: Assistant Administrator for Europe and the New Independent States of Eurasia at USAID, 1993–97

DOLE, ROBERT: U.S. senator, Kansas (Rep.), 1961–96

DONNELLY, CHRIS: NATO Special Adviser for Central and Eastern European Affairs, 1989–2003

DRACULA: Fictional character in Gothic horror novel by Irish author Bram Stoker

DREW, NELSON: U.S. Air Force colonel and European Affairs Staff director at National Security Council; killed in auto accident in Yugoslavia in 1995

DUCARU, SORIN: Romanian ambassador to the United States, 2001–06; Permanent Representative of Romania to the United Nations, 2000–01; Permanent Representative of Romania to NATO, 2006–13

DUGUAY, GILLES HORACE J.: Canadian ambassador to Romania, 1995–98

EHRENWALD, PETER: International sales director, the Boeing Company

EINIK, MICHAEL: Deputy Chief of Mission, U.S. embassy, Bucharest, 1995–99

EISENHOWER, DWIGHT D.: President of the United States, 1953–61

EIZENSTAT, STUART E.: U.S. ambassador to the European Union, 1993–96; Under Secretary of Commerce for International Trade, 1996–97; U.S. Under Secretary of State for Economic, Business and Agricultural Affairs, 1997–99; U.S. Deputy Secretary of the Treasury, 1999–2001

EMANUEL, RAHM: Senior Adviser to President Clinton, 1993–98

ENESCU, GEORGE: Romanian composer

FAHD, KING: Saudi Arabia's ruling monarch, 1982–2005

FEINE, ZVI: Director of Joint Distribution Committee programs in Eastern Europe

FERDINAND, KING (AND QUEEN MARIE): Romania's ruling monarch, 1914–27

FILDERMAN, WILHELM: Head of Romanian Jewish community, 1919–47

FISHER, JOSEPH: U.S. congressman, Virginia (Dem.), 1975–81

FLORANCE, COLDEN: Washington, D.C., architect

FOGG, KAREN: Head, European Commission Delegation, Bucharest, 1993–98

FOGLEMAN, RONALD R. (AND MISS JANE): U.S. Air Force Chief of Staff, 1994–97

FORD, GERALD: President of the United States, 1974–77

FOXMAN, ABRAHAM: National Director, Anti-Defamation League, 1987–2015

FRANK, MONIQUE: Netherlands ambassador to Romania

FRASURE, ROBERT: Deputy Assistant Secretary of State for European and Canadian Affairs, 1994–95; died in car crash near Sarajevo, Bosnia, 1995

FRIED, DANIEL: Staff of U.S. National Security Council, 1993–97; U.S. ambassador to Poland, 1997–2000; U.S. Assistant Secretary of State for European and Eurasian Affairs, 2005–09

FRIENDLY, NICK: Head of President Clinton's advance team in Bucharest, July 1997

FUNAR, GEORGHE: Mayor of Cluj, 1992–2004

FUNDERBURK, DAVID: U.S. ambassador to Romania, 1981–85; U.S. congressman, North Carolina (Rep.), 1995–97

GAFFNEY, FRANK: Founder, President, and CEO of Center for Security Policy, Washington, D.C.

GARNER, DAVID: Citibank representative, Bucharest, 1996–97

GAVRILESCU, DINU: Assistant to Romanian Chamber of Deputies President Adrian Nastase

GEOANA, MIRCEA: Romanian ambassador to the United States, 1996–2000; Romanian Foreign Minister, 2000–04

GEORGESCU, FLORIN: Romanian Minister of Finance, 1992–96

GHEORGHIU-DEJ, GHEORGHE: Communist leader of Romania, 1947–65

GHERMAN, OLIVIU: President of Romanian Senate, 1992–96

GILMAN, BENJAMIN: U.S. congressman, New York (Rep.), 1973–2003

GINGRICH, NEWT: U.S. congressman, Georgia (Rep.), 1979–99

GORBACHEV, MIKHAIL: General Secretary of the Communist Party, Soviet Union, 1985–91

GORE, ALBERT: Vice President of the United States, 1993–2001

GOTT, IZU: Director, Romanian Jewish Choir

GRASSLEY, CHARLES: U.S. senator, Iowa (Rep.), 1981–

GREAT SYNAGOGUE: Historic synagogue, Bucharest, Romania

GREEN, DORA: Wife of Joshua Green

GREEN, JOSHUA: IMF representative, Bucharest, Romania

GROSSMAN, MARC: U.S. ambassador to Turkey, 1995–97; Assistant Secretary of State for European and Canadian Affairs, 1997–2000; Under Secretary of State for Political Affairs, 2001–05

HACHOMI, EMILY: Israel Deputy Chief of Mission, Romania

HACHOMI, ITZAK: Husband of Emily

HAGI, GHEORGHE: Romania's most famous soccer player

HALAICU, CRIN: Mayor of Bucharest, 1992–96

HARDYMON, JAMES F.: Chairman and CEO, Textron, 1993–98

HARRIS, DAVID: Executive Director, the American Jewish Committee, 1990–

HARTMANN, ARNA: World Bank representative, Bucharest, Romania

HAWLEY, GENERAL RICHARD E.: U.S. Air Force general

HELMS, JESSE, JR.: U.S. senator, North Carolina (Rep.), 1973–2003

HOAGLAND, JIM: Journalist and editor, the *Washington Post*

HOLBROOKE, RICHARD: U.S. Assistant Secretary of State for European and Canadian Affairs, 1994–96

HORBULYN, VOLODYMYR: National Security Adviser to the President of Ukraine, 1994–96

HORN, GYULA: Prime Minister of Hungary, 1994-98

HREBENCIUC, VIOREL: Head of General Secretariat of Romanian Government, 1993–96

HUNTER, ROBERT E.: U.S. ambassador to NATO, 1993–98

HUSSEIN, KING: King of Jordan, 1952–99

ILIE, VASILE (PREFECT OF SUCEAVA): Prefect of Suceava Judet

ILIESCU, ION: President of Romania, 1990–96, 2000–04

IOANID, RADU: U.S. Holocaust Memorial Museum, Washington, D.C.

IOHANNIS, KLAUS: President of Romania, 2014–

IONESCU, CONSTANTIN DUDU: Romanian Deputy Minister of Defense, 1996–98

ISARESCU, MUGUR: Governor of the National Bank of Romania, 1990–

JACOBS, SUSAN: Consul-General, U.S. embassy, Bucharest, 1995–98

JOHNSON, RALPH R.: U.S. ambassador to Slovakia, 1996–99

JOINER, WEBB: President, Bell Helicopter, 1991–95; Chairman, 1995–98

JOULWAN, GENERAL GEORGE: U.S. Army general, Commander-in-Chief, U.S. European Command and Supreme Allied Commander, 1993–97

KAHN, PETER: Publisher, the *Wall Street Journal*

KAISER, ROBERT G.: Managing Editor, the *Washington Post*, 1991–98

KENNELLY, BARBARA: U.S. congresswoman, Connecticut (Dem.), 1982–99

KINKEL, KLAUS: German Foreign Minister, 1992–98

KIRK, ROGER: U.S. ambassador to Romania, 1985–89

KIRKLAND, IRENA: Wife of Lane Kirkland

KIRKLAND, LANE: President, AFL-CIO, 1979–95

KOHL, HELMUT: German Chancellor, 1982–98

KORNBLUM, JOHN C.: U.S. Assistant Secretary of State for European Affairs and Special Envoy to the Balkans, 1995–97; U.S. ambassador to Germany, 1997–2001

KOVÁCS, LÁSZLÓ: Hungarian Foreign Minister, 1994–98

KRUZEL, JOSEPH J.: U.S. Deputy Assistant Secretary of Defense for European and NATO Policy, 1993–95; killed in auto accident in Yugoslavia, 1995

KRYS, SHELDON: U.S. Foreign Service officer, ambassador, and Co-director of State Department Ambassador School

KUCHMA, LEONID: President of Ukraine, 1994–2005

KWAŚNIEWSKI, ALEKSANDER: President of Poland, 1995–2005

LAKE, ANTHONY: U.S. National Security Adviser, 1993–97

LANTOS, ANNETTE: Wife of Tom Lantos

LANTOS, TOM: U.S. congressman, California (Dem.), 1981–2008

LAUDER, RONALD: Son of Estée Lauder, founder of Estee Lauder Company; U.S. ambassador to Austria, 1986–87

LAZAR, GILDA: Romanian Foreign Ministry spokesperson, 1997–99

LERMAN, MILES: Chairman, U.S. Holocaust Memorial Museum, 1993–2000

LEVANON, NEHEMIAH: Adviser to Israel's Prime Minister in matters affecting Jewish emigration from Romania

LI FENGLIN: Chinese ambassador to Romania, 1991–95

LIEBERMAN, JOSEPH: U.S. senator, Connecticut (Dem.), 1989–2013

LINOWITZ, SOL: President Carter's personal representative to the Middle East peace negotiations, 1979–81

LIPPMAN, THOMAS: Middle East Bureau chief, the Washington Post

LIVINGSTON, BOB: U.S. congressman, Louisiana (Rep.), 1977–99

LUFT, BOGUMIŁ: Polish ambassador to Romania, 1993–99

LUGAR, RICHARD: U.S. senator, Indiana (Rep.), 1977–2013

LUPESCU, ELENA (MAGDA): Consort and later wife of Romanian King Carol II

MAGUREANU, VIRGIL: Director of Romania's Internal Security Service (SRI), 1990–97

MAJOR, SIR JOHN: British Prime Minister, 1990–97

MALOVANY, YOSSI: Cantor, Fifth Avenue Synagogue, New York, 1973–

MANIU, IULIU: Co-founder, Romania's National Peasants' Party; Romanian Prime Minister, 1928–33

MARGARETA, PRINCESS: Eldest child of King Michael I and Queen Anne of Romania

MARKO, BELA: Long-time head of ethnic Hungarian political party in Romania, UDMR

MARTON, KATI: Wife of Richard Holbrooke

MCCAIN, JOHN: U.S. senator, Arizona (Rep.), 1987–

MCDONNELL, JOHN: Chairman of McDonnell Douglas, 1988–97 (until its merger with Boeing in 1997)

MEAD, DANA G.: President, chairman, and CEO, Tenneco, Inc., 1992–2000

MEČIAR, VLADIMIR: Prime Minister of Slovakia, 1990–91, 1992–94, 1994–98

MELEŞCANU, TEODOR: Romanian Minister of Foreign Affairs, 1992–96, 2017–

MEYER, MARK: Founder and president, Romanian-American Chamber of Commerce

MIKVA, ABNER: Chief Judge, U.S. Court of Appeals for the District of Columbia Circuit, 1991–94; counsel to President Clinton, 1994–95

MILLER, WILLIAM G.: U.S. ambassador to Ukraine, 1993–98

MILO, AVI: Israeli ambassador to Romania

MILOŠEVIĆ, SLOBODAN: First president of Serbia, 1991–97

MOTLEY, LANGHORNE: U.S. Foreign Service officer, ambassador, and Co-director of State Department Ambassador School

MURESAN, SEVER: Romanian Davis Cup tennis player; later president of Banca Dacia Felix

NASTASE, ADRIAN: President, Romanian Chamber of Deputies, 1992–96; Prime Minister of Romania, 2000–04

NASTASE, DANA: Spouse of Adrian Nastase

NEGRITOIU, MISU: Adviser to Romanian President Iliescu for economic and reform issues

NICOLAE, NICOLAE M.: Romanian ambassador to United States, 1976–78

NIMETZ, MATTHEW: Counselor, U.S. State Department, 1977–79

NIXON, RICHARD M.: President of the United States, 1969–74

NYE, JOSEPH S., JR.: Assistant Secretary of Defense for International Security Affairs, 1994–96

OGRYZKO, VOLODYMYR: Director, Foreign Policy Department, under Ukrainian President Kuchma

ORTIZ, SOLOMON: U.S. congressman, Texas (Dem.), 1983–2011

OSTROVENKO, YEVGENY: Russian ambassador to Romania

PALMER, MARK: U.S. ambassador to Hungary, 1986–90

PAPAS, CLAUDE: General manager of Procter & Gamble operations in Romania

PAŞCU, IOAN MIRCEA: State Secretary for Defense Policy and International Relations, Romanian Ministry of National Defense, 1993–96

PAUKER, ANA: Foreign Minister of Romania, 1947–52

PAUNESCU, GEORGE: Romanian businessman and first President of RASDAQ

PELL, CLAIBORNE: U.S. senator, Rhode Island (Dem.), 1961–97

PELLETREAU, NANCY: U.S. Consul General, Bucharest, Romania, 1992–95

PENDIUC, TUDOR: Mayor of Piteşti, Romania, 1992–2016

PEPPER, JOHN E., JR.: Chairman and CEO, Procter & Gamble, 1995–2002

PERES, SHIMON: President of Israel, 2007–14; former Prime Minister, Foreign Affairs Minister, Defense Minister, Finance Minister, and Transportation Minister

PERRY, WILLIAM: U.S. Secretary of Defense, 1994–97

PETRE, ZOE: Presidential aide on foreign affairs to Romanian President Constantinescu, 1996–2000

PFAFF, WILLIAM: Op-ed columnist, *International Herald Tribune*

POPESCU-TĂRICEANU, CĂLIN: Romanian Minister of Industry and Commerce, 1996–97

POWELL, GENERAL COLIN: Chairman, U.S. Joint Chiefs of Staff, 1989–93; U.S. Secretary of State, 2001–05

PRITZKER, JAY: Philanthropist and co-founder, Hyatt Hotels Corporation

RABIN, YITZHAK: Prime Minister of Israel, 1974–77, 1992–95

RACEANU, MIRCEA: First Secretary, Romanian embassy, Washington, D.C., 1974–77; later served in Romanian Foreign Ministry; indicted for treason by Ceauşescu regime; became a U.S. citizen in 1992

RAMSEY, LOUIS: Chairman and CEO, Simmons First National Bank, Pine Bluff, Arkansas

RATIU, ION: Vice President, Romanian National Peasants' Party, founder of *Romanul Liber* (English/Romanian monthly newspaper), co-founder of Romanian newspapaper *Cotidianul*

REDMAN, CHARLES: U.S. ambassador to Germany, 1994–96

REED, JOHN S.: Chairman, Citibank/Citicorp, 1984–2000

RICKERT, JONATHAN: Deputy Chief of Mission, U.S. embassy, Bucharest, 1993–95

RIDGWAY, ROZANNE: U.S. Assistant Secretary of State for European and Canadian Affairs, 1985–89

RIFKIND, MALCOLM: U.K. Minister of Defense, 1992–95

RODHAM, TONY: Brother of Hillary Rodham Clinton

ROMAN, PETRE: Romanian Prime Minister, 1989–91; later Chairman of Romania's Democratic Party (PD)

RORVIG, RICHARD: Economic Affairs Counselor, U.S. embassy, Bucharest, 1994–97

ROSEN, MOSES DAVID: Chief Rabbi of Romania, 1948–94

ROSENFELD, STEPHEN S.: Senior editor, the *Washington Post*

ROSENNE, MEIR: Israeli ambassador to the United States, 1983–87

ROSSBACH, ANTON: German ambassador to Romania, 1993–96

RUBIN, ROBERT: U.S. Secretary of the Treasury, 1995–99

RUBINSTEIN, ELYAKIM: Deputy Chief of Mission, Israeli embassy, Washington, D.C., 1985–86; later vice president, Supreme Court of Israel

ŞAFRAN, ALEXANDRU: Chief Rabbi of Romania, 1940–48

SARBU, ADRIAN: Head of Romania's PRO-TV

SCHIFTER, RICHARD: Special Assistant, U.S. National Security Council, 1993–2001

SCHMIDT, CARL: Career Foreign Service officer, U.S. State Department

SCHNEIER, ARTHUR: Senior Rabbi, Park East Synagogue, New York

SCHULZE, RICHARD: U.S. congressman, Pennsylvania (Rep.), 1975–93

SCHIFTER, RICHARD: Special Assistant, U.S. National Security Council, 1993–2001

SEVERIN, ADRIAN: Romanian Foreign Minister, 1996-97

SHALIKASHVILI, GENERAL JOHN: Chairman, U.S. Joint Chiefs of Staff and Supreme Allied Commander, 1993–97

SHOPPA, LLOYD: President, Bell Helicopter, 1995–97

SHTEYERMAN, RABBI JACOB: Joint Representative, Kiev

SHULTZ, GEORGE: U.S. Secretary of State, 1982–89

SIMON, PAUL: U.S. senator, Illinois (Dem.), 1985–97

SIMONS, THOMAS W., JR.: Career Foreign Service officer, U.S. ambassador to Poland, 1990–93

SINGER, ISRAEL: Secretary General, World Jewish Congress, 1986–2001

SION, MIHAI: Romanian Consul-General, Los Angeles, California, 1994–98; "foster son" of Ion Iliescu

SLOCOMBE, WALTER B.: U.S. Under Secretary of Defense for Policy, 1994–2001

SMITH, CHRISTOPHER H.: U.S. congressman, New Jersey (Rep.), 1981–

SMITH, JED: U.S. Treasury financial expert

SOLBERG, SARAH: Director, General Services Officer, U.S. embassy, Bucharest, 1993–96

SOMOGYI, FERENC: Hungarian Deputy Foreign Minister, 1994–97

SPECTRE, GEORGE: Associate Director, B'nai B'rith, Washington, D.C.

SPENCE, FLOYD: U.S. congressman, South Carolina (Rep.), 1971–2001

SPINEANU, ULM: Romanian Minister of Economic Reform, 1996–98

SPITZER, JACK J.: President, B'nai B'rith International, 1978–82

SPOLAR, CHRISTINE: Correspondent, the *Washington Post*

STEVENSON, ADLAI, III: U.S. senator, Illinois (Dem.), 1970–81

STOICA, VALERIU: Romanian Minister of Justice, 1996–2000

STOLOJAN, THEODOR: Romanian Prime Minister, 1991–92

TAHER, FATHI: Kuwaiti businessman active in Bucharest; worked closely with the U.S. embassy in building the American School

TALBOTT, STROBE: U.S. Deputy Secretary of State, 1994–2001

TALISMAN, MARK: Washington Director, Council of Jewish Federations

TALPES, IOAN: Director of Romanian External Security Service (SIE), 1992–97

TARACILA, DORU IOAN: Romanian Minister of Interior, 1994–96

TARNOFF, PETER: U.S. Under Secretary of State for Political Affairs, 1993–97

TEITELBAUM, JOEL: Founder and first Grand Rabbi of the ultra-Orthodox Satmar Hasidim

TEMEŞAN, RAZVAN: President of the Romanian bank Bancorex, 1992–97

TENET, GEORGE J.: Director, U.S. Central Intelligence Agency, 1997–2004

TEOCTIST, ARAPAŞU: Patriarch, Romanian Orthodox Church, 1986–2007

TERRE DES HOMMES: Swiss relief agency caring for street children in Romania

TINCA, GHEORGHE: Romanian Minister of National Defense, 1994–96

ŢIRIAC, ION: Romanian Davis Cup tennis player and later businessman

TÖKÉS, BISHOP LÁSZLÓ: Bishop, Hungarian Church in Romania. His removal by Ceauşescu forces led to Timisoara demonstration and massacre, December 1989

TUDOR, CORNELIU VADIM: Co-founder and head of Greater Romanian Party (PRM); Romanian senator, 1992–2008

UDOVENKO, HENNADIY: Ukrainian Minister of Foreign Affairs, 1994–98

UNDERSTEIN, BOB: American businessman representing Marriott and other companies in Bucharest

VACAROIU, NICOLAE: Prime Minister of Romania, 1992–96

VALENTI, JACK: President, Motion Picture Association of America, 1966–2004

VAN DER STOEL, MAX: High Commissioner on National Minorities of the Organization for Security and Cooperation in Europe, 1993–2001

VAN STEENBERGEN, IGNACE: Belgian ambassador to Romania, 1993–95

VANIK, CHARLES: U.S. congressman, Ohio (Dem.), 1955–81

VASILE, RADU: Member of political party PNT-CD; Prime Minister of Romania, 1998–99

VITEAZUL, MIHAI: Romania's legendary "Michael the Brave"

VOICULESCU, DAN: Romanian businessman; former Securitate operator in Cyprus

WALD, ROBERT L.: Chairman, Romanian American Enterprise Fund, 1993–95

WEIZMAN, EZER: President of Israel, 1993–2000

WENICK, MARTIN: Career Foreign Service officer, U.S. State Department

WHITEHEAD, JOHN C.: U.S. Deputy Secretary of State, 1985–89

WIDNALL, SHEILA: U.S. Secretary of the Air Force, 1993–97

WIESEL, ELIE: Romanian-born Nobel laureate

WOLF, FRANK R.: U.S. congressman, Virginia (Rep.), 1981–2015

WOLFENSOHN, JAMES: President, World Bank, 1995–2005

ZAHARIA, GENERAL DAN: Romanian Deputy Defense Minister

ZANC, GRIGORE: Prefect, Cluj County, Romania, 1990–96

Index

Abortion, 75–76, 107, 341
Acheson, Dean G., 38
Ackerson, Sarah, 261
Adair, Marshall, 168, 221, 227
Adoptions, 243
AFL-CIO, 40
Aggrey, Reuben, 23
Aiken, Hugh, 207–08
Albright, Madeleine, 41, 309, 318, 328, 330–33, 347, 349–52
Alexandris, Christos, 339
Ambassador school, 41–42, 60
American International School of Bucharest, 224, 301–02
American Jewish Committee (AJC): author as national president of, 35, 43, 77; and choir visit to Washington D.C., 30; on emigration of Romanian Jews to Israel, 8; executive director of, 5; Iliescu address to, 170; Romanian delegation sent to by, 3; "What Being Jewish Means to Me" series from, 259–60
Amoco, 49, 72, 320
Andrei, Stefan, 13
Anghelescu, Gheorghe, 164
Anti-Semitism: decline of, 35; at diplomatic reception, 97, 98; history in

Romania, 21, 24, 34, 42; in political parties, xx, 20, 43, 50, 182; stereotypes regarding Jews, 13; vandalism of Jewish cemetery, 156. See also Holocaust
Antonescu, Ion: controversial nature of, 51; execution of, 51; and Iron Guard, 50–51; Jewish community under, 18, 325, 334–35; monument proposals in memory of, 58, 87, 106; opposition and overthrow of, 51, 104; rehabilitation of reputation, 79, 112
Ant trade, 212
Appeal of Conscience Foundation, 25
Arad, Moshe, 335
Arms Proliferation Control Agency (APCA), 186–87, 192
Asmus, Ron, 333
"Assessing Democracy Assistance: The Case of Romania" (Carothers), 210
Augustine, Norman, 304–05

Baal Shem Tov, 28
Babiuc, Victor, 280, 283, 289
Bacanu, Mihai, 322
Bache, Andrew, 145
Balanzino, Sergio, 214
Bales, Peter, 161

Banking sector: Banca Agricola, 92, 302; Banca Dacia Felix, 92, 123, 180, 193–94, 294; Banca Tiriac, 92; Bancorex, 92, 236, 254–55; privatization of, 84, 92, 109, 160–61, 282; reform of, 282. *See also* International Bank for Reconstruction and Development; National Bank of Romania; World Bank

Bankruptcy procedure training, 281

Barnes, Harry, 178–79

Basescu, Traian, 244–45, 270, 289, 304, 358

Baucus, Max, 221

Bavaria, Ed, 320

Bechtel, 209

Beck, Ernest, 174–75

Begin, Menachem, 21, 36, 125

Bell Helicopter. *See* Cobra helicopter deal

Berger, Sandy: on candidate for Romanian ambassador, 41; on Clinton (Bill) visit to Romania, 337, 338; on Cyprus special envoy, 335; on Hungarian-Romanian Basic Treaty, 258–59; on Iliescu trip to Washington, D.C., 146, 168; Nastase meeting with, 115; and NATO expansion, 94, 245, 328, 332; support for MFN status for Romania, 222

Berlin Wall, destruction of, xv, 52

Bias. *See* Prejudice and discrimination

Biden, Joseph R., 41, 295

Billygate affair, 39

Birth control. *See* Contraception ban

Bismarck, Otto von, 46

Black Sea: author's tour of shipyards on, 164; deployment of U.S. forces in, 152; NATO presence in, xvii, 214; oil exploration and production rights in, 141–43, 216; territorial disputes in, 141–43, 216, 264–65, 307–10, 313

Blandiana, Ana, 298, 322

Blinken, Donald, 207, 258, 259

B'nai B'rith International, 8, 15, 17, 170

Boeing, 136, 193, 195, 304

Bogdan, Corneliu, 15–16, 21, 24

Bogdan, Radu, 204

Bond financing, 192, 195–96, 210

Bosnian civil war (1992–1995), 125, 159–60, 211–12, 250

Botez, Magda, 154

Botez, Mihai, 64, 97, 106–07, 147, 154, 298

Boyd, Alberta, 74

Boyd, Frank, Jr., 73–74, 80

Boyer, Bernard, 204, 223, 268, 275, 280, 305–06, 345

Bratianu, Gheorghe, 57, 104, 257, 298

Bratianu, Ionel, 57, 257

Brody, Kenneth, 171

Bronfman, Edgar, 30, 177

Brown, Hank, 170, 221, 222

Brown, Ronald H., 95, 96, 158, 172

Browning, Robert, 275

Brucan, Silviu, 57, 129–31

Brzezinski, Zbigniew, 13, 82, 93, 259

Bureau of European Affairs at State, 45

Burg, Avram, 26

Burns, Nicholas, 290–91

Bush, Barbara, xix, 123–24

Bush, George H. W., xix, 31, 113, 123–26, 179–80, 341

Bush, George W., 359

Buteyko, Victor, 309, 312–13

Buyer, Steve, 163

Cajal, Nicolae, 154, 162

Calciu-Dumitreasa, Gheorghe, 111

Camdessus, Michel, 159, 171, 173, 189, 284, 292, 327

Capital markets program, 109, 148, 151, 168, 261–63

Carol I (king of Romania), 48

Carol II (king of Romania), 49–50

Carothers, Tom, 210, 291

Carp, Mihai, 290, 296, 297, 324, 326, 352

Carson, Johnnie, 41

Carter, Billy, 39, 188

Carter, Jimmy: Bush (G.H.W.) on, 124–25; on emigration of Romanian Jews to Israel, 13–14; Habitat for Humanity supported by, 114; meeting with Ceausescu, 10, 13–14; support for author's ambassadorship from, 39; UN vote on Israeli settlement policy, 36

Catuna, Anuta, 353

CD. *See* Christian Democratic Party

Ceausescu, Elena, 12, 21, 33, 43, 53, 254

Ceausescu, Nicolae: author's meetings with, 13, 20–22, 29, 43; background of,

12; building programs under, 31–32, 254; diplomatic relations established by, 9–10; economy under, 65; on emigration of Romanian Jews to Israel, xv, 8, 12–13, 21; execution of, xv, 33, 53; foreign debt elimination by, 31; Gorbachev on, 315; meetings with U.S. officials, 10, 13–14, 20–22, 24, 29; overthrow of, xx, 11, 58, 125; role models for, 11, 52

Ceausu, Dumitru, 307–09

Central and Eastern Europe: aid programs in, 72–73, 108, 149, 210–11; end of communism in, xv–xvi, xix; free trade association in, 160; Jewish communities in, 6–7, 19–20, 311–12; military capability limitations on, 81; NATO expansion in, 92–94; restitution of Jewish property in, 128–29, 161–62; U.S. objectives in, 43; White House Conference on Trade and Investment in, 94–95. *See also specific countries*

Chaly, Oleksandr, 141, 142, 216, 264, 307–10, 312, 315–16, 346

Chebeleu, Traian: archival assistance by, 226; on arm sales to pariah states, 186; author's meetings with, 111, 183, 248; on Dacia Felix debt, 180; on economic reform, 268; Iliescu campaign preparation by, 234; at NATO ambassadors' lunch, 203; visit to U.S. by, 177–78

Cheney, Richard, 125

Chernomyrdin, Viktor, 93, 137–38

Chilija River navigation rights, 310, 313

China, ambassadors sent to Romania by, 138

Chirac, Jacques, 283, 292, 305–06

Chiuzbaian, Iosif, 101

Choral Synagogue: author's memories of, 19, 70; diplomatic tours of, 161–62; establishment of, 4; evening services at, 22; forceful removal of Jews from, 51; location of, 4, 5, 17; memorial services at, 19, 57, 102

Christian Democratic Party (CD), 55, 58, 61, 197. *See also* PNT-CD

Christopher, Warren, 63, 115, 129, 140, 149–50, 246

Chumak, Volodymyr, 311

Churchill, Winston, 236

Cioflina, Dumitru, 143, 213–14, 226, 280

Ciorbea, Victor: city clean-up projects by, 237; on Cobra helicopter deal, 291–93; dismissal from office, 328; on economic reform program, 302–03; on International Republican Institute, 235; on investment opportunities, 320–21; mayoral experience of, 195, 225, 233, 234; meetings with U.S. officials, 239, 284, 336, 341–42, 346–47; at NATO ambassadors' lunch, 237, 328; press relationships with, 322; as prime minister, 66, 77, 223, 271; visit to U.S. by, 336–37

Ciumara, Mircea, 266, 267, 304, 328

Clift, Denis, 281

Clinton, Bill: authorization of author's ambassadorship, 77, 79; on Cobra helicopter deal, 350; Constantinescu meeting with, xix, 349–51; criticism of privatization efforts, xvii; Cyprus conflict special envoy sent by, 41, 318, 319, 335; on democracy, 363; on Hungarian-Romanian Basic Treaty, 149; Iliescu meeting with, xix, 113, 146, 167–68; NAFTA support by, 40; on NATO expansion, 68, 92, 349–50, 354–57; on restitution of Jewish property, 104, 168; on U.S.-Romania strategic partnership, 333, 350, 355; visits to Romania by, xix, 337–38, 343, 344, 349–58

Clinton, Chelsea, 357, 358

Clinton, Hillary, xix, 59, 113, 237–41

CNVM (Romanian National Securities Commission), 261

Coal miner raids, 35, 55–56, 58, 293–95, 361

Cobra helicopter deal: Clinton (Bill) on, 350; economic benefits of, 81, 216, 217; financial concerns in, 192, 217–18, 223, 292; IFM objections to, 81, 247, 292, 293, 327; significance for U.S.-Romanian relations, 228; sovereign guarantee given in, 291; and State Ownership Fund, 217, 218, 247, 327; termination of, 284, 327

Coca-Cola, 72, 153, 229, 320

CODELs. *See* Congressional delegations

Codreanu, Corneliu, 50
Comaneci, Nadia, xix, 225
Communism and communists: crypto-communists, 62, 344, 346, 361; end in Eastern Europe, xv–xvi, xix; Iliescu ties to, 55, 61, 361; John Paul II challenge against, 12; oppression under, xix, xxi, 11, 25, 300; in Romania, xv–xvi, 8–12, 19–20, 29, 52–53, 130
C-130 Hercules aircraft, 81, 110, 169, 213, 266
Conference of Presidents of Major American Jewish Organizations, 8, 15, 17
Congressional delegations (CODELs), 17, 23–24, 163, 295
Congress of Berlin (1878), 3, 7, 48
Conner, Bart, xix, 225
Conover, Bill, 345
Constantinescu, Emil: account of coal miner raids by, 58; anti-corruption campaign initiated by, 267, 294; author's meetings with, 82–83, 116, 194–95, 331–32; "Contract with Romania," 58, 267, 362; democratization under, 360, 362–63; economic reform efforts, 66, 77; educational background, 154; election as president, 56, 59, 145, 272; foreign policy powers of, 342–43; historical revisionism of, 284; Iliescu on, 272–73, 346; on investment opportunities, 320–21; meetings with U.S. officials, xix, 274, 284, 296–97, 329–30, 339, 349–51; at NATO ambassadors' lunch, 280; on NATO expansion, 348; press relationships with, 322; prime minister appointments by, 223; religious orientation of, 234; on Ukrainian friendship treaty, 142, 308, 315
Constantinescu, Romulus, 133
Constitutional reform, 35, 65
Containment policies, 11
Contraception ban, 75–76, 107, 243
"Contract with Romania" (Constantinescu), 58, 267, 362
Conventional Armed Forces in Europe Treaty (1990), 81
Cook, Robin, 328, 331
Cooper, Jerome Gary, 41

Coposu, Corneliu: author's meetings with, 197; on coal miner raids, 56; condemnation of Iliescu by, 58, 61; death of, 61, 104; imprisonment of, 55, 104; political ideology of, 104–05; rejection of offer to join coalition government, 62, 83, 97; on Ukrainian friendship treaty, 142
Copyright law, 118–19, 200
Corruption: in airports, 4; anti-corruption campaign, 267, 294; convictions for, 35; in customs service, 4, 211; Foreign Corrupt Practices Act, 72; of government officials, 83, 103, 125, 242, 247–48; persistence of, xviii; of police, 99
Coşea, Mircea: author's meeting with, 83–84, 105–06; political views of, 63; privatization assistance from, 150, 160; RASDAQ assistance from, 262, 263; at White House Conference on Trade and Investment, 94
Cosma, Miron, 293, 294
Costa, Mircea, 327
Council of Europe Recommendation 1201, 116, 127, 140, 150, 206
Counterterrorism operations, 121, 231
Country team meetings, 95–96
Crabbie, Christopher, 249, 259
Crane, Phil, 221
Craner, Lorne, 149, 270, 319, 335
Crypto-communists, 62, 344, 346, 361
Crypto-fascists, 20, 62, 221
Cultural life, 7, 103, 253, 301
Currency stabilization, xvii, 75
Customs service, 4, 211
Cutler, Lloyd, 36
Cuza, Alexandru Ion, 48
Cyprus, special presidential envoy to, 41, 318–19, 335
Czech Republic: enterprise funds in, 149; NATO admission for, 82, 93–94, 144, 245, 328, 330; Warsaw Initiative grant for, 109

Daley, William M., 327
Danforth, John, 8
Danube Delta, 56, 141, 171, 287
Daschle, Tom, 170, 173
Datculescu, Petre, 272

Davis, John, 37, 60, 69, 79
Dayton Accords (1995), 160, 250, 335
Degeratu, Constantin, 280, 322
Democratic Liberal Party (PDL), 267
Democratic Party (PD): anti-Semitism directed at, 97; formation of, 56; in government coalition, 197, 242, 267, 285; ministries held by, 270, 272, 343
Democratic Union of Hungarians in Romania (UDMR): author's meetings with, 197, 219–20; on ethnic conflict, 100–101, 103; extremist nature of, 140, 220; in government coalition, 267, 268; on Hungarian-Romanian Basic Treaty, 139, 140; in ministry positions, 197
Democratization, xvi, xx, 65, 75, 262, 360–63
Deng Xiaoping, 10
Diaconescu, Ion: appointment of prime minister, 223; author's meetings with, 191, 197, 242, 270–71; election as PNT-CD leader, 190; imprisonment of, 55; meetings with U.S. officials, 339
Dima, Emil, 119–20, 134, 150, 218, 235–36, 247
Dimitriu, Sorin, 302–03, 327
Dine, Thomas A., 91
Direct foreign investment, 66, 84, 136, 265, 303
Discrimination. *See* Prejudice and discrimination
Dole, Robert, xix, 123, 173, 339–41
Donnelly, Chris, 248–49
Dracula legend, historical basis for, 56–57, 236
Drew, Nelson, 169
Duguay, Gilles, 345

Eastern Europe. *See* Central and Eastern Europe
Economic reform: acceleration of, 269, 275; barriers to, 65, 67, 120, 206; and foreign investment, 84, 268; funding for, xvii; IFM assistance with, 106; importance of, 287–88; politics in, 66, 67, 77; program for, 302–03, 317; public support for, 328; RASDAQ as element of, 91; USAID assistance with, 317; World Bank assistance with, 106

Economy: bond financing, 192, 195–96, 210; capital markets program, 109, 148, 151, 168, 261–63; collapse following end of communist rule, xvi; currency stabilization for, xvii, 75; direct foreign investment in, 66, 84, 136, 265, 303; external debt, 168; foreign debt elimination and impact on, 31; in interwar period, 49; market-based systems, 65; restructuring of, 75, 84, 94–95; social market economy, 362. *See also* Economic reform; Gross domestic product; Inflation; Oil and oil industry; Privatization; Trade
Education. *See* Training
Ehrenwald, Peter, 136
Einik, Michael, 74, 224, 345, 346
Einik, Sarah, 345
Eizenstat, Stuart, 36, 128, 161–62
Emanuel, Rahm, 40
Emigration of Romanian Jews to Israel: author's assistance with, xv, 8, 12, 15–17, 21, 98; Ceaușescu on, xv, 8, 12–13, 21; historical trends, 7; Israeli government involvement with, 9, 14–17; most favored nation status as bargaining tool for, 9–11, 14–17, 25–26; procedural constraints on, 21; Rosen on, 8, 16
Energy conference (1995), 173, 175, 180–81
Energy sector, xviii, 84, 209
Enterprise funds, 149, 178–79
Ethnic conflict with Hungarian minority: history of, 10, 47; Iliescu on, 59, 79, 139; political nature of, 100–101, 103, 133, 220; U.S. concerns regarding, 79
Ethnic politics, 10, 140
European Union (EU): economic reform assistance from, 106; financial and technical support from, xvi, xix–xx; opposition to adoption of Romanian orphans, 243; PHARE assistance program of, 109, 262; Romania's admission into, 359; standards for admission to, 211
EXIM (U.S. Export-Import) Bank, 171, 195
External Security Service (SIE), 63–64, 97, 121
Exxon, 148

Fascists and fascism: crypto-fascists, 20, 62, 221; in Iron Guard, 104; murder of Jews by, 5, 300; rise of, 50

FCPA (Foreign Corrupt Practices Act of 1977), 72

Ferdinand I (king of Romania), 48–50

Filderman, Wilhelm, 334

Financial Enterprise Structural Adjustment Loan (FESAL), 76, 119, 134, 146, 147, 205–06

Fisher, Joseph, 23

Fisher, Stanley, 177

Florance, Colden, 224

Fly trade, 212

Fogg, Karen, 120

Fogleman, Ronald R., 143, 242

Ford, Gerald, 10

Foreign Corrupt Practices Act of 1977 (FCPA), 72

Foreign policy: key actors in, 63; moral foreign policy, 348; NATO admission as main objective of, 68, 73, 78, 80–82; presidential powers in, 342–43; Romanian acts of independence from Soviet Union in, 9. *See also* Hungarian-Romanian Basic Treaty; Partnership for Peace; Romanian-Ukrainian friendship treaty

Fourth of July celebrations, 143, 153–54

Foxman, Abraham, 179

Frank, Monique, 220

Frasure, Robert, 169

Freedom of religion, 65, 352

Fried, Dan, 168, 199, 221, 285–87, 337

Friendly, Nick, 338

Fuerth, Leon, 168

Funar, Gheorghe: attacks on Iliescu, 194, 258; author's meetings with, 100–101, 132–33; characterization of, 133; in ethnic conflict with Hungarians, 100; extremism of, 140, 172; on Hungarian-Romanian Basic Treaty, 258; Iliescu on, 174; Magureanu on Russian use of, 157

Funderburk, David, 61, 110, 149, 170, 222

Gaffney, Frank, 82

Garner, David, 345

Gavrilescu, Dinu, 289

GDP. *See* Gross domestic product

Genocide, 58, 220

Geoana, Mircea: on arm sales to pariah states, 186; author's suggestion of ambassadorship for, 154, 179; characterization of, 199; criticisms of, 342, 348; intergovernment support for, 274; MFN status assistance from, 221–22

Georgescu, Florin: on bond financing, 210; characterization of, 63; in Cobra helicopter deal, 218; IMF negotiations by, 166–67; on Intercontinental Hotel sale, 157; on late payments, 195; on privatization, 136, 150; RASDAQ assistance from, 262; on State Ownership Fund, 135; tennis diplomacy by, 128; at White House Conference on Trade and Investment, 94

Gheorghiu-Dej, Gheorghe, 19, 52, 104, 129

Gherman, Oliviu, 64, 83, 126, 220–21, 239, 240, 263

Gilman, Ben, 226

Gingrich, Newt, 115, 173, 267

Glasnost (openness), 29, 52

Göncz, Árpád, 329

Gorbachev, Mikhail, 29, 52, 125, 130, 315, 361

Gore, Albert: Constantinescu meeting with, 274, 284; Iliescu meeting with, 115, 158, 159, 168, 171–72; on NATO expansion, 93; request to visit Romania, 113–14; on Romanian-Ukrainian friendship treaty, 142

Gott, Izu, 30, 31, 102

Grassley, Charles, 170, 221

Greater Romania Party. *See* Romania Mare Party

Great Synagogue, 5–6, 32–33

Great War. *See* World War I

Green, Peter S., 291

Green, Joshua, 77, 102, 103

Gross domestic product (GDP): budget deficit as percentage of, 265, 269, 292, 293, 302; deflator as inflation barometer, 166; growth of (1999–2004), 67; IMF figures on (1990–1996), 65–66; state-owned enterprises and *régies autonomes* as percentage of, 134

Grossman, Marc, 36–38, 41, 318

Gypsy (Roma) populations, 7, 99, 251, 264, 290

Habitat for Humanity, 114
Hachomi, Itzak and Emily, 102
Hagi, Gheorghe, 236
Halaicu, Crin, 122
Hardymon, Jim, 247
Harris, David, 259
Hartmann, Arna, 77, 119
Havel, Václav, xvi
Hawley, Richard E., 143
Healthcare services, xviii, 91–92
Helms, Jesse, 43, 61, 97, 110–11, 149, 173, 341
Helsinki Accords (1975), 11, 308
Hezbollah, 231
Hitler, Adolf, 50, 159, 206
Holbrooke, Richard A.: author's meetings with, 45, 60, 91, 107; characterization of, 42–43; as CS First Boston advocate, 317–18; as Cyprus special envoy, 319, 335; marriage of, 115–16; on NATO expansion, 92–93
Holocaust: comparison of other tragedies to, 58; emigration of survivors, 7; heroes of, 300, 301; memorial ceremonies, 29; old age home for survivors of, 6; Romania's role in, 233
Holocaust Museum, 9, 35, 113, 170, 184, 226
Horbulin, Volodymyr, 141, 312
Horn, Gyula, 55, 112, 139, 149–50
Hrebenciuc, Viorel: archival access provided by, 226; on cancellation of Jehovah's Witness conference, 238; characterization of, 63, 103; dismissal of, 247–48; economic reform efforts of, 120; on ethnic conflict with Hungarian minority, 103; on IMF negotiations, 177; on Intercontinental Hotel sale, 157–58; privatization efforts of, 150–51; on restitution of Jewish property, 104, 128–29, 162
Human rights, 87, 111, 116, 118, 221, 295
Hungarian-Romanian Basic Treaty (1996): autonomy considerations in, 101, 116, 127, 139–40, 150; as condition for NATO membership, 88, 107, 147; negotiations regarding, 139–40, 206–07, 226, 246; opposition to, 258; signing of, 258–59; U.S. support for, 112, 149–50

Hungarian-Slovakian Basic Treaty (1995), 127, 140, 150, 206, 226
Hungary: Basic Treaty with Slovakia, 127, 140, 150, 206, 226; border disputes with Romania, 50, 51; enterprise funds in, 149; NATO admission for, 82, 93–94, 144, 245, 328, 330; religion in, 47; Warsaw Initiative grant for, 109. *See also* Ethnic conflict with Hungarian minority; Hungarian-Romanian Basic Treaty
Hunter, Robert E., 259

IBM, 304
ICJ. *See* International Court of Justice
IFM. *See* International Monetary Fund
IFOR (International Peace Keeping Force), 250
Ilie, Vasile, 324
Iliescu, Ion: author's meetings with, 34–35, 64, 111–13, 183–84, 196, 199–200, 285–86; on Basic Treaty with Hungary, 139; on Bosnian civil war, 212; campaign preparations, 234, 242, 248; characterization of, 34, 54, 153–54, 360; coal miner raids engineered by, 35, 55–56, 58, 294–95, 361; on Cobra helicopter deal, 217; communist ties to, 55, 61, 361; on Constantinescu, 272–73, 346; democratization under, xx, 360, 362–63; diplomatic reception hosted by, 96–98; economic reform efforts, 66, 77, 362; efforts to overthrow Ceaușescu, 58; election as president, xvi, 54–55, 58–59, 62, 359, 360; energy conference attended by, 173, 175, 180–81; on ethnic conflict with Hungarians, 59, 79, 139; Hungarian-Romanian Basic Treaty signed by, 258; on IMF negotiations, 189; Interministerial Committee formed by, 235; meetings with U.S. officials, xix, 59, 113, 125, 146, 167–72, 240, 344; on penal code amendments, 170, 183–84; in RASDAQ implementation, 262; rural support for, 62; on Ukrainian friendship treaty, 141; visit to U.S. by, 146–48, 157–59, 167–74, 177–81
Iliescu, Nina, 361

IMET (International Military Education and Training), 73, 169, 213
Inflation: economic measures for reduction of, 67, 75; GDP deflator as indication of, 166; post-revolution, 34; predicted growth of, 265, 269, 302
Interministerial Committee, 235
Internal Security Service (SRI), 63–64, 120–21, 156–57, 231, 250–51, 287–88
International Bank for Reconstruction and Development, xvii
International Court of Justice (ICJ), 142–43, 264, 308–10, 313
International Military Education and Training (IMET), 73, 169, 213
International Monetary Fund (IFM): on bond financing, 195–96; Cobra helicopter deal objections from, 81, 247, 292, 293, 327; currency stabilization loans from, xvii, 75; economic reform assistance from, 106; GDP figures from, 65–66; macro stabilization plan from, 265; monetary restraints imposed by, 75; representatives from, 76–77; standby loans from, 146, 161, 166–67, 174, 189, 191–92, 206; support for ambassadorship from, 61
International Peace Keeping Force (IFOR), 250
International Republican Institute (IRI): author's correspondence with, 270, 285, 335–36; Ciorbea on, 235; opposition to Iliescu government, 61; political interference by, 149, 291, 319
Ioanid, Radu, 9, 226
Iohannis, Klaus, xx, 48
Ionescu, Christian, 98
Ionescu, Constantin Dudu, 341–42
Iran, Romanian arm sales to, 152–53, 186–87, 192–93, 199, 351
Iraq, Romanian arm sales to, 152–53, 186–87, 192–93, 199
IRI. *See* International Republican Institute
Iron Guard, 19, 50, 51, 104, 156
Isarescu, Mugur: on Banca Dacia Felix, 180, 194; on bond financing, 210; on Dracula legend, 56–57, 236; economic report by, 265, 303; as governor of National Bank of Romania, 63, 358;

IMF and World Bank negotiations by, 166–67, 191–92, 195; on late payments, 195; as prime minister, 67, 223, 265; at White House Conference on Trade and Investment, 94
Israel: author's visit to, 43–44; on Great Synagogue preservation efforts, 33; Oslo Accords signed by, 43; on restitution of Jewish property, 162; right of return for Jews, 7–8; settlement policy in occupied Arab territories, 36. *See also* Emigration of Romanian Jews to Israel

Jackson-Vanik Amendment, 9, 14, 17, 221
Jacobs, Susan, 241, 297
Japan, ambassadors sent to Romania by, 138–39
Jehovah's Witnesses, 237–38
Jewish communities: challenges faced by, 6–7, 19–20; population decline following World War II, 7; reaction to UN vote on Israeli settlement policy, 36; in Soviet Union, 14, 15; in Ukraine, 311–14. *See also* Anti-Semitism; Holocaust; Romanian Jewish community
John Paul II (pope), 12
Johnson, Ralph, 108–09, 229
Joiner, Webb, 326, 327
Joulwan, George A., 138, 249–50, 311, 323

Kadar, Janos, 361
Karski, Jan, 300
Keay, Justin, 291
Kennedy, John F., 38, 73
Kennelly, Barbara, 221
Kien, Peter, 301
Kim Il-sung, 11, 52
Kinkel, Klaus, 283, 285, 306, 319
Kirk, Roger, 19, 29
Kirkland, Lane, 39–40
Klipper, John, 178–79
Kohl, Helmut, 112–13, 145, 290
Kornblum, John, 227, 289–90, 348
Kovács, László, 116, 139, 246
Kruzel, Jospeph J., 109, 110, 169
Krys, Sheldon J., 41
Kuchma, Leonid, 141, 312, 315, 350
Kwaśniewski, Aleksander, 55

Lake, Tony, 41, 158–60, 168
Land reform programs, 76
Lantos, Annette, 296, 329
Lantos, Tom, 209, 222, 290, 295–97, 329–30
Lauder, Ronald, 122, 123
Lavie, Neftali, 128
Lazar, Gilda, 343
Legionnaires. *See* Iron Guard
Levanon, Nehemiah, 9, 15
Lieberman, Joseph I., 40
Li Fenglin, 138
Linowitz, Sol, 36
Livingston, Robert, 149
Lockheed Martin, 81, 136, 193, 213, 304–05
Luft, Bogumil, 249
Lugar, Richard, 246
Lupescu, Elena, 50

Magureanu, Virgil, 58, 63–64, 119–21, 156–57, 231, 287–88
Major, John, 189, 249
Malovany, Yossi, 323
Management/employee buy-outs (MEBOs), 76, 134, 135
Maniu, Iuliu, 50, 57, 61, 104, 145, 298
Mann, Theodore, 15
Mao Zedong, 10
Margareta (princess of Romania), 58, 107–08
Marie (queen of Romania), 48
Marko, Bela, 100, 101, 219–20
Marriott Corporation, 114, 151, 157–58
Marsh, Virginia, 174
Marshall Plan, xix
Marton, Kati, 115–16
Mass Privatization Program (MPP), 67, 77, 83–84, 109, 120, 134
McCain, John, 149, 319, 335–36
McDonald's, 136, 151, 153, 185, 303
McDonnell, John, 208–09, 304
McDonnell Douglas, 193, 209, 304, 320
Mead, Dana, 208
MEBOs (management/employee buy-outs), 76, 134, 135
Meçiar, Vladimir, 206
Megiddon, Avshalom, 102
Meleşcanu, Teodor: on arm sales to pariah states, 186; author's meetings with,

77–82, 116; Basic Treaty negotiations by, 139–40; on Bosnian civil war, 159–60; characterization of, 63; criticisms of, 130; as foreign minister, 63, 64; on Hungarian-Romanian Basic Treaty, 127, 150, 246, 258; and Iliescu campaign, 248; on IMF negotiations, 189; on Interministerial Committee, 235; meetings with U.S. officials, 125; on Molotov-Ribbentrop Pact, 141; on NATO admission, 78, 81–82, 144; and tennis diplomacy, 126; Ukrainian friendship treaty negotiations by, 141; visit to U.S. by, 177–79, 246
Mencken, H. L., 174
Merry Cemetery, 299
Meyer, Mark, 180
MFN status. *See* Most favored nation status
Michael I (king of Romania), 50, 52, 101, 104, 108, 344, 362
Michael the Brave (king of Romania), 48, 49, 59, 80, 324
Mikva, Abner, 188
Military: arm sales to pariah states, 152–53, 186–87, 192–93, 199, 351; civilian control of, 63, 169; C-130 Hercules aircraft for, 81, 110, 169, 213, 266; downsizing, 73; equipment maintenance, 110; financial needs of, 143; missile stockpiling, 152–53; modernization of, xix; reform of, 87, 152, 322; reorganization of, xvi; training and education for, 73, 169, 213. *See also* Cobra helicopter deal
Miller, William, 308–09
Milošević, Slobodan, 212
Minnow trade, 212
Molotov-Ribbentrop Pact (1939), 50, 140–42, 226–27, 264, 307–08, 324, 325
Moral foreign policy, 348
Moses, Alfred H.: ambassadorship training and confirmation, 41–43, 60; on American Jewish Committee, 3, 35, 43, 77; background and family, xxi, 33, 35; Black Sea shipyards toured by, 164; Ceauşescu in meetings with, 13, 20–22, 29, 43; Constantinescu in meetings with, 82–83, 116, 194–95,

Moses, Alfred H. (*cont.*)
331–32; cultural life experienced
by, 103, 253, 301; as Cyprus special
envoy, 41, 319; economic reform
efforts by, 77; emigration assistance
for Romanian Jews, xv, 8, 12, 15–17,
21, 98; fundraising for choir visit
to Washington, D.C., 30; Great
Synagogue preservation efforts by,
32–33; Hanukkah tours by, 26–29;
Iliescu in meetings with, 34–35, 64,
111–13, 183–84, 196, 199–200, 285–
86; initial visit to Romania, 3–6; in
Israel, 43–44; as Jewish Affairs advisor,
36–37; Meleşcanu in meetings with,
77–82, 116; Nastase in meetings with,
35, 83, 116–19; post-ambassadorship,
357–58; on replacement of Romanian
ambassador to U.S., 154, 179;
resignation as U.S. ambassador, 318,
343, 345–47; in Romanian-Ukrainian
friendship treaty negotiations, 307–13;
Rosen, relationship with, 18, 34; in
Saudi Arabia, 43–44; support for
ambassadorship nomination, 37–41;
tennis diplomacy by, 126, 128; U.S.-
Romania strategic partnership initiated
by, xviii–xix, 333; in "What Being
Jewish Means to Me" series, 259–60
Moses, Amalie, 70, 324
Moses, Barbara, 39, 68–70, 79, 81
Moses, Carol: on ambassadorship, 39;
cancer diagnosis for, 44–45; children
and grandchildren, 33, 35, 358; death of,
358; visits to Romania, 4, 6, 198, 255
Most favored nation (MFN) status: as
bargaining tool, 9–11, 14–17, 25–26;
non-paper on, 199; permanent approval
of, 111, 113, 168, 172, 221–22
Motley, Langhorne A., 41
MPP. *See* Mass Privatization Program
Mureşan, Sever, 92, 123–26, 180, 193–94,
293–94

NAFTA (North American Free Trade
Agreement), 40
NAP (National Agency for Privatization),
262, 263, 327
Nastase, Adrian: author's meetings with,
35, 83, 116–19; characterization of,

64, 83; on Cobra helicopter deal, 247;
criticisms of, 151; on Hungarian-
Romanian Basic Treaty, 127, 150;
imprisonment of, 35, 83; on local
elections, 233; meetings with U.S.
officials, 114–15, 239, 240; on penal code
amendments, 183, 184; on PNT-CD
rejection of national unity government,
97; privatization legislation passed by, 77;
in RASDAQ implementation, 262; and
tennis diplomacy, 126
Nastase, Dana, 127, 239
Nastase, Ilie, 225, 233
National Agency for Privatization (NAP),
262, 263, 327
National Bank of Romania: building
of foreign reserves by, 191; debt
instrument terms negotiated by, 282;
foreign exchange regulation by, 191,
196, 206; IMF negotiations with,
166–67; late payments from, 195;
leadership of, 56, 63, 166–67, 193–95,
358; privatization of, 282; support
for Dacia Felix by, 193; technical
assistance for, 210
National Democratic Institute (NDI), 149
National identity, relationship with
religion, 12, 155
National Liberal Party, 50, 57, 139, 257
National Peasants Party (PNT), 50, 55,
57, 61, 145, 284. *See also* PNT-CD
National Salvation Front (NSF), xvi, 34,
53–55, 83, 360, 361
NATO. *See* North Atlantic Treaty
Organization
Nazi Germany, xix, 3, 5, 51, 58, 140
NDI (National Democratic Institute), 149
Negritoiu, Misu, 120
Nicolae, Nicolae, 13
Nimetz, Matt, 17
Nixon, Richard, 10, 337
Non-papers, 81–82, 107, 111, 198–99
North American Free Trade Agreement
(NAFTA), 40
North Atlantic Treaty Organization
(NATO): ambassadors' lunches, 144–45,
190, 203, 220–21, 237, 259, 273–75, 280,
328; Article 5 guarantee, 87, 245, 359; in
Black Sea region, xvii, 214; competition
among applicants, 249, 290, 291,

305–06; expansion of, 68, 92–94, 137–38, 213, 245, 328–33; as foreign policy objective, 68, 73, 78, 80–82; Madrid Summit, 292, 332, 336, 348; peacekeeping missions, xvii, 250; Perry Principles of, 87, 139, 152, 170; preconditions for admission to, 87–88, 107, 164–65; Romania's admission into, 359; schedule for review of aspiring members, 355. *See also* Partnership for Peace

NSF. *See* National Salvation Front

Nye, Joseph S., Jr., 109–10

Ogryzko, Volodymyr, 312

Oil and oil industry: Black Sea exploration and production rights, 141–43, 216; exports, 49; illegal imports to Serbia, 212; investment opportunities in, 207; modernization of, 175, 320; privatization of, 148, 176; refinery evacuation drills, 255–56; technical assistance in, 209

O'Neill, Tip, 122

Oppression: under communism, xix, xxi, 11, 25, 300; political, xix, 29

Organization for Security and Cooperation, 220

Orphans and orphanages, 107, 108, 237, 243–45

Ortiz, Solomon, 163

Oslo Accords (1993), 43

Ostrovenko, Yevgeny, 137–38

Overseas Private Investment Corporation, 149

Paik Nak-whan, 139

Palmer, Mark, 32, 122, 123

Papas, Claude, 208, 345–46

Partnership for Peace (NATO): civilian defense minister requirement in, 80; Clinton (Bill) on, 350, 354; Romanian participation in, 165, 168, 169, 228, 245, 248; as stepping stone to NATO membership, 92; and Warsaw Initiative, 109

Pascu, Ion Mircea, 34

Pauker, Ana, 70, 257

Paunescu, George, 114, 151, 234, 261–63

PD. *See* Democratic Party

PDL (Democratic Liberal Party), 267

PDSR. *See* Social Democratic Party of Romania

Peace Corps, 73, 149

Peacekeeping missions, xvii, 198, 250, 350, 354

Pell, Claiborne, 170, 173

Pelletreau, Nancy, 69

Penal code amendments, 170, 173, 183–84, 200

Pendiuc, Tudor, 255

Pepper, John, 304, 320

Perestroika (restructuring), 29, 52, 361

Perry, William J., 87, 152–53, 169–70, 223

Perry Principles (NATO), 87, 139, 152, 170

Petre, Zoe, 280–81, 295–96, 338, 347

Petroleum. *See* Oil and oil industry

Pfaff, William, 291

PHARE assistance program, 109, 262

PNT. *See* National Peasants Party

PNT-CD: author's meeting with, 222, 242; on coal miner raids, 56; decline of, 191; economic reform efforts, 66; formation of, 55; generational issues for, 191; in government coalition, 267, 268; IRI funding of, 149; ministries held by, 272; political platform of, 104, 110–11; rejection of offer to join coalition government, 83, 97; training of government officials by, 194–95, 266–67; urban support for, 62

Pocepa, Ion, 157

POFs (private ownership funds), 76, 135

Poland: division of, 46, 50; enterprise funds in, 149; NATO admission for, 68, 82, 93–94, 144, 245, 328, 330; religion in, 47; Solidarity Movement in, xvi; Warsaw Initiative grant for, 109

Police: in cemetery vandalism case, 156; corruption of, 99; counterfeit packaging halted by, 208; in Jewish communities, 7; training courses for, 281

Political oppression, xix, 29

Political system: and constitutional reform, 35, 65; democratization of, xvi, xx, 65, 75, 262, 360–63; disarray following end of communist rule, xvi; ethnic politics in, 10, 140; in interwar period, 49–51. *See also specific political parties*

Popa, Dumitru, 169, 187
Pop family, 300, 301
Powell, Colin, 123, 125
Prejudice and discrimination, 48, 59, 220, 263–64. *See also* Anti-Semitism; Xenophobia
Pritzker, Jay, 319–20
Private ownership funds (POFs), 76, 135
Privatization: acceleration of, xvii, 120, 150–51, 273, 303; of agricultural land, 66, 76, 302; of banking sector, 84, 92, 109, 160–61, 282; displacement of workers due to, 282; of housing and retail businesses, 66, 76; management/employee buy-outs in, 76, 134, 135; Mass Privatization Program, 67, 77, 83–84, 109, 120, 134; of national television, 88, 112, 123; of oil industry, 176; planning and preparation for, 105–06, 108–09; RASDAQ as element of, 76, 91, 227, 261–63; of state-owned enterprises and *régies autonomes*, 77, 84, 94, 134, 150; USAID assistance on, 108–09, 151; World Bank guidance on, 67, 76, 136–37
PRM. *See* Romania Mare Party
Procter & Gamble, 136, 208, 303–04, 320, 345–46
PSM. *See* Socialist Party of Romania
Public diplomacy, 71, 181
PUNR. *See* Romanian National Unity Party
Putna Monastery, 325–26
Puwak, Hildegard, 160

Rabin, Yitzhak, 44, 188–89
Raceanu, Mircea, 24
Ramsey, Louis, 40
The Ransom of the Jews: The Story of the Extraordinary Secret Bargain between Romania and Israel (Ioanid), 9
RAs. *See Régies autonomes*
RASDAQ. *See* Romanian Association of Securities Dealers Automated Quotations
Ratiu, Ion, 58, 145, 146–47, 174, 242
Reagan, Ronald, 17
Redman, Charles E., 41
Reed, John, 320
Reform: of banking sector, 282; constitutional, 35, 65; of Internal

Security Service, 287; land reform programs, 76; of military, 87, 152, 322. *See also* Economic reform
Régies autonomes (RAs): as barrier to economic reform, 65, 67, 206; employment in, 66, 134; privatization of, 77, 84, 94, 134; subsidies for, xviii
Reigart, Keith, 324
Religion: freedom of, 65, 352; hybrid culture of, 47; and national identity, 12, 155; and private enterprise, 233. *See also* Jewish communities
Rickert, Jonathan, 69, 74, 79, 111, 126, 221
Ridge, Tom, 341
Ridgway, Rozanne, 32
Rifkind, Malcolm, 249, 283, 290
Rodham, Tony, 187–88
Roman, Petre: Airbus purchases by, 193; author's meetings with, 116, 197; background of, 97; on coal miner raids, 58, 294–95; criticisms of, 294; meetings with U.S. officials, 339–40; in presidential election, 197, 269, 270; as prime minister, xvi, 54, 130; as Senate president, 272; split with Iliescu, 35, 55–56, 242, 361
Roman, Valter, 54, 97
Romania: anti-Russian sentiment in, 47, 82; border disputes with Hungary, 50, 51; communism in, xv–xvi, 8–12, 19–20, 29, 52–53, 130; cultural life in, 7, 103, 253, 301; energy sector in, xviii, 84, 209; geographical location, 46–47; government offices in, 100; healthcare services in, xviii, 91–92; as independent state, 3, 48; interwar period in, 49–51; orphans and orphanages in, 107, 108, 237, 243–45; per-capita annual income in, xvii, 72; political history of, 46–56; religion in, 12, 47, 65, 155, 233, 352; Soviet relations with, 9–10, 52–53, 284; strategic partnership with U.S., xvii–xix, 144, 152, 333, 350–52, 355; trade relations with U.S., 98; transportation industry in, xviii, 84; U.S. military presence in, 73–74; Warsaw Initiative grant for, 109–10; in World War I, 3, 49; in World War II, 3, 51. *See also* Economy; Ethnic conflict with

Hungarian minority; Foreign policy; Military; Political system; Romanian Jewish community

Romania Mare Party (PRM): anti-Semitism in, xx, 20, 97; extremist nature of, 106, 194, 215; opposition to mainstream politics, xx; in parliamentary coalition, 111, 174, 194; severing of ties with PDSR, 182, 220–21

Romanian American Enterprise Fund, 149, 178–79

Romanian Association of Securities Dealers Automated Quotations (RASDAQ), 76, 91, 227, 261–63, 291

Romanian Jewish community: challenges faced by, 6–7, 19–20, 334–35; choir visit to Washington D.C., 30–31; government surveillance of, 19; Hanukkah tours of, 26–29; history of, 7; leadership of, 5, 11, 18, 22; population estimates, 4, 7, 18, 325; restitution of property for, 104, 128–29, 161–62, 168; vandalism of cemetery belonging to, 156; World War II losses of, 42. *See also* Emigration of Romanian Jews to Israel

Romanian Jewish Federation, 4, 16, 17, 19, 154, 162

Romanian National Securities Commission (CNVM), 261

Romanian National Unity Party (PUNR): anti-Semitism in, 43, 97; conflict with Hungarian minority, 100–101, 103; extremist nature of, 62, 106, 194, 215; ineffectiveness of, 84; opposition to author's ambassadorship, 43; in parliamentary coalition, 62, 111, 182, 194; severing of ties with PRM and PUNR, 258

Romanian Orthodox Church, 12, 47, 155, 237–38, 299, 316

Romanian-Ukrainian friendship treaty (1997): and Black Sea territorial disputes, 141–43, 216, 264–65, 307–10, 313; on Chilija and Sulina navigation rights, 310, 313; as condition for NATO membership, 88, 107; and Molotov-Ribbentrop Pact, 140–42, 226–27, 264, 307–08; negotiations regarding, 140–43, 216, 226–27,

307–13; signing of, 315–16

Roma (Gypsy) populations, 7, 99, 251, 264, 290

Rorvig, Richard, 134, 205, 236

Rosen, Amalia, 22, 26, 28, 30

Rosen, Moses: activism of, 25; author's relationship with, 18, 34; characterization of, 19, 86, 335; on choir visit to Washington, D.C., 30, 31; death of, 11, 18, 19, 40; on emigration of Romanian Jews, 8, 16; Great Synagogue preservation efforts by, 32; Hanukkah tours by, 26–29; as leader of Romanian Jewish community, 5, 11, 18, 22; meetings with U.S. officials, 23–25; parliamentary position held by, 18; travel freedom granted to, 9

Rosenne, Meir, 30–31

Rossbach, Anton, 112, 144, 145

Rubin, Robert, 170

Rubinstein, Elyakim, 33

Russia: ambassadors sent to Romania by, 137–38; anti-Russian sentiment in Romania, 47, 82; mafia in, 156–57; on NATO expansion, 93, 137–38, 290. *See also* Soviet Union

Sadat, Anwar, 21, 125

Şafran, Alexandru, 18, 334, 335

SALs. *See* Structural adjustment loans

Sarbu, Adrian, 122

Saudi Arabia, author's visit to, 43–44

Saunders, Hal, 37

Schifter, Richard, 40, 41, 221

Schmidt, Carl, 17

Schneier, Arthur, 25

Schuld, Norman, 148

Schulze, Richard, 23

Securitate: in banking sector, 92; demonstrations quashed by, 52; dismantling of, 76; political connections of, 151; tactics of, 231; Teoctist compromised by, 155; union infiltration by, 294; white paper on operations of, 157

Securities and Exchange Commission, U.S., 91

Security sector. *See* External Security Service; Internal Security Service; Police; Securitate

Sephardic Synagogue, 5, 32
Serbia, in Bosnian civil war, 125, 159–60, 211–12
Serpent Island, 141, 142, 216, 264, 308–10, 313
Severin, Adrian: on Clinton (Bill) visit to Romania, 337; concordat between Uniate and Romanian Orthodox churches attempted by, 316; on Constantinescu, 285, 342–43; government experience of, 289; integrity of, 286; meetings with U.S. officials, 339, 347, 351; on moral foreign policy, 348; at NATO ambassadors' lunch, 273–74; on NATO expansion, 305–06; on Ukrainian friendship treaty, 309, 312, 313, 315
Shalikashvili, John, 212–14, 322
Shapiro, Paul, 226
Shell Oil, 49
Shoppa, Lloyd, 216, 218, 293
Shteyerman, Jacob, 311
SIE (External Security Service), 63–64, 97, 121
Simon, Paul, 40, 221
Simons, Thomas W., Jr., 32
Singer, Israel, 30, 128, 129, 177
Sion, Mihai, 147
Slocombe, Walter, 283–85
Slovakia: Basic Treaty with Hungary, 127, 140, 150, 206, 226; NATO admission for, 94; religion in, 47
Smith, Chris, 61, 222
Smith, Jed, 160, 192
Snell, Terry, 221
Social Democratic Party of Romania (PDSR): economic reform efforts, 66, 67; image considerations, 181; local election losses, 233–34, 247–48; misinformation campaigns by, 286–87; in parliamentary coalition, 62, 111, 194; relationship with extremist parties, 62, 97; Roman split from, 56; rural support for, 62; severing of ties with PRM and PUNR, 182, 220–21, 258; as successor to NSF, 83
Social market economy, 362
Social support programs, 302
Socialist Party of Romania (PSM), 97, 106, 112, 194, 215

SOEs. *See* State-owned enterprises
SOF. *See* State Ownership Fund
Solberg, Sarah, 257–58
Solidarity Movement, xvi
Somogyi, Ferenc, 246
South Korea, ambassadors sent to Romania by, 139
Soviet Union: Black Sea gentleman's agreement made by, 216; Jewish communities in, 14, 15; *perestroika* and *glasnost* policies in, 29, 52, 361; Romanian relations with, 9–10, 52–53, 284; U.S. containment policies toward, 11. *See also* Russia
Spectre, George, 15
Spence, Floyd, 163
Spineanu, Ulm, 266–67, 271, 291–93, 320, 328
Spitzer, Jack, 17, 22, 29
Spolar, Christine, 268–69
SRI. *See* Internal Security Service
Stabreit, Immo and Barbara, 44
Stalin, Josef, 12, 70, 253
State-owned enterprises (SOEs): as barrier to economic reform, 65, 67; employment in, 66, 134; privatization of, 77, 84, 94, 134, 150; subsidies for, xviii, 92
State Ownership Fund (SOF): and Cobra helicopter deal, 217, 218, 247, 327; creation of, 76; ineffectiveness of, 235; leadership of, 119, 302–03; privatization efforts of, 134–35, 150–51, 205, 208; technical assistance for, 317
Steenbergen, Ignace van, 97–98
Steinberg, Mel, 179
Stephen the Great (prince of Moldavia), 325
Stevenson, Adlai, 8
Stoica, Valeriu, 339
Stolojan, Theodor, 34–35, 59, 130
Strauss-Tiron, Gabriela, 300, 301
Street children, 243–45
Structural adjustment loans (SALs), xvii, 75, 94. *See also* Financial Enterprise Structural Adjustment Loan
Sucevița Monastery, 325
Sugiura, Yoshiki, 138–39
Sulina River navigation rights, 310, 313

Taher, Fathi, 186, 224, 345

Talbott, Strobe: on author's ambassadorship, 45; on Clinton (Bill) visit to Romania, 337; on embassy communications, 341–42; Iliescu meeting with, 168, 170; on NATO expansion, 285, 319, 328; on U.S.-Romania strategic partnership, 333

Talisman, Mark, 15

Talpes, Ioan, 64, 97, 121, 141

Taracila, Doru, 99

Tarnoff, Peter, 246, 258

Teitelbaum, Joel, 297

Temeşan, Razvan, 236

Tenneco, 208, 303–04, 352

Tennis diplomacy, 126, 128

Teoctist (Orthodox Patriarch), 111, 155, 238, 344

Terrorism, 42, 120–21, 157, 231

Textron, 217, 247

Thatcher, Margaret, 144

Timişoara massacre (1989), 52

Tinca, Gheorghe: on Cobra helicopter deal, 192, 217–18, 228; on International Hotel sale, 151; meetings with U.S. officials, 143, 152–53, 163, 213–14; selection as defense minister, 63, 64; on U.S.-Romania bilateral military relationship, 80

Tiriac, Ion, 92, 122–23, 339

Tito, Josip Broz, 10

Tökés, László, 58, 133

Totu, Ioan, 32

Towry, Debra, 132

Trade: U.S.-Romania trade relations, 98; White House Conference on Trade and Investment in Central and Eastern Europe, 94–95; World Trade Organization, 98. *See also* Most favored nation status; North American Free Trade Agreement

Training: for ambassadorship, 41–43, 60; on bankruptcy procedures, 281; for government officials, 194–95, 266–67; for management and professionals, 137; for military, 73, 169, 213; for police, 281

Trajan (Roman emperor), 47, 56

TransChem, 235, 316–17, 321

Transportation industry, xviii, 84

Treaties. *See specific name of treaty*

Tudor, Corneliu Vadim, xx–xxi, 20, 97, 174, 182, 340

TWA Airline hijacking (1985), 120

UDMR. *See* Democratic Union of Hungarians in Romania

Udovenko, Hennadiy, 141, 309, 312

Ukrainian-Romanian friendship treaty. *See* Romanian-Ukrainian friendship treaty

Ullmann, Viktor, 301

Understein, Bob, 114–15

United Nations, xvii, 36, 198

United States: containment policies toward Soviet Union, 11; economic reform assistance from, 106; financial and technical support from, xvi, xix–xx, 88, 137, 209–11; military presence in Romania, 73–74; RASDAQ implementation assistance from, 261–62; Romanian ambassador to, 64, 97, 106–07, 147, 154, 179; strategic partnership with Romania, xvii–xix, 144, 152, 333, 350–52, 355; trade relations with Romania, 98

U.S. Agency for International Development (USAID): budgeting by, 190; bureaucracy of, 72–73; enterprise funds administered by, 148–49; privatization assistance from, 108–09, 151; RASDAQ funding from, 91, 291; school bathroom facilities provided by, 234–35; technical assistance from, 209–11, 317

U.S. Export-Import (EXIM) Bank, 171, 195

U.S. Information Agency (USIA), 71, 93, 132, 133

U.S. Trade and Development Agency, 149

Vacaroiu, Nicolae: archival access provided by, 226; characterization of, 85, 130; on Cobra helicopter deal, 217; economic report by, 269; foreign reserves under, 195; meetings with U.S. officials, 240; as prime minister, 64, 195; properties owned by, 236; RASDAQ assistance from, 262; Romanian-Ukrainian friendship treaty negotiations by, 141; strike settlements by, 84, 94; tennis diplomacy by, 128

Valenti, Jack, 119
Valmont Industries, 321
Vance, Cyrus, 36
Van der Stoel, Max, 220
Vanik, Charles, 16, 17, 23, 24
Vasile, Radu, 197, 204, 222–23, 271–72
Viteazul, Mihai. *See* Michael the Brave
Vlad the Impaler (prince of Wallachia),
    56–57, 236
Volcker, Paul, 67

Wald, Bob, 178
Wałęsa, Lech, xvi
Warsaw Initiative, 109–10
Wasserman, Reb, 28
Weizman, Ezer, 189
Wenick, Martin, 32
Whitehead, Bob, 248–49
Whitehead, John, 25
White House Conference on Trade and
    Investment in Central and Eastern
    Europe, 94–95
Whitman, Christine, 341
Widnall, Sheila E., 143
Wiehens, Michael, 119
Wiesel, Elie, 42, 57, 297–98
WJC. *See* World Jewish Congress
WJRO (World Jewish Restitution
    Organization), 162

Wojtyła, Karol Józef, 12
Wolf, Frank, 61
Wolfensohn, James, 159, 171
Worby, Rachel, 301
World Bank: currency stabilization loans
    from, xvii; economic reform assistance
    from, 106; loans and grants from, 66,
    191–92, 265; privatization guidance
    from, 67, 76–77, 136–37; support for
    ambassadorship from, 61. *See also*
    International Bank for Reconstruction
    and Development; Structural
    adjustment loans
World Jewish Congress (WJC), 30, 128,
    129, 177
World Jewish Restitution Organization
    (WJRO), 162
World Trade Organization, 98
World War I (1914–1918), 3, 48, 49
World War II (1939–1945), 3, 18, 42,
    51

Xenophobia, xx, 43, 182, 290

Yeltsin, Boris, 93, 137–38

Zanc, Grigore, 132–33
Zhelev, Zhelyu, 138
Zhirinovsky, Vladimir, 174

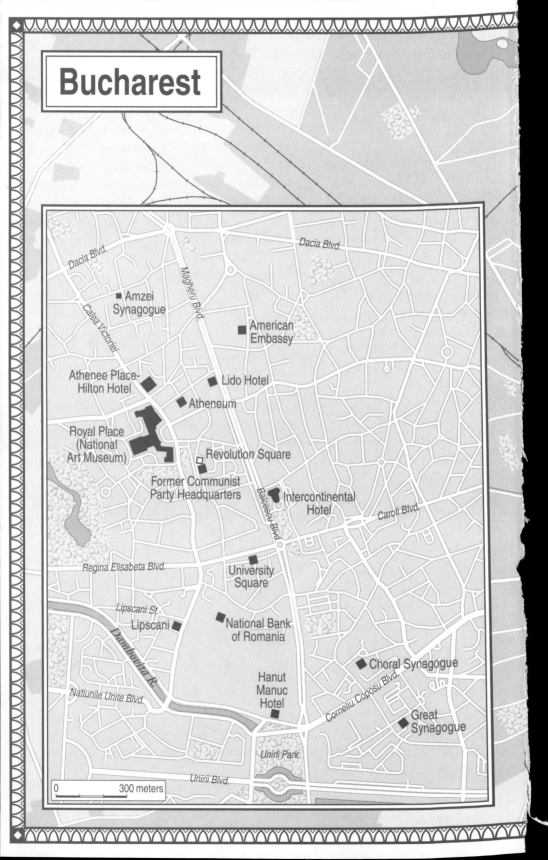

Bucharest

Dacia Blvd.

Dacia Blvd.

Magheru Blvd.

Calea Victoriei

Amzei
Synagogue

American
Embassy

Athenee Place-
Hilton Hotel

Lido Hotel

Atheneum

Royal Place
(National
Art Museum)

Revolution Square

Former Communist
Party Headquarters

Balcescu Blvd.

Intercontinental
Hotel

Caroli Blvd.

Regina Elisabeta Blvd.

University
Square

Lipscani St.

Lipscani

National Bank
of Romania

Dambovita R.

Choral Synagogue

Natiunile Unite Blvd.

Hanut
Manuc
Hotel

Corneliu Coposu Blvd.

Great
Synagogue

Unirii Park

Unirii Blvd.

0   300 meters